The Harvest of Sorrow

By the Same Author

THE HARVEST OF SORROW

Soviet Collectivization and the Terror–Famine

ROBERT CONQUEST

*The University of Alberta Press
in Association with the
Canadian Institute of Ukrainian Studies*

First Published in Canada by
The University of Alberta Press
141 Athabasca Hall
Edmonton, Alberta, Canada T6G 2E8
in Association with the
Canadian Institute of Ukrainian Studies
1986

Canadian Cataloguing in Publication Data
Conquest, Robert
The harvest of sorrow
ISBN 0-88864-110-9
1. Ukraine—History—1921-1944.
2. Famines—Ukraine.
3. Peasantry—Ukraine—History.
4. Collectivization of agriculture
—Ukraine—History. I. Title.
DK508.8.C65   1986   363.8′0947′71   C85-091011-3

First published in the United States of America by
Oxford University Press
200 Madison Avenue
New York, New York 10016

Printed in the United States of America
on acid free paper.

For
Elizabeth Neece Conquest

Contents

Contents

The black earth
Was sown with bones
And watered with blood
For a harvest of sorrow
On the land of Rus´

The Armament of Igor

The Harvest of Sorrow

Preface

The task of the historian is the notoriously difficult one of trying to represent clearly and truly in a few hundred pages events which cover years of time and nations of men and women. We may perhaps put this in perspective in the present case by saying that in the actions here recorded about twenty human lives were lost for, not every word, but every letter, in this book.

Heartfelt acknowledgements are therefore due to all who supported and assisted me. In the first place to the Harvard University Ukrainian Research Institute and the Ukrainian National Association which were my prime sponsors; and to Professors Omeljan Pritsak, Ihor Ševčenko and Adam Ulam (all of Harvard) who were instrumental in providing or suggesting this sponsorship.

In the actual work, I have to acknowledge above all the major co-operation and contribution of Dr James Mace, also of Harvard, in both massive research and detailed discussion. I am also most grateful to Dr Mikhail Bernstam, of the Hoover Institution, Stanford University, especially for his expert assistance on the demographic and economic side; and to Helena Stone, also of Stanford, for truly invaluable help both in the general research and in checking innumerable references. Of the many who have, in different ways, usefully drawn my attention to particular lines of evidence, I would thank particularly Professor Martha Brill Olcutt, Professor Bohdan Struminsky, Professor Taras Lukach and Dr Dana Dalrymple.

I have normally used the Ukrainian spelling of Ukrainian place and personal names, except for Kiev, Kharkov and Odessa (though I have not been entirely consistent with minor localities which are variously transliterated in English language sources). On a lesser point, I write of 'the Ukraine' rather than simply 'Ukraine'. A few Ukrainians regard this as in some way slightly derogatory, implying a local or dependent rather

1

than a national status. But I find that in almost all cases works by Western scholars sympathetic to Ukrainian nationality, and even translations from prominent Ukrainian writers, use 'the Ukraine', which is also countenanced by the Harvard Ukrainian Research Institute. It is a matter of current English usage, and certainly no more indicative of non-independence than for example, 'The' Netherlands. I ask those readers who may nevertheless feel irritated to forgive me, and to consider the larger number who would feel the omission strained or unnatural.

Devoted and lengthy secretarial work, often from barely legible manuscript, was performed with her usual cheerful efficiency by Mrs Amy Desai. Mr John Beichman is also to be thanked for helping with this, as is my wife, who took time from her own writing to deal with some of the more impenetrable parts of the MS – though also, as ever, for her more general support and encouragement.

Of the various resources in America and Europe on which I have relied, I would make special acknowledgement to the Hoover Institution's incomparable Library and Archives.

Stanford, California   R. C.
1985

Introduction

Fifty years ago as I write these words, the Ukraine and the Ukrainian, Cossack and other areas to its east – a great stretch of territory with some forty million inhabitants – was like one vast Belsen. A quarter of the rural population, men, women and children, lay dead or dying, the rest in various stages of debilitation with no strength to bury their families or neighbours. At the same time, (as at Belsen), well-fed squads of police or party officials supervised the victims.

This was the climax of the 'revolution from above', as Stalin put it, in which he and his associates crushed two elements seen as irremediably hostile to the regime: the peasantry of the USSR as a whole, and the Ukrainian nation.

In terms of regimes and policies fifty years is a long time. In terms of individual lives, not so long. I have met men and women who went through the experiences you will read of as children or even as young adults. Among them were people with 'survivors' guilt' – that irrational shame that they should be the ones to live on when their friends, parents, brothers and sisters died, which is also to be found among the survivors of the Nazi camps.

At a different level, what occurred was all part of the normal political experience of the senior members of today's ruling group in the Kremlin. And the system then established in the countryside is part of the Soviet order as it exists today. Nor have the methods employed to create it been repudiated, except as to inessentials.

★

The events with which we deal may be summed up as follows: In 1929–1932 the Soviet Communist Party under Stalin's leadership, for reasons that will emerge in the course of our narrative, struck a double blow at the peasantry of the USSR as a whole: dekulakization and collectivization. Dekulakization meant the killing, or deportation to the Arctic with their families, of millions of peasants, in principle the better-off, in practice the most influential and the most recalcitrant to the Party's plans. Collectivization meant the effective abolition of private property in land, and the concentration of the remaining peasantry in 'collective' farms under Party control. These two measures resulted in millions of deaths – among the deportees in particular, but also among the undeported in certain areas such as Kazakhstan.

Then in 1932–3 came what may be described as a terror-famine inflicted on the collectivized peasants of the Ukraine and the largely Ukrainian Kuban (together with the Don and Volga areas) by the methods of setting for them grain quotas far above the possible, removing every handful of food, and preventing help from outside – even from other areas of the USSR – from reaching the starving. This action, even more destructive of life than those of 1929–1932, was accompanied by a wide-ranging attack on all Ukrainian cultural and intellectual centres and leaders, and on the Ukrainian churches. The supposed contumaciousness of the Ukrainian peasants in not surrendering grain they did not have was explicitly blamed on nationalism: all of which was in accord with Stalin's dictum that the national problem was in essence a peasant problem. The Ukrainian peasant thus suffered in double guise – as a peasant and as a Ukrainian.

Thus there are two distinct, or partly distinct, elements before us: the Party's struggle with the peasantry, and the Party's struggle with Ukrainian national feeling. And before telling of the climaxes of this history, we must examine the backgrounds of both. This we do in the first part of this book.

The centre of our narrative is nevertheless in the events of 1929 to 1933. In this period, of about the same length as that of the First World War, a struggle on the same scale took place in the Soviet countryside. Though confined to a single state, the number dying in Stalin's war against the peasants was higher than the total deaths for all countries in World War I. There were differences: in the Soviet case, for practical purposes, only one side was armed, and the casualties (as might be expected) were almost all on the other side. They included, moreover, women, children and the old.

There are hundreds of histories and other works on the First World War. It would not be true to say that there are no books on the collectivization and the terror-famine. Much has in fact been published, but it has almost all been either documentary or of a specialist nature (and I have been greatly indebted to both). But no history in the ordinary sense of the word has previously appeared.

The purpose of this book is thus a strange one. It is to register in the public consciousness of the West a knowledge of and feeling for major events, involving millions of people and millions of deaths, which took place within living memory.

But how is it possible that these events are not already fully registered in our public consciousness?

There are, I think, three main reasons.

First, they seem far removed from Western experience. The very word 'peasant' is strange to an American or a Briton, referring to a condition in distant lands, or in times long past. And indeed, the story of the Russian or Ukrainian peasant is very different from that of the British or American farmer.

The Ukraine, too, does not declare itself as a nation in the Western consciousness as Poland or Hungary or even Lithuania do. In modern times it had a precarious and interrupted independence for only a few years. It has appeared on our maps for two centuries as merely part of the Russian Empire or the Soviet Union. Its language is comparatively close to Russian – as Dutch is to German, or Norwegian to Swedish – not in itself a touchstone of political feeling, yet tending to appear so in the absence of other knowledge.

Finally, one of the most important obstacles to an understanding was the ability of Stalin and the Soviet authorities to conceal or confuse the facts. Moreover, they were abetted by many Westerners who for one reason or another wished to deceive or be deceived. And even when the facts, or some of them, percolated in a general way into the Western mind, there were Soviet formulae which tended to justify or at least excuse them. In particular, the image was projected of the exploiting 'kulak' – rich, powerful and unpopular, purged (even if a trifle inhumanely) as an enemy of the Party, of progress, and of the peasant masses. In fact this figure, to the extent that he had existed at all, had disappeared by 1918, and the word was used of a farmer with two or three cows, or even of a poorer farmer friendly to the first. And by the time of the terror-famine, even these were no longer to be found in the villages.

★

These actions by the Soviet government were interlinked. On the face of it, there was no necessary connection. Logically, dekulakization could have taken place without collectivization (and something of the sort had indeed happened in 1918). Collectivization could have taken place without dekulakization – and some Communists had urged just that. And

5

the famine need not have followed.

The reasons why the regime inflicted each and all of the components of this triple blow will emerge in our text.

★

A further element in the story is that there are social and economic implications, and matters of intra-party doctrinal dispute.

The economic side, though covered as sparingly and digestibly as possible, is indeed dealt with here; though in their essentials the problems, and the struggles, were not economic ones in the normal sense. Fifty years later it would be hard to maintain that economic forces are properly understood even in the West where the study has flourished without constraint. In the Soviet Union in the 1920s understanding was at a far lower level. Moreover, the available information and statistics were erroneous or inadequate to a marked degree. The Party's economic theorists held views which had even then been long superseded in serious academic circles. But, above all, the Party thought of genuine economic trends as obstacles to be overcome by the power of State decrees.

Most useful recent work has appeared in the West by skilled economists who have lately studied the themes fully, and are yet not inclined – as most of their predecessors were – to seek an economic rationality, or a reliability of official figures, in areas where neither apply. (There are, indeed, a number of questions on which specialists hold various opinions. In many cases the story can be told in a way general enough to avoid controversial points; in others I advance the alternatives, or take a view and explain why. But this is, in any case, a minor element in the story, and it is not our purpose to chew on economic detail).

The other theme of the period on which much has been written is the factional struggle within the Communist Party, and Stalin's rise to power. This too is covered here, but mainly to the degree that it is relevant to the vaster events in the countryside; and even then not, as has been so often done, taking the various arguments at their ideological face value so much as in the context of the prospects actually facing the Party mind.

For the events we recount here were the result not simply of an urge to power, an insistence on suppressing all autonomous forces in the country, but also of a set of doctrines about the social and economic results achievable by terror and falsehood. The expected results did not emerge: but it may in any case be thought that to make such sacrifices in the name of hitherto untested dogma was a moral as well as a mental perversion. And this is even apart from the unstated or unconscious motivations to be met with here as elsewhere.

6

That is, not merely at the level of personal advancement, of personal vendetta, of personal gain, but even more profoundly in the sense which Orwell so clearly saw it, the Communists 'pretended, perhaps they even believed that they had seized power unwillingly and for a limited time, and that just around the corner there lay a paradise where human beings would be free and equal', but in reality, 'Power is not a means, it is an end'.

Whatever view be taken of this, (and even accepting the Stalinists' motivations at their face value), it is at least clear that, at more than one level, the sort of rationality sometimes allowed even by critics opposed to the programme was not really much in evidence, or only at a shallow level inappropriate to the complexities of reality.

Stalin looms over the whole human tragedy of 1930–33. Above all, what characterizes the period is the special brand of hypocrisy or evasion which he brought to it. These are not the necessary concomitants of terror. But in this case, deception was the crux of every move. In his campaign against the Right, he never admitted (until the last moment) that he was attacking them, and compromised, if only verbally, when they protested; in the dekulakization, he pretended that there really was a 'class' of rich peasants whom the poorer peasants spontaneously ejected from their homes; in the collectivization, his public line was that it was a voluntary movement, and that any use of force was a deplorable aberration; and when it came to the terror-famine of 1932–3, he simply denied that it existed.

★

It is a very appropriate moment to establish the true story beyond controversy. For we now have so much evidence, and from such a variety of mutually confirmatory sources, that no serious doubts remain about any aspect of the period.

Our types of evidence may be summed up. First, a great deal of material directly bearing on these events became available, often in driblets inserted into masses of orthodox sentiment, from Soviet scholars – though more in the Khrushchev interlude, and especially the early 1960s, than later.[1] (Indeed after Khrushchev's fall attacks were made on those scholars who, while keeping within prescribed limits, had endeavoured to show some of the errors, and the terrors, of the Stalin approach to peasants).[2]

Soviet scholars also in effect rehabilitated and made public the basic figures of the suppressed 1937 census. So we can now compare them with Soviet estimates of the 'natural rate of growth' of the period; and thus, with reasonable accuracy, estimate the huge death roll of 1930–33. (It may be added that even accepting the figures of the falsified census of

7

1939, this remains devastating).

Then, official evidence contemporary with these events includes some extraordinarily frank material in the Soviet press, in particular that outside Moscow, some of it only recently available. In addition, a number of confidential documents at a local level have reached the West, in the 'Smolensk Archives' now at Harvard, and in other ways.

Then, we have the testimony of former Party activists who took part in the infliction of the regime's policies on the peasantry. These include such distinguished dissidents, now in exile, as General Petro Grigorenko and Dr Lev Kopelev.

Another important source is the accounts of some of the foreign correspondents then in Russia (even though at the time they were considerably hindered in their efforts, and outflanked, by others concerned to placate, or even become accomplices of, the regime – as we shall examine in Chapter 17). There are the reports of foreign citizens visiting their original homes and of foreign Communists working in the USSR. There are letters written from villagers to co-religionists, relatives, and others in the West.

Above all, there are a great number of first-hand reports by survivors both of the deportations and of the famine. Some of these come in individual books or articles; many more in the devoted work of documentation by Ukrainian scholars who actively sought testimony from witnesses scattered the world over. In addition, a great number of individual accounts are to be found, for example, in the Harvard Research Interview Project. And as the acknowledgements in the Preface inadequately indicate, a great deal of scattered information from all over the world has been made available to me. The most remarkable feature of such testimony, especially from peasants themselves, is the plain and matter-of-fact tone in which terrible events are usually narrated.

It is especially gratifying to be able to confirm and give full credit to this first-hand evidence. For a long time testimony which was both honest and true was doubted or denounced – by Soviet spokesmen, of course, but also by many in the West who for various reasons were not ready to face the appalling facts. It is a great satisfaction to be able to say that these sturdy witnesses to the truth, so long calumniated or ignored, are now wholly vindicated.

Then there is fiction, or reality appearing in fiction. One of the world's leading scholars in the field of Soviet economics, Professor Alec Nove, has noted that in the USSR 'the best material about the village appears in the literary monthlies'.

Some fiction actually published in the USSR is clearly autobiographical and veridical. Mikhail Sholokhov's *Virgin Soil Upturned*, published in the 1930s, even if somewhat restrained by his Communist point of view, already contains remarkably frank and clear accounts of the events in the villages.

In more recent times, fiction published in the USSR in the Khrushchev period, and another cycle of work by the new 'country writers', appearing before 1982, give very frank accounts.

One modern Soviet author published in 1964 an account of the famine and its reasons: 'In accordance with one order or another, all the grain and all the fodder were taken away. Horses began to die en masse and in 1933 there was a terrible famine. Whole families died, houses fell apart, village streets grew empty . . .'[3] In 1972 the same writer could complain: 'one thing is striking: in not a single textbook on contemporary history will you find the merest reference to 1933, the year marked by a terrible tragedy'.[4]

Unpublished *samizdat* work is, of course, franker and more overtly condemnatory. We must note above all *Forever Flowing* by the Stalin Prize-winning novelist Vasily Grossman, whose chapter on the collectivization and the famine is among the most moving writing on the period. Grossman, himself Jewish, was co-editor of the Soviet section of the *Black Book* on the Nazi holocaust (never published in the USSR), and the author of a terrible documentary work, *The Hell of Treblinka*.

In general, two things should be noted. First, the sheer amount of evidence is enormous. Almost every particular incident in the villages recounted here could be matched by a dozen, sometimes even a hundred, more.

More important yet, the material is mutually confirmatory. The accounts of the emigré survivors, which might have been thought distorted by anti-Soviet sentiment, are exactly paralleled in the other sources. Indeed, the reader will in many cases probably find it hard to guess whether testimony is Soviet or emigré.

This mutual reinforcement of evidence is clearly of the greatest value; and in general one can say that the course of events is now put beyond question.

★

This was not the only terror to afflict the subjects of the Soviet regime. The death roll of 1918–22 was devastating enough. The present writer has elsewhere recounted the history of the 'Great Terror' of 1936–8; and the post-war terror was little better. But it remains true that the rural terror of 1930–33 was more deadly yet, and has been less adequately recorded.

The story is a terrible one. Pasternak writes in his unpublished memoirs, 'In the early 1930s, there was a movement among writers to travel to the collective farms and gather material about the new life of the village. I wanted to be with everyone else and likewise made such a trip with the aim of writing a book. What I saw could not be expressed in words. There was such inhuman, unimaginable misery, such a terrible disaster, that it began to seem almost abstract, it would not fit within the bounds of consciousness. I fell ill. For an entire year I could not write'.[5] A modern Soviet author who experienced the famine as a boy, similarly remarks, 'I should probably write a whole book about 1933, but I cannot raise enough courage: I would have to relive everything again.'[6]

For the present writer too, though under far less direct impressions, the task has often been so distressing that he has sometimes hardly felt able to proceed.

It is for the historian to discover and register what actually happened, to put the facts beyond doubt and in their context. This central duty done, it cannot mean that he has taken no view of the matters he describes. The present writer does not pretend to a moral neutrality; and indeed believes that there can be few nowadays who would not share his estimate of the events recorded in the pages which follow.

★

PART I

The Protagonists: Party, Peasants and Nation

The Communist revolution is carried
through by the class which is itself
the expression of the dissolution of
all classes, nationalities, etc.

Marx and Engels

1

The Peasants and the Party

C'est dur, l'agriculture

Zola

At the beginning of 1927, the Soviet peasant, whether Russian, Ukrainian, or of other nationality, had good reason to look forward to a tolerable future. The land was his; and he was reasonably free to dispose of his crop. The fearful period of grain-seizure, of peasant risings suppressed in blood, of devastating famine, were over, and the Bolshevik government seemed to have adopted a reasonable settlement of the countryside's interests.

There were, it was true, many imperfections in the prospect before him. The authorities were changeable and inconsistent in their price and tax policies. And suspicions of their long term intentions could not be wholly put aside. The government and its agents remained alien to the peasant, as governments always had been – the *vlast*, or 'power', to be watched with circumspection and handled with care and cunning.

But meanwhile, there was comparative prosperity. Under the New Economic Policy which had granted the peasant his economic freedom, the ruined countryside had made a great recovery.

All in all, it was a moment to savour. For the first time in history, almost all the country's land was in the possession of those who tilled it, and its product at their disposal. And if Ukrainian they were, in their national capacity, in a far better position than at any time since the extinction of the remnants of the old Ukrainian state a century and a half before: now, at least, their language and culture were allowed to flourish.

This nationality aspect we shall consider in a later chapter, and here deal only with the past and the present shared by all the peasantry.

13

The details of peasant history are complex, with variations from province to province, widespread anomalies of tenure, and legal provisions so muddled and complicated as to be virtually impenetrable. It will be sufficient to our purpose to present in a general fashion the conditions of life of the peasantry in the main areas.

The system of cultivation was of the sort we read of in Western Europe's Middle Ages. The 'three field system', where one field in three was left fallow, prevailed; and each peasant household owned strips of land in each of the fields, and observed the cycle laid down by the village as a whole. Or such was the norm: in fact fields might be left fallow for several years, or abandoned altogether.

Generally speaking, the country's soil fell into two main zones, with important social consequences.

In the north, the country was and still is to a considerable degree naturally forest. The villages were settled in clearings, typically no more than a dozen or so two-storeyed houses of logs thatched with straw, with outbuildings. That is, the peasants were in effect, and often in reality, one large family, with its holdings naturally held in common. The soil was poor, and much effort went into hunting and fishing on the one hand and household industries on the other.

In the south, and particularly the bulk of the Ukraine, lies the steppe, most of it the fertile 'black earth' belt. There the villages are typically much larger. Perhaps a couple of hundred houses of poles plastered with yellow clay would line the two sides of one of the rare streams in its little valley, their fields being up on the steppe. The soil was much richer, but also more liable to variations of weather affecting the crop. A large village like Khmeliv in the Poltava Province numbered, with its outlying hamlets, nearly 2,500 farms. It had two churches, sixteen windmills, a steam-mill, a clinic, a village school of five classes and (nearby) a large commercial granary.

The peasant's position was, until 1861, that of a serf – one usual Russian word (*rab*) meaning in fact 'slave' – whom his landlord actually owned, subject to higher authority. This sounds like what prevailed in the West in the period often characterized as 'feudal'· But 'feudalism' is such a broad word that to apply it to Mediaeval England and 18th-19th century Russia alike is to miss the major differences. In the first place, under Western 'feudalism' the serf had rights vis-à-vis the lord, and the lord vis-à-vis the King. In Russia, after Mongol times, the lower simply had obligations to the higher.

Then, in the West serfdom gradually died out. In Russia, it became more widespread, more onerous, and more inhuman right into the 19th century, as more and more was demanded from them in labour and taxes.

14

By the turn of the century 34 million of a population of 36 million were serfs.

Under serfdom, especially in Russia proper, the village commune, or *mir*, held joint responsibility for taxes, and for the redistribution of land within the village which took place from time to time. This 'repartition', though known earlier, became common from the 17th century. (Tools and livestock remained family property and the plots round the actual household were allotted hereditarily.)

In the Ukraine west of the Dnieper (and in Byelorussia) the commune existed but did not, generally speaking, possess the right of repartition. Instead hereditary household tenure existed – though there was communal control over choice of crop, and of field rotation, a co-ordination necessary under the strip system of cultivation.

*

The Emancipation of the Serfs carried out by Tsar Alexander II in 1861 was a remarkable, if severely flawed, advance. The peasant was henceforth a free man, and held his own land. The snags were that he was not given all the land he had previously cultivated and for the land he was given he had to make redemption payments over a long period.

Emancipation had been seen for some time by most educated subjects of the Tsar as a necessity if the country was not to remain a stagnant backwater; and the defeat and humiliation of the Crimean War was held to show that the older order could no longer compete. But a reform organized from above, and designed not to revolutionize society, inevitably carried with it a desire to protect the landlord's interest as well as that of the peasant. Throughout the ensuing period it is clear that the peasant remained unsatisfied, and continued to regard the remaining land held by the landlord as rightfully his own.

Still, up to a point the peasant benefited, and knew that he benefited. Figures given by a recent Soviet authority on the number of peasant disorders in 1859–63 and 1878–82 respectively are illuminating: 3,579 in the earlier period, 136 in the later. Clearly the emancipated peasant had less resentment than is sometimes supposed.[1]

Nevertheless, redemption charges were based on an economic over-valuation (except in Western provinces, including the West-bank Ukraine) and were a fearful strain on the peasantry. Moreover, increasing population meant that the size of peasant holdings diminished – by up to a quarter in the Black Earth districts. Arrears piled up. But finally the debt was reduced or cancelled by a series of government decrees.

Meanwhile, between 1860 and 1897 the peasant population of the empire's European section grew from 57 to 79 million, and land-hunger increased. Yet in 1877, the average peasant allotment was about 35.5 acres. In France, at the time, the average of *all* holdings, peasant and landlord, was less than nine acres: three-quarters of French holdings were less than five acres. In fact, after every allowance for climate and so on, the real trouble was that the Russian peasant did not use his land efficiently.

There were some good signs: annual yield per acre increased from 387 lbs in 1861–70 to 520 lbs in 1896–1900. Moreover, the allotment figures are not the whole truth, since the average peasant rented a further acre for every six in his own possession; and the poorer peasant leased some of his land, and also (less than two million of them) might work as a wage labourer as well. However, in 1900 there was on average only one horse per peasant household.

After the Emancipation the communes continued to be responsible for taxes and village administration. The General Statute of Emancipation constituted for the village commune the 'village assembly' of heads of households – *skhod* (Ukrainian *hromada*) – to run its political and economic affairs. In 1905, more than three-quarters of peasant households belonged to 'repartitional' communes, though almost half of the communes had not in effect *practised* 'repartition' from Emancipation to the turn of the century.[2] Meanwhile, in the Ukraine the communal tenure was less pervasive, and in lands west of the Dnieper, covered less than a quarter of the households in 1905.

★

The fact that on the whole the peasants maintained their traditional ways so stubbornly may lead us to think of them as isolated in their villages, wholly out of contact with the world of the cities. Nothing could be falser. To a far higher degree than in most Western countries, large numbers of the peasants had for centuries regularly migrated to the cities for seasonal work as carpenters, construction workers, factory workers, tradesmen and so on.

In the northern region in Russia proper where the agricultural product was not enough to provide subsistence, almost all peasant households were also engaged in side-work – on average 44% of their income was so derived. Even on the steppe some three-quarters of the households did such work, though to the extent of only 12% of their income.

In 1912 90% of all households in Moscow Province had members in outside non-agricultural work. And at the end of the first decade of the 20th century, one-third of all commercial and industrial establishments in Moscow itself were owned by peasants, who were also the most numerous class in all trade or business, except textiles.[3]

★

The economic pressure on the peasants was great. But in addition they almost universally regarded the landlord as an enemy, and his land as rightfully theirs.

The traditional forms for peasant resistance were many – timber-cutting, unlawful pasturing, the carting off of hay and grain from the fields, pillage and arson, renters' strikes, and occasional open appropriation and seeding of land. In 1902, in the Ukrainian provinces of Kharkov and Poltava a serious rebellion broke out involving more than 160 villages, and some eighty landlords' estates were attacked in a few days. And by 1905–1906, there were very frequent outbreaks all over the country.

★

All parties agreed that only a modernization of agricultural methods could save the situation. The main problem is simply stated: given the primitive techniques in use, the amount of land was inadequate, and increasingly so, to the growing rural population. The amount of land available, in the abstract, was more than sufficient, as we have seen. The change must be in the organization of the peasant economy and in technical advance. And by the end of the 19th century, (as Esther Kingston-Mann points out[4]), a cult of modernization had arisen that 'justified any action to render the peasant obsolete long before "history" or the laws of economic development had succeeded in doing the job'. Many natural assumptions seem, however, to be untrue, at least in the 1880s: that the non-communal lands as such were much more productive than the communal; that there was anything like economic equality within the commune; that communal agricultural practice was the more backward.[5] Peasant demand for the newer type of plough exceeded the supply.[6]

But even in 1917 only half of the peasant holdings had iron ploughs. Sickles were used for reaping, flails for threshing. And, even in the 1920s, the wheat and rye yield of seven to nine centners a hectare was only slightly higher than on 14th century English estates.[7]

The crucial consideration for all suggestions of modernization was that the three field strip system was uneconomic, and not to be reconciled with modern methods of farming.

The conclusions drawn by conservatives was that the more enterprising peasants must be given the right to secede from the commune, but also to

17

exchange their strips for a consolidated acreage, and thus become farmers in the Western sense, with both the possibility and the incentive to improve their land and its output.

One of the concessions extracted by the 1905 Revolution was an increase in the funding of the Peasant Bank, and a modification of its rules to give advances of 90% or more to peasants purchasing land. (In 1906, moreover, the peasant gained the right to an internal passport like anyone else).

As early as January 1906, the then Prime Minister Witte had obtained approval in principle for the breakup of 'repartitional' land into private holdings, and soon afterwards Stolypin, with whom the plan is chiefly associated, succeeded him. His intention was, as he put it, based on the idea that 'The Government has placed its wager, not on the needy and the drunken, but on the sturdy and the strong – on the sturdy individual proprietor who is called upon to play a part in the reconstruction of our Tsardom on strong monarchical foundations'.

Lenin called Stolypin's plans 'progressive in the scientific economic sense'.[8]

By laws of 9 November 1906, 4 June 1910, and 29 May 1911, such a programme was put into some sort of effect. Under these decrees, any peasant householder might demand separate title to the land held by the household. This did not at once lead to consolidation of the strips into single discrete holdings – by 1917 it is believed that three-quarters of hereditary holdings were still in strips; but nevertheless physical consolidation was provided for, and began to take place on a significant scale.

The task of converting the mediaeval system into individual farms was 'of almost incomparable difficulty'. In 1905 9.5 million peasant households were in communes and 2.8 in hereditary tenure. Over the years to 1916, about 2.5 million households are generally estimated to have left the commune.[9] And by 1917 the 13–14 million peasant allotments are thought to have been divided as follows:–

5 million in unchanged repartitional tenure
1.3 million legally, but not actually, 'hereditarized'
1.7 million in transition
4.3 million hereditarized, but still in strips
1.3 million partly or wholly consolidated

In the Ukraine in particular, though also elsewhere, new farms set up in the ploughland rather than in the old village became fairly common. About 75,000 of those, forming small hamlets of their own, are reported in 1915.

These consolidated farms immediately showed great improvements in production.[10] But the extent of consolidation by 1917 was not enough to have produced the revolution in Russian agriculture which had been foreseen. Stolypin himself had spoken of the need for 20 years' peace, and his plans had had less than ten. The reforms were almost entirely aborted by the Revolutions of 1917, among whose major results were the 'black repartition' – spontaneous seizure of the landlords' lands; the strong revival of the commune; and the disappearance of many of the new individual farms.

★

The Russian intelligentsia had taken two contrary views of the peasantry. On the one hand they were the People incarnate, the soul of the country, suffering, patient, the hope of the future. On the other, they appeared as the 'dark people', backward, mulish, deaf to argument, an oafish impediment to all progress.

There were elements of truth in both views, and some of the country's clearest minds saw this. Pushkin praised the peasants' many good qualities, such as industry and tolerance. The memorist Nikitenko called the peasant 'almost a perfect savage' and a drunkard and a thief into the bargain, but added that he was nevertheless 'incomparably superior to the so-called educated and intellectual. The muzhik is sincere. He does not try to seem what he is not'. Herzen held, if rather sanguinely, that inter-muzhik agreements needed no documents, and were rarely broken; in the peasant's relationship to the authorities, on the other hand, his weapon was deceit and subterfuge, the only means available to him – and he continued to use it in Communist times, as can be seen in the work of all schools of Soviet writers from Sholokhov to Solzhenitsyn.

But for the Utopian intellectual it was one or the other, devil or angel. The young radicals of the 1870s, to the number of several thousand, 'Went to the people' – stayed for months in the villages and tried to enlist the peasants in a socialist and revolutionary programme. This was a complete failure, producing negative effects on both sides. Turgenev's 'Bazarov' gives some of the feeling: 'I felt such hatred for this poorest peasant, this Philip or Sidor, for whom I'm to be ready to jump out of my skin, and who won't even thank me for it' – and even Bazarov did not suspect that in the eyes of the peasants he was 'something in the nature of a buffooning clown.'

It would not be true to say that all the intelligentsia suffered this revulsion, and early in the next century the Socialist Revolutionary Party took up the peasant cause in a more sophisticated manner. But meanwhile

19

Marxism had won over a large section of the radicals, and they were given ideological reason for dismissing the peasantry as the hope of Russia. This change of view was, of course, little more than a transfer of hopes and illusions from an imaginary peasant to an almost equally imaginary proletarian.

But as regards the 'backward' peasantry, one now finds expressions of hatred and contempt among the Marxist, and especially among the Bolshevik, intellectuals going far beyond Marxist theoretical disdain; and one can hardly dismiss this in accounting for the events which followed the October Revolution.

The townsman, particularly the Marxist townsman, was not even consistent in his view of what was wrong with the peasantry, varying between 'apathetic' and 'stupidly greedy and competitive'.[11] Maxim Gorki, giving a view shared by many, felt that 'the fundamental obstacle in the way of Russian progress towards Westernization and culture' lay in the 'deadweight of illiterate village life which stifles the town'; and he denounced 'the animal-like individualism of the peasantry, and the peasants' almost total lack of social consciousness'.[12] He also expressed the hope that 'the uncivilized, stupid, turgid people in the Russian villages will die out, all those almost terrifying people I spoke of above, and a new race of literate, rational, energetic people will take their place'.[13]

The founder of Russian Marxism, Georgi Plekhanov, saw them as 'barbarian tillers of the soil, cruel and merciless, beasts of burden whose life provided no opportunity for the luxury of thought'.[14] Marx had spoken of 'the idiocy of rural life', a remark much quoted by Lenin. (In its original context it was in praise of capitalism for freeing much of the population from this 'idiocy'). Lenin himself referred to 'rural seclusion, unsociability and savagery';[15] in general he believed the peasant 'far from being an instinctive or traditional collectivist, is in fact fiercely and meanly individualistic'.[16] While, of a younger Bolshevik, Khrushchev tells us that 'for Stalin, peasants were scum'.[17]

★

But if Lenin shared the Bolshevik antipathy to the peasants as the archaic element in Russia, his main concerns were to understand them in Marxist terms, to work out tactics to use them in an intermediate period before their disappearance from the scene, and to decide how to organize the countryside when his party gained power.

In the first place Marxism held that the central developments of the future would consist of a confrontation between the new (in his day) working 'class' and the capitalist owners of industry. In every advanced society, and increasingly so the more advanced it became, the population would be largely concentrated in these two main categories, with intermediate, or 'petty bourgeois', elements – in which the peasantry were specifically included – tending to the proletarian side in so far as they themselves were becoming proletarianized, but to the capitalist in so far as their attachment to private property remained.

Marx's study of agrarian matters as such, apart from these class analyses, was meagre. But he made it clear that in the socialist society he foresaw, the 'contradictions' between town and country would disappear. He envisaged a triumph of capitalism in the countryside, followed, with a socialist victory, by a proletarianizing of the countryside. Meanwhile he held that all the peasants together were only like 'a sack of potatoes', in that the isolation of individual farms prevented any true social development of relations.[18]

As to the action to be taken after a Marxist victory, the Communist Manifesto demands 'The abolition of property in land ... the improvement of the soil generally in accordance with a common plan. Establishment of industrial armies especially for agriculture. Combination of agriculture with manufacturing industries; gradual abolition of the distinction between town and country'.

By this Marx meant that in the country, as in the town, a concentration of production and employment would take place, until agriculture became little more than a sort of rural factory work. Small scale production, in the eyes of city-centred Marxian economics, could not in any case long survive, let alone flourish. As David Mitrany puts it, Marx and his disciples looked on the peasant 'with a dislike in which the townsman's contempt for all things rural and the economist's disapproval of small scale production mingled with the bitterness of the revolutionary collectivist against the stubbornly individualistic tiller of the soil'.[19]

As Engels wrote in *Anti-Dühring*, the socialist revolution was to 'put an end to commodity production, and therewith the domination of the product over the producer'. He went on to imagine that the laws of man's 'social activity' hitherto confronting him as external, 'will then be applied by man with a complete understanding'.

'Complete understanding' . . . : over a hundred years later there are few who would claim that we yet have such understanding of the laws of the economy and of society. And part of the reason for such scepticism arises from the results of the Marxist principles in actual application.

When it comes to analysis of what was actually going on, Marx's conviction was that in agriculture, as in industry, property was becoming increasingly concentrated. This was, in fact, fallacious: in Germany, which he knew best, the number of small (2–20 hectare) holdings

21

increased their total area between 1882 and 1895, and the same was true elsewhere. (The German census of 1907 showed that large estates and farms were still losing ground).

Lenin's early work on the industrial side of capital development in Russia is well researched and documented. When he comes to the peasants, however, this evaporates, as in Marx's case, and we are left with ill-supported 'class' analysis. Indeed, the economists of the late 19th century on whom the Russian Marxists relied had done no independent research. They simply asserted that the commune was disintegrating because of the conflict between rural proletarians and peasant capitalists, producing no solid evidence, since none such existed.

Lenin's general analysis of the (non-kulak) peasant in Marxist terms is clear enough: 'He is partly a property owner, partly a worker. He does not exploit other workers. For years he had to defend his position against the greatest odds. He suffered exploitation at the hands of the landlords and the capitalists. He put up with everything. Nevertheless he is a property owner. For this reason, the problem of our attitude to the class is one of enormous difficulty'. And, in a much quoted formulation, he adds 'day by day, hour by hour, small scale production is engendering capitalism . . .'[20]

Marx had indeed written that Russia might go forward to socialism using the old commune as one of its constituents (he seems to have thought that it was a sort of survival from the Marxist phase of 'primitive communism'). But his main expression of this opinion, an 1881 letter to Vera Zasulich, was not published until 1924; and even what was known of it earlier was regarded by Russian Marxists as an unfortunate concession to their Populist enemies, based on false information. Lenin himself saw the commune as a system which 'confines the peasants, as in a ghetto, in petty mediaeval associations of a fiscal, tax-extorting character, in associations for the ownership of allotted land'.[21]

He foresaw the modernization of Russian agriculture on the Marxist basis of large co-operative farms working to a plan. The only other method, he believed, was the capitalist one pursued by Stolypin, of which he remarked, 'the Stolypin Constitution and the Stolypin agrarian reform mark a new phase in the breakdown of the old, semi-patriarchal and semi-feudal system of tsarism, a new manoeuvre towards its transformation into a middle class monarchy . . . It would be empty and stupid to say that the success of such a policy in Russia is "impossible". It is possible! If Stolypin's policy is continued . . . then the agrarian structure of Russia will become completely bourgeois'.[22] As Lenin saw, the poor peasants managed their land very badly, and production would rise if the rich peasants took over.[23]

The advantage of the Stolypin approach is that, in one form or another, it had actually worked in modernizing agriculture in the advanced countries. The disadvantage of Lenin's (taken simply as a method of modernization) is that it was untried and theoretical. This did not, of course, prove that it could not work, a point which remained to be seen.

Lenin's views on the tactics to be pursued vis-à-vis the peasants by his party, supposedly representing the proletariat, were carefully developed on the basis of a remark of Marx's that the proletarian revolution might be supported by a new version of the 16th century German Peasant War.

In his *Two Tactics of Social Democracy* (1905), Lenin urged an intervening stage of the 'Democratic Dictatorship of the Proletariat and Peasantry'; but this was quite openly no more than a temporary tactical move. In the same pages he says that after this coalition is in power, 'then it will be ridiculous to speak of unity of will of the proletariat and peasantry, of democratic rule; then we shall have to think of the Socialist, of the proletarian dictatorship'.[24]

And here we find a flaw, a schematism, in the Bolshevik view of the countryside which was to be powerfully present over the whole period we cover – the invention or exaggeration of class or economic distinctions within the peasantry. A 'rural proletariat' was indeed discoverable: in 1897 1,837,000 listed employment in wage-work in agriculture and other non-industrial employment as their chief – though not usually their only – occupation; and in the summer season, many more short-term labourers were taken on. But as we shall see these carried little social weight, and had little proletarian consciousness in any Marxist sense.

Similarly with Lenin's, and later, attempts to define poor and 'middle' peasants. Even Lenin was aware that a peasant dairy farmer near a big town might not be poor even if he had no horse at all, and that a peasant on the steppe with three horses might not be rich. But theory was never adjusted to take such things into account.[25]

Indeed, and partly for such reasons, Lenin's notions of the peasantry and its divisions were both varied and inconsistent. But on one point he and his successors remained insistent, and this was to prove decisive in the years that follow: the 'kulak' (in Ukrainian *kurkul*) enemy. Lenin hypothesized the 'kulak' as a rich exploiting peasant class against whom, after the removal of the landlords proper, peasant hatred could be equally directed.

'Kulak' – 'fist' – properly speaking meant a village moneylender and mortgager, of whom there was usually at least one in a village or group of villages. Any rich peasant might make an occasional loan, would indeed be expected to. Only when moneylending became a major source of income, and of manipulation, was he seen as a 'kulak' by the villagers. O.P. Aptekman, one of the Populists who has left a really frank account of his experiences with the Russian peasantry, notes that when told that the 'kulak' sucked the blood of the peasantry, a peasant would retort 'these fine gentlemen cannot stand the fact that some peasants are now better off'; or say that not every well-to-do peasant was a kulak, and that these city people don't understand peasant life.

Lenin, on the other hand, even in 1899, while using kulak in its correct sense of rural usurer, rejected the idea that such exploiters and those who hired labour were quite different, insisting that they were 'two forms of the same economic phenomenon'.[26] Neither he nor his followers were in fact ever able to define the kulak, middle peasant and poor peasant in economic terms. Lenin himself, when asked what a kulak was, replied impatiently, 'they will know on the spot who is a kulak'.[27]

At any rate, a minority hostile class, more or less automatically involved in bitter struggle with the rest of the peasantry, was taken to exist in the villages; and if the peasant would not hate him, at least the Party could.

There was, moreover, an implicit assumption in the Bolshevik attitude to class struggle which was not often given direct expression. A conversation took place in August 1917 in the Smolny Institute canteen between Dzerzhinsky (shortly to be Lenin's Police Commissar) and Rafael Abramovich, the Menshevik leader. Dzerzhinsky said:

'Abramovich, do you remember Lasalle's speech on the essence of a constitution?'

'Yes, of course'.

'He said that a constitution is determined by the correlation of real forces in the country. How does such a correlation of political and social forces change?'

'Oh well, through the process of economic and political development, the evolution of new forms of economy, the rise of different social classes, etc, as you know perfectly well yourself'.

'But couldn't this correlation be altered? Say, through the subjection or extermination of some classes of society?'[28]

A year later Zinoviev, then one of the top leaders of the new Soviet state, remarked in a public speech in Leningrad that 'We must carry along with us 90 million out of the 100 million Soviet Russian population. As for the rest, we have nothing to say to them. They must be annihilated'.[29] As it turned out, Zinoviev's figures were an underestimate, and it was the classes constituting the majority who provided the victims.

★

2

The Ukrainian Nationality and Leninism

> The interests of socialism are above
> the interests of the right of
> nations to self-determination
>
> *Lenin*

A major reason why the events we shall be describing never truly gripped the Western mind appears to be a lack of understanding or knowledge of the power of Ukrainian national feeling, of Ukrainian nationhood. In this century an independent Ukrainian state only lasted a few years, and then with interruptions, and was never able to establish itself either physically or in the world's consciousness. In fact the Ukraine, as large as France and more populous than Poland, was far the largest nation in Europe not to emerge as an independent entity (except briefly) in the period between the two World Wars.

To make these points about Ukrainian nationhood is not in the least anti-Russian. Indeed, Solzhenitsyn, the epitome of Russian national feeling, though hoping for a brotherly relationship between the three East Slav nations of Russia, Byelorussia and the Ukraine, grants without question that any decision on union, federation or secession must be a matter for the free choice of the Ukrainian people, that no Russian can decide for them.

The Ukraine's long independent cultural tradition was little known in the West. It had appeared on the maps as part of the Russian Empire, often shown merely as 'Little Russia'; its inhabitants were known, at most, to speak a tongue whose closeness to or distinctiveness from Russian was not clearly grasped. The distinction of language was, in fact, there from long before the subjugation of the Republic on the Waterfalls by Catherine the Great. But it was, thereafter, treated by the Russian rulers, and even other Russians of theoretically liberal spirit, as no more than a dialect.

For the Tsars, as later for at least some of the Soviet rulers, an eventual linguistic and national assimilation seemed natural.

Why did it not take place?

First, the roots of the old Ukrainian language in the millions of the peasant population were deeper and firmer than had been supposed. There was no tendency to merge. People spoke either Russian or Ukrainian.

It is true that in the cities, and among men from the Ukraine who were absorbed into the ruling culture, Russian naturally became the usual language. But apart from the central bastion of peasant speech, there were – as elsewhere – a number of educated Ukrainians who found in their own Ukrainian language and culture a special character which they were not willing to see disappear in the name of 'progress'.

In fact Ukrainian and Russian are merely members branching out from the same linguistic family – the East Slavic: just as Swedish and Norwegian are members of the Scandinavian branch of the Germanic family, or Spanish and Portuguese of the Iberian branch of the Romance family. In any case, linguistic closeness is not of decisive political and cultural significance. Norway demonstrated its overwhelming desire for independence from Sweden in the referendum of 1905. Dutch is, historically, a dialect of Low German: Dutch unwillingness to submit to Germany has been demonstrated on numerous occasions, one of them quite recently.

Similarly with the idea of the Ukraine as having always been a part, even a natural part, of the Russian Empire, or the Soviet Union.

★

Historically the Ukrainians are an ancient nation which has persisted and survived through terrible calamities. The Kiev Grand Princes of Rus' ruled all the East Slavs: but when Kiev finally fell to the Mongols in 1240, that realm was shattered. The Slavic populations to the North, living a century and a half under the Mongols, eventually became Muscovy and Great Russia. Those in the South were largely driven westward, becoming the Ukrainians, and developing under the influence of the European states. They first united with the Grand Duchy of Lithuania, of which Ukrainian was an official language, and later came under – less satisfactory – Polish control.

It was under Polish rule that the first Ukrainian printing presses and schools appear in the last half of the 16th century. It was thus as part of that sprawling and heterogeneous commonwealth that the Ukrainians re-emerged, with much of their land half empty and subject to devastating raids by the Crimean Tatars. The Cossacks now appear – Ukrainian freebooters who first went to the steppe to hunt and fish, then learnt to fight off the Tatars, and by the end of the 16th century set up their own forts and became a military factor in their own right. In the 1540s they founded the Sich, the great fortified encampment below the Dnieper rapids, on the borders of Tatar invasion. The Sich was, for more than two centuries, a military republic, of a type found occasionally elsewhere in similar conditions – democratic in peacetime, a disciplined army in war. The Cossacks were soon leading peasant revolts against their nominal lords, the Poles. Over the next century endless wars and agreements finally led to the effective establishment of a Ukrainian state by Hetman Bohdan Khmelnytsky in 1649. From now on there were constant attempts by Moscow to intervene and finally the Hetman Ivan Mazepa chose an alliance with Charles XII of Sweden against the encroachments of Peter the Great, and was supported by the Sich. The defeat of Charles at Poltava in 1709 was a disaster for the Ukraine.

Over the 18th century, Moscow at first continued to recognize the autonomy of the Hetmanate, while tightening its power to nominate for the post, and putting increasing pressure on the nominees. Finally in 1764 the Hetmanate was abolished, a few of its outward forms persisting until 1781. The Sich republic, which had fought on the Russian side against the Turks in the war of 1769–74, was suddenly destroyed by its allies in 1775. Its *otaman* was sent to the Solovki Islands in the White Sea, and his colonels to Siberia – an almost exact foreshadowing of the fate of their successors in the 1920s and 1930s. Ukrainian statehood, which had existed for over a century, fell, like that of Poland, through insufficient strength to combat large and powerful adversaries.

Like Poland, the Cossack-Hetman state had been of a constitutional parliamentary type – imperfect in these fields by many standards, yet not at all in the tradition of the extreme serfdom and despotism which now descended on it from St Petersburg. Meanwhile those Ukrainians who had remained under Polish rule – and maintained for years a series of peasant-cossack *Haidamak* rebellions – soon also fell in part to Russia, in part to Russia's accomplice in the partitions of Poland, Austria. Throughout the following centuries this 'West Ukrainian' element which Russia did not rule, though smaller, had greater opportunity for political and cultural development and remained a powerful seedbed of national feeling.

Russian-style feudalism followed the flag. Huge estates were handed out to royal favourites; and decrees, starting in 1765 and ending 1796, destroyed the liberties of the Ukrainian peasant, reducing him to the level of his Russian counterpart. It should be remembered nevertheless that only just over a couple of generations in the Ukraine suffered full serfdom; and it typically takes more than two generations – Macaulay says five – to destroy the popular memory of earlier times.

But all in all, as Herzen wrote, 'the unfortunate country protested, but could not withstand that fatal avalanche rolling from the North to the Black Sea and covering everything . . . with a uniform shroud of slavery'.[1]

And this general enslavement of the peasantry went with an attack on the Ukrainian language and culture. Russian rituals were introduced into the church. In 1740 there had been 866 schools in Left-bank Ukraine; in 1800 there were none. The Academy of Kiev, founded in 1631, was turned into a purely theological institution in 1819.

The end of the Ukrainian state, and the introduction of the bureaucratic serfdom and autocracy of central Russia, did not destroy Ukrainian national feeling. But over the next century, it did succeed in driving it down into a low level of consciousness.

Individual Ukrainian leaders sought to gain foreign support for the idea of a separate Ukrainian state at various times from the 1790s to the 1850s. But the key to Ukrainian national survival lay elsewhere. The peasantry went on speaking Ukrainian, and the songs and ballads of the Cossack past were part of their natural heritage, never uprooted.

On the more conscious side, the first work in modern Ukrainian, Ivan Kotlyarevsky's 'travesty' of the Aeneid, appeared in 1798. Through the first half of the century there was a great deal of work done in the collection of Ukrainian folklore material. And in 1840 the country's leading poet, Taras Shevchenko (1814–61) born a Ukrainian serf, began to publish his magnificent pastoral and patriotic poetry, whose influence cannot be exaggerated.

Shevchenko was arrested in 1847 and banished as a common soldier to Siberia, where he spent ten years. His works were banned, and it was not until 1907 that they were published in complete form in Russia.

★

There was many a people in the early 19th century which seemed to be, in the German phrase, a *Naturvolk*. That is, they spoke a language, often differentiated into dozens of overlapping, unregistered dialects. But they had no 'consciousness' of the type provided by intellectual leadership. Such might be found among the Balkan nations, and elsewhere.

The Ukrainians now had some of these characteristics. But their older national consciousness never quite perished. What distinguished them

28

from the Russians persisted – and their Russian or Russified landlords appeared alien in a way which sharpened and maintained differences. And Shevchenko, above all, positively identified the ignominy of serfdom with the ignominy of Russification.

In general, the Russian Empire's yoke lay heavy on a whole range of nations, and the phrase 'prison of the peoples' was a valid one. In Central Asia, the Caucasus, Poland, the Baltic, foreign nations were brought under Russian control in war after war. These were, however, generally recognized to be alien elements, and the prospect of assimilation, though never abandoned, correspondingly remote.

With the Ukraine it was different. And as the century came to a close, and even more in the new epoch of revolution, the idea that this great region which Russian imperialists had always considered a part, even if an as yet inadequately assimilated part, of Russia proper, might indeed wish to be free of control from the north, was a more devastating thought than the resistance of more recently conquered, or lesser, or non-East Slav areas. Even most of the liberal intelligentsia of Russia, totally absorbed in the struggle with absolutism, rejected the Ukraine, and generally opposed even token autonomy for the country.

As with other nations – the Czechs, for instance – the Ukrainians appeared as a people consisting almost wholly of peasants and priests. Moreover when industry was developed, the peasants of Russia, poorer than their Ukrainian counterparts, swarmed in to take on the work, and the industrialization of the 19th century thus meant the intrusion of foreigners and a Russian city population.

For a few years at the beginning of the 1860s the Russian government pursued a comparatively liberal policy, and Ukrainian societies and periodicals proliferated. But in 1863 an edict declared that there was no Ukrainian language, merely a dialect of Russian, and banned works in Ukrainian except for *belles–lettres*, in particular forbidding books which were 'religious and educational, and books generally intended for elementary reading by the people'. A number of Ukrainian figures were deported to North Russia, and Ukrainian schools and newspapers were closed down.

In spite of the government's measures, Ukrainian 'societies' (*Hromada*) persisted in the 1870s, limited legally to research, but nourishing the national idea. This resulted in a further decree in 1876 wholly confining Ukrainian publication to historical documents, forbidding Ukrainian theatrical or musical performances, and closing the main organs – in Russian but pro-Ukrainian – of the movement.

The active Russification campaign which followed did not greatly Russify the Ukrainian peasantry, succeeding only in its first task of

29

denying them books and schools in their own language: it thus led simply to an unprecedented increase in illiteracy, to some 80% of the population, a huge decline. As Petro Grigorenko (himself a Ukrainian) puts it, even if in dramatically emphasized form, 'during the centuries they spent in the Russian imperial state, the Ukrainians forgot their national name and became accustomed to the name their colonizers imposed on them – the Malorosi, or Little Russians'.[2]

Yet among the peasantry, the old ballads of the great national heroes of the Hetmanate and the Sich persisted. Throughout the period the national idea was preserved by the poets and intellectuals. And in 1897 a General Ukrainian Democratic Organization was illegally founded, to co-ordinate their cultural and social groups.

Nevertheless, until the early years of the century, almost nothing was visible in the way of a mass movement of the Ukrainian population. The rebirth of the nation was sudden and overwhelming. A leading figure in the Ukrainian national movement held that it obtained a true mass following only in 1912.[3]

There had been signs that this breakthrough of the national spirit was coming. Peasant risings in 1902 were repeated in 1908. The propertied classes were overwhelmingly non-Ukrainian, and the Ukrainians were overwhelmingly peasants. And the incipient nationalist movement in the Ukraine (as in Poland, the future Czechoslovakia, and elsewhere) was predominantly of socialist cast. The first real political party – the Revolutionary Ukrainian Party founded in 1900, soon came under Marxist influence. It split, and one faction joined the Russian Social Democratic Labour Party, but soon ceased to function, and the other, now called the Ukrainian Social Democratic Party, became estranged from Lenin on the issue of home rule.

The next, and in the end more important Ukrainian party was the Ukrainian Party of Socialist Revolutionaries, though of minor influence until 1917.

In 1905, the first Ukrainian language newspaper in the Russian Empire, *Khilorob*, appeared, and many others followed, in particular the first Ukrainian daily, *Rada*. In 1907 the first complete edition of Shevchenko's poems came out. In the State Dumas elected under the Constitution resulting from the 1905 Revolution, Ukrainian members formed a bloc of 40 members in the First Duma, and in the Second they put demands for autonomy.

Stolypin, however progressive on the economic issues, was a complete Russian imperialist on the national issue. In 1910 he, in effect, ordered the closing of the Ukrainian cultural societies and publishing houses and banned lectures in Ukrainian at the universities – indeed banning the

30

'public' use of the language. Nor was he opposed, on this issue, by the Russian 'progressive' or 'radical' press, though some moderate liberals spoke up for the Ukrainian cultural – as against political – demands.

But the centenary of Shevchenko's birth, in 1914, though hotly opposed by the authorities, saw an outburst of national feeling in which the villages were now directly involved.

It was this comparative lateness of the Ukrainian renaissance (though no later than that of other East European peoples); the misidentification of linguistic cousinhood with linguistic identity; and the absence of political frontiers between Russia and the Ukraine, which gave the inattentive West the impression that there was no real Ukrainian nationhood as there was Polish or Russian nationhood. These conceptions, though entirely false, still bedevil at least our reflex attitudes to the Ukrainian nation; and need to be consciously examined.

When World War I broke out the entire Ukrainian press was shut down, and all Ukrainian educational work was stopped. The leading Ukrainian figures, in spite of declarations of loyalty, were arrested and exiled.

★

In principle, nationality means nothing in strict Marxism: 'The proletarian has no country'. Indeed, in *The German Ideology* Marx and Engels define their proletariat as 'the expression of the dissolution of all classes, nationalities, etc. within present society'.

Lenin, writing in 1916, says flatly that 'the aim of Socialism is not only to abolish the present division of mankind into small states and all-national isolation, not only to bring the nations closer to each other, but to merge them'.[4] And he defines nationhood as a historical category marking a particular economic epoch, that of capitalism.[5]

But he also held (writing in 1914) that 'it is precisely and solely because Russia and the neighbouring countries are going through this epoch that we require an item in our programme on the right of nations to self-determination'.[6]

Having admitted that national aspirations do exist over an undefined transitional period, Lenin considers how to utilize them. It was, indeed, in connection with nationalist movements that he said, in a famous passage:

> The General Staffs in the present war assiduously strive to utilize all national and revolutionary movements in the camp of their enemy . . . We would be very poor revolutionaries if, in the great proletarian war for emancipation and Socialism, we did not know how to utilize every popular movement against

31

each separate disaster caused by imperialism in order to sharpen and extend the crisis.[7]

Thus, for Leninism national movements and questions of national sovereignty are transitional phenomena of a bourgeois nature, but can be utilized by the Communists in the more important class struggle. From this the conclusion was drawn that it might or might not be possible to turn particular national movements to the advantage of the Communists. Those which could not be so used were to be ruthlessly opposed. Even before the Russian revolution Lenin wrote,

> If . . . a number of peoples were to start a Socialist revolution . . . and if other peoples were found to be serving as the main bulwarks of bourgeois reaction – then we would be in favour of a revolutionary war against the latter, in favour of 'crushing' them, destroying all their outposts, no matter what small national movements arose . . .

because

> The various demands of democracy, including self-determination, are not an absolute, they are a particle of the general democratic (at present general Socialist) world movement. In individual concrete cases, a particle may contradict the whole; if it does, then it must be rejected.

Any particular national movement might thus be sacrificed, on the principle that:

> . . . the interests of the democracy of one country must be subordinated to the interests of the democracy of several and of all countries.[8]

Lenin noted that as early as 1849 Engels was writing that Germans, Hungarians, Poles, and Italians 'represent the revolution', while the South Slavs 'represent the counter-revolution', and that this had been the case for a thousand years.[9] Marx himself had indeed written (at a time when the Germans were considered the 'progressive nation'):

> Except for the Poles, the Russians, and at best the Slavs in Turkey, no Slavic people has a future, for the simple reason that all Slavs lack the most basic historic, geographic, political and industrial prerequisites for independence and vitality.[10]

And Engels commented:

> Now you may ask me whether I have no sympathy whatever for the small Slavic peoples, and remnants of peoples . . . In fact, I have damned little sympathy for them; (he was equally contemptuous of 'such miserably powerless so-called nations as the Danes, the Dutch, the Belgians, the Swiss etc').[11]

Stalin's central essay in *Marxism and the National and Colonial Question*

32

was written in pre-revolutionary times and approved by Lenin, who appointed him Commissar for Nationalities in the first Soviet Government in 1917. Elaborating Lenin's points Stalin writes:

> Cases occur when the national movements in certain oppressed countries come into conflict with the interests of the development of the proletarian movement. In such cases support is, of course, entirely out of the question. The question of the rights of nations is not an isolated self-sufficient question; it is a part of the general problem of the proletarian revolution, subordinate to the whole, and must be considered from the point of view of the whole.[12]

And again:

> There are cases when the right of self-determination conflicts with another, a higher right – the right of the working class that has come to power to consolidate that power. In such cases – this must be said bluntly – the right of self-determination cannot and must not serve as an obstacle to the working class in exercising its right to dictatorship.[13]

Immediately after the revolution, Lenin himself wrote:

> There is not a single Marxist who, without making a total break with the foundations of Marxism and Socialism, could deny that the interests of Socialism are above the interests of the right of nations to self-determination. Our Socialist Republic has done and is continuing to do everything possible for implementing the right of self-determination for Finland, Ukraine, etc. But if the concrete position that has arisen is such that the existence of the Socialist Republic is endangered at a given moment in respect of an infringement of the right to self-determination of a few nations (Poland, Lithuania, Courland, etc) then it stands to reason that the interests of the preservation of the Socialist Republic must take preference.[14]

As to the actual form of the state in multinational Russia, the original view of the Bolsheviks was hostile to a federal solution. Lenin had stated in 1913:

> Federation means a union of equals depending upon consent . . . We reject federation on principle; it weakens economic links; it is an unsuitable form for our State.[15]

The experiences of the next few years showed that he and the Bolsheviks had greatly underestimated and misunderstood the question of nationality, learning their main lessons in the Ukraine. After the experiences we shall be recounting below, Lenin settled for all the trappings of Federation, and all measures of cultural autonomy, so long as the actualities of power remained centralized.

★

In March 1917, soon after the collapse of Tsardom, a Ukrainian Central Rada (Council) was formed by the Ukrainian parties, headed by the most distinguished figure in the country, the historian Mykhailo Hrushevsky, in politics a Ukrainian Social-Revolutionary.

In June the Rada issued an appeal for autonomy, and the first Ukrainian government was formed, with the writer Volodymyr Vynnychenko (a Social-Democrat) as Premier and Mikhaylo Tuhan-Baranovsky, an eminent economist, the most prominent member. Representatives of the minorities – Jews, Poles and Russians – joined it in July.

The Rada did not at first make specific claims to independence, but extracted various concessions from the Russian Provisional Government in Petrograd. Effective power, and the support of the vast majority of the people, and even of the local Soviets, was with the Rada. This was the reality which faced Lenin when he seized power in November.

The Ukraine was to be the first great example of the extension of Soviet rule by force over an independent East European country – recognized as such by Lenin in 1918. Its conquest, and the establishment of puppet governments, some of whose members eventually felt the pull of their deeper natural feelings, closely parallels the experiences of the Baltic States twenty years later, of Poland and Hungary twenty-five years later.

The Rada took over full authority in the Ukraine on 16 November 1917, and on 20 November declared the creation of the Ukrainian People's Republic, though even now still speaking of 'federative' relations with Russia (but since the Rada did not recognize the Bolshevik Government, there was at this time no 'Russia' with which to federate).

In the elections for the Constituent Assembly, held on 27–9 November, 1917, the Bolsheviks only got 10% of the vote in the Ukraine, the Ukrainian Social-Revolutionaries receiving 52%, and the bulk of the rest going to other national parties, in particular the Ukrainian Social-Democrats and the Ukrainian Party of Socialist Independents.

A Congress of Soviets was called in Kiev on 16–18 December 1917, and the Bolsheviks were voted down by huge majorities, only getting 11% of the ballots. Their delegates then decamped to Kharkov, which had just been occupied by the Red Army, and called their own Congress of Soviets, all but a handful of the delegates being Russian. Here, on 25 December 1917, they proclaimed a 'Soviet Government' under H. Kotsyubinsky. On 22 January 1918, the Rada declared the Ukraine an independent sovereign republic. But on 12 February 1918 the Kharkov puppet government was able to enter Kiev in the wake of the Red Army, the Rada moving to Zhytomyr.

The Bolshevik invaders were accompanied by 'food detachments' who were diverted into ten-man squads to seize the grain in the villages, under Lenin's instructions to 'send grain, grain and more grain'.[16] Between 18 February and 9 March 1918, 1,090 railroad cars of grain were shipped to Russia from the Kherson Province alone.[17]

The Bolsheviks were, at best, lukewarm towards even an appearance of Ukrainian political devolution at the Party level. Lenin's chief subordinate Yakov Sverdlov said, 'the creation of a separate, Ukrainian Party, whatever it might be called, whatever programme it might adopt, we consider undesirable'.[18] The first Soviet government in the Ukraine only lasted for a few weeks, and was almost overtly an imposition of Russian, if Russian revolutionary, rule. It suppressed Ukrainian schools, cultural institutions and so forth. In fact, the Russianizing tendency in the early Ukrainian Soviet regimes was intensely anti-Ukrainian. A leading Ukrainian Communist, Zatonsky, even told later of how the first Cheka chief in Kiev, the notorious Lacis (Latsis), shot people for speaking Ukrainian in the streets, and that he himself narrowly avoided this fate.[19] Attempts were made to prevent the foundation of even a nominally Ukrainian Communist Party, or the survival of a nominally Ukrainian Trade Union Movement.

As the Germans and Austrians advanced the Bolsheviks had to withdraw, and in April declared their Ukrainian Soviet Government dissolved.

★

The Rada government sent delegates to Brest Litovsk, where the Bolsheviks were negotiating with the Germans, and in the event, on Lenin's instructions, the Bolshevik Government renounced claims over the Ukraine, and implicitly recognized the independent Ukrainian Government.

German and Austrian troops, in the guise of allies, now exploited the Ukraine – whose resources the Central Powers wished to use in the last phase of the war against France, Britain and the United States. The Rada proving unforthcoming, they sponsored on 29 April 1918 a coup d'état by General Pavel Skoropadsky, who proclaimed himself Hetman, and ruled until December in collaboration with Russian and landlord elements.

A Communist Party of the Ukraine was now at last formed, and on 2–12 July 1918 its First Congress was held in Moscow. Against the resistance of Ukrainian Communists headed by Mykola Skrypnyk it became an integral part of the Russian Communist Party. On 17–22 October 1918 a Second Congress – also in Moscow – noted that the Party's main task was 'the unification of the Ukraine with Russia'.[20] On behalf of the Moscow Politburo, Kamenev announced to this Congress that in Finland, Poland and the Ukraine 'the slogan of the self-determination of the nationalities has been turned into a weapon of the counter-revolution'.[21]

It is quite clear that the Bolsheviks, like most other Russians, had been caught by surprise at the astonishingly rapid and profound re-emergence of the Ukrainian nation. And in the case of many of them, the notion of Ukrainian as a peasant dialect of Russian never really left their minds. Lenin had earlier spoken of the rights of the Ukrainians, among other nationalities of the Russian Empire. But at the Eighth Congress (1919) he declared that any national feeling that might have existed in the Ukraine had been knocked out of it by the Germans, and even wondered aloud whether Ukrainian was really a mass language.[22]

In the Party Programme of 1918 it was plainly asserted that:

The Ukraine, Latvia, Lithuania and Byelorussia exist at the present time as separate Soviet republics. Thus is solved for now the question of state structure.

But this does not in the least mean that the Russian Communist Party should, in turn, reorganize itself as a federation of independent Communist Parties.

The Eighth Congress of the R.K.P. resolves: there must exist a *single* centralized Communist Party with a single Central Committee ... All decisions of the R.K.P. and its directing organs are unconditionally binding on all branches of the party, regardless of their national composition. The Central Committees of the Ukrainian, Latvian, Lithuanian Communists enjoy the rights of regional committees of the party, and are entirely subordinated to the Central Committee of the R.K.P.

And Lenin was writing, a few years later, when faced with tendencies to insubordination

The Ukraine is an independent republic. That is very good, but in Party matters it sometimes – what is the politest way of saying it? – takes a roundabout course, and we have to get at them somehow, because the people there are sly, and I will not say deceive the Central Committee but somehow or other edge away from us.[23]

★

Following the collapse of Germany in November 1918 a Ukrainian revolt against Skoropadsky soon restored the republic, and the Ukrainian National Union set up a Directorate headed by Vynnychenko, Simon Petliura and others.

Moscow reached an agreement not to interfere with the re-established People's Republic, if the Communist Party of the Ukraine were allowed to function legally, and Lenin does not seem to have decided on an invasion until the end of the year.

But the Ukrainian regime was militarily weak. Petliura, the War Minister of the Ukraine, had led a large-scale peasant revolt against the Hetmanate. But when his government was re-established the peasants went home, and the state was left almost defenceless. He had little choice but to offer commissions, and money, to anyone who could raise troops, and these *otamans* proved impossible to control, often becoming local warlords, changing their allegiance, even committing pogroms.

But this proved insufficient against the renewed Soviet attack, and on 5 February 1919 the Ukrainian government again had to leave Kiev, remaining for most of 1919 at Kamianets-Podilsky (Kamenets-Podolsk). Moscow withdrew recognition of Ukrainian independence, and the Soviet government in the Ukraine, for this and other reasons, was obnoxious to the people. It attempted, for one thing, to preserve the old landed estates as state farms or collectives; but 75% of the land so designated was seized by the peasantry.

This second Soviet regime in the Ukraine was in part based on Lenin's expectation (22 October 1918) that an 'international proletarian revolution' would soon break out.[24] It consisted of four Russians and two Ukrainians. Khristian Rakovsky (a Bulgarian) was named Head of State of the new Ukrainian Soviet Republic. He had negotiated for Lenin in Kiev with the Hetman government, and returned to Moscow to write a series of articles saying, in effect, that Ukrainian nationalism was a fad of a few intellectuals, while the peasants wanted to be addressed in Russian.[25]

He is now actually quoted as saying, in February 1919, that recognition of Ukrainian as the national language of the Ukraine would be a 'reactionary' measure, benefitting only kulaks and the nationalist intelligentsia.[26]

★

Lenin would in any case have wished to reincorporate the Ukraine into his new system. But it is clear that, like the Germans in *their* desperate struggle, he regarded Ukrainian resources as vital. On 11 February 1919, Moscow ordered the requisition without payment of all grain 'surplus' above a consumption quota of 286 pounds per capita. On 19 March 1919 Lenin himself demanded 50 million poods of grain, as necessary to the Bolsheviks' survival.[27] A Ukrainian scholar plausibly maintains that this was not literally true; but that Lenin's alternative was to provoke the *Russian* peasantry with even more excessive requisitions than they suffered already, and that it was preferable to transfer the burden.[28] In any case the result was 93 Ukrainian revolts in April 1919, and 29 in the first half of May. From 1–19 June there were 63.[29] In all some 300 seem to have occurred in the short period April–July. Instead of the planned loot of 2,317,000 tons of grain the Bolsheviks were only able to collect 423,000 in 1919. In effect the Communist writ hardly ran outside the cities.

The White offensive under Denikin in August 1919 once more drove out the Bolsheviks from the eastern part of the Ukraine, while the Ukrainian National Republic re-established itself west of the Dnieper.

On 2 October 1919, Moscow ordered its Ukrainian Soviet Government to disband, (this time also dissolving the Ukrainian Central Committee, which had been producing 'nationalist' deviations). This was followed by a variety of 'illegal' or oppositional activity among the Ukrainian Communists, and in December 1919 Lenin finally insisted on new tactics. In principle these amounted to accepting the aspirations of the Ukrainian people, while keeping the Ukrainian Communists under firm Moscow control.

This change of tactics was clearly the result of the failure of strong-arm centralization methods. At the Tenth Congress of the Russian Communist Party, the Ukrainian Communist V. Zatonsky said flatly:

> The national movement has apparently been engendered by the revolution. It must be said bluntly that this we have overlooked and most certainly let pass. This has been the greatest mistake of the Communist Party working in the Ukraine . . . We have missed the upsurge of the national movement which was perfectly natural at the moment when the broad peasant masses awoke to conscious life. We have missed the moment when a perfectly natural feeling of self-respect arose in these masses, and the peasant, who before had regarded himself and his peasant language, etc, with disdain, began to lift up his head and to demand much more than he had demanded in tsarist times. The revolution has aroused a cultural movement, awakened a wide national movement, but we have not managed to direct this national movement into our own course, we have let it pass, and it has gone wholly along the road where the local petty-bourgeois intelligentsia and the kulaks led it. This had been our greatest mistake.[30]

Or, as another leading Ukrainian Communist, Grinko (Hrynko), was to say, in 1919–20 the nationality factor was 'the weapon of the peasantry that went against us'.[31]

In fact the failure of the first two Soviet attempts on the Ukraine were evaluated in Moscow, and the conclusion was reached that the Ukraine nationality and language was indeed a major factor; and that a regime which ignored this too ostentatiously was doomed to be considered by the population as a mere imposition.

Organizationally the new line meant collaboration with the Borotbists – a 'left' faction of the Ukrainian Socialist Revolutionary Party, which accepted Soviet rule, but held strong national principles, and had shown itself capable of arousing at least some support in the countryside where the Bolsheviks had failed entirely.

Indigenous Bolshevism was, in fact, so weak that no plausibly Ukrainian-looking leadership could be obtained from it. But now, when Moscow decided on playing the Ukrainian card, there were these new men available. This alliance, followed by the entry of Borotbists into the Communist Party, meant that in the future there were many of the Ukrainian leadership who had a nationalist rather than a Leninist past. In fact, the Ukrainian Communist Party can be looked on as having 'two roots', as early Soviet historians put it. Whereas in Russia only a few former non-Bolsheviks, and at a low level, are to be seen in the ruling group (Vyshinksky, for example), in the Ukraine we find an ex-Borotbist, Liubchenko, later rising to be Chairman of the local Council of People's Commissars, and others, such as Grinko, in equally high position.

Though many Poles (like Dzerzhinsky, Radek, Kossior, Menzhinsky, Unshlikht) and Latvians (like Rudzutak, Eikhe, Berzin) had been veterans in the Bolshevik movement, few Ukrainians had appeared. Of the few that did some – in particular Skrypnyk and Chubar, both involved in revolutionary action at the centre – also tended to become defenders of Ukrainian national aspirations when they were transferred to the Ukraine. In many ways, as we have said, this anticipates what was to happen in Eastern Europe in the 1940s and 1950s with Communists thought completely susceptible to Moscow's orders, like Nagy and Kostov.

In this chaotic period, it should be remembered, the full implications of Leninism were not yet clear to many. A few Left-wing non-Communist parties remained precariously legal for some years, while within the Communist Party itself groupings with diverse views emerged publicly.

As far as the Ukraine is concerned, the essential point is that the regime was now strengthened by a group with real connections with the Ukrainian people; but at the same time, a source of nationalist demands.

★

None of the substance of power was, in fact, granted, nor could it have been without fissiparous results. A Conference of the (largely spurious) Communist Party of the Ukraine held outside the republic at Gomel in Byelorussia in October 1919, passed a realistic resolution (published seven years later) to the effect that 'the movement to the south and the organization of Soviet power in the Ukraine will be possible only with the aid of regular disciplined detachments (who must on no account be of local extraction)'.[32] At this period the membership of the Communist Party of the Ukraine was still only 23% Ukrainian.[33]

Among the various differences between Soviet rule in Russia proper and in the Ukraine, one of the most revealing was in the administration in the villages. Over the 'War Communism' period, the regime's main agency of power in the countryside was the Committee of Poor Peasants, consisting of the pro-Communists among the poor peasants and 'rural proletarians', in Russia overruling the village Soviets, in the Ukraine taking their place entirely. The Committees were dissolved late in 1918, but were recreated, *in the Ukraine alone*, on 9 May 1920, under the title Committees of Unwealthy Peasants (*Komnezamy*), with provision for the entry into them of the least well-to-do village peasants. In the rest of the USSR only the village Soviets remained. These were also formed in the Ukraine, but there the Committees had the right to denounce any village Soviet measure to higher authority, to expel members of the village Soviet executive, to dissolve the village Soviet and call new elections. They were also empowered to requisition foodstuffs.

Their position was explained as follows in a circular letter of the Central Committee: 'in the Ukrainian villages power really resides in the hands of the wealthy peasants, the kulaks, who by their nature are implacable foes of the proletarian revolution' and who were 'organized and armed to the teeth'. The Committees of Unwealthy Peasants were to organize the village poor, 'disarm the kulaks, and eliminate banditism'.[34]

The leading figures in the Committees, the Party's main support in the countryside, were largely non-Ukrainian. At their first Congress only 22.7% of delegates spoke in Ukrainian, at the second only 24.7%;[35] they were moreover an insufficient basis of Soviet power, and several thousand city Communists were sent to the countryside to assist them.

Nor did the Ukrainianizers within the Party even now meet with understanding, even at the cultural level, from the Bolsheviks as a whole. A Ukrainian delegate to the Twelfth Party Congress spoke of 'highly responsible comrades from the Ukraine' who argued 'I have travelled all over the Ukraine, I have spoken to the peasants, and I have gained the impression that they don't want the Ukrainian language'.[36]

Rakovsky, at least, had learnt his lesson, but had to complain of the difficult time they had 'forcing' the 'Ukrainian' Party organizations 'to understand the significance of the nationalities question'. The current nationality policy was understood 'by the majority in the Ukraine, and here in Russia even more, to be a certain strategic game of diplomacy . . .

"we are a country that has gone beyond the stage of nationalities", as one comrade expressed himself, "we are a country where material and economic culture opposes national culture. National culture is for backward countries on the other side of the barricade, for capitalist countries, and we are a Communist country"'.[37] An important section of the Bolsheviks, such veterans as D.Z. Lebed, held a theory of a 'struggle of two cultures' in which 'proletarian Russia' confronted the 'peasant Ukraine', with the corollary that no Ukrainianization was needed, since Russian culture must prevail. An attempt was made as late as the Ukrainian Party's Fifth Congress, 17–20 November 1920, (by no less a figure than Lenin's leading lieutenant Zinoviev), to limit the Ukrainian language to the rural areas, taking into account the final triumph of the 'more highly cultured Russian language'; but this was rejected.[38]

Through 1920–21 there was continual intra-party strife on the issue, with many of the Ukrainian Communists fighting hard to keep the formal liberties they had won, and to extend the cultural and linguistic Ukrainianization.

Skrypnyk, now the most distinguished Bolshevik on the Ukrainian side, fought on the basis (as he put it at the Tenth Congress of the Russian Communist Party, March 1921) that 'comrades must get out of their minds the idea that the Soviet federation is nothing more than a Russian federation, because the important fact is not that it is Russian, but that it is Soviet'.[39] The struggle on this issue was to continue.

★

The third Soviet occupation of the Ukraine was complete by March 1920. The temporary conquest of much of the western part, including Kiev, by the Poles in May 1920 was the last important interruption of Soviet rule.

The last regular Ukrainian units were overwhelmed in November 1920, and their remnants crossed the Polish frontier and were interned, though major guerilla raids went on until the end of 1921. In April 1921 there were 102 armed anti-Communist bands of from twenty or thirty to fifty or even 500 men operating in the Ukraine and the Crimea, not counting the anarchist Makhno's army, still numbering ten to fifteen thousand. Minor guerilla warfare, as Soviet sources confirm, and as we shall see in the next chapter, dragged on for years after the main anti-Soviet forces were crushed in 1921.[40]

But the Ukraine, in fact, was now by and large subdued, the first independent East European state to be successfully taken over by the Kremlin. The attempt on Poland proved a failure in 1920: otherwise people would perhaps even now, in that case too, be taking as natural what was merely historical, a long established subjection to Moscow,

41

interrupted by only a few years of independence.

Three successive Soviet Governments were thus installed in the Ukraine in 1918–20, each of them arriving in the wake of a Red Army invasion. The first two were expelled by rival invading forces, but not before they had shown an almost total incapacity to gain Ukrainian support. It was only on the third effort that Lenin and the Bolsheviks finally learnt that without serious, or serious-looking, concessions to Ukrainian national feeling, their rule would remain rootless and precarious. Once Lenin himself had mastered this lesson about the importance of not offending national susceptibilities, he held to it strongly, attacking Stalin and others when he felt them to be acting as overt Great Russian chauvinists. And 'independence' was now granted.

For the next ten years, the Ukraine was to enjoy a considerable measure of cultural and linguistic freedom, and governments were concerned not to enforce Moscow's political will too crudely or ostentatiously. It was, however, a continual struggle, and it remained clear that an important section of the Party continued to regard Ukrainian national feeling as a divisive element in the USSR, and the urge to independence as inadequately extinguished. Stalin shared this conviction, and when the time arrived, he was to act on that principle, and with the utmost ruthlessness, against the Ukrainian nation.

★

3
Revolution, Peasant War and Famine, 1917–21

> It loves blood
> The Russian earth
>
> *Akhmatova*

By 1917 the peasants already owned or rented out four times the land held by other owners, (including the intrusive 'townsmen' whose share in 1911 had already been over 20%). 89% of the cropped ploughland was in peasant hands.[1]

The collapse of the old regime in March 1917 resulted in the forcible takeover by the peasantry of the large estates. In 1917 108 million acres were taken from 110,000 landlords, and 140 million acres from two million 'peasants' – these latter being, as the figures of an average of seventy acres each indicate, better describable as small landlords. Through 1917–18 (in thirty-six evidently representative provinces) the peasants increased their holdings from 80% to 96.8% of all usable land,[2] while the average peasant holding increased by about 20%, (in the Ukraine it was nearly doubled).[3]

The number of landless peasantry dropped by nearly half between 1917–19, and the number who owned over 10 *desyatinas* (c. 27.5 acres) went down by over two-thirds.[4] A true levelling had taken place in the villages.

In accordance with Lenin's tactical estimates, The Land Decree of 8 November 1917, immediately following the Bolshevik seizure of power, was based on peasant demands voiced by the Social-Revolutionaries; and was a conscious manoeuvre to gain peasant support. It declared that only the Constituent Assembly (to be in fact dispersed by the Bolsheviks when it met in January 1918) could decide the land question, but asserted that 'the most just solution' would be the conversion of all land, including State land, 'to the use of all who work on it', and that 'forms of land tenure must be completely free . . . as may be decided by individual villages'. Lenin subsequently explained this as a manoeuvre,

We Bolsheviks were opposed to the law . . . Yet we signed it, because we did not want to oppose the will of the majority of peasants . . . We did not want to impose on the peasants the idea that the equal division of the land was useless, an idea which was alien to them. Far better, we thought, if, by their own experience and suffering, the peasants themselves came to realize that equal division is nonsense . . . That is why we helped to divide the land, although we realized it was no solution.[5]

A decree for 'socialization' of the land, on 19 February 1918, spoke of the virtues of collectivization, but was in effect largely concerned with distribution under the 8 November law.

The commune re-emerged, or rather was reinvigorated, spontaneously; it was allowed to deal with the redistribution of landlord and other land, the Bolsheviks seeming to believe that it could be restricted to this single duty, and the rest of village administration be taken over by Soviets. In fact, generally speaking, the commune became the effective village leadership.

The commune's re-emergence involved at least the partial destruction of the Stolypin peasantry as a class, and the 'separators' were now often forced back into the commune.[6] Their individual farms, or hamlets of several individual farms, called *khutors* (Ukrainian *khutirs*), were often in any case large or prosperous enough to qualify their owners as kulaks under the Communists' rough and ready rules. In Siberia, and in the Ukraine – where it was almost always a matter of hamlets rather than separate farmsteads – a fair number of khutirs after all survived for the time being, but in the USSR taken as a whole by 1922 less than half of the original 'separated' farms remained.[7] (Though the method was later to receive some encouragement from the authorities, in the period when productivity appeared more important than doctrinal considerations).

Recommunalization was, however, the essential. On the eve of the Revolution fewer than 50% of the peasants in forty-seven European provinces were still members of the village commune. But by 1927 95.5% of the holdings were in the old communes, with only 3.5% in individual farms of the Stolypin type. The – ironic – result was that 'Socialism' was not forwarded in any way. The commune perpetuated agrarian backwardness; but at the same time became, as a genuine peasant organization, a bulwark against socialization, as the Communists saw. And from the Communist point of view, the whole 'black repartition' itself meant that 'when the villages succeeded in getting hold of the landlords' property, they turned a completely deaf ear to ideas of Socialism'.[8]

Lenin put his view of this phenomenon on a number of occasions. He presented the doctrinal problem clearly:

Petty bourgeois proprietors are willing to help us, the proletariat, to throw out the landed gentry and the capitalists. But after that our roads part.

And he concluded

Then we shall have to engage in the most decisive, ruthless struggle against them.[9]

★

In May 1918, then, the Bolsheviks decided that the initial phase of alliance with the peasantry as a whole was over and that the socialist revolution could now begin in earnest. Lenin remarked that if a few hundred thousand noblemen could rule Russia, so could a few hundred thousand Communists. And this, rather than a more scholastic class or social analysis, may seem the right perspective.

The downgrading of the peasantry as a whole was formalized in July 1918 when the new Soviet Constitution provided for a heavy weighting of votes in favour of the worker against the peasant – (for the former one representative for 25,000 *voters*, for the latter one for 125,000 of the *population* – probably a difference of about 3–1). In the central Soviet organs where this imbalance mainly showed itself Party control in any case vitiated any real voting. But the symbolic effect, while defensible as good Marxism, was not calculated to woo the peasantry. The formula in the countryside for the new Socialist phase was an alliance with the poor peasant and the 'village proletarian' against the 'kulak', with the 'middle peasant' neutralized (though at a critical point in the Civil War the middle peasant became an 'ally' again).

However satisfactory in terms of class doctrine, there were many difficulties about this formulation in practice. In the first place the kulak in the sense of a rich exploiting peasant against whom the rest would make war, was by now a more or less mythical figure. Indeed, the moneylending and mortgaging which had been the original mark of the kulak, were no longer practical, being forbidden by law. However, we are told, 'the first blow' came in the summer of 1918, when the number of 'kulak' households was reduced to a third, and 50 million hectares were expropriated,[10] the 'kulaks' losing over 60% of their land.[11] In August 1918 Lenin spoke of two million kulak exploiters, but in April 1920 of only one million 'exploiting the labour of others'. The seizure and redistribution of 'kulak' land and property continued, at least in the Ukraine, until mid-1923, and one can be sure that no one who could by the remotest test be dubbed 'kulak' escaped.

But more awkward still, the 'rural proletariat' was, almost by definition, the weakest element in the village, in no way playing a productive role comparable to that of an urban proletariat. It included, as Communist

45

commentators were to admit, the lazy, the drunks, in general those least respected by the village as a whole. Where Stolypin had 'bet on the strong' Lenin was betting on the weak.

Yet he had no other method of obtaining or creating some sort of following in the countryside. The Party itself was extraordinarily weak in the villages. Before the revolution only 494 peasants belonged to the Bolshevik Party, and only four rural party cells existed.[12]

Bolshevik leaders were frank about the necessity of *creating* the otherwise virtually non-existent class war in the village. Sverdlov said in an address to the Central Executive Committee in May 1918,

> We must place before ourselves most seriously the problem of dividing the village by classes, of creating in it two opposite hostile camps, setting the poorest layers of the population against the kulak elements. Only if we are able to split the village into two camps, to arouse there the same class war as in the cities, only then will we achieve in the villages what we have achieved in the cities.[13]

★

The struggle was bitter, and became increasingly bitter. For it was not at all a mere matter of poor versus rich in the village. Far more than the class struggle, the central issue was by now the abolition of the peasant's right to sell his grain, and the battle simply to seize it in the name of the state.

A decree of 9 May 1918 'on the monopoly of food' empowered the Commissariat of Food to extract from the peasants any grain held in excess of quotas set by the Commissariat, adding that 'this grain is in the hands of kulaks'. The decree called on 'all working and propertyless peasants to unite immediately for a merciless war on the kulaks' for this purpose. A later decree, on 27 May, authorized the Food Commissariat to raise special 'food detachments' of reliable workers for the forcible collection of grain; 10,000 strong in July 1918, these detachments had risen to 45,000 by 1920. How these troops tended to behave can be gauged by a description, by Lenin, of their common behaviour: arbitrary arrests, beating or threatening with execution without sufficient reason, distilling vodka from the grain they had collected, and drunkenness.[14]

The decree of May 1918 had referred to 'surplus' grain beyond a calculation of double the peasant's 'needs'; but in January 1919 a decree 'on food requisition' was calculated the other way round, from the 'needs' of the state, and it became legal to requisition regardless of what was left the peasant. Lenin admitted later, 'Practically, we took all the surplus grain – and sometimes even not only surplus grain but part of the grain the peasant required for food'.[15]

A Soviet scholar tells us in a recent work that originally the food requisitioning detachments tried to extract grain directly from those suspected of hoarding it, without involving the rest of the peasantry; but found that 'without pressure from their fellow-villagers, [the kulaks] refused to turn over the surplus and, moreover, hid part of the grain in the houses of the poor, promising them a hand-out'.[16] In fact village solidarity was not broken.

To pursue the new class war, 'Committees of Poor Peasants' (of which we have already spoken in the Ukrainian context) were set up by a decree of 11 June 1918. Lenin described them as marking the transition from the attack on landlordism to the beginning of the socialist revolution in the countryside.[17]

From the provincial figures available, it emerges that the Committees of Poor Peasants (Russian *Kombedy*) were only just over half composed of peasants of any sort;[18] (and in 1919 they were in Russia proper dissolved into the village Soviets, similarly manned). The activists in both were, in fact, city Communists – over 125,000 of these were sent to man the defective village organizations.[19]

In speech after speech Lenin first urged, then announced, the sending of detachments of 'thousands and thousands' of 'politically advanced' workers from the two capitals to the countryside, to head the food requisitioning detachments and provide leadership to the Committees of Poor Peasants.

Though the bulk of even the poorest peasants remained aloof, the regime succeeded in building up some sort of base in the countryside. As the antagonisms grew worse in the villages, small gangs which had accepted Communist patronage and had the support of the armed intruders from the cities, began to plunder and murder more or less at will.[20] In addition Lenin proposed in late August 1918 that hostages be taken in each region: '25–30 hostages from among the rich who would be responsible with their lives for the collection and loading of all surpluses'.[21] He also suggested that part of the requisitioned grain be shared with informers.[22]

A Soviet scholar gives estimates that in 1919 about 15–20% of the agricultural product was requisitioned, increasing in 1920 to 30%.[23] (And compulsory delivery was extended, by a decree of 5 August 1919, to 'cottage industry products'.)

This attitude to the products of the peasantry is often spoken of as 'War Communism', the implication being that it was an emergency policy dictated by the exigencies of the Civil War. This is quite untrue. Not only had the Civil War not really started at the time of the original decrees, but

Lenin in June 1918 already defined the grain monopoly from quite a different point of view, as 'one of the most important methods of gradual transition from capitalist commodity exchange to socialist product-exchange'.[24]

That is to say, far from being a 'war' measure the 'War Communism' policy was a conscious attempt to create a new social order, to effect the immediate transformation of the country into full socialism. Even after the débâcle Lenin admitted this clearly, speaking of 'an attempt to attain Communism straight away', and saying 'Generally, we thought it possible . . . to begin without transition to build up socialism'.[25] In October 1921, he said 'We calculated . . . or we presumed without sufficient calculation – that an immediate transition would take place from the old Russian economy to state production and distribution on Communist principles';[26] and, on the specific policy of requisition,

> We made the mistake of deciding to change over directly to Communist production and distribution. We sought to obtain a sufficient quantity of grain from the peasants by the way of the *Razverstka* [compulsory grain delivery quotas], then to apportion it to the industries, and that thus we would obtain Communist production and distribution. I would not affirm that this was exactly how we visualized it, but we did act in this spirit.[27]

One of the regime's leading economists was to write of the War Communism period that it lacked planning, so that any shortfall was attacked as a 'shock' target and given top priority. This inevitably resulted in economic anarchy,[28] and it was particularly applied to the problem of getting the peasants' grain, with force the only method available – though Nikolay Bukharin, in his *Economics of the Transformation Period*, maintained with strange logic that coercion of the peasantry could not be considered 'pure constraint' because it 'lies on the path of general economic development'. Lenin commented 'Very good'.[29]

More generally Socialism was conceived as a matter of centralization, planning and the abolition of money. The system now established was one of nationalized industry and finance, and grain procurement by force, under a highly centralized governmental machine. This was regarded by the Party, from Lenin down, as not merely socialism, but even communism. Lenin, indeed, at one point presented requisitioning as the essence of socialism; and held that direct State-peasant relations were socialist and market relations capitalist.[30]

One of the most striking conclusions from this is that Lenin saw the establishment of socialism, or of socialist relations, without regard to any collectivization of the peasantry. The criterion, in fact, was merely the abolition of market relationships.

The question at issue was thus how to obtain the peasant's grain without buying it. As we come to the collectivization of 1930, it is sensible to think of it, if anything, less in the social terms of collective ownership and work but more in terms of it providing a method of putting it beyond the power of the peasant to withhold his product from the state.

Meanwhile in 1918–21 such highly subsidized collective farms as were formed were few and inefficient, and Lenin spoke of them contemptuously, as 'alms-houses'. A number of large estates were transformed into State Farms (*Sovkhozy*), regarded as the highest form of socialist agriculture – the true rural factory envisaged by Marxists. The law on Socialist Land Tenure of 14 February 1919 said that they were being organized 'to create the conditions for a complete shift to communist agriculture'. But they too were not in fact either efficient or popular, in spite of the various advantages showered on them. And neither State nor collective farms were of any real significance under War Communism, or until much later.

As to effective modernization in the future, the tractor, newly heard of from America, was already seen to be the instrument for modernizing the farms. Lenin thought, or said, in 1919, that 100,000 tractors would turn the peasants into Communists.[31]

The end of the Civil War was not accompanied by relaxation of 'War Communism'. In fact further Utopian measures were put in train: communications and rents were made free; the abolition of money was in the planning stage, together with the abolition of the central bank; and at the end of 1920 the last small enterprises were nationalized – at the same time as a further state intervention in the peasants' affairs in the form of orders on what crops to produce.

As late as 8 March 1921, while the Kronstadt rebellion was at its height, Lenin was still telling the Tenth Party Congress that abandoning grain requisitions in favour of free trade 'would still unfailingly lead to the rule of the White Guard, to the triumph of capitalism, to complete restoration of the old regime. And I repeat: one must clearly recognize this political danger'.

★

While the Civil War raged, the peasants saw little hope from the Whites either. Denikin – as the *Large Soviet Encyclopaedia* surprisingly admits – was an adherent not of Landlord–Tsardom but of the Constitutional Democrats. But the absence of unity or uniformity in the White ranks allowed scope for the accusation that they wished to restore the landlords, as some undoubtedly did. Moreover Denikin stood for a 'Russia one and indivisible', and refused to admit the existence of the Ukrainians.

A further fatal flaw in the policies of Denikin's and most of the other anti-Soviet regimes was that their attitude to the immediate agrarian problem – the urgent need of any regime or army of the time for grain – led to non-market policies. Or rather, this is true of all the White regimes before Wrangel. He, for the first time, began to rely on the market forces and free trade in grain. And his breakout with a small and often defeated army from the Crimea in 1920, on the face of it desperate, for the first time brought peasant volunteers in large numbers to a White army in the Ukraine.

Yet in general the Civil War was a contest between two well armed but unpopular minorities. And if in considering the period from 1918, we are habituated to turn our main attention to it, it is for inadequate reasons: it was a regular war, of organized armies, rival governments, high commands; conducted for the capture of key points, of central cities. Its campaigns and battles are clear on the ground; its prominence in the eyes of the world plain and dramatic.

Yet in its scope, and even more in its casualties and its effect on the country, it may reasonably be held as less pervasive and less massive than the Peasant War of 1918–22 which overlapped it and outlasted it. As late as 1921, with all the Whites gone, the Soviets' leading historian describes the situation:

> The centre of the RSFSR is almost totally encircled by peasant insurrection, from Makhno on the Dnieper to Antonov on the Volga.[32]

There were still active risings, too, in Byelorussia, the South East, Siberia, Karelia, the Caucasus, and Central Asia.[33]

Already in 1918 official figures give 108 'kulak revolts' in the Soviet republic from July to November 1918. For 1918 as a whole, no fewer than '245 important anti-Soviet rebellions broke out in only 20 regions of central Russia';[34] while 99 are listed in about a third of Bolshevik territory, in seven months of 1919.[35]

In some areas a food requisitioning plenipotentiary would reach a village and be shot; a punitive expedition would follow, shooting half a dozen peasants and arresting others; a new plenipotentiary with assistants would arrive and be shot in a day or two; another punitive expedition – and so on.[36] These small clashes were widespread, and merged into larger rebellions, with the 'Greens' presenting at least as great a threat as the Whites or the Poles.

Lenin's attitude to his various enemies emerges strikingly in one of his notes to a leading Red Army commissar: 'A beautiful plan. Finish it off with Dzerzhinsky. Under the guise of "Greens" (and we will pin it on them later) we shall go forward for ten-twenty versts and hang the kulaks, priests and landowners. Bounty: 100,000 roubles for each man hanged'.[37]

Early in 1919 a major revolt took place in the Volga region, (followed by another in 1920). In the summer of 1919, a Russian peasant 'army' in Fergana formed for defence against the Moslem inhabitants threw in its lot with the Moslems against the Reds. In the North Caucasus real insurrectional armies were reported by the Communist authorities and several Soviet divisions were annihilated.[38] There were other major rebellions elsewhere in the minority territories. On 13 February 1921 the Armenians rose, capturing the capital Erevan five days later.

In West Siberia a rising in January 1921 mobilized 55,000–60,000 peasants, spread over twelve districts,[39] and effectively cut Soviet communications, capturing a number of towns – even ones as important as Tobolsk.[40]

The celebrated Antonov rebellion starting on 19 August 1920 overran most of the Tambov Province and parts of adjoining provinces, and fielded an army of over 40,000 peasant fighters. A congress of these Tambov rebels adopted a programme for the abolition of Soviet power and the convocation of a Constituent Assembly under equal voting, with the land given to those who worked it. Similar documents were produced by the Volga rebels, which also called for power to the people 'with no subdivision into classes or parties'.[41]

It was impossible to label the rebels kulaks as such, since official reports showed that from 25–80% of villagers actively fighting in Antonov's forces[42] were poor or middle peasants. They held large Bolshevik forces to a stalemate for many months, so that it was not until May 1921 that the revolt was effectively suppressed by regular forces under Tukhachevsky. Even after that smaller groups were in action at least until mid-1922. Reprisals were savage, involving the Lidice treatment for whole villages.

In the Ukraine, the great rising of Grigoriev in May 1919, had 20,000 men, 50 cannons, even 6 armoured trains; Soviet historians hold it responsible for preventing the projected Red Army invasion of Rumania to aid Bela Kun's Hungarian Soviet Republic.[43] Among many other rebel forces the bands of the anarchist Makhno became the most famous, at one period mustering some 40,000 men. It was for a time in alliance with the Reds against the Whites, but after January 1920 there were eight months of fierce fighting between Makhno and the Bolsheviks. A brief restoration of that alliance in October and November 1920, against the last White threat by Wrangel, was followed by renewed fighting which went on until August 1921. The appeal of Makhno's anarchism was readily explained by him: the peasantry was against 'the landlord and rich kulak' but also against 'their servant the political and administrative power of the official'.[44] An analysis which gives point to that advanced in Pasternak's *Doctor Zhivago*:

> The peasants are in revolt, there are ceaseless risings. You'll say that they are fighting the Reds or Whites indiscriminately, whoever may be in power, that they are simply against any established authority because they don't know what they want. Allow me to differ. The peasant knows very well what he wants, better than you or I do, but he wants something quite different. When the revolution came and woke him up, he decided that this was the fulfilment of his dreams, his ancient dream of living anarchically on his own land by the work of his hands, in complete independence and without owing anything to anyone. Instead of that, he found he had only exchanged the old oppression of the Czarist state for the new, much harsher yoke of the revolutionary super-state. Can you wonder that the villages are restless and can't settle down! . . .[45]

Grigoriev and Makhno were not the only Ukrainian rebels. The Partisan leader 'Zeleny' led a great rising over a large territory near Kiev, and there were many others. All in all, in February 1921, 118 risings are reported by the Cheka as in progress.[46]

When it comes to lesser clashes, in the Ukraine in a single four day period as late as April 1921, the Cheka reports a band of ten seizing grain and killing an official in the Podilia Province; a band of fifty mounted men armed with machine guns attacking a sugar plant, killing five guards and making off with eighteen horses, 306,000 roubles and two typewriters, in the Poltava Province; a band of two hundred mounted men attacking a railway station and killing twenty-six Red Army men before being driven off by an armoured train, in the Kharkov Province.[47]

In the same area, partisan warfare on a minor scale went on for years. In the Lebedyn district, Sumy Province, a partisan band was active until 1928.[48] Another band of twenty-odd Ukrainian partisans were also operating near Bila Tserkva, Kiev Province, until 1928;[49] and there are numbers of similar reports elsewhere, especially in the North Caucasus and Central Asia.

It is noteworthy that Antonov's men had been joined by workers, 'including some railwaymen', as official reports complained.[50] It is not our purpose to deal with the workers' movement, but it is indeed significant that the working class was equally, or almost equally, turning against the Communists. Even in 1918 there were powerful workers' strikes and demonstrations even in Petrograd, while in the industrial region of the Urals, a Soviet historian notes, 'the Left SRs raised against us backward elements of the factory workers in Kuchva, Rudyansk, Shaytansk, Yugovsk, Setkino, Kasliono and elsewhere'.[51] At the great industrial centre of Izhevsk and elsewhere major worker risings took place; an

'Izhevsk People's Army' of 30,000 men being formed, and eventually going over to the Whites and serving with Kolchak.

Moreover the workers made, as a Soviet authority puts it, 'purely peasant' demands, such as the end of forced requisition and of the confiscation of peasant household goods.[52]

More sinister still, from the Soviet point of view, was the increasing unreliability of the Red Army. Desertion, or failure to report for the draft, averaged 20% and in some areas it was as high as 90%.[53] A Soviet source estimates the number of Red Army deserters in Tambov Province alone, in the autumn of 1920, as 250,000.[54]

In March 1919, a brigade mainly recruited from Russian peasants in the Tula region mutinied in Byelorussia, and made common cause with the local peasant rebels, setting up a 'People's Republic'.[55]

The Red Army commander Sepozhkov led a force of 2,700 soldiers in revolt on the Volga in July 1920, a movement which, after his death, his successor Serov kept in the field for more than two years, even capturing towns, and deploying 3,000 men as late as January 1922. In December 1920 another Red Army officer, Vakulin, rebelled in the Don region, soon increasing his force of some five hundred to 3,200 and after his death his successor, Popov, deployed 6,000 men by March 1921. In February 1921 yet another Red Army commander, Maslak, took his brigade over from Stalin's favourite First Cavalry Army and joined Makhno.

But the most critical point was reached with the revolt of the Kronstadt naval base on 2 March 1921. The Kronstadt rebels had a clear notion of the peasants' grievances. In their newspaper they wrote, 'In exchange for almost totally requisitioned grain, and confiscated cows and horses, they got Cheka raids and firing squads'.[56] As Trotsky was to declare at the Fifteenth Party Conference in 1926, at Kronstadt 'the middle peasant talked with the Soviet Government through naval guns'.

It is little wonder that on 15 March 1921 Lenin was saying, though not in public, 'we are barely holding on'.[57]

★

The human destructiveness of the Peasant War can be gauged from the figures. Even before the great famine of 1921–2, which took some five million lives, Soviet official data makes it clear that in 1918–20 just over nine million perished[58] (this is to omit the two million Russian dead of World War I – and the one million odd refugees).

The deaths from typhus,[59] typhoid, dysentry and cholera in 1918–23 are estimated as just under three million, (mainly from typhus), and many of these were in the famine period, and among the deaths attributed to it.

But even if we take two million of them as from 1918–20, we are left with seven million other excess deaths in those years.

The leading Soviet authority, B.T. Urlanis,[60] estimates the killed on both sides in the Civil War as approximately 300,000 – including many Poles and Finns. Even if we add all the massacres, killings of prisoners and so on, we can hardly envisage a Civil War death roll of a million, which indeed seems a high figure.

The other six million died of local famines, and in the Peasant War. The latter, of course, was mainly a matter of male dead. The 1926 census shows nearly five million fewer men than women, far the greater part of the deficit in the age group 25–65 years old.[61] This must roughly indicate that with two million men killed in World War I, and a million (or less) in the Civil War, there were some two million (or more) more men than women dead from other causes – that is, almost entirely, in the Peasant War.

These were not necessarily killed in battle. For it is reasonably clear that the death roll from executions was at least as high as that in the fighting. Of one group of uprisings, a senior Cheka officer writes that 3,057 insurgents were killed in battle and 3,437 shot afterwards.[62]

These figures of the dead in the Peasant War are only rough. But they are a sufficient indication of the extent and persistence of the peasant resistance, and of the sacrifices they were prepared to make in the attempt to prevent the subjugation of their livelihood to the requisition system.

★

The events of 1918–21 had produced a disruption of the social and economic order of a type only comparable to the effect of the Thirty Years War in Germany. In the First World War, millions of the Tsar's subjects – as of every other major European nation – had been moved to the front; afterwards their peasant majority had returned to take part in the seizure of the land of the nobility; the latter, a small class, had collapsed. But these events had not much shaken society as a whole. On the contrary, the division of the land had consolidated and further settled the peasant majority. The true disintegration took place in the Lenin period. A large part of society disappeared through death and emigration. Millions more had moved all over the countryside, fleeing 'from one hunger-stricken area to another, from one theatre of war to another'.[63] Meanwhile the economy simply collapsed. And, as we have noted, the results of Communist policies in the countryside were economically retrogressive. The more advanced peasantry were dispossessed or killed off, and, in much of the land, the old three strip system re-emerged where it had died out.

But mere disruption was far more important. The decline in agriculture only began in 1919, but by 1922 work horses were down 35.1% (from 1916), cattle 24.4%, hogs 42.2%, sheep and goats 24.8%,[64] – livestock, in fact being at about two-thirds of the pre-war level.

In 1913 about 700,000 tons of fertilizer had been used, in 1921 about 20,000 tons. The area sown had gone down from 214 million acres in 1916 to c. 133 million in 1922. The grain crop (including potatoes) had gone down by about 57% between 1909–1913 and 1921. These are in some cases estimates which are by no means as precise as the figures might imply: but they cannot be far wrong.[65]

The great famine of 1921 was not due to any conscious decision that the peasant should starve. Nevertheless, to attribute it simply to drought is quite untrue. The weather, though bad, was not at the disaster level. The factor which turned the scale was, in fact, the Soviet Government's methods of crop requisition – partly because it took more of the peasant's product than would leave him with subsistence; partly because, over the past three years, it had effectively removed much of the incentive to produce.

The starvation which now possessed the land followed inevitably from the ruling that, (as with Lenin's frank admission), the peasant's needs were not to be taken into account.

★

The famine was worst in the Volga basin. The misery and death was of the same nature as we shall be describing when we come to the even worse famine of 1932–3, with a single major difference. In 1921–2 the existence of the famine was admitted, and relief from abroad was actively encouraged.

On 13 July 1921 the Soviet Government allowed Maxim Gorki to appeal for foreign aid. The future President Hoover's American Relief Administration, which had already done much humanitarian work in Central and Eastern Europe, started moving stocks into Russia soon after 20 August. The US Congress appropriated $20 million in December; and Americans were also encouraged to sponsor individual packages, and subscribed $6 million. The total amount of American funds made available was about $45 million.

In Moscow Gorki assembled a group of distinguished citizens, mostly of non-Communist or non-political backgrounds, as the Soviet element in the work of relief.

At the maximum, the American Relief Administration and its associated organizations were feeding over 10,400,000 mouths, and various other organizations nearly two million more, for a total of more than 12,300,000.

There had been famines in Russia before – in 1891, in 1906, in 1911, but none of these had been as profound or had affected such large populations. In the worst of previous famines the peasants who could not get enough seed grain never exceeded three million, but in 1921 such peasants numbered thirteen million.

The American Commission on Russian Relief estimated about three million homeless children in 1922,[66] (with two million more in danger of starvation at home). Of these 1,600,000 were in permanent or temporary institutions – 1.5 million being fed by foreign relief organizations.

Even at this stage there was a tendency to leave the Ukrainian peasantry unassisted, (though Soviet official figures were to give 800,000 deaths from famine and related diseases in the Ukraine in the first half of 1922 and this is reported as not covering some of the worst areas).[67] In the Ukraine the famine was at first concealed, according to official American Relief Administration reports, by 'estimating the crop at almost exactly twice the figure accepted by the local authorities'.[68] And the Ukrainian famine areas were not at first made accessible to the American aid organizations. 'The Government in Moscow', as an American scholar noted, 'not only failed to inform the American Relief Administration of the situation in the Ukraine, as it had done in the case of other much more remote regions, but deliberately placed obstacles in the way of everything which might bring the Americans into touch with the Ukraine . . .'[69]

Indeed, between 1 August 1921 and 1 August 1922 10.6 million hundredweight of grain was actually taken from the Ukraine for distribution elsewhere. But finally American Relief was in April–June 1922 admitted to the Ukraine, (as Soviet President Kalinin put it) 'at the height of the famine when thousands were already dying and other thousands resigned to death'.[70] Relief Administration representatives said that it was 'astonishing' that trainloads of food from Kiev and Poltava were 'sent hundreds of miles to the hungry along the Volga' instead of being transported a score or so miles to Odessa or Mikolaiv, where 'famine was raging'.[71] It was only in January 1922 that the Donets Province had been permitted to suspend shipments.[72] All this certainly represents not mere inefficiency, but an official tendency to put the maximum burden on the least 'loyal', (though the temporary exclusion of the Americans may be due in part to a reluctance to let them visit a Kiev still under martial law).

The *Large Soviet Encyclopaedia* in its 1926 edition gives a fair account of the American Relief Administration's work, acknowledging that it was feeding about ten million people at the height of its activity, and that it had spent 137 million gold roubles. In 1930 the *Small Soviet Encyclopaedia* told that 'under the pretext of good works' the American Relief Administration had really been concerned to lessen a crisis of production in the USA. By 1950 the *Large Soviet Encyclopaedia's* new (2nd) edition was saying that the ARA had used its apparatus 'to deploy espionage activity and support counter-revolutionary elements. The counter-revolutionary acts of the ARA aroused energetic protests on the part of the broad toiling masses'. And the view of the newest (3rd) edition (in 1970) is that the ARA 'provided a certain aid in the struggle against famine' but that at the same time leading circles in the USA used it 'to support counter-revolutionary elements and sabotage and espionage activity'.

In fact, the non-Communist Russian relief representatives in Moscow were arrested in the autumn of 1921 (at a time when Maxim Gorki was out of the country). Intervention by Hoover personally resulted in the commutation of death sentences, and several members, after a period of Siberian exile, were even allowed to leave the country.

Between 1918 and 1922 one-tenth of the population had perished. The famine was for the moment a last sacrifice by the peasantry to the delusive and oppressive agrarian policies of the regime. For meanwhile, their struggle against the attempt totally to subjugate the countryside and destroy the peasant economy had been successful. Their own insurgents, and finally the Kronstadt sailors, had brought the government in Moscow to a realization that disaster faced it if it continued to impose its essential programme; and to an acceptance, at least for the time being, of a retreat, a truce which left the free peasantry in existence.

*

4

Stalemate, 1921–7

Hope and fear, and peace and strife
Scott

Finally, at the last moment, Lenin had listened to the voice of reality, to the peasant speaking with the naval guns of Kronstadt, the machine guns of Makhno and Antonov. On 15 March 1921, at the Tenth Congress, only seven days after he had declared that there would be no relaxation of the party's policies and doctrines, he saw that ruin faced the regime. He settled for temporarily abandoning the attempt to socialize the countryside, while using the breathing space to consolidate the Party's grip on political power. The New Economic Policy (NEP) was proclaimed.

Even now, the retreat was reluctant. At first Lenin hoped to placate the peasantry without reinstituting market relations, by organized direct barter between state industry and peasants. This failed, and he 'retreated to markets, money and capitalists'.[1] Unlimited requisitioning of grain was replaced by tax measures (though this was delayed for some months in the Ukraine, with a view to securing further grain for immediate needs). Money was restored, and all limitations on holding it repealed.

Railway fares, postal charges, and other such things abolished in the last phase of 'War Communism' were restored by decrees of 9 July 1921, 1 August 1921, and 15 September 1921. And in October 1921 industries regained the right to sell their products on the open market.

The veteran D.B. Ryazanov characterized NEP at the Tenth Party Congress as a 'peasant Brest' – the equivalent retreat in the face of peasant power that had been necessary at the Treaty of Brest–Litovsk in the face of German power.

Lenin himself spoke of NEP as a 'breathing space' when strength was lacking for a full revolutionary transition. He added, 'We are engaged in a strategic retreat that will allow us to advance on a broad front in the very near future'.[2]

It was customary in Khrushchev's time for Soviet scholars to quote Lenin, over this period, as saying that collectivization of the land must be a slow process, depending on persuasion and the free consent of the peasantry; and that expropriation even of the richer peasantry should only be undertaken when the material, technical and social conditions were suitable. He did indeed go on record to this effect.[3]

Though at first calling NEP a 'retreat', one of many the Bolsheviks had at one time or another had to make, as NEP took hold Lenin sometimes even justified it as in itself a method of achieving socialism: not the last of the changes of mind he made on such issues. In August 1922 he was calling peasant trading cooperatives 'cooperative capitalism'. In a couple of brief notes in January 1923, when he was already largely incapacitated by his stroke, he thought that 'given socialist ownership of the means of production and the victory of the proletariat over the bourgeoisie' such cooperatives would add up to 'a socialist regime'.[4] He went so far as to urge skilled modern-style trading as a means of imposing the commercial side of cooperation, calling (as in other matters) for a 'cultural revolution' to improve Russia in this sphere.[5] (In fact, the cooperative movement in credit, buying and selling had benefited the richer peasantry, and produced no trend whatever to collective farming).

At the same time a statement of Engels to the effect that the Social-Democrats would never force, but only persuade, the German peasantry into collective ways became much referred to in the Party literature. But the fact that NEP was given a broad theoretical basis by many of the leaders, sometimes including Lenin, does not in itself seem as significant as is sometimes made out. *All* actions, however pragmatic, by a highly doctrinal and theoreticizing sect like the Bolsheviks almost automatically generated such interpretations. But at any rate the 'Rightists' in the Party who were to propose a fairly long period of gradual development under NEP were able to cite Lenin's words, as well as the obvious fact that it was he after all who had instituted NEP in the first place.

Yet it would probably be a mistake to seek for a real basis to any particular policy in Lenin's remarks during this period. At times one has the feeling (as in earlier phases of the Revolution) that he was merely uncertain of the best way forward, and casting about for policies and theories. For example, at the Eleventh Congress in 1922, he announced that the retreat had gone too far and that it was time to advance again. However, he seems to have changed his mind again, and no action resulted.[6]

The restoration of industry was also a part of NEP, and also involved concessions to capitalism. As Lenin put it, in October 1921, owing to the collapse of industrial production 'the proletariat has ceased to exist as a class', and the licensed capitalists would assist in the 'restoration of the industrial proletarian class'.[7] At one point he even held that the big capitalists could be turned into allies against the peasant smallholder, seen as the main enemy,[8] thus repeating a formula he had already advanced in 1918, that 'in our country the main enemy of socialism is the petty bourgeois element'.[9]

When not calling for a swift resumption of the advance – that is when at his most pro-NEP – Lenin saw the struggle for the allegiance of the middle peasants as perhaps lasting generations – but at best 'ten or twenty' years.[10] (NEP in fact officially lasted for just under 9 years). But, as against such tactical advice, Lenin always maintained his more profound theoretical position: that the peasantry 'engenders capitalism and the bourgeoisie constantly, daily, hourly, and on a mass scale',[11] which justified the utmost vigilance, and the seizing of the earliest possible opportunity to put a stop to such a state of affairs.

He also said that in the given world conditions the period of peaceful construction would 'obviously not be for very long'.[12] And in a letter to Kamenev on 3 March 1922 (not printed until 1959) he added, 'It is a great mistake to think that the NEP put an end to terror; we shall again have recourse to terror and to economic terror'.[13]

In his classic work on Lenin, Adam Ulam concludes that if he had lived, Lenin would have ended NEP earlier than Stalin did[14] – the latter having to consolidate his own position before acting. However that may be, his gradual disappearance from public life, and his death on 21 January 1924, left the Party with the problem of sooner or later, and by one means or another, eliminating the independent peasant.

*

Lenin's uncertainties reflected the fact that there was now an innate contradiction in Party policy. On the one hand (on the economic side) it wished to encourage agricultural production, and this meant encouraging the effective producers. On the other (on the political and doctrinal side) it regarded these effective producers as, eventually, the class enemy, and in principle relied on the less effective, but even more on the ineffective, elements of the peasantry.

Moreover, every time the 'poor peasant' was helped to strengthen his economic position, he ceased to be a poor peasant; and giving land to a landless peasant similarly moved him into a less acceptable category;

while as the 'middle peasant' prospered further, he automatically became a 'kulak' in Communist eyes.

These contradictions were not resolved until Stalin's Revolution of 1930. Meanwhile, the most urgent task was the reestablishment of agriculture. And this could only be accomplished through real encouragement, real incentives, to the 'kulak' producers.

The national problem, too, could only be handled by temporary retreat. In the Civil War, while neither Lenin nor Denikin had any intention of granting real independence to the Ukraine or other nations, Lenin had (or finally came round to) the better tactical line, and of the two it appeared that his policies might give some promise. The Whites were, in actual fact, not as blind to the national problem as is sometimes said, and Kolchak urged a recognition of the independence of Finland, Poland and other lands: but at the crucial moment this was ignored and Denikin had struck for Moscow under Russian 'Unity' slogans.

Lenin is nowadays often quoted by Ukrainian Communist dissidents to support the idea that he was in sympathy in principle with minority nationhood. But in fact, it is clear that he now understood the dangers to the regime of the national feelings of Ukrainians and others, and believed they should be neutralized, though without giving up for a moment the principles of centralization and Moscow control.

The failure of the first Communist regimes to establish themselves in the Ukraine had led to second thoughts. Just as Ryazanov called the New Economic Policy a 'peasant Brest', the new policy towards the Ukraine which came at this time might be called a 'Ukrainian Brest Litovsk'. In both, the concessions were enough to ensure an abatement of immediate hostility to the Communist regime. The peasant was no longer persecuted for peasant conduct; the Ukrainian was allowed a certain cultural autonomy.

As we have seen, the concessions to Ukrainian feeling, like the concessions to the peasantry, had been made as a matter of political necessity. The first Soviet regime in the Ukraine was actively against Ukrainianism, and perished in a storm of mass hostility. The national attitudes of the second, rather more circumspect, still aroused profound resistance. The third and successful incursion of Communism was strongly resisted, but was militarily better prepared: while politically it manoeuvred to take some of the edge off resistance by a more careful and systematic policy of attention to Ukrainian nationhood, or such of it as did not seem irremediably anti-Communist.

In December 1922 the still supposedly independent Ukraine, Transcaucasia and Byelorussia entered the new Union of Soviet Socialist Republics. A policy of 'Ukrainianization' was formalized in April 1923, at the Twelfth Congress of the Russian Communist Party. For the first time since the 18th century, a government firmly established in the Ukraine had as one of its professed aims the protection and development of the Ukrainian language and culture.

Prominent scholars and writers, even those who had strongly supported the Rada Republic, came back from emigration. They included the great historian Mykhailo Hrushevsky, who had actually been Chairman of the Rada, together with other Ministers and soldiers of that regime.

At the same time, several of the Ukrainian Social Revolutionaries who had been tried and sentenced to short terms of imprisonment in 1921 were pardoned and given posts. For example, Vsevolod Holubovych, former Prime Minister of the Ukrainian Republic, was made Chairman of the Ukrainian Supreme Economic Council, and others took lesser cultural and economic posts.[15]

In fact, very unlike in Russia proper, the new policy extended to the high figures of the pre-Bolshevik regime.

Almost all, it is true, took non-political, academic positions – though ex-Premier Vynnychenko was actually admitted to the Ukrainian Communist Party and its Central Committee, and appointed Deputy Premier and Commissar for Foreign Affairs, before wisely choosing to return to exile . . .

'Ukrainianization' went further than similar concessions to nationalism elsewhere. Ukrainian cultural figures who returned to the country came in the genuine hope that even a Soviet Ukraine might be the scene of a national revival. And, to a high degree, they were right – for a few years. Poetry and fiction, linguistic and historical writing, established themselves on a scale and with an intensity extremely exciting to all classes, while the older literature was reprinted on a massive scale.

Moreover, the countryside, the peasantry, were reached in a devoted campaign by Ukrainian cultural organizations. Permitted by the Bolsheviks under the new tactics, these were naturally composed of men who, even if thinking of themselves as Communists, were mainly concerned with the nation's history and literature. General Grigorenko describes how, as a youth, he first heard of Ukrainian music and literature from a branch found in his village: 'And from them I learned that I belonged to the same nationality as the great Shevchenko, that I was a Ukrainian'.[16]

Even Stalin, at the Tenth Party Congress in 1921, spoke approvingly of the eventual Ukrainianization of the Ukraine's cities: 'It is clear that whereas Russian elements still predominate in the Ukrainian towns, in the course of time these towns will inevitably be *Ukrainianized*', instancing

Prague, which had been largely German before the 1880s, and then became Czech.

*

Lenin's death was followed by the struggle for power which brought Stalin to unchallenged supremacy six years later. In brief, Stalin first crushed the 'Left' and then the 'Right'. Leon Trotsky was out-manoeuvred by an alliance of Grigori Zinoviev, Lev Kamenev, and Stalin. Zinoviev and Kamenev were then defeated by Stalin and the Rightists Nikolay Bukharin, Alexey Rykov and Mikhail Tomsky, and a newly formed alliance of Trotsky, Zinoviev and Kamenev was similarly dealt with. (As each vacancy occurred in the Politburo, it was filled with figures who in the next phase generally supported Stalin). And then, with the Left crushed, by the end of 1927, Stalin turned against the Right, who were effectively defeated within two years.

This struggle was, of course, fought out in terms of policies. Here we are only concerned with the agrarian side of that dispute – though this was indeed a major controversy.

The most important elements in it can be simply stated. Everyone approved in principle of the New Economic Policy. Everyone wished to go on as soon as possible to a socialization of agriculture. No one claimed that the peasantry should be forcibly socialized; but no one objected to the use of a considerable amount of pressure.

The discussion in the Party about the future of the countryside, and indeed Stalin's final decisions on the matter in 1929–30, may be considered at two levels. First, the specific views advanced by the various factions, which are of interest in themselves and also highly indicative, taken together, of the enormous difficulties the minority Marxist–Leninist Party now faced in its efforts to impose its doctrines, and even to maintain its rule.

Second, this was not simply a struggle of ideas but also a struggle for power. Even Lenin, in his 'Testament', while attributing faction in the Party to the two-class nature of Soviet society, saw that mere personal hostility between leading figures was a major crux. The period 1924–30 saw not only the institution of Stalinist policies in the countryside, but also Stalin's elimination of all those apart from himself who had been members of the Politburo under Lenin.

The mere doctrinal discussions in the Party about what steps to take next are thus of much interest, but it is arguable that they have been given greater attention than is perhaps justified by their intrinsic significance. At the same time, we need not take at their face value each shift in the leadership's public statements, or each speech by one or another leading figure of the second rank, for tactical considerations often dominated.

Having said which, it remains true that the party leadership, after Lenin's effective disappearance from the scene, was divided about policy towards the peasant.

All the ruling group were adherents of a doctrine which required them to regard 'commodity' and market relations as unacceptable. Their attempts to do away with them had proved economically and socially disastrous, and for the time being at any rate they had had to abandon their true policies and were faced with coping with these deplorable phenomena.

At the same time, their doctrine had led them to an analysis of the 'class' structure of the countryside, under which the prosperous and efficient peasant was not only the enemy of the Party, but also the natural foe of all the rest of the peasantry. This analysis may have proved defective in practice, but they were not prepared to give it up in considering rural problems.

In the early years of NEP, all factions of the Party agreed that cooperative farming was necessary in the countryside, and held that it should proceed through getting the peasant used to cooperation in credit and merchandising matters, and only later in agriculture itself. In fact, on paper this orthodoxy remains. As a modern western scholar puts it, 'Nowadays it is still claimed, though with lessening conviction, that this is the way in which things actually happened . . .'[17]

The struggle within the Party is often represented as though the 'Right' of Bukharin and his associates accepted some sort of liberal-type future. The first things to be said are that they too were devoted to one-party rule; that they too thought of the extinction of the market economy as an essential aim; and that they too accepted the idea that the 'kulak' represented the class enemy.

The differences within the leadership were not on these issues, but merely on how long the market relationship with the peasantry, and private property in land, were to last; to what degree they should be restricted by State action; and how they should be brought to an end.

But if the range of policies put forward by the rival factions was not on the face of it very great, their tones and attitudes differed strikingly. Bukharin went to the length of saying in April 1925:

Our policy in relation to the countryside should develop in the direction *of removing, and in part abolishing, many restrictions which put the brake on the growth of the well-to-do and kulak farm.* To the peasants we must say 'enrich yourselves, develop your farms, and do not fear that restrictions will be put on you'.

However paradoxical it may appear, *we must develop the well-to-do farm in order to help the poor peasant and the middle peasant*.[18]

Thus not merely some vague well-to-do peasant, but the 'kulak' himself, by definition the class enemy, was appealed to, in the interest of economic growth – just as Lenin had actually called on the capitalist proper. And Bukharin added that any fear of the kulak becoming a new landlord class was mythical, so that no 'second revolution' in the countryside would be necessary.

Bukharin's formulation was highly unpalatable in the Party, and he had to retract the order to 'enrich yourselves' in the autumn. Nevertheless he was only expressing, in provocative terms, what lay at the heart of the NEP tactic. He saw, moreover, that the Party's attempt to combine the two contradictory approaches of concession and repression resulted in 'a situation where the peasant is afraid to instal an iron roof for fear of being declared a kulak; if he buys a machine, then he does it in such a way that the Communists will not notice. Higher technique becomes conspiratorial!'[19]

Bukharin and the Right stuck to the idea that the peasant could, over a longish period, be persuaded of the advantages of collectivization, yet it seems quite clear that the peasants would never have voluntarily collectivized. Indeed, Lenin's analysis of the 'middle peasant' masses gives no encouragement to the idea. Some pressure, economic or other, was needed and implied in Lenin's position at its softest – and even in that of most of the Right. The question was how much pressure, and when.

Though even Bukharin was later to say that the kulaks 'may be hunted down at will', he now seems to have envisaged kulak cooperatives surrounded by the economic power of State banks and the State industrial sector, and forced to compete, with increasingly poor prospects, against the State-owned cooperatives of the other peasant strata. So they would have no choice but to become integrated into the Socialist economy, even though an 'alien element' within it. He went on to argue that this supposed integration would in fact be elimination, since the cooperatives would defeat the kulak capitalist, in the same way that the petty NEP capitalist of the cities would be defeated by the socialist sector.

The attitudes of the 'Left', out of power but still able to argue, were presented by Preobrazhensky. The key to progress was industrialization; apart from anything else, only thus would the power of the Socialist sector become greater than that of the non-Socialist countryside. The phrase 'primitive Socialist accumulation', originally Trotsky's, shocked the Right with its implication of 'exploitation' of the peasants. Preobrazhensky even used the phrase 'internal colony' of them. But in effect, the funds for any industrialization (or re-industrialization) had, in one way or another, to be wrung out of the population somehow, with the peasant's production as the largest and most obvious source.

In Meiji Japan up to 60% of the peasant income had gone, via taxes and rent, to financing industrialization, but with incentive enough to get the farmers to increase production (so that from 1885–1915 the productivity of agricultural labour doubled). For Preobrazhensky, similarly, increased levies on the peasantry would be made on an increased peasant surplus, produced by improved methods of cultivation.

Bukharin argued against Preobrazhensky that the exploitation of the countryside to finance industry was mistaken even on economic grounds, in that the peasantry – if it were to survive at all – must do so as a market for industrial goods and these must therefore be forthcoming from the start. But in fact Trotsky, and the Left in general, also saw that at least a supply of necessities like matches, soap, paraffin, must be purchasable by the peasantry.

Thus the views of the 'Right' and 'Left' at this point were not very divergent. Bukharin himself emphasized the crucial importance of developing the State sector more rapidly than its competitor. He seems to have believed that socialist industry, owing to its supposed inherent superiority, would leap ahead automatically, but by 1926 he too seems to have realized that its growth must somehow be accelerated, and that the peasant would inevitably have to supply much of the investment.[20]

He nevertheless took the view that the peasant would not accept socialism unless and until it showed its superior economic attractiveness. Mere hypothetical argument would not (and could not in a Marxist view) have much prospect of changing a consciousness deeply rooted in class economic attitudes. But in this, again, there was not much difference with the Left. As Trotsky saw, the best way to overcome the disparity between the prices of manufactured goods and agricultural products was to improve the efficiency and productivity of industry. While noting the increase in class differentiation in the countryside, and 'the growth of the kulak stratum',[21] he argued that, properly managed the growth of industry would 'forestall the process of class differentiation within the peasantry and nullify its effects'.[22] And in general the Left felt that collectivization should follow industrialization, and be made possible by it. (This too, it may be added, is represented in some current Soviet scholarship as what actually happened).

The Left still spoke of the 'alliance' with the middle peasantry, though stressing that the interests of the proletariat must come first. Nor did they, as sometimes supposed, urge forced collectivization. They believed that the individual peasant, and even the kulak, would persist for a long time.

'A forced loan of 150 million pounds of grain from 10% of the richest peasants was the most sweeping measure that the Left ever called for'.[23] Even Trotsky, in exile, was to write that the Left had not wanted the liquidation of classes in five years, and only wished to tax the kulak income enough for industrialization.[24] The Left's position like the Right's was, in fact, that the socialist sector must be continually strengthened, so that it would come inevitably to dominate and eventually control the whole economy.

On the other hand, the Left, all in all, had little in the way of a specific programme, just a few suggestions on taxation and agricultural improvement, their main emphasis being on industry – though they did urge serious steps to increase the (then very meagre) numbers of collective farms, especially for poor peasants. But Bukharin too presented little in the way of a real approach to modernizing or socializing the countryside, except in some vague future when peasant attitudes would have changed. What the Left and Right had in common at this stage was a belief that fiscal measures (even if sometimes pretty rough ones) should be used in the direction of the rural economy; and that 'forced' collectivization would be disastrous.

The core of the dispute lay elsewhere. To the extent that Party policy was now winning support, or at least tolerance, from the more prosperous sector of the peasantry, the Left faction grew increasingly worried that Communist ideals were being compromised, and the Communist view of class-struggle being eroded. Almost no one in the Party was really reconciled to the market system. But, on all sides of the debate, we find the very shaky assumption that a planned central economy would be coexistent with a market.

As has been pointed out, and not only by the then Left and the later Stalinists, Bukharin's attitude in particular at least *appeared* to postpone rural socialism until the unlikely epoch of peasant acquiescence in the new scheme. The Soviet regime would meanwhile remain to some degree at the mercy of market forces it did not control (or, in Marxist terms, of a class inherently no better than an ally, and often worse).

There was a further, and associated, doctrinal debate. The view held by Lenin and the Bolsheviks from the beginning had been that Socialism could not be achieved in one country, or anyhow a backward one like Russia; and in the years after 1917 they had often made it clear that they expected revolutions in Western Europe to provide the necessary Marxist basis for a socialist proletarian order. It would be superfluous to adduce the many quotations from Lenin and others to the effect first that these would occur, and second that the Russian 'Socialist' revolution could not survive without them.

The feeling behind this was rational enough, not only in commonsense, but also in doctrinal terms. The Russian level of industrialization, and the size and 'maturity' of the proletariat, were in principle insufficient to cope with the transformation of a huge agrarian majority. In fact, the task which now actually faced the leadership was impossible.

But it will be seen that the Bolsheviks had in practice already *acted* as if Russia could be made over without outside support. The arguments of the NEP period all imply at least the possibility of a long haul before any rise of revolutionary regimes elsewhere. But the Left in particular still looked to the world revolution. And it was only gradually, and as a highly controversial doctrinal innovation, that the *idea* of 'Socialism in One Country' was advanced, and eventually became orthodox.

As late as May 1924 Stalin himself had proposed the traditional view: 'the final victory of socialism and the organization of socialist production will never be brought about by the effort of one single country, least of all an agrarian country like Russia. If this end is to be attained, the efforts of several developed countries will be indispensable'.[25]

The true originator of the theory of Socialism in One Country was in fact Bukharin. It was Stalin, though, who made it the central issue of inner-Party controversy. And he was certainly right in this. For though Trotsky and others might argue that it was unMarxist to try to sustain a revolution in a single country admittedly not far advanced enough for it in theoretical terms, one thing was now clear: after the defeat of direct Soviet military efforts in Poland in 1920, and of the Comintern's last throw in the West, the German Communist fiasco of 1923, the revolution was not going to be successfully established in the advanced countries which were theoretically necessary to sustain a revolutionary Russia. In practical terms, this meant either that the Soviet regime should throw all its efforts into an evidently doomed pursuit of European revolution, or it should abdicate, or at least retreat to a 'bourgeois-democratic' stage. But the Party activists were in practice not prepared for political suicide, and were ripe to accept as orthodox a doctrine, however strange, which gave support to their real will.

Stalin, in the usual manner, tried to father Socialism in One Country on Lenin, the latter having referred to the possibility once – though in the quite different context of the possibility of socialism in one *advanced* country.

★

The way in which these and other disputes were argued may remind us that the Communist Party leadership was not a group of rational economists, considering ways of producing a rationalized society – though they sometimes thought of themselves as such, and represented their actions as such to observers in the West. They were a group which had accepted a millenarian doctrine, and their rationale for holding power was that they would translate this into practice to produce a new and superior society. Its superiority consisted, essentially, in that it supposedly brought into effect the theories of Karl Marx: which is to say the notion that a 'proletarian' regime (which that of the Soviet Union was by definition) would produce a 'socialist' order. This implied certain doctrinally prescribed forms. These were both in economic fundamentals – in that 'commodity', or market relations, must disappear; and in class relations, in that classes dependent on private ownership and the market must in one way or another be eliminated.

The concessions made by the Communists in 1921 were only to be justified as maintaining the Party in power. But its retention of power could only be justified if it took the earliest feasible opportunity to move on to the creation of the social order prescribed by doctrine, and eliminate the classes doctrinally known as barriers to the necessary future envisaged by the motivating theory.

As Lenin frankly admitted, the Communists in fact knew very little about economic reality. And this must be borne in mind continually when we consider the efforts of the Soviet government to guide, or to master, the rural economy.

The famous proposition about a 'scissors crisis' was first propounded at the Twelfth Party Congress in 1923. The 'scissors' were the two diverging lines on a graph, the one showing the increasingly high prices of industrial goods, the other the excessively low prices paid for agricultural goods.

This original 'scissors crisis' was a short-lived phenomenon following a period of great dislocation, and in the absence of grain reserves.[26] It was simply due to a government over-pricing of industrial and under-pricing of agricultural goods, and disappeared as soon as this was corrected.

But it was a striking example of the regime's touchiness and impatience with the market phenomenon, which it both detested and misunderstood. Whenever the terms of trade turned against the government, or even appeared to do so, there were to be these signs of excessive anxiety, of a lack of the patience needed if the market mechanism was to find its most effective level.

Meanwhile, recovery had nevertheless begun. Groman, the country's chief economist, wrote that '1922–3 was the first normal year of economic life after eight abnormal years.'[27] The price structure was still in bad shape, but all in all the improvement was already notable, and entirely due to the establishment of market relations and peasant ownership. The Agrarian Code of October 1922 declared the land still the property of the nation, but guaranteed perpetual hereditary use to the cultivator. It even adopted Stolypin's ideas of consolidating the peasant strips; and in some areas new individual farms began to emerge again. In fact, the code recognized three forms of ownership – cooperative (involving in the 1920 1–2% of the holdings); private ownership including individual farms of the Stolypin type; and communal, in the traditional sense.

At the beginning of 1925 restrictions on the hiring of wage-labour were lifted. As a result of these measures the initial economic recovery in the countryside was striking. Gross agricultural production was reported up to pre-war figures as early as 1925–6.[28] Grain production rose from 57.7 million tons per annum in 1922–5 to 73.5 million tons in 1926–9,[29] though it never quite reached its prewar level, especially in the Ukraine and the North Caucasus.

This recovery, as General Grigorenko, who then worked on his father's farm, points out, was the work of 'the people of the ruined countryside, ploughing with cows, or harnessing themselves to the plough'.[30]

★

As Lenin foresaw, successful individual agriculture meant prosperity for the most efficient peasantry, and the 'kulak' bugbear once again raised its head.

Even among Soviet writers on the subject there is some dispute about who the new 'kulaks' were. On one view, they were the old kulaks who had lain low, and now emerged to start again. On the other, they were a new stratum of former middle and poor peasants, economically on the rise. No doubt both views have some truth, and things seem in addition to have varied from place to place. At any rate, as was to become clear later, many of the new rich peasants were men who had been out of the village and in the Red Army or partisans during the Civil War – men, often enough, who had shown exceptional initiative, and who had come into contact with outside life and ideas. On the other side of the coin, these ex-soldiers, as those with the most pro-Soviet record, were at this time in a strong position to put pressure on local officials, and get the best terms available when it came to taxes.

For the time being, no measures were seriously taken against them. Indeed, in these years, terror was, by earlier and later standards, hardly noticeable, remaining at what was in the Soviet context a minimal level. Amnesties were even granted to peasant rebels. A typical scene was when 126 peasant partisans surrendered under an amnesty personally witnessed by Petrovsky in March 1922 in the town of Lokhvytsia in the Ukraine (all were to perish seven years later in the new terror).[31]

The notion that this peaceful period could not and would not last was already pervasive in Party and police spheres. As a Moscow observer put it, 'the Party, particularly in its lower cells, was instinctively, subconsciously, hostile towards NEP'.[32] In general Party activists in the countryside who had fully understood the clear instructions of 1918–21, were baffled and disconcerted by the truce with the middle peasant and even the 'kulak'. They often acted accordingly. As early as 1924 a leading Communist, M.M. Khatayevich, had noted the conviction among both the ordinary peasants and the Party members themselves 'that one need only be a member of the Party cell in order to make requisitions, or arrests, or to confiscate whatever one will without any special authorization from the appropriate authority'. He added that 'It was difficult to tell where the Party cell ended and the tribunal or the police or the land commission began'.[33]

As to the peasants, their 'attitude to the Soviet regime was never enthusiastic, except in the case of some of the bednyaks (poor peasants), and then only in certain periods'.[34] As to the other strata, they took what advantage was possible of the situation. In Siberia there was even a concerted move by 'kulaks' in 1925–6 to create their own party, the 'Peasant Union', supported by petitions involving several thousand people![35]

A leading OGPU official, Peters, wrote publicly that 'we must not forget that under the conditions of the NEP our worst enemies still surround us';[36] while a secret OGPU circular of June 1925 notes that:

> It has been ascertained that counter-revolutionary organizations and groups in the Ukraine are well aware of the fact that the OGPU is at present forced, so to speak, to a certain passivity, caused by the New Economic Policy and also by governmental considerations of a higher nature. That this situation is only temporary is clear to every one of us. The OGPU should therefore not lose a good opportunity to unmask our enemies, in order to deal them a crushing blow when the time comes.[37]

Police preparation for the next phase included instructions for the keeping of records on 'suspected counter-revolutionaries'. These are listed in the Ukraine (in a secret circular of February 1924):

Political Parties and Organizations

1. All former members of pre-revolutionary bourgeois political parties.
2. All former members of monarchical unions and organizations (Black

Hundreds).

3. All former members of the Union of Independent Grain Growers (at the time of the Central Rada in the Ukraine).
4. All former members of the gentry and titled persons of the old aristocracy.
5. All former members of youth organizations (Boy Scouts and others).
6. All nationalists of all shades of opinion.

Officials and Employees in the Active Service of Tsarism

1. Officials of the former Ministry of Internal Affairs: all officials of the *Okhrana* [secret political police], police and gendarmerie, secret agents of the *Okhrana* and police. All members of the frontier corps of gendarmerie, etc.
2. Officials of the former Ministry of Justice: members of the district and provincial courts, jurymen, prosecutors of all ranks, justices of the peace and examining magistrates, court executors, heads of county courts, etc.
3. All commissioned and non-commissioned officers, without exception, of the former tsarist army and fleet.

Secret Enemies of the Soviet Regime

1. All former commissioned officers, non-commissioned officers and enlisted men of the White movements and armies, the Ukrainian Petliurist formations, and various rebel units and bands who actively resisted Soviet rule. People amnestied by the Soviet authorities are not excluded.
2. All those employed in a civil capacity in the departments and local offices of White governments, the armies of the Ukrainian Central Rada, the Hetman's state police, etc.
3. All servants of religious bodies: bishops, Orthodox and Catholic priests, rabbis, deacons, churchwardens, choirmasters, monks, etc.
4. All former merchants, shopkeepers and 'Nepmen'.
5. All former landowners, big land-leasers, well-to-do peasants (who formerly employed hired labour), big craftsmen and proprietors of industrial establishments.
6. All persons having someone among their near relatives who at the present time is in an illegal position or is conducting armed resistance against the Soviet regime in the ranks of anti-Soviet bands.
7. All foreigners, irrespective of nationality.
8. All those with relatives or acquaintances abroad.
9. All members of religious sects and communities (Baptists in particular).
10. All scholars and specialists of the old school, particularly those whose political orientation is undeclared up to this day.
11. All persons previously convicted or suspected of contraband, espionage, etc.[38]

A sizeable portion of the population.

Meanwhile, it is at least symptomatic that 67% of those shot by order of courts in 1923 were peasants.[39]

★

The loss of direct economic control of the Soviet village was accompanied by a parallel loss of what administrative control had been available at the local level.

The old commune largely remained the true centre of economic power in the Russian countryside. There were many Party complaints about 'dual power', with the local Soviets weaker than the communes.

The village Soviet was in principle elected on universal adult suffrage, but from the start it had been controlled by the authorities as the 'rural arm of the dictatorship of the proletariat'.[40] Even Soviet sources make clear that at first all the decisions were taken by the Chairman, invariably a Party nominee. And analysis of lists of individual members of district and village Party cells shows that many of them came from outside, or had long lived in other regions and returned on Party orders, while the 'loyal' locals were mainly good-for-nothings, apart from a few village teachers.[41]

But now over wide areas the middle and richer peasants gained control of the village Soviets. Thus the village commune, which had in practice carried out most of the non-coercive side of the great redistributions following the revolution, became, even more than before, the dominant element in the Russian villages, with the Soviet as little more than its agent for certain official purposes.[42] In 1926 90% of village households belonged to the communes; and they 'in practice controlled the economic life of the village'.[43]

The membership of the *skhod*, the village meeting, was now all who belonged to households and were over eighteen. In theory all could vote, but in practice only heads of households did so, as before. Indeed, even the Soviet Agrarian Code laid down that a quorum should consist not of a percentage of members but of half the representatives of households.[44]

In 1927 serious moves were made to give the village Soviets more power, and purge them of unreliable elements, but it was clearly seen that the real problem was the commune. At the Fifteenth Congress Molotov said that, driven from the Soviets, the kulaks had 'tried to entrench themselves in the commune' (Kaganovich: 'Right'!), 'Now we will finally beat them out of even these last trenches'.

★

But who were the 'kulaks'? The attempt at defining the class enemy in the

73

village, and determining his numbers, was to have devastating effects on millions of lives in the forthcoming period. In fact it is clear that, however defined, the kulak was, as an economic class, no more than a Party construct. As we noted of the War Communism period, and earlier, Lenin had transferred a word from its original meaning to cover an alleged 'class' in the villages. This was now sometimes admitted. Bukharin, in a pamphlet published in 1925, distinguished between 'the better-off innkeeper, the village usurer, the kulak' and the well-off farmer who employed several labourers – the latter not to be considered as a kulak.[45] The Commissar for Agriculture, A.P. Smirnov, also tried to extricate the prosperous peasant from the semantic distortion Lenin had inflicted on him, pointing out that a kulak was, properly speaking, a pre-revolutionary exploiting type which had now virtually disappeared.[46] Milyutin (Lenin's first Commissar for Agriculture) asked on the same occasion, 'What is a kulak? So far there has been no clear, concise definition of the kulak's role in the process of stratification'.[47] Nor was one ever made.

One contributor to the Party's agrarian discussion wrote that any one familiar with real conditions 'knows perfectly well that the village kulak cannot be traced directly (i.e. by direct reference to statistics on the employment of wage-labour). He cannot be identified by straightforward means, nor is it possible to determine whether or not he is a capitalist'.[48] Thus a more or less psychological or political identification remained open, as was indeed to be the actual, if not admitted, practice in the crucial years ahead.

Though one writer in the official organ *Bolshevik* actually proposed abandoning the term kulak altogether,[49] the concept was essential to the Party view of the villages, and efforts were made not only to define, but to calculate the number of the class enemy.

Figures of kulak numbers varied widely. In 1924 a Soviet scholar noted that 'One might admit, straining the figures considerably, that kulak exploitations are 2–3%, but in fact, these exploitations have not sufficiently established their kulak character'.[50]

But in 1927–9 estimates ranged between 3.7% and 5% of the peasantry (each 1% representing 1.25 million people). Even Molotov, while accepting 3.7%, said that it was 'an almost impossible task' to estimate kulak numbers.[51]

The official *Statistical Handbook USSR 1928*, whose figures were often used by the political leadership (though, in fact, as merely economic analysis, the term it employs is 'entrepreneur') gives 3.9 of the households or 5.2 of the rural population as such, and defines them as those who either

(a) possess means of production valued at more than 1,600 roubles and let or lease means of production or hire labour for over 50 days during the year, or

(b) possess means of production valued at more than 800 roubles and hire labour for over 75 days during the year, or

(c) possess means of production valued at more than 400 roubles and hire labour for more than 150 days a year.

It is worth noting, for any for whom the word kulak still conjures up a rich exploiter on the grand scale, that the most prosperous peasants in 1927 had two or three cows and up to ten hectares of sowing area, for an average family of seven people.[52] And the richest peasant group received only 50–56% greater income per capita than the lowest.[53]

The more crucial point, for the moment, was that the 'kulaks', 3–5% of the peasant households, produced around 20% of the grain.[54]

*

At the height of NEP, the Party felt the necessity of appeasing the 'kulak' economically; but politically, it never failed to emphasize the need, arising out of the kulak's new economic strength, to strengthen against them the alliance of the proletariat and the poor peasantry.[55] But if the kulak was hard to define, so was the poor peasantry.

Even the 'agricultural wage-labourers', a simple enough sounding category, gave trouble. Many of them (63%) owned farms, and some 20% even livestock, and they were often employed on a daily, rather than a seasonal or yearly basis: thus they were hard to distinguish from 'poor peasants' who might equally do wage labour from time to time; or if not the peasant himself, one of his family.

So the 'poor peasant' was sometimes defined as a husbandman with a small plot and no horses who did occasional outside work. Another definition (by Stalin's leading economist, Strumilin) was that he owned a farm whose revenue did not exceed the average pay of an agricultural worker. And there were other definitions still, some of which allowed the poor peasant to have a horse.

When it came to the 'middle peasant', muddle persisted – indeed was aggravated by schemes to divide them into 'weak' and 'well-off' middle peasants. The common criterion which distinguished both from the 'poor peasant' by ownership of a horse was, as we have said, controversial in the Party. And the division between them and the kulak depended in most definitions on taking the kulak as one who employed labour, and who was hence, in the theory-bound eyes of Party experts, a sort of capitalist. But middle peasants, and even poor peasants, might also employ labour. Indeed during the struggle with the Left opposition, the Agitation and

Propaganda Department of the Central Committee said clearly that 'a significant share in the hiring of labourers falls to middle-peasant households'.[56]

So other criteria emerged – for example that of the size of the farm's sown area. But in fact a big farm often belonged to a large family of otherwise impeccably defined 'middle peasants', while one who appeared an obvious kulak in that he was far more prosperous, might have a smaller farm, and rent out agricultural machinery, traffic in grain and so on.[57] Indeed, yet another criterion, described as 'basic', was the kulak's hiring out of implements and draft animals:[58] but some theoreticians held that hiring out of animals or equipment was a 'commercial' relationship not a 'class' one.[59]

Then there were attempts to define kulaks (like middle peasants) by the possession of livestock. But one who was a middle peasant in that he did not hire labour and was little involved in trade, might yet (if he had a large family) hold three cows and two horses.

Moreover, as Kritsman, representing the Agrarian Section of the Communist Academy, remarked, while advancing a complicated system of his own, 'our statistical materials are unfortunately ill-adapted to such comparatively subtle research'.[60] Another respected Soviet economist reported (though in a book only published posthumously in 1956) that 'we have no statistical data, however incomplete or approximate, on the evolution of class structure in the Soviet villages over any given period of years'.[61] In fact, a Western scholar is able to quote four major estimates of the numbers in each category of peasants made in 1925–8, and adds that he could have given a dozen more, differing in both criteria and results.[62]

★

Moreover, even with the categories sorted out, the 'labourers' were, as ever, not a useful power base. Only a quarter of them were even members of the State's Agricultural Workers Union (itself, in the view of Party observers, of little use).[63] By the end of 1927 only 14,000 of them (out of an estimated 2.75 to 3 million) were members of the Communist Party.[64]

And of course, as long as the agricultural worker remained in his category, he felt that the Soviet government had not helped him. But as soon as he prospered he entered a group on which the Party looked with doubt or hostility.

On the other hand, if the village poor did not prosper in spite of all the official advantages provided for their categories, they were despised by the local Party. Even Communist officials are quoted in the Party's theoretical organ as refusing to have anything to do with them, because 'they are all drunkards'.[65] This is in accord with the view attributed to the middle peasants by a Soviet agrarian publication of the time: 'How can we learn from the poor peasantry, when they cannot even make their own borshch'?[66]

Thus economic aid to the village poor was either useless to the Soviet economy, merely increasing their consumption, or it enabled them to become middle peasants. In any case, there are many official reports which make clear that the sums allotted to credits for the peasants were in themselves wholly inadequate, and subject too to gross administrative misuse.[67]

Nor, as ever, did the poorer strata reliably take a hostile attitude to the richer. Peasant delegates to the Fifth Congress of Soviets state that the failure of government-sponsored credit associations made it impossible to appeal to the masses; while 'the kulak and subkulak touch the most sensitive strings'.[68]

As to the middle peasant, in principle the Party adhered to the formula of alliance with him against the kulak, and this remained the official line through a period of great changes in real policy, while the actual treatment of the middle peasantry, indeed of the whole peasantry, ranged between encouragement and repression. In fact, it has been said of an important section of the Party, to which Stalin now began to adhere, 'the more those of this persuasion emphasized the watchword of alliance with the middle peasant the more pronounced, in practice, grew their hostility towards him'.[69]

But the whole differentiation, however done, was largely based on a false view of supposed class attitudes. The only advantage the poor had was that, on principle, they were first choice for political perks such as membership of the village Soviet. But even there they usually took the same line as the rest of the peasantry, and through the coming period, during all the troubles over grain collection and prices policy in general, 'the poor reacted in exactly the same way as the other producers'.[70]

★

During the political and ideological struggle of the 1920s Stalin's main concern was, of course, to build up his strength in the Party through the control which his leadership of the secretariat gave over all appointments.

The supposed working class base of the regime had by now been largely (not of course entirely) reduced to a matter of organizational *force majeure* on the one hand, and mere fiction on the other. But there was a countervailing source of strength. The Party itself, in possession of all the positions of power, had become an 'interest'. A bureaucracy had been born, a huge group for whom power and perquisites had to a considerable degree replaced, or at least distorted, the old motivations. What Rakovsky already described in terms of 'the car-harem syndrome' was in fact evolving into a new social stratum. It was not only a matter of the more recent 'careerist' intake into the party, but also of the evolution of its old membership into the ways of a ruling elite. Nor did it necessarily imply any abandonment of ruthless or revolutionary measures. On the one hand the preservation of power was in question. On the other, Leninist ideology remained both the driving force and the justification of the ruling elite.

On the whole, both Left and Right had reservations about the propriety of the new priviligentsia, and its members inclined to look rather to Stalin.

But it is also true that many of the younger generation who had been local militants in Tsarist times, and risen in the turmoil of the Civil War, were inclined to resent the Europeanized intellectuals, both Left and Right, who dominated theoretical discussion; and these too (often of working class origin) were a pool of future Stalinists.

On the actual political issues, concerned to defeat Trotsky and Zinoviev, Stalin at first subscribed in general to Bukharin's views, in particular that socialist principles would reach the peasant through marketing cooperatives, gradually leading him to production cooperatives too; and that State credits were the key weapon. Even the words 'collective farm' are not to be found in Stalin's writings prior to the Fifteenth Party Congress in December 1927. He still argued, too, that industrialization was only feasible if 'based on a progressive improvement of the material condition of the peasantry'.[71]

Stalin nevertheless was already beginning to tone down the Bukharinist pronouncements in some small ways, perhaps (as Isaac Deutscher suggests) to keep his appeal to Party activists more flexible than the Right's. Thus in early 1926, Stalin was writing confidentially that the peasantry was a 'rather unstable' ally, that in the Civil War it was 'sometimes siding with the workers, and sometimes with the generals'.[72] This reflected the attitude of most Communists to the peasantry.

The defeat of the Trotskyites, then of Zinoviev and Kamenev, then of the 'United Opposition' formed by the three of them, was complete in December 1927, when Trotsky and Zinoviev were expelled from the Party at the Fifteenth Party Congress. At this Congress the main political consideration was to preserve the appearance of unity among the victorious Stalin-Bukharin leadership in the phase which marked the final attack on the Left. But it is now that we see the first overt moves of Stalin and his followers to appropriate the Left's policies. While the official Congress documents were in terms of 'limiting' the kulak, Stalin and Molotov both spoke of 'liquidating' that class; and it was becoming 'common knowledge' in leading circles that Stalin was moving Left. He now started sending out instructions[73] on extraordinary measures against the kulaks in a tone contradicting the speeches at the Congress.

The Right, nevertheless, while pressing for the need for economic equilibrium, also itself came round to a greater emphasis on industry, and harder measures against the kulak. Bukharin had already, in October, claimed that the alliance with the middle peasantry was now secure, so that a 'forced offensive against the kulak' to limit 'his exploiting tendencies', was now possible, by taxation, and the curtailment of employment of labour. Both Bukharin and Rykov spoke at the Fifteenth Congress of the need for pressures on the peasantry, though they still warned against any departure from NEP, which would lead to violent crisis.

It is conventional for Soviet writers to take Bukharin and his allies as devoted to restoring capitalism in the countryside – either consciously (in the extreme Stalinist view) or 'objectively'. A similar notion is held among some Western writers: the Rightists were moderate men who would have helped the private farmer, as the buttress of the country's rural economy, and only sought collectivization when the peasantry was ready for it and all the tractors and so forth needed to make it attractive were there.

Up to a point this was their original policy. But by late 1928 it was expressed in such terms, already rather harder, as Bukharin's view:

> It is a matter of making large capital investments in agriculture. . . . A rise in the individual peasant sector, especially that devoted to grain, a limiting of the kulak sector, the construction of the sovkhozes and kolkhozes, in combination with a correct price policy, and along with a development of co-operatives embracing the mass of the peasantry.[74]

In the first flush of NEP Bukharin had indeed gone overboard in print for the private sector; and (in 1929) he and the Right were to have severe qualms about the methods of crash collectivization which Stalin enforced. But what seems more important is that the 'Rights' never for a moment suggested the only real alternative of true private-peasant modernization: and that they 'gave unstinting support' to the decisions of the Fifteenth Party Congress about a long-term collectivization programme (20% by 1933). Bukharin, in fact, never really revised Party agrarian theory – and nothing in that line is to be found in his last *Notes of an Economist* (1928).

The Right had never for a moment abandoned the idea of socialized agriculture. Nor did they deny the Leninist notion of the class struggle in the countryside. Bukharin's defence of the alliance with the middle peasant was the context of his remark about hunting down the kulaks at will, and the formulation remained orthodox right through collectivization.[75]

The most accurate way of putting it seems to be that in both agriculture and industry Bukharin stood against 'maximum' aims such as excessive taxation of the peasantry, leading to a fall in agricultural production; and in favour of a balanced attention to light as well as heavy industry.

Stalin's tactics in the new phase, that is in 1927–30, when his main political concern was to defeat the Right, were tortuous and ambiguous. On the one hand, he was working to use his organizational powers to place his own men in key posts in the party apparatus both centrally and throughout the country. On the other, while winning over the now leaderless left-inclined elements among the Party masses, he moved slowly enough to carry with him as many as possible of the elements which had been devoted to NEP, increasingly isolating the Right leaders ideologically as well as organizationally. Moreover, as a certain stability and even prosperity began to emerge in the cities, and a 'proletariat' again established itself, a strong feeling grew in the Party, and among all factions, that some fresh effort in the direction of 'Socialism' could now be made.

This was generally envisaged in terms of a further strengthening of the largely restored industrial base, and a slow expansion of the rudimentary collective farm system in the village. The decisions of the Fifteenth Congress envisaged a Plan, of which these were to be the main contents – Bukharin and Tomsky assenting.

★

In the Ukraine, the intra-party struggle took a form quite different from that in Moscow. Lazar Kaganovich was sent as First Secretary of the Communist Party of the Ukraine in April 1925 – replacing the Volga German Kviring who had been obstructing Ukrainianization. Kaganovich, very much Stalin's man, had such a fearful reputation in later years that his appointment now is sometimes taken as a bad one for the Ukraine – and indeed Oleksander Shumsky, Ukrainian Commissar for Education, objected that Vlas Chubar, as a Ukrainian, should get the job. But in fact Kaganovich, though alert for national deviation which might shake Moscow control, was at this time an active patron of 'moderate' Ukrainianization[76] on the cultural and linguistic side. And for a few years the Ukrainian culture continued to flourish, though not without setbacks. (Kaganovich, though not an ethnic Ukrainian, was in fact Ukrainian-born, and could speak the language fluently).

By 1926, the degree of Ukrainian national self-expression seemed to Moscow to have got out of hand. Shumsky was demanding fuller cultural, economic and political autonomy. He was accused of national deviation and removed with his supporters, the scandal being worse because he was defended by the Communist Party of the Western Ukraine (then on Polish territory) and had his case brought before the Executive Committee of the Comintern. Stalin commented that Shumsky's attitude had attractions for the local intelligentsia, but amounted to 'a struggle for the alienation of Ukrainian cultural and social life from the common Soviet cultural life, of a struggle against Moscow and Russians in general, against Russian culture'[77] – as, in a sense, was true.

The fall of Shumsky and the attack of 'Shumskyism' did not lead to a reversion to full Russification, but only to the avoidance of the more confrontational ways of opposing it. Shumsky was succeeded as Commissar of Education by Skrypnyk, who remained the chief party figure defending his country's culture over the next seven years.

Mykola Skrypnyk, son of a Ukrainian railway employee, is in many ways the key figure in the period which follows. He had joined the Russian Social-Democratic Party in 1897, and was first arrested for party work in 1901. When the Party split came in 1903, he became a Bolshevik. By 1913 he was serving on the board of *Pravda*; and at the Sixth Party Congress in 1917 he became a member of the – then very small – central Committee. When he went back to Kiev as Lenin's plenipotentiary in December 1917, he does not seem to have given much thought to the Ukrainian national problem. It was only on his return in April 1920, after brief stints in which he had taken a fairly centralist view, that we see his development into the spokesman for an independent though Soviet Ukraine. And by sheer force of character he was able to keep these contraries in some sort of equilibrium almost until his death in 1933.

As J.E. Mace has pointed out, Skrypnyk's apparently humble post of Commissar of Education is misleading, for he was *de facto* in charge of the nationality question, ideology and culture. This involved a constant, but initially successful, struggle.

Skrypnyk was frank about what he was up against. He spoke indignantly at the Twelfth Party Congress about high-level Communists who accepted Ukrainianization because it was the current policy, but made no practical application of it. One of those who had voted for it at the recent Ukrainian Party Conference, he said, had been approached while leaving the hall by a worker who addressed him in Ukrainian, and had replied 'Why don't you speak in an intelligible tongue?'[78]

His associate, the Communist writer Mykola Khvylovy, wrote forthrightly in 1926, in the Ukrainian Party's official organ, 'the Ukrainian economy is not Russian and cannot be so, if only because the Ukrainian culture, which emanates from the economic structure and in

81

turn influences it, bears characteristic forms and features . . . In a word, the Union remains a Union, and the Ukraine is an independent state'.[79] (An appeal, for purposes of political struggle, to the verbal forms of the USSR Constitution, rather than to its allocation of the realities of power). Similarly, the official in charge of Ukrainian political education, Mikhaylo Volobuev, complained that the Ukraine was still in effect being economically exploited through the survival of pre-revolutionary fiscal patterns.

The Ukrainian tendency in the Communist Party of the Ukraine was supported by a number of Ukrainian Jewish figures such as Kulyk, Lifshits, Hurevich and Ravich-Cherkassky. The last-named criticized Russian Party members who (he said), 'believe that the Ukrainian SSR and the Communist Party of the Ukraine are fictitious or else merely playing at independence. At best they concede that during the period of struggle against the nationalist Central Rada and Directory, it was imperative for the Communist Party and the Soviet Government in the Ukraine to adorn themselves with defensive national and independent colours. Now that the Soviet government in the Ukraine has been firmly established, they agree that the role of the Ukrainian SSR and the Communist Party of the Ukraine is finished'.[80]

From the other side there were orthodox Communist reservations expressed about the fissiparous effects of national feeling. Stalin, for the time being, steered a middle course – until he had crushed Bukharin and his supporters, and until the struggle with the peasantry became the most important item on the agenda.

In July 1928, Kaganovich, who had handled the Ukraine with at least comparative tact, was nevertheless recalled to Moscow. Stalin, in Bukharin's view, 'bought the Ukrainians by withdrawing Kaganovich from the Ukraine'.[81] Stalin himself writes of a demand from the Ukraine that Kaganovich be replaced by Grinko or Chubar.[82] However, the new Ukrainian First Secretary was the Pole Stanislav Kossior, with Chubar Chairman of the local Council of People's Commissars.

★

Thus it is clear that the Ukrainian Party intelligentsia was still restive: and the regime had also failed to establish itself in the countryside, where the new order may have been accepted as a *fait accompli*, but had never struck roots. In 1926, as a prominent local Communist wrote, those connected with the regime, even in such harmless capacities as village newspaper correspondents, were 'shunned'.[83]

Partly for this reason, the much-resented Committees of Unwealthy

82

Peasants had been maintained in the Ukraine after their dissolution elsewhere. Though stripped of most of their power in 1925, in mid-NEP, they regained much of it in 1927–8, with special commissions to 'bring to light grain surpluses'[84] – a presage of Stalin's attitude when he established his complete rule, and when his true policies came into their own.

★

PART II

To Crush the Peasantry

The harvest is past, the summer is
ended, and we are not saved.

Jeremiah

5

Collision Course, 1928–9

Je sors d'un mal pour tomber dans un pire.

Corneille

At the beginning of 1928 there came a grain crisis – or rather what appeared in the minds of the leadership to be a grain crisis. In fact, it was no more than a temporary disequilibrium in the grain market, easily correctable if normal measures had been applied. But once again, the Party's inherent distrust or ignorance of the whole market system and incompetent price policy led to a sort of panic.

There were indeed problems. By 1928 the export of grain had virtually ceased. Before World War I half the grain production had come from landlord and 'kulak' farms. Moreover, these had produced over 71% of the grain available for the market, and for export.

In 1927 the peasants owned 314 million hectares, as against 210 million before the revolution – though the number of holdings had grown from 16 million to 25 million.[1] And the (non-kulak) peasant who had produced 50% of the grain before the war, and consumed 60% of what he produced, now produced 85% of the grain and consumed 80% of that.[2] The state's problem was how to get hold of the grain. But as the veteran G.Ya. Sokolnikov had said flatly at the Fifteenth Congress in December 1927 'we must not think that the peasants' grain reserves are a sign of some kind of kulak war against the proletarian economic system, and that we should launch a crusade to take it away. If we do this, we will only be returning to requisition'.[3]

Yet the alternative was intelligent use of market and fiscal measures; and a certain amount of forethought. Both were lacking. As a writer generally sympathetic to the regime puts it, 'the policy of the Soviet government, which gambled every year that the harvest of the year concerned would be a good one, was inherently unrealistic'.[4]

And more generally 'the regime had no idea where it was going, the decisions it took lacked coherence and served only to disrupt agricultural production'.[5] At the Fifteenth Party Congress, several speakers had spoken of this situation, Kaminsky, for example, condemning the 'fluctuations and uncertainties in the prices of agricultural production'.[6] He took an example from the officially set price of flax, which had been changed five times in two years.

One of the West's leading analysts of the problem, the late Professor Jerzy F. Karcz, speaks of the failure to build up a grain reserve in the good years as 'negligence bordering on folly'; and adds that when 'inept price and fiscal policies produced the procurement crisis of 1927–8', the government's ability to react intelligently was much affected by 'the parallel and almost unbelievable crisis in information'.[7] For in fact, as Karcz puts it, 'the apprehension that did exist at that time over the ability of the Soviet peasant to supply marketed output to the economy . . . appears to have been completely unfounded'.[8] It has been estimated that in 1927–9 an additional investment of only 131.5 million roubles in higher grain prices would have brought the market into equilibrium.[9]

Moreover it has been shown, and tacitly confirmed by Soviet economists, that the basic figures on which Stalin relied in considering the grain problem were highly distorted,[10] (and indeed that Soviet figures even for the grain harvest of any particular year varied considerably).[11] In fact Stalin based himself on a considerable underestimate of the grain marketed in 1926–7, which was far from being as low as his inexpert and ill-informed advisers assumed.[12] A Soviet scholar has recently indicated (in a tactful manner) that Stalin accepted an estimate of 10.3 million tons for gross 1926–7 grain marketing, while the true figure was 16.2 million tons . . .[13]

Indeed, throughout the period with which we deal, and in all its various crises and supposed crises, the figures on which the regime relied were almost as unreliable as those it forecast or 'planned'. A modern Soviet scholar notes, too, how the men on the spot, overwhelmed by forms and questionnaires, responded: 'We cannot understand half the questions. We just put down the first thing that comes into our heads .. .'[14] Meanwhile the Central Statistical Office, the State Planning Commission (Gosplan), the Commissariat of Inspection and the statistical departments of the cooperative movement, 'were producing widely conflicting figures on identical problems, sometimes on matters of great importance, such as procurements, sown areas, or the five year plans'.[15]

Stalin claimed, erroneously, that 'the marketable grain in our country is now half what it was before the war, although the gross output of grain has reached the prewar level'.[16] He added – a swing to the Left in theory even beyond the immediate hard line now to be put into practice – that the blame lay primarily on the 'kulak', and that 'the solution lies in the transition from individual peasant farming to collective, socially conducted agriculture' and 'a struggle against the capitalist elements of the peasantry, against the kulaks'.[17]

At a meeting of the Central Committee and Central Executive Committee in April 1928, the line was that the crisis had been due to various economic factors, with the kulak merely taking advantage of a disequilibrium. Stalin, however, was almost at once shifting the main blame back on the kulaks, a position supported by his experts in later years, one of whom writes, for example, 'The kulaks organized sabotage of grain-collection in 1927–8. Holding a great reserve of grain, they refused to sell it to the state at the price laid down by the Soviet government'.[18]

Nowadays, however, most Soviet historians, even including the 'dogmatic' Sergey Trapeznikov, list reasons for the grain crisis of 1928 in the same general terms as Western scholars – an incorrect relation between industrial and agricultural prices; a lack of industrial goods aimed at the rural market, and hence a lack of incentive to sell rural produce; and faulty administration of the grain purchase programme, which encouraged the peasants to hoard grain if prices were too low. And the decrease in 'kulak' numbers meant that those with much excess grain were now fewer.[19]

In any case the deficit in grain in January 1928 was only some 2,160,000 tons[20] by no means a 'crisis' or 'danger' as Stalin insisted.[21] Indeed, though grain output had decreased, other agricultural production, including livestock, was rising – so that the gross output of agriculture actually went up by about 2.4% in 1928;[22] while even at the time a Soviet expert estimated the annual rate of growth of peasant productive capital as 5–5½%, a very reasonable rate.[23] Moreover, as Trapeznikov notes, peasant sales of industrial crops, which commanded a high purchase rate, grew rapidly.[24]

In fact the peasantry was simply reacting normally to the market situation, to the unrealistically low grain prices set by the state.

However, in January 1928 came what the American scholar Stephen F. Cohen rightly calls 'the pivotal event'. Faced with, or believing themselves to be faced with, a grain shortage, the Politburo voted unanimously for 'extraordinary' or 'emergency' measures. The Rightists saw these as a limited expropriation of 'kulak' grain, and when it developed into a mass confiscation of grain from the peasantry as a whole, conducted with almost as great brutality as in 1919–21, they complained.

But, basically, it was the whole decision – even though granted by all factions to be temporary and not to involve the end of NEP – which was fatal. For the party was seizing grain which had been produced for profit under supposedly guaranteed market conditions. The seizures provided the state with the grain it wanted. But it demonstrated to the agricultural producers that market conditions could no longer be relied on: so the economic incentive to produce, already shaken, was largely destroyed. At the same time, the Party's success in confiscating the grain gave it the false, and shallow, idea that here was a simple method of solving the problem.

For the grain deficit of just over 2 million tons was more than made up, the emergency measures producing nearly 2.5 million tons.[25]

Stalin described the emergency measures as 'absolutely exceptional' But the methods employed could not fail to remind the peasant of War Communism. There was a mobilization of cadres. 30,000 activists were sent to the grain growing regions. In the villages emergency 'troikas' were set up, with full power to overrule local authorities. The village, district and provincial party organizations were harassed with purges of 'weaklings'. The grain markets were closed. The amount of grain which peasants could have ground in the mills was limited to a minimum for their own consumption. In effect, though the Centre from time to time deplored 'excesses', the requisitions of the Civil War had indeed returned. Stalin's policy of attack on the 'kulak' and requisitioning in the village was in fact close to the more extreme variants of the Left programme, and Preobrazhensky gave it full support.

And now, again as in 1919, the middle peasant, by far the largest category, began no longer to have adequate representatives in the village Soviets. In some of the Ukrainian provinces their share fell to under 30%. Moreover, such organs as the electoral committees, which in effect determined the composition of these Soviets, often had only a bare majority of peasants of any sort, as against officials and others.[26]

A law of 10 January 1928 changed the quorum rules for the village commune meeting, so that a third of the members might bind the rest.[27] Peasants deprived of the Soviet vote were not to vote at the village meeting; whereas labourers without a household gained that right; and decisions of the meeting could be questioned by the village Soviet if thought to be contrary to Soviet policy.[28] This was the beginning of the end of the independence of the commune, and at the same time a blow at the middle peasant.

The commune's role under the Tsars, of 'self taxation', now began to be used again on a wide scale. That is, the commune was made responsible for extracting 'surplus money' from the village, after its new style meeting had been made to accept a given figure, (though since it was laid down that the commune must impose higher taxes on kulaks whatever the villagers' own view, the traditional freedoms of self-taxation no longer applied). In fact, official documents make it quite clear that even the poor peasants gave little support to the Party's scheme; and that the harsh administrative measures then imposed alienated all elements in the villages.[29]

Though the Ukraine, the North Caucasus and the Volga were also singled out for special attention, this time Siberia was the main target. Stalin personally went there (the last visit he was ever to make to the countryside). He addressed the Territory Party Committee and other bodies, and denounced them for incompetence bordering on sabotage. When they protested that the amount of grain asked for was excessive, he told them that while the poor and middle peasantry had sold their surplus the kulaks had huge reserves, fifty or sixty thousand poods per farm. This was pure guesswork. Moreover he contradicted himself, admitting that the largest amount of unsold grain was in the hands of the middle peasant.[30]

When it came to local practice, officials who listed all those definable as kulaks, but still had not met their quotas, were told to 'find the rest'.[31] But, since the kulaks, under any definition, did not in fact have surpluses adequate to meet the procurement demands transmitted to local officials, the latter in fact had no recourse but to make up the deficit from the stores of the peasantry as a whole.

Indeed, a letter sent by Stalin to Party organizations admitted that the kulak was not the major source of surplus grain, but was to be combated rather as the economic leader of the peasantry 'with the middle peasant following behind'.[32]

As the crisis grew less, it was admitted by Stalin and his supporter Bauman that the 'emergency measures' had included searches, confiscation and so on, and that the middle peasant's 'safety margin' had been tapped. Stalin himself was to explain with breathtaking frankness what was going wrong. In April and May 1928 there was a shortfall in the grain collection. 'Well, the grain still had to be collected. So we fell once again into extraordinary measures, administrative wilfulness, the violation of revolutionary legality, going round to farms, making illegal searches, and so on, which have caused the political situation in the country to deteriorate, threatening the alliance of the workers and peasants'.[33]

The major 'legal' weapon used against the peasantry was 'Article 107', in force since 1926. It laid down prison terms and confiscation for persons causing a deliberate rise in prices, or failing to offer their goods for sale. It had never been intended for use against the peasantry, but as a measure against the 'speculator' middleman. At the Central Committee's plenum in July 1928, Rykov was able to reveal that in an apparently typical district the application of Article 107 had involved poor peasants in 25% of the cases and middle peasants in 64%, with 'kulaks' proper only accounting for 7%![34] – And a published poll of poor peasants later in the year showed clearly that the expected support for government measures was not forthcoming from them.[35]

At this July 1928 plenum it was announced that the extraordinary measures had been repealed – (NEP had already been reaffirmed in principle at the plenum in April). Stalin gave his support, if in a typically oblique way, to the 'Left' thesis on getting industrialization capital from the peasant; while also covering his NEP flank:

> The way matters stand with the peasantry in this respect is as follows: it not only pays the State the usual taxes, direct and indirect; it also overpays – in relatively high prices for manufactured goods, in the first place, and it is more or less *underpaid* in the prices for agricultural produce, in the second place . . .
>
> It is something in the nature of a 'tribute', of a supertax, which we are temporarily compelled to levy in order to maintain and develop our present rate of industrial development, in order to ensure an industry for the whole country, further raise the well-being of the rural population and then abolish altogether this additional tax, these 'scissors' between town and country . . . unfortunately, our industry and our country cannot *at present* dispense with this additional tax on the peasantry . . .

But, Stalin continued:

> Are the peasants capable of bearing this burden? They undoubtedly are: firstly because this burden will grow lighter from year to year, and secondly, because this additional tax is being levied . . . under Soviet conditions, when exploitation of the peasants by the Socialist State is out of the question, and when this additional tax is being paid in a situation in which the living standards of the peasantry are steadily rising.[36]

Yet he was also able to tell the plenum that pressure was being kept up on the 'capitalist' element in the countryside to the extent of 'sometimes' ruining them.[37]

On one view Stalin had only wanted, by the emergency measures, to 'frighten the kulaks into submission'.[38] At any rate new directives went out to stop extraordinary measures, raise grain prices, send manufactured goods to the countryside.

But the more prosperous peasants had indeed taken fright. Some planted less, others sold up their property. For by now prices did not even cover the cost of production, as was admitted by Stalin's chief economist, Strumilin.[39] And in general the grain producers naturally responded to the compulsory seizures by losing any desire to increase production, and the sheer hard work by which the peasant had revived the country's agriculture started to fade away.

So at the end of 1928 the Party was faced with the results of its handling of the agricultural problem come back to roost in worse form yet. Both grain and livestock production began to show a decline by the autumn of 1928. Moreover, with the increase in population since 1914 taken into account, grain production per capita had gone down from 584 kg to 484.4 kg.[40]

When the market mechanism had failed to give satisfaction, requisition made up the shortfall, and the government then went back to the market. But from the peasant point of view, the market was no longer a reasonably secure outlet, but one that might be superseded at any moment by requisition. And in the further deterioration of market relations thus produced, the government remembered the success it had had with forced requisition, and did not reflect that it was the requisition of grain produced with the incentive of the market, and that in the new circumstances this was certain to shrink in quantity.

It is perfectly clear that it was not 'hoarding' but low production that was the essential.[41] Bukharin spoke of 'fairy tales' of grain hoarding.[42]

★

Meanwhile, throughout the struggle for grain in the countryside, Stalin used the situation to attack the Right. His line was that there were 'certain elements which are alien to the Party and blind to the class positions in the villages' and who wanted 'to live at peace with the kulak'.[43] At the April 1928 plenum of the Central Committee he made a very sharp attack on party members 'tagging along behind the enemies of socialism'. By mid-1928 Bukharin saw that Stalin was determined on a course which would produce risings which he would have to 'drown in blood'.[44] And as early as June 1928, Bukharin and Stalin were not on speaking terms. Yet the appearances were preserved.

Bukharin complained that the average Central Committee member did not understand the dispute. But he made little effort to explain it to them. The Right combated Stalin in private while concealing the split in public. Stalin, meanwhile, made no attacks on the Rightist leaders, but his representatives attacked unspecified deviations of those who were 'reluctant to quarrel with the kulaks', and finally 'a fundamentally Right-wing attitude' came under general attack in *Pravda*.[45]

But it was Bukharin who now urged 'the offensive against the kulak'. Kalinin, at this time on Bukharin's side, glossed over this with the explanation that no violent expropriation would be permitted – sensibly adding that so long as private holdings remained more 'kulaks' would always emerge to replace ones dispossessed.

Stalin, too, still foreswore handing the kulaks 'over to the GPU', though in less convincing language, and explicitly reserving the right to use 'administrative' as well as economic methods against them. When it came to personalities Stalin directed his public attack at lesser, and more forthright Rightists – in particular Frumkin, Deputy Commissar of Finance and Commissar of Foreign Trade. Frumkin came out openly with a letter to the Central Committee on 15 June 1928. Stalin attacked him in November, before that Committee, as representing the 'Right deviation'. At the same time he said that the Politburo was united, though criticizing the fourth most important Rightist, Uglanov, as a 'conciliator'. At this plenum in November 1928, Bukharin and Tomsky were nevertheless driven into submitting their resignations. But Stalin was not ready for this, and induced them to withdraw – conceding their demand that rumours about a split should be stopped!

Over 1928 and 1929, the Right were simply outwitted by Stalin. Their position was gradually destroyed without their finding the occasion to make a serious effort to engage in a public confrontation even to the level of Trotsky's, let alone Zinoviev's.

As Robert V. Daniels has put it, 'the history of the Right opposition affords the singular spectacle of a political group's being defeated first, and attacked afterwards'.

★

As the grain crisis started to return late in 1928, even the State Planning Commission took the view that the 'falling tendency' in grain collection was a seasonal phenomenon.[46] And as late as November 1928 Stalin was denouncing the idea that 'extraordinary measures' should be permanent policy.[47]

The new shortage of grain in the hands of the State was therefore coped with by measures of which it was simply denied that they were 'extraordinary' or amounted to crude confiscation. The 'Ural-Siberian method', officially based on recommendations from the party organs in those two areas, was adopted by the Politburo (Rykov dissenting) and was applied on a nation-wide scale from about February 1929 (though only given legal form in June). It based itself on the idea that there were large hoards of grain, mainly in the hands of 'kulaks', and insisted on higher grain quotas for the villages. The 'method' consisted in theory of 'a form of consensus voiced by the mass of the peasants'. The party plenipotentiaries sent to the villages did not simply order grain requisition. They assembled the village meeting and induced them to accept higher collection figures, to apply 'self-taxation' to grain as well as money, and to decide against which 'kulaks' to exert 'social influence' and 'mass pressure'. The village meetings were induced to carry out their role in this by pressures in fact indistinguishable from force. They almost invariably voted against the new proposals. Thereupon their leading spokesmen were denounced as kulaks or 'sub-kulaks': 'there are sometimes arrests, house-searches, fines, confiscation of property, or even shooting'.[48] The meetings were kept in session until those remaining voted acceptance. Any question of quorums was ignored. State power was then used, supposedly in the service of the village commune, against those believed to have grain.

Any recalcitrants were expelled from cooperatives, refused milling rights, and so on: in fact cases are quoted in the Soviet press of refusal to admit their children to schools, boycotts, deportations, fines . . .[49]

By the spring of 1929 meat, too, began to be collected by force – Siberia supplied 19,000 tons in this way as against 700 tons the previous year.[50]

In addition to requisition, backed by fines and imprisonment, there were many incidents of the confiscation of 'kulak' implements and draft of animals, and sometimes of his land as well, especially in the Ukraine. This was approaching the full 'dekulakization' which the Party still denied was necessary.

In theory the 'kulak' could only be 'coerced' because this was the will of the peasant masses. This 'social influence' was, in fact quite spurious. And, as against the ideological or cosmetic side of the campaign, we may note some of the empirical evidence. In one district, the official press reported, neither poor nor middle peasants were attracted to the side of the party. In another, 40% of the villages voted against the system; in yet another 30%: indeed *Izvestiya* admitted that the village meetings often decided against the party.[51]

However, the campaign proceeded, with more emphasis on party workers from the towns – said in one report to be forcing the 'meetings' with 'cavalry methods'.[52] The 'Leftist' Sosnovsky, now in exile in Siberia, wrote that the authorities 'fell on the peasant' with a concerted ferocity seldom seen since the days of 1918–19; the peasant was required to 'give' – grain, taxes (before they were due), loans, levies, insurance . . .[53]

In report after report, it becomes clear that the meetings were simply bullied into submission. Moreover, (as we shall see later), these methods united rather than divided the peasants, including the poor peasants.[54] For once again the pressure supposedly to be put on the 'kulaks' did not yield adequate results. So, though never openly instructed to do so, officials once again started applying the confiscations to the middle peasantry.

In the interests of inflaming the class struggle in the villages, one of the measures ordered was the allotting of 25% of grain confiscated from the kulak to the poor peasants and labourers. Even with this inducement, the village poor were slow to respond. And by the beginning of spring, when the authorities most needed them, it became necessary to stop this bribe – all the grain was now required for the state. As a result, according to Bauman, the poor peasant, though helpful earlier, in this phase 'frequently did not have enough to eat, and so he too has gone cap in hand to the kulak'.[55] Mikoyan also spoke of the poor peasant's 'wavering' under the influence of the kulaks.[56] A leading article in *Pravda* noted that the kulaks were attracting the rest of the peasantry to their side under slogans supporting the equality of the commune.[57]

But the Ural-Siberian method in itself could not be regarded as a wholly successful technique. It suffered from the fact that the grain was in the hands of the man who had reaped it, and could only be got from him by a concentrated effort, largely implemented by temporary intruders unfamiliar with the village. In addition, the Ural-Siberian method was an attempt to use the coercion suitable to a command economy in a context which was still in principle a market economy.

Yet the crushing of the 'kulaks' and the destruction of the free market were inextricably linked. For crushing the 'kulaks' simply meant, in economic terms, destroying the peasants' incentive to produce for the market.

★

Nor was the campaign in the countryside the sole sign of a move to the left. The whole atmosphere in the country from 1928 on was one of increasing terror and hysteria, of a turn against the comparative peace of early NEP.

The opening signal of this campaign was the first of the notorious faked public trials, the Shakhty Case where Stalin in March 1928 framed a group of 'bourgeois specialist' engineers against the wishes of the Right, of the moderate Stalinist Kuibyshev in charge of economic matters, and even of Menzhinsky, Head of the OGPU. (Nor was Shakhty unique: wreckers were everywhere exposed in 1928–9, including 'bourgeois specialists' in Kazakhstan allegedly connected with 'the British capitalist Urquhart').[58]

The Shakhty Trial and similar cases were a clear signal that the intensities of class warfare were to be resumed. At this time a third of all specialists working in the national economy were from the pre-revolutionary intelligentsia, and among those with higher education they formed a clear majority. 60% of teachers in higher education were of the same provenance. But everywhere the old intelligentsia was hounded from its posts, and often enough into exile or death as well. Their children were expelled from the universities – indeed the universities virtually collapsed until 1934.

By 1930 more than half the engineers had no proper training: only 11.4% had had higher education, and some had not even been put through crash courses.

In the Ukraine, the 'Cultural Revolution' had a somewhat different tone from that in Moscow. The attack was made not only on the older Ukrainian cultural establishment, but equally on the 'nationalist' inclined Communist intelligentsia.

At the local level – and back in the villages – teachers, usually of suspect social origin, were in frequent trouble, often fined – illegally – as class enemies, or on such grounds as having a priest as a relative, such cases being very common.[59]

As things got worse, in 1929, it is given as a typical instance that local officials 'especially went to Yablonskaya school to see teacher Orlova, the daughter of a kulak sentenced to eight years for anti-Soviet activity, and Kustova, the daughter of a priest. There they organized a drunken party and forced the teachers to sleep with them . . . [One of them] motivated his infamous suggestion with the statement: 'I am [Soviet] power; I can do anything', knowing that such statements would have particular effect on Orlova and Kustova, since they are of alien class origin. As a result of his tormenting, Kustova came close to suicide'.[60]

★

In general, the Marxist view that class feeling must be the motive force of social change had to be accommodated, so it was once more incited and subsidized and, where that failed, invented, in the villages.

In a speech to the Central Executive Committee in December 1928 the Soviet President Kalinin himself gave some of the reasons why the 'kulak', (even in the strained Communist definitions), was not properly hated even by the poor peasant. The kulak, he reported 'also has a positive part to play in the rural economy', making loans to the poor peasant and thus 'rescuing him from his difficulties in times of distress' – an oblique admission that the government was *not* helping. And when the kulak killed a cow, he added, the poor peasant could buy some of the meat.[61]

Class struggle was hard to maintain. A typical complaint was still that: 'Sometimes the kulak leads the poor and middling strata. There are cases when peasants of a collective farm vote against the expulsion of kulaks.

97

Occasionally, the poor follow the kulak owing to bad organization. The cause of this, beside the weak organization of the poor, are intimidation on the part of the kulak, lack of culture, and family connections'.[62]

Poor peasants too, as official reports tell us, would say 'there are no kulaks in our village'; and – even more strikingly – 'now they are confiscating bread from the kulak; tomorrow they will turn against the poor and middle peasant'.[63]

In a speech, (unpublished at the time), to the North Caucasian Party Conference in March 1929 Mikoyan said frankly that the middle peasant saw the kulak as an example, and accepted his authority, while regarding the poor peasant as economically inefficient. Only the large collective farm, Mikoyan added (reflecting the new Stalinist thinking), would retrieve the situation.[64] Again, at the April 1929 Sixteenth Party Conference, Sergei Syrtsov, shortly to be promoted to Politburo candidacy, said that not only some of the middle peasantry but some of the poor peasantry as well supported the kulaks. In fact the Head of the Central Committee Agricultural Department said flatly 'the middle peasant has turned against us and sided with the kulak'[65] Through 1928–29 there are scores of such admissions that the 'kulak' and the rest of the peasantry took the same position – even from men like Kaganovich.[66]

However, the 'kulak' mania was in one way helpful to the party, as Stalin himself noted: for if the middle peasant saw that the private prosperity he sought would only lead to his becoming a kulak and being repressed – or if he was simply 'prevented . . . from becoming a kulak' – he might come round to the idea that the collective farm was the only remaining way to prosperity.[67]

As to their number: taxes imposed in November 1928 on 'the wealthiest strata in the village'[68] in theory hit 2–3% of the peasantry (to discourage 'apathy', the tax was altered to being based on the area sown, regardless of the actual harvest).[69] But in practice, as Stalin admitted, up to 12%, in some areas even more, were affected.[70] And other sources show that the 'surtax' affected 16% of all households in the RSFSR,[71] *Pravda* was to speak of entire kulak villages.[72] In one such, in the North Caucasus, not even members of the local Soviet would attend meetings about the grain collection.[73] The number treated as kulaks in 1929 grain quotas is undiscoverable by Soviet researchers, but one Soviet historian estimates that it was about 7–10% of all rural households,[74] while the joint pseudo-category of kulaks and 'better-off' were later to be described by Stalin as amounting to 15% of all rural households.

★

98

The crucial year 1929, in fact, found the grain problem, and the peasant problem, still unsolved. Bread rationing had been introduced in the towns in the winter of 1928–9, (and in the autumn of 1929 meat rationing followed). In the spring of 1929 Rykov (supported by Bukharin) proposed the import of grain – the expedient to which the USSR was finally driven in the 1960s. But this was now rejected after a 'very heated discussion'.[75]

In the Politburo, Bukharin now spoke of a 'military feudal exploitation of the peasantry', and over the early part of the year the Right continued to make a strong effort to stabilize relations with the peasantry, the end of coercive measures, a return to NEP and the free market.[76]

By the spring of 1929 Stalin was speaking (in a then unpublished speech) of Bukharin's 'treacherous behaviour'.[77] Bukharin had made and published his central point, quoting Lenin to the effect that it would be disastrous for the Communist course to apply strict communist principles in the villages 'so long as the material basis for Communism does not exist in the countryside'.[78] Nearly all the non-party, i.e. professional, economists supported this, and the Right's idea of restoring the equilibrium of the market: in particular Vladimir Groman, the chief brain of the State Planning Commission (Gosplan). Even Strumilin, closest to Stalin among the Gosplan economists, held that the rate of growth should not outpace the resources needed for it.

The Five Year Plan was officially approved in April-May 1929, before it had been properly completed.

It was in any case not really a 'plan' at all. Though some measure of co-ordination, and a fair amount of attention to the relation between resources and possibilities was preserved, in effect it was (and even more in the event) 'merely a body of figures which were constantly being scaled upward, and this was its sole function'.[79]

The planners put forward two versions, one less ambitious than the 'optional' other one, which was made conditional on five good harvests, a good international market for grain, no necessity for high defence expenditure, and other factors. Even this was to be scaled up. And, in so far as the plan still retained some remnant of the coordination Gosplan economists had called for, this disappeared as each industry and individual plant sank into a series of ever more unattainable crash programmes, without regard to the resources of the economy as a whole.

Nevertheless if the original Five Year Plan had in fact been followed, the individual sector would only have declined by the odd percent of the population by 1932–3, and it would have retained almost 90% of gross peasant production.[80] This adequately indicates what overt party policy still was in the spring of 1929.

The Party's actions in the countryside had in fact largely destroyed

NEP. But it is not clear that the leadership yet understood what it had done. Even now, and as late as mid-1929, there was general assent to the ideas of NEP, of a long continuing private sector in agriculture, and of market relations. In particular, such were the ideas to be found among the economists, not only in Gosplan but also in the Commissariat of Agriculture.

In April 1929 even Stalin was saying that between 4.9 and 5.7 of the 8.2 million tons of grain required by the State could be obtained in the market, with the remaining 2.5 million tons needing 'organized pressure on the kulaks' on the Ural-Siberian model[81] – an extraordinary and chimerical mix of two economic methods, but at least not calling for total control.

The comparatively slow way in which Stalin carried out his double operation of crushing the Right and embarking on crash collectivization seems to have been largely due to the fact that an important section of his own supporters were not quite ready for either, even in the early part of 1929, or at least to Stalin sensing something of the sort. The defeat of the Right in April 1929 was a rallying of Central Committee veterans to what still appeared a fairly moderate economic course, and having opted for Stalin, they were led step by step into the full implementation of the extreme policies of the winter.

★

The endless struggle against the kulak was much discussed in the Party and its organs in the earlier part of 1929, but no decision on how to deal with him was then reached. It was only in May 1929 that the Council of People's Commissars produced a formal definition of a kulak farm. It regularly hired labour; or had a mill or buttermaking or similar establishment; or hired out agricultural machinery or premises; or had members engaged in commercial activities or usury or other income not from work – specifically including the priesthood.[82]

Under these definitions almost any peasant could have been penalized. Moreover republican, territorial and provincial authorities were given the right to modify them to suit local conditions!

Meanwhile even the most radical speakers said that there was no intention of physically liquidating the kulak, and mass deportation was not mentioned until a subcommittee on the question submitted, towards the end of the year, a proposal that the worst of three categories of kulak, active enemies guilty of hostile acts, should be imprisoned or deported.[83] Yet 'dekulakization' – the beginnings of the mass action we shall be dealing with in the next chapter – begins sporadically early in 1929. For

100

example, in the village of Shampaivka, Kiev Province, with about 3,000 households, fifteen peasants were dekulakized and sent north as early as March 1929.[84]

Such dekulakization was activated by the most eager Stalinists at the provincial level. On 20 May 1929 the Central Volga party committee ruled that kulak counter-revolutionaries should be removed; on 14 June, the North Caucasus committee laid down that troublesome kulaks should be expropriated and exiled – though only if they had been caught with concealed grain, and then no more than one or two per *stanitsa*.[85] More generally, we are told in a Soviet publication that local government organs were given the power, 'by decision of general meetings of the working peasantry' to exile kulaks by administrative order *early in 1929*.[86]

But the position remained ambiguous. The normal weapon was a series of successive grain quotas and taxes. According to Strumilin the kulak, with average earnings five times greater than those of a poor peasant, paid thirty times as much tax per head.[87] A decree of 28 June 1929 'allowed' village Soviets to inflict fines five times the value of the individual farm's procurement, if it failed to meet its quota. This was the 'legal' basis of action in the village, including dekulakization, until February 1930. Failure to pay the fines meant the selling up of the kulak's farm, dispossession. A typical order from the Dnipropetrovsk Province ran 'Citizen Andriy Berezhny, wealthy farmer, is obliged to deliver corn at the 40% rate. He has not delivered 203 poods, and now refuses to make further delivery. He is to pay 500 roubles fine within twenty-four hours. In the case of not paying, forced collection of fines by means of selling up must take place'.[88]

In 1928–9, as a result of all this, the 'kulaks' lost 30 to 40% of their means of production.[89]

'Loss of electoral rights' was a penalty often inflicted in conjunction with others. It may be asked why the peasant minded this removal of a virtually non-existent privilege. The reason is that it appeared on his personal documents, and would instantly brand him wherever in the country he sought refuge or employment. And deprivation of the right to vote 'was often followed by denial of lodging, food ration and medical services, and especially by exile'.[90]

We should note that, apart from the kulak, another element tolerated by NEP in the interests of the market now disappeared. This other new 'bourgeoisie' – the notorious Nepmen – amounted to half a million, mainly small shopkeepers without employees. The shops they ran in the villages were assessed in 1927 as having an average capital value of 711 roubles, (even at the official rate, some $375, or £80). Their disappearance led to a virtual collapse of the distribution of consumer goods. 'Even the meagre goods available could not be distributed'.[91]

As against the idea of exiling or selling up the kulak over 1929 Kalinin made an attempt to permit 'kulaks' (after giving up their property) to be assimilated into collective agriculture. As late as mid-1929 Party spokesmen were to be found strongly inclining to allow the kulaks to join the collective farms 'if they completely renounce their personal ownership of means of production'. Others took the opposite view.[92] In August Bauman authoritatively stated that the question had not been finally resolved by the Party.[93] However, in the later half of the year we hear little more of the possibility of kulak admission to the kolkhozes. By October those suggesting it were being accused of Right deviation.

★

But all this was far from the winning over of the peasantry *en masse*, and the isolation of the class enemy, which was desired. The main body of the peasantry was now thoroughly alienated. They used all the weapons available to them, including massive complaint to their sons serving in the Army.[94]

Pravda, in an editorial on 2 February 1929, complained bitterly that the peasant had not yet realized 'the basic difference between the laws of the old regime and Soviet laws', still regarding the *vlast* as automatically hostile. *Pravda* was particularly annoyed at such persisting sayings as 'what is the use of laws when the judges know each other' and 'the law is a spider's web, the bumblebee gets through, the fly is caught'.

The comparative peace of the villages at the height of NEP had totally disappeared. Already in 1928, from all over the country came reports of looting, civil disorder, resistance, riots, in which workers also participated.[95] One official history quotes case after case of party and other activists attacked – three 'kulaks' killing an Ivanovo party secretary on 7 June 1928; the shooting of a kolkhoz chairman in Kostroma on 7 November 1928; of another activist in the same region the same day; of the chairman of a village Soviet in Penza on 19 December 1928; and a dozen others all over the USSR.[96] From 1927 to 1929 300 procurement agents are reported killed.[97]

The number of 'registered kulak terrorist acts' in the Ukraine quadrupled between 1927 and 1929, 1,262 being reported in the latter year.[98] Resistance grew ever stronger. Official figures for nine months of 1929 alone, and only in the central provinces of the RSFSR, show 1,002 'terrorist acts' were organized by 'kulaks', with 384 deaths. For these 3,281 people were sentenced – and of these only 1,924 – 31.2% – were 'kulaks': the others were 1,896 'middle peasant sub-kulaks', 296 poor

102

peasants and 67 officials. Since in such cases the pressure to call the accused a kulak was obviously great, it constitutes an admission that the rank-and-file peasantry were hostile.[99]

In the autumn of 1929 a further increase in 'terrorism' is registered.[100] Nevertheless, in spite of a certain degree of sporadic armed resistance, there was not at this stage anything in the way of a serious rebellion, and these are still isolated incidents compared with what was to come.

Meanwhile large scale resistance of a more passive type was even more significant. In particular grain was buried – first on the peasants' own land, then in odd waste areas, haystacks, churches, out in the steppe, in the ravines and the forest. Kulaks put their grain in their relatives' names, sold it to poor peasants at low prices, or to illegal private traders who smuggled it in parcels, on rafts, in carts at night. Middle and poor peasants did the same as far as they could. Even collective farm peasants evaded the collection as best they could. When they could not hide or sell their grain, they turned the crop into hay, burnt it, or threw it in the rivers.[101]

★

In the villages, the party still had inadequate means of control. The number of rural members of the Party in the 1917–21 period had been about one-sixth of the total, and many of these were workers. Moreover, in 1922–3, a Soviet writer notes, 'only an infinitesimal number of Communists in the villages' had renewed their membership.[102] In 1929, therefore, the bulk of the village Communists were recruits of the NEP period, who had been largely untouched by the militant party doctrines of the earlier phase.

It was noted in the Party literature that a poor peasant activist previously loyal to the regime, who might even be a party member, moved easily 'from a favourable class position to a hostile one'.[103] In the villages, moreover, (as Molotov complained in 1928), agricultural workers and poor peasants only made up 5% of the Party membership.[104] And a resolution of the November 1928 plenum of the Party Central Committee noted that in the Ukraine the rural party contained 'a considerable number of better-off peasants and near-kulak elements, which are degenerate and totally alien to the working class'.[105] In any case, the great majority of the rural membership was not peasant at all but, in the main, local officials.

Moreover, however looked at, their numbers were inadequate. In September 1924, there were only 13,558 party cells in the villages, with a membership of 152,993, the cells typically numbering four to six members and being spread over three or four villages sometimes five or six miles apart.[106] Even in October 1928, there were only 198,000 peasant party members (out of 1,360,000) – one Communist peasant per 125 peasant households. Only 20,700 rural party cells existed in the 70,000 villages. By 1929 there were 333,300 village (not necessarily peasant) members in 23,300 cells, (though some of these cells were, a prominent Communist commented, fictitious).[107] In the Ukraine the Party membership in the villages was smaller still – 25,000 members employed in agriculture out of 25 million rural inhabitants.[108]

Even in 1929, there was approximately only one Party cell to three village Soviets. In the village Soviets themselves, the 'poor peasants' who had only held about 16% of the membership under NEP, went up from 28.7 to 37.8 in 1929, but even this was denounced as inadequate. Nor did this influx of 'poor peasants', however Marxist, prove effective. When the offensive against the peasants began to gather momentum the village Soviets, and even the district Soviets, opposed the attack, Moscow noting that they 'were forming a bloc with the kulaks' and 'degenerating'.[109]

The Chairman of one District Executive Committee is quoted as saying that the pressure on the kulak 'will turn him and the whole population against us'. Not merely ordinary peasants, but local Party members would tell plenipotentiaries 'We have no kulaks here'. Even the plenipotentiaries 'grow pacifist'.[110]

Local party members – and even local GPU militia organs – were kept under pressure from above, being attacked for being insufficiently militant. Many were dismissed – in some cases entire district committees and even all the party cells in a district;[111] and party officials who tried to preserve some order and legality were denounced as accomplices of the Right.[112]

More generally *Pravda* complained that Communists were 'often . . . opponents of the rapid development of collective farms and state farms, "principled" supporters of the "free development of peasant economy", defenders of peaceful co-existence with the kulak, people who do not see classes in the countryside'.[113]

This purge of party 'opportunists' unenthusiastic about the new policies assumed a mass character.[114] In fact even the 'peasant correspondents' were officially attacked as 'to a considerable degree alien elements'.[115]

Of course, none of this is to say that the authorities had no reliable agents at all in the countryside. In a village of two thousand or more inhabitants, it was not difficult to find an adequate 'brigade' of activists. A report of one such names fourteen – some farm labourers, some ex-partisans, some budding police-apprentices. Many of them were, as ten years previously, a semi-criminal element.[116]

104

One of the best known of modern Soviet 'country novels', Vasilii Belov's *Kanuny*,[117] gives a very depressing account of the end of NEP in the Vologda area under such characters. One of the main adherents of the regime in the village has as his motives vengeance, meanness, and compensation for his knowledge of his inferiority, denounces anonymously, and in general behaves revoltingly. 'He never forgave people, and saw only enemies in them and that engendered fear, and he did not hope for anything, but believed only in his own power and cunning. And having believed in that, another idea was entrenched in him: all people are like him and all the world lives under the sign of fear and power, as he does. Force creates everything, but a greater force subdues it and people take into consideration only force. They are afraid of it'.

But in general, rural Communism was to a large degree a broken reed. So, once again, in the summer of 1929 a hundred thousand urban party members were sent into the countryside to help the grain collection; and other agents of the government, perhaps as many again, later joined them. In the North Caucasus alone 15,000 town dwellers descended on the peasantry.[118]

★

The transition from the phase of direct Party intervention camouflaged as mass action to the next phase was not difficult. In the press, from every platform, a lynching mood towards the class enemy had already been launched. For it had at least been shown over 1928–9 that the appearance of lynch law – of popular or mass feeling – rather than 'naked administrative methods', could be created in these campaigns, even though the real feeling of the peasantry was unenthusiastic.

Moreover the lynching mood was extended, though as yet less literally, to the problem of the defeated Right. Tomsky was removed as Head of the Trade Unions in June 1929, and Bukharin from the Comintern in July, though still for the time being remaining members of the Politburo. Their followers were eliminated from all sensitive posts. And over the following period came the purge of their many supporters among the rank-and-file. In spite of Bukharin's failure to organize his opposition as the Left had done, modern Soviet works tell us that entire party organizations supported him, and that 100,000 party members were eventually expelled as Rightists[119] – compared with 1,500 Trotskyites.

On the other hand, the atmosphere of crisis appealed to the old Left, and at this time a group of important 'leftists' – Preobrazhensky, Radek and Smilga – broke with Trotsky and accepted the new Stalinist line.

Nor was it the case that the authorities neglected, at least in theory, to provide incentives as well as coercion. Scarcity of goods for the countryside was called 'one of the most serious obstacles'.[120] However, in the Central Committee Resolution of 29 July 1929, it was laid down that the supply of goods 'must chiefly be related to the fulfilment of the grain collection plans',[121] and it was ruled that this should be done on a class basis, for example exempting the poor peasant from this condition.[122]

But the goods were not in fact forthcoming, and there was no suggestion that policy should wait for them. On 28 June 1929 it had been ruled that a peasant could be penalized for not delivering grain even if it could not be shown that he was 'hoarding' any: he could be fined, and if the fine was not paid, expropriated. Another decree on the same day laid down penalties for 'failure to carry out general state instructions': first fines, and on the second offence a year's imprisonment, or if in a concerted group up to two years, with full or partial expropriation and exile.[123] Many 'kulaks' now sold up and moved into the towns to avoid this.[124]

All sorts of shifts were meanwhile introduced to make up the looming grain deficit. 'Voluntary' gifts of corn to the Government were ordered: for example in October 1929 villages in the Ukraine were told to send in an extra twenty pounds of wheat per family within a few days.[125]

The facts of the period have been to some extent obscured by Stalin's deceptive and devious style. In his struggle against the Right, he was able to undermine them while not attacking them. He was able to maintain that an artificial agitation got up by his nominees was a genuine wave of class struggle in the villages. And finally, he was always able to blame deviationists for the 'excesses' which were an unavoidable result of his policies.

There were party members who understood perfectly well that the fight was not only against the kulak, but also the middle peasant, but held that this was correct Leninist policy and should be proclaimed as such.[126] But this accurate analysis could only be regarded, in the realm of theory, as Left deviationism.

At every point, policy had to be decked out in appropriate Marxist terms. So, first an almost entirely artificial class war in the village had to be posited, and rubbed in to the point of extreme tedium, even when the leaders knew it to be false. And then, at the end of 1929, a purely imaginary switch of the middle peasantry to a love of collectivization became the crux. No party spokesman could omit, let alone rebut, this piece of doctrinal piety.

★

In this atmosphere of conceptual confusion and fantasy, with policy shifting while verbalizations remained the same, it was hard for party members to adjust themselves to the tempo of change. Nor, even at this stage, can we be sure when exactly it was that Stalin determined on crash collectivization.

On a purely agricultural view, Stalin's thinking has been described in terms of having rediscovered in the early part of the year the 'short-term effectiveness' of coercive methods, and then 'trying to solve a long-term, structural problem by means of short-term, war-economy measures, including collectivization'.[127] It seems that the partial success, and partial failure, of the Ural-Siberian method and later actions converted him to the view that only total control over the countryside would solve the Party's problem.

The Five Year Plan had envisaged five million households in the collective farms by 1932–3. But the Government's newly formed 'Kolkhoz Centre' was already in June 1929 talking of seven to eight million during 1930, while aiming at collectivizing half the population during the Plan period, and trebling the acreage envisaged in the Plan.[128] At this point, in fact, the Plan's agricultural component had collapsed. But even these figures were to be overtaken by far higher ones. By November they had already nearly doubled, to double again during December.

For, while the Right had held that collectivization would only make sense when the peasantry had adequate machinery and other goods from the towns, a different consideration prevailed among the Stalinists. As Mikoyan put it in June 1929, 'if there were no grain difficulties' collectivization would not have been urgent.[129]

★

In the early days of the regime great efforts had been made to establish collective farms. Many were set up by administrative pressure, and most of them disappeared when NEP came into force. Many had been largely staffed by workers, who now began to return to the cities. In other cases richer peasants who had joined them to save their property went back to private farming[130] – a phenomenon to be seen again in 1930. In any case, these early kolkhozes, though often comparatively successful, were always a minor feature. By mid-1928 less than 2% of households belonged to them.

A decree of the Council of People's Commissars and the Central Executive Committee of 16 March 1927 shows no trend towards them. And as late as the end of 1928 there was still no suggestion of the collectivization of the mass of the middle peasants – though a Decree of 15 December recommended favoured treatment for any rural collectives[131] (and now also gave the authorities the right to forbid the setting up of new 'consolidated' individual farms in cases where this would reinforce the 'kulak' stratum).[132]

Even half-way through 1929 the Commissariat of Agriculture estimated that there were 40,000 kolkhozes then in existence, but only 10–15,000 of them with chairmen competent to run them.[133] Most were of the 'TOZ' type – in fact not really collective farms at all but merely associations for joint tillage, ploughing, harvesting and sharing the proceeds: it was, of course, the quite different 'artel' type kolkhoz, with the land, implements and produce properly under 'collective' – that is, state – control, that was the chosen vehicle of the Stalin era.

★

Apart from the political and social reasons given for collectivization, a most important justification runs that small-scale farming is unproductive, so that either large-scale socialist farms or large-scale capitalist farms are inevitable. During this period, there is also a further outburst of expressions of faith in a technological revolution which would (for example) stop any 'archaic' ideas of 'animal husbandry allegedly requiring a kind of individual treatment'.[134]

Lenin had, of course, been quite orthodox in envisaging an eventual system of huge Marxist factory-farms. But it had been realized by Soviet economists in the 1920s, from the experience of excessively large collective farms set up at the time, that a smaller size would be more efficient.[135] Some of these economists who were former Social-Revolutionaries, in particular the major figure Chayanov, had written sensibly throughout, and still defended small scale agriculture in 1929 – but soon had to repudiate this position.

For Stalin came out in favour of the 'giant kolkhozes', saying, 'The objections of "science" to the possibility and expediency of organizing large grain factories of 50,000 to 100,000 hectares has been exploded and turned to ashes'.[136] This formulation was indeed toned down when Stalin's *Works* appeared years later, to '40–50,000'; but meanwhile the agricultural experts perforce followed his lead, in fact acceptably putting the emphasis on 100,000 rather than the lower figure. And other scholars were soon speaking of the kolkhoz in classical Marxist terms as a 'transition to the large collectivized agricultural factory'.[137]

Stalin himself went to the length of predicting that, by these methods, 'Our country will, in some three years time, have become one of the

108

richest granaries, if not the richest, in the whole world'.[138] And Bukharin too was soon enthusing about giant farms, each encompassing a whole District![139]

Typical of the time is the tale of the Khoper area on the Lower Don, which had been made a crash collectivization model. It came forward at the end of 1929 with a plan, worked out in three days, for a 'socialist agrotown' of 44,000 people in flats, with libraries, restaurants, reading rooms, gymnasiums[140] . . . a fantasy to persist through Soviet history.

This urge to the giant farm had no basis except an urge to urbanize the countryside and produce the grain-factories hypothesized by a German scholar a couple of generations previously. The merest look at agricultural reality would have raised the question of why successful capitalist farms were not of this giant size. For, leaving all political theory aside, if huge farms were the more productive they would have emerged under capitalism just as huge factories did. Moreover, even with non-Soviet co-operative farming, as one of the West's leading scholars in the field has pointed out, 'Outside the USSR . . . attempts to combine small farms into large scale production co-operatives have thus far proved unsuccessful'.[141]

Partly for such doctrinal reasons, intensive farming was simply never tried. But it is quite clear that there was room for considerable increases in the productivity of the small farms. In 1861–76 to 1901–10 Russian grain yields had increased by as much as 45%; and in 1924–9 were again 22% higher than the average yields of 1901–10.[142] In fact peasant agriculture had not reached its limits of expansion; as we have seen Soviet estimates gave an annual rate of growth of peasant productive capital as 5.5%.

Regardless of the form of agriculture, there seems little doubt that output could have been raised by fairly simple methods. Steel ploughs substituted for the five million wooden ploughs still in use; the better use of seed; and similar measures taken in other countries, would have proved very effective. All that was needed was a rise in productivity to something like that of other Eastern European countries of the period.

*

The initiative for mass collectivization is still supposed to have arisen on the Lower Volga and to have spread 'spontaneously'.[143] Through 1929 other local party committees came forward with ever increasing schedules for their own collectivization, to fulfil what they rightly saw as the leadership's intentions, (though often inflating their collectivization figures without actually increasing collectivization, or so it was complained).[144]

The Collective Farm Centre set up in the summer at first decided to concentrate on selected 'districts of comprehensive collectivization', in which a very high proportion of kolkhozes would be set up. In July, the largely Cossack North Caucasus Territory announced that its programme would be based on the collectivization of whole *stanitsas*.[145] The phenomenon, at this point, was thus highly localized and concentrated; by November with only 7.6 of the households in the USSR as a whole (about two million of them) collectivized, provinces and territories show up to 19%, and some districts within them up to 50% or more, with, in the end, entire provinces reaching this level.

The principle of a majority vote for the kolkhoz in a village forcing the minority also to join now became normal. And the voting was, as usual, under strong pressure. Even then the 'majority', as a leading Party figure pointed out, might be eighteen to fourteen out of seventy-seven households (in one case he listed); while in another village lack of any votes against was followed by the refusal of *all* the fifteen individual peasants elected to the collectivization committee to serve, having instead to be fined and imprisoned. Moreover, the individual peasants thus finding themselves destined for the kolkhoz, at this stage often sold off their livestock and implements before joining.[146]

The lesson drawn by the authorities was that the highly collectivized areas should serve as pilot models for the whole country; and over the last part of the year this 'method' of mass collectivization was declared by Stalin himself to be an essential precondition to fulfilling the Plan.[147]

As always during Soviet agricultural turmoil, the detailed planning was thoroughly defective, and the press often carried stories of large amounts of grain being wasted: 'Twelve carloads of wheat are rotting in the basement of the Red Star flour mill at Zheleznyany in the Donbas';[148] 'at the Byelorussian branch of the Grain Association 2,500 tons of grain are piled out in the open. In Voronkovo 100 tons of grain have rotted in the granaries . . . In many parts of the Odessa Province grain is lying in heaps on the ground, not even covered . . . tens of thousands of tons of grain are thus piled on the ground under the open sky'.[149]

In mid-1929 it was still roughly accepted that the rate of collectivization would depend on the availability of tractors. But as the year advanced it came to be argued, as Stalin did in an address to agrarian Marxists,[150] that a mere aggregation of ploughs, under collectivized conditions, would greatly improve agricultural efficiency.

With all the increase of pressure, Stalin played his cards so carefully that even in early September of his leading followers Ordzhonikidze could speak of 'years and years' being necessary and Andreyev could deny that complete collectivization was possible under the Five Year Plan.[151]

But the real tendency, the implicit momentum of the Stalin leadership, ran the other way. A surer view was given by Pyatakov, as a former Leftist of the highest influence speaking in October 1929 at the Council of People's Commissars. He said that 'We are obliged to adopt extreme rates of collectivization of agriculture', and went on to invoke 'the same tension with which we worked in the time of armed struggle with the class enemy. The heroic period of our socialist construction has arrived'.[152] In fact, party traditionalism now rallied to Stalin partly because of a belief that, however crude his methods, he was fighting the decisive battle of the regime, partly because the very dangers of the new phase seemed to demand party unity. The atmosphere of the Civil War was, as Pyatakov urged, in effect recreated. This was not only useful against the peasantry. It also gave all the benefits of an emergency to the feelings of the Party activists. Moderation was, or was to be, crushed or swept away on a wave of partisan emotion.

*

The more serious party economists had held that an industrial growth of 18–20% (then already achieved, at least on paper) should be maintained, with the emphasis on efficiency. No plans should be made without an adequate look at the available resources. But Stalin and his followers now insisted on a doubling of the growth rate; (in the event the actual results in industrial production in 1930 were to be – even on official figures – an increase of 22% instead of 35%, and so with the figures of productivity and production costs).[153]

As to the economists, as 1929 wore on there were a number of statements which made it clear that they had the choice of supporting the politicians' new plans or going to prison.[154] The Stalinists began, in fact, to attack them openly, Molotov speaking of 'bourgeois-kulak ideologists at the centre and in the localities'.[155] In October Groman was removed from the Expert Council of the Central Statistical Administration, and at the end of the year that body was put directly under Gosplan.[156] Non-Party economists like Chayanov renounced their views as if they were Communists, though this resulted in attacks on their renunciations as insincere. Still, they survived for the moment, to die in Secret Police hands a few years later, implicated in the Menshevik Trial and other frame-ups.

The political leadership not only rebuffed the economists, but even imposed an end to economic research in 'mathematical models of growth, studies of investment allocations and effectiveness, models of accumulation and consumption, research on management models,

111

studies on scientific organization of labour and many other endeavours'.[157] Stalin's economist Strumilin said, 'Our task is not to study economics but to change it. We are bound by no laws. There are no fortresses which Bolsheviks cannot storm. The question of tempo is subject to decision by human beings'.

It was now laid down that the country's capital stock was to be doubled in five years. But agricultural output too was to increase – by 55%, while consumption was to rise by 85%.

By 1 July 1929 4% of the households were in kolkhozes, and by November 7.6%. Except where total forced collectivization had already been put through the collective farms were still almost everywhere 'weak' and overwhelmingly made up of poor peasants.

Stalin, however, now parlayed this not very impressive 'upsurge' into a vast, irresistible movement. On 7 November he announced 'the *radical change* that has taken place in the development of our agriculture from small, backward *individual* farming to large-scale, advanced *collective* agriculture, to cultivation of the land in common . . . The new and decisive feature of the peasant collective farm movement is that the peasants are joining the collective farms not in separate groups, as was formerly the case, but in whole villages, whole regions, whole districts and even whole provinces. And what does that mean? It means that *the middle peasant has joined the collective farm movement*. And that is the basis of the radical change in the development of agriculture which represents the most important achievement of Soviet power during the past year'.[158] (Soviet experts of the Khrushchev period criticized this claim as fallacious,[159] as well they might. But the later tendency of official scholars is to accept much of Stalin's case, including support for his view that the possession of a small proportion of the land by collectives proved that the conditions existed 'for total collectivization').[160]

The pressures for extreme measures now grew sharply. The key moment was the Plenum of the Central Committee which met on 10–17 November 1929. The members were told that mass voluntary collectivization was already happening, and put under pressure – in particular by Molotov as Stalin's chief spokesman – to seize within weeks or months an opportunity which 'should not be missed' to solve the agrarian question once and for all.

Molotov called for collectivized provinces and republics 'as soon as next year' and spoke of a 'decisive advance' over the next four and a half months. On the 'kulaks', he warned against their penetrating the collective farms; 'treat the kulak as a most cunning and still undefeated enemy'.[161]

Molotov also made it clear that the supposed material conditions for collectivization would not be fulfilled: 'the amount of material assistance cannot be very great . . . all that the State can give, despite its efforts, is a very small sum'.[162] Instead, the Central Committee called for major investment by the peasants themselves.

With all this, Molotov – still! – attacked the Right for wrongly accusing the Party 'of building Socialism through policies of extraordinary measures, i.e. through a policy of administrative repression'.[163]

In their defence, Rykov read a statement by himself and the other two Rightist leaders 'withdrawing' their disagreement with the majority, saying that they had had nothing against the industrialization and collectivization tempo nor the policy of 'decisive action' against the kulak. However, he still claimed that the Right's tactical methods would have proved a 'less painful path' and was strongly attacked by many speakers, including Stalin. Their repentance was rejected as inadequate. And the political victory was celebrated by Mikoyan stating that while the Party's hands the previous years had been 'to some extent tied by the vacillation and opposition of Right wing members of the Politburo', now 'a clear and understanding line' on grain was possible.[164]

In addition to the attack on the Right, there was, as ever, some conventional criticism of minor 'excesses'. Kaminsky, the Chairman of the crucial Collective Farm Centre, admitted to the plenum that 'administrative measures' might have been applied 'in some places', but dismissed this as 'of minimal importance'.[165]

The plenum's resolutions on agriculture were that: it resolved that a 'radical solution' was needed and that 'this task lies in the direction of further speed-up of the processes of collectivization'; it ordered all Party organizations 'to put as a keystone the task of further developing mass productive co-operation, collectivization of the peasant households'; it called for the 'mobilization . . . for work in the collective farms' of 'at least 25,000' industrial workers belonging to the Party; it demanded 'the most decisive measures' against the kulaks.

In a separate resolution it declared that 'the Ukraine must, in the course of a very short period of time, set examples for the organization of large-scale socialized farming'.

It condemned the Right Opposition for having 'declared that the tempo of collectivization that has been undertaken is unrealistic', that the 'material and technical prerequisites are absent and that there is no desire on the part of the poor and "middle" peasantry to go over to collective forms of land ownership'. And it expelled Bukharin from the Politburo for having 'slandered the Party with demagogic accusations' and for having 'maintained that "extraordinary measures" had pushed the "middle" peasant toward the kulak'.[166]

Following the plenum Bukharin, Tomsky and Rykov recanted in more acceptable terms, and other ex-oppositionists like Shlyapnikov and Pyatakov called strongly for Party unity.

A vast new administrative body was now formed: the All Union People's Commissariat of Agriculture, with overriding planning powers. And a Commission was set up on 5 December to deal with the whole collectivization schedule. Headed by the new Commissar of Agriculture, Yakovlev, it made a report of 22 December suggesting complete collectivization of the grain-producing areas within two to three years.

Even now Yakovlev warned against 'ecstasy' in plunging in to do everything administratively, thus frightening off the middle peasant, and against mere competitiveness to reach 100% collectivization before other areas. This last was an only too true description of the frivolous and careerist attitudes of many local leaders. Yakovlev was now criticized by super-Stalinists like Sheboldayev: even so the Commission only recommended that 'at least a third' of the sown area be cultivated collectively by the spring of 1930.[167]

This was not radical enough for Stalin, whose fiftieth birthday in December 1929 was the occasion of a great glorification of the General Secretary, accompanied by falsification of Party history of the type to become more extreme as the years passed.

Molotov described the draft as unsatisfactory, and Stalin sent it back for improvement: he indicated that the deadline for collectivizing the grain producing areas should be the autumn of 1930 – and this was laid down for the Ukraine.[168]

The revised plan was approved on 4 January, and by now the North Caucasus and Volga were set to complete their collectivization by Spring 1931 at the latest, and the remaining grain areas by Spring 1932 at the latest.

As to dekulakization, Stalin laid down that 'Dekulakization is now an essential element in forming and developing the collective farms . . . of course it is wrong to admit the kulak into the collective farm. It is wrong because he is an accursed enemy of the collective farm movement'.[169] By this time, *Pravda* was complaining that kulaks were not being arrested in sufficient number,[170] not forced to hand in grain 'surpluses', and so on.[171]

A subcommission on kulaks of the Politburo Commission reported that 'the time is ripe for the question of the elimination of the kulak to be posed in a specific form',[172] since the political conditions for this now existed – the middle peasant having turned to the kolkhoz.

At any rate, the subcommission now made the division of the kulaks into three categories, of which the first should be arrested and shot or imprisoned, and their families exiled; and the second exiled merely; while (at this stage) the 'non-hostile' third section might be admitted to the collective farm on probation. The striking crux here is that it is the first call for the systematic deportation of the kulaks.

Stalin issued the key formula for the new phase: 'We have gone over from a policy of limiting the exploiting tendencies of the kulak to a policy of liquidating the kulak as a class'.[173]

★

To sum up the period leading up to the 'Second Revolution' and the new cycle of mass terror and inhumanity: the Party had always intended, as soon as it became feasible, to bring individual farming and the rural market economy to an end; its first attempt to destroy the market had ended in disaster, and it had been forced for some years to accommodate its rule to the existence in the countryside of conditions unpalatable to its doctrines; when so situated it had failed to understand or properly manage the market, and at the first signs of trouble had reverted to force, on a supposedly temporary basis, failing to recognize that 'temporary' compulsion tends to destroy the market incentive past revival; it was driven by growing failure of those incentives into a policy of further force; and finally, finding that 'exceptional' measures to seize the crop were expensive and difficult, it had turned to collectivization as a means of insuring that the crop remained from the start under Party control and out of the hands of the peasantry – at the same time being ideologically sound.

Three successive winters had seen three approaches. In 1927–8, it was virtually a matter of simple seizure of grain; in 1928–9, the appearance of mass support and village initiative was insisted on for the same result; in 1929–30 this faked spontaneity was harnessed to collectivization, a permanent method of securing control of the grain.

In effecting these ends, the Party had relied continually on a spurious doctrinal analysis to show it a supposed class enemy of a minority in the countryside, whereas in fact almost the entire peasantry was opposed to it and its policies. This doctrinal fantasy had, however, practical advantages, in that it could be used against the natural leaders of the peasantry, to cripple the villages' resistance.

The economic results of these decisions were to be, on one view, disastrous. They included the destruction of the most efficient element of the peasantry, and the removal of incentives to the remainder. It is possible that Stalin and his colleagues did not foresee the extent of the disaster; certainly their pronouncements about huge productive progress in agriculture under the new system sound that way. But when the disaster came, they did not consider more than very temporary retreat; and all in

115

all it appears that the advantage of having control of the crop outweighed for them the disadvantage of that crop's shrinkage.

When it comes to the human side, the final end of the partial independence of the peasantry, the crushing of the power of the market and of the last petty-bourgeois class, and the imposition of the state's power in every corner of the countryside were felt to be positive goods. Not merely did they outweigh humane considerations: the 'struggle' with the hostile 'kulak', the revival of class war, were positively invigorating to the Party, restoring its faith in its *raison d'être*.

And so we enter the epoch of dekulakization, of collectivization, and of the terror-famine; of war against the Soviet peasantry, and later against the Ukrainian nation. It may be seen as one of the most significant, as well as one of the most dreadful, periods of modern times.

★

6

The Fate of the 'Kulaks'

They buried him in alien soil

Shevchenko

From the point of view of the sequence of events, it is misleading to treat dekulakization separately from collectivization. For they went on at the same time, and were aspects of the same policies. But the fate of the 'kulaks' is at this point so different from that of the collectivized peasant that it nevertheless seems to warrant separate treatment; though in the narrative which follows, it should be remembered that the non-kulak peasantry was at the same time going through the painful process of collectivization described in the next chapter – indeed that the destruction of the kulaks was in part designed to decapitate the peasantry in its resistance to the imposition of the new order.

It was on 27 December 1929 that, as we have seen, Stalin announced the aim of 'the liquidation of the kulaks as a class'.[1]

The official Party ruling on dekulakization only came on 30 January 1930, when a resolution 'On Measures for the Elimination of Kulak Households in Districts of Comprehensive Collectivization' was approved by the Politburo and sent out to local Party bodies;[2] actual legalization was finally forthcoming in a decree of 4 February.

As we have seen, mass dekulakization had already been taking place in a number of areas led by the more extreme Stalinists. It had become more and more common as 1929 wore on. 'Individual kulak groups' were exiled from various Ukrainian villages, Cossack stanitsas, and elsewhere.[3] And this was already understood as the beginning of the destruction of the kulaks 'as a class'.[4]

But the campaign was now brought to its final fruition, and in an atmosphere of intense 'class' bitterness. Official statements held that

117

'The kulaks will not leave the historical stage without the most savage opposition';[5] and the view was taken that 'We must deal with the kulak as we dealt with the bourgeoisie in 1918. The malicious kulak, actively opposing our construction, must be cast into Solovki,' (the notorious concentration camp complex on the White Sea).[6]

Of course, as we have said, the use of the term 'kulak' had been a distortion of the truth right from the beginning of the regime. But by now it was hardly applicable as an economic class even in its perverse post-revolutionary definitions. Many 'kulaks' even on the definitions of the late '20s, had already been ruined, as is clearly stated in Soviet sources.[7] And the others were hardly either rich or exploitative. Only a minority owned three or four cows and two or three horses. Only 1% of farms employed more than one paid worker.

The value of goods confiscated from the 'kulaks' was indicative. A figure of 170 million roubles has been given, though a more recent figure is 400 million – that is between 170 and 400 roubles a household (about $90–$210, even at the official rate of exchange), even if the total dekulakized was as low as the official million families. As one commentator says, the mere cost of deportation was probably higher than this.[8]

In one province (Kryvyi Rih) 4,080 farms were dekulakized in January–February 1930, yielding to the kolkhoz only a total of 2,367 buildings, 3,750 horses, 2,460 cattle, 1,105 pigs, 446 threshing machines, 1,747 ploughs, 1,304 planters, 2,021 tons of grain and millet! The Soviet author detailing this explains the meagreness of these totals by the fact that much of the kulak's property had been seized in the 1928–9 offensive.[9] In either case, he was now already a poor man. Of a typical 'kulak' an activist noted, 'He has a sick wife, five children and not a crumb of bread in the house. And that's what we call a kulak! The kids are in rags and tatters. They all look like ghosts. I saw the pot on the oven – a few potatoes in water. That was their supper tonight'.[10]

Peasants were particularly shaken by the expropriation of former poor peasants who had worked hard through NEP and managed to buy a horse or a cow.[11]

To cap it all, moreover, the average kulak's income was lower than that of the average rural official who was persecuting him as a representative of a wealthy class.[12]

But economic classification was by now a chimera. The use of tax lists to decide on dekulakization, a method at least rational on the face of it, did not really fit the official line. An OGPU report held that it 'frequently did not correspond to reality and was not justified by serious real reasons'![13] And in practice the whole anti-kulak operation got out of hand, and involved large numbers of peasants of every economic situation.

A Soviet writer quotes a village in which even a local Communist feels that only five families (of 'five to eight persons') out of sixteen dekulakised were really definable as kulaks.[14] Soviet economists of the Khrushchev period gave as an example the village of Plovitsy in the Ukraine, where sixty-six of the seventy-eight 'kulak' households were 'really' middle peasants.[15]

As E.H. Carr put it, 'It was no longer true that class analysis determined policy. Policy determined what form of class analysis was appropriate to the given situation'.[16] For example, even a very poor farmer, if a devout churchman, would be a kulak.[17] And at any given moment almost 2.5 million households of middle peasants could readily be transferred from the category of 'ally' to that of 'class enemy'.

Stalin's policies were presented in terms of a class analysis which made little apparent sense. They were also economically destructive in that they led to the 'liquidation' of the most efficient producers in the countryside. But there is a level at which his policies were after all rational. If, more realistically than the Marxists, we envisage peasant society as generally speaking a reasonably integrated whole, the Stalin's blow can be seen as the elimination of the natural leaders of the peasants against the Communist subjugation of the countryside. That the term 'kulak' began to be used in a sense far wider than even the Party's economic definition substantiates the point; while this becomes even clearer with the formalisation of the category 'subkulak', a term without any real social content even by Stalinist standards, but merely rather unconvincingly masquerading as such.

As was officially stated, 'by "kulak", we mean the carrier of certain political tendencies which are most frequently discernible in the subkulak, male and female'.[18] By this means, any peasant whatever was liable to dekulakisation; and the 'subkulak' notion was widely employed, enlarging the category of victims greatly beyond the official estimate of kulaks proper even at its most strained.

Moreover, contrary to the original instructions, dekulakization was in no way confined to the maximum collectivization regions.[19]

★

By 1931, it began to be officially admitted that former kulaks on any of the varied Soviet definitions were kulaks no more: for example the West Siberian Territory Committee of the Party reported in May to the Central Committee that the 'kulaks' deported in March 'had very limited property' – i.e. were poor.[20] A Soviet historian notes that 'the kulaks had lost the majority of features characteristic of them: systematic use of hired labour, renting out implements and horses, their own workshops, etc.' – so that 'in 1931 it became increasingly difficult to expose a kulak who disguised his class essence'.[21] This is a classic expression of the Marxist notion that economics determines consciousness – that a man's having at some time in the past fulfilled the conditions of a Marxist-devised class categorization is a matter of 'essence' which no later change can alter.

On 9 May 1931, M.I. Kalinin himself, at a conference of secretaries and members of the Central Executive Committee, said that the government had intended to introduce changes in the law on the definition of a kulak, but after discussion had to give up the project. The grounds given in one Soviet comment are that 'the old attitudes of a kulak have almost disappeared, and the new ones do not lend themselves to recognition'![22]

Pravda also warned that 'even the best activists often cannot spot the kulak', because they failed to realise that given a good harvest sale, 'certain middle peasant households are rapidly transformed into well-to-do and kulak households'.[23] – The perennial problem which all along had stultified the scheme for class war in the countryside.

Thus, by a strange logic, a middle peasant could become a kulak by gaining property, but a kulak could not become a middle peasant by losing his. In fact the kulak had no escape. He was 'essentially' a class enemy, a sub-human. Yet the naming of the kulak enemy satisfied the Marxist preconceptions of the Party activist. It presented a flesh-and-blood foe accursed by history; and such a target made for a far more satisfactory campaign than mere abstract organizational change. And it provided a means of destroying the leadership of the villagers, which might have greatly strengthened the resistance, strong enough in all conscience, which they offered to collectivization.

★

The Party's plan for the kulak was formalised in the resolution of 30 January, based on the report of Bauman's sub-commission, which gave the three categories of kulak, and laid down the imprisonment or execution of the first group, to number no more than 63,000.

However, the figures for group I, (those to be shot or imprisoned) which were decided entirely by the local OGPU, were well over the local quotas in the areas of which we have reports, implying an actual figure of about 100,000 instead of the planned 63,000, and this is confirmed by recent Soviet historians.[24]

The second group, to include the families of the first group, were to be sent to the North, Siberia, the Urals or Kazakhstan, or remote areas of their own region; and not more than 150,000 households were to be involved. A top secret letter of 12 February 1930 repeated the three categories, with orders that group II confiscations should be done gradually, to coincide with their eventual deportation.[25]

The third group, described as 'loyal', were now to be partly expropriated and moved out of the kolkhoz to land elsewhere in the district. It appears that they were to come under government control and be used in such work as 'labour detachments and colonies in forestry, roads, land improvement', etc.[26] A typical resolution allotted to category III kulaks dispersed within their province poor quality land of not more than one hectare per person.[27]

The Party Secretary for Siberia, Robert Eikhe (a member of the Commission on whose report the Politburo based itself), wrote at the time that the 'most hostile and reactionary' kulaks should be sent to concentration camps in such 'distant areas' of the North as Arctic Narym and Turukhansk; all the others should work in 'labour colonies', a euphemism for labour camps of less strict regime, and not be left in their villages. Kulak labour could build new roads and enterprises in the uninhabited taiga.[28]

It can be concluded from an analysis of recent Soviet work that the original planned total for all three categories was 1,065,000 families.[29] The Politburo, in December 1929, had used a figure of five to six million persons to be dekulakized,[30] which amounts to about the same figure. (The average 'kulak' family is in fact given in 1927 as seven persons, which would give 7–7.5 million).[31] But it is clear, in any case, that local inflation of the targets and the addition of 'subkulaks' increased the total to a considerable degree. One chairman of a village Soviet boasted in 1930, 'At the plenums of the village Soviet we create kulaks as we see fit. For example, on 4 January during the plenum of the village Soviet the population of two villages spoke up on the question about deportations of kulaks from the area of Shuisk village in defence of citizen Petukhov; they insisted that he be considered a middle peasant. But we fought back and decided – deport him'.[32]

For various provincial and other committees were soon exceeding their allotted numbers. In Moscow Province, the exile quota was about doubled in practice, and similarly in Ivanovo-Voznesensk, according to a Soviet study.[33] In fact it is officially established in the most formal party documents that in some regions instead of the correct dekulakization of 4–5% of the farms, the figure was as high as 14–20%.[34]

This seems to be confirmed, as far as that is possible, by figures we chance to have for individual villages. In one village of 1,189 farms, 202 were arrested or exiled and 140 evicted.[35] In another, of 1,200 house-holds, 160 were dekulakized; in another of 120–31; in another of 800–90. A statistician reports of three villages in Vinnytsia Province, in one of 312 households, 24 deported; in another of 283 – 40; in another of 128 – 13.[36] And a work of modern Soviet fiction gives us a village in which 'one peasant in every twenty has been put under arrest', the informant commenting merely that 'they will be lucky if it stops there'.[37]

Another modern Soviet author has written of collectivization in Siberia: the best peasants are deliberately wiped out; a rabble of loafers, windbags and demagogues come to the top; and any strong personality is persecuted regardless of social background.[38] Two other such writers tell the same story. In one (Astafiev) the dregs of the population, now in power, commonly provoke the best peasants so that they can get them sent to the 'Gulag'.[39]

As to the division into categories, figures we have (from a district of the Western Province) show 3,551 households listed as kulak – 447 in the first category, 1,307 in the second, and only 1,297 in the third. That is, 63% of the kulaks were to be shot, imprisoned or deported even at this stage. Moreover, the local instruction orders that those remaining, allotted marshland or eroded forest land and made to carry out forest or road labour, were to be prosecuted upon any failure to meet compulsory procurements, and so were also well on their way to deportation.[40] (If these figures are to be taken as roughly applicable in general, then of the million odd 'kulak' families, 630,000 were in groups I and II, and 370,000 in group III. In any case the definition of categories was flexible, just as that of the kulak himself was, and soon these figures were to be greatly exceeded.)

The first mass arrests (starting in late 1929) had been made by the GPU only. Heads of families were taken, many of them former soldiers in the White Armies. All were shot.

Then in December, again heads of families were taken, held in prison for two or three months, then sent off to camp. For the moment their families were left untouched, but inventories were made of their property.

At the beginning of 1930, the families were rounded up. By now the operation had become too large for the GPU, and Party activists were mobilized to assist in the actual deportation.[41]

We chance to have the instructions in the Western Province, mentioned above. The local Party took the decisions on dekulakization on 21 January 1930 – before official instructions were formalized. Two GPU officers drew up the plans. The GPU apparatus was reinforced, and the local 'militia' taken off other duties. All concerned were issued arms. 'Troikas', traditional in the Civil War, were set up, consisting of the local

Party, government and GPU chiefs.[42]

A further decree of 3 February 1930 instructed the OGPU, in conjunction with the Council of People's Commissars of the Russian Republic, to submit proposals for the resettlement of kulaks and their families 'deported to remote localities of the RSFSR, and for their employment at work'. This emphasis on the police responsibility was realistic.

The categories were of no lasting benefit to the supposedly lucky kulaks of category III. We are told by recent Soviet historians that since the third category 'likewise opposed the kolkhozes, it became necessary to remove them too to more distant regions'.[43]

In the first weeks of 1931 hitherto undeported Ukrainian kulaks failing to meet their quotas were expropriated and exiled, and this developed, as also in the North Caucasus and Lower Volga, into 'a new wave of the elimination of the kulaks as a class'.[44] In one hamlet of nineteen farmers in the Dnipropetrovsk province ten were dekulakized in the first wave, and five later.[45] (Another hamlet, of sixteen small farmers and about 950 acres, Hrushka, in the Kiev province, was already totally destroyed in 1930).[46] In one North Caucasian village sixteen kulak households previously categorized as non-kulak were 'exposed' in the winter of 1930, and twenty-two horses, thirty cows and nineteen sheep taken from them. These wealthy exploiters had therefore averaged 1.4 horses, 1.8 cows and 1.2 sheep per household![47]

The formal decision for the second wave of deportation of kulaks was taken in February 1931.[48] It was more thoroughly prepared than the first; lists were obtained, OGPU questionnaires disguised as tax checking were sent out. On 18 March 1931, in the Western Province, a special operation was mounted. But the programme leaked and in one district all but 32 of the 74 families to be seized escaped.[49]

Escape was, indeed, almost the sole resource left – and that a million or more families were prepared to abandon their property and homes in this way is in itself indicative. Right at the start, *Pravda* complained of kulaks who 'began to sell their property, dividing the proceeds among their middle peasant relations, and let their livestock go unfed'.[50] They are also accused of breaking their machinery rather than handing it over.[51]

Sometimes they tried to move elsewhere with their cattle, though to little purpose. In the Stavropol area in the North Caucasus, 'kulaks drove herds of oxen, dairy cows, horses and sheep from district to district'.[52]

When mass rebellion came in the villages, as we shall be discussing in the next chapter, formerly prosperous peasants were often, though not always, among the leaders. But otherwise there was little they could do in the way of resistance. There are many stories of the men in a family attacking their persecutors with sticks or axes, and being shot down. Otherwise the commonest form of protest was destruction of their property – including arson, as with one woman in the Ukrainian village of Pidhorodne in the Dnipropetrovsk Province, who in 1931 tossed a burning sheaf on to the thatched roof of the house the GPU was confiscating from her, crying 'We worked all our lives for our house, you won't have it. The flames will have it'![53] Even in the earliest phases, the Soviet press gave many accounts of arson committed against the authorities and their agents.[54]

*

It is sometimes suggested that driving the 'kulaks' from the land had at least some economic rationale in that they joined the urban labour force, much in need of recruits because of the crash industrialization policy.

Kulaks were indeed used in new mines and other establishments in their areas of exile: and in Siberia 'a significant part' of category III kulaks were 'owing to the shortage of labour' sent into the construction of new industrial projects, and into lumbering.[55] But elsewhere, to the important extent that they managed to leave the countryside and merge into the proletariat in the main industrial areas, this was done against the strongest legal and other measures to prevent it.

A top secret decree of 12 February 1930 spoke of special vigilance to stop kulaks leaving the countryside for industry.[56] And the introduction of internal passports on 27 December 1932 was openly motivated in part as a move to 'purge kulaks, criminals, and other anti-social elements from the cities'.[57]

It is true that many desperate 'kulaks' did indeed swarm to the towns. The need for workers was so great that factory managers took them on, clandestinely, on a fair scale. *Pravda* strongly attacked such managers: in February 1930 there were fifty kulaks in a group of 1,100 newly employed at a works in the Kherson district, and of course they idled, drank and sabotaged, and must be removed.[58] In the Donets basin kulaks who managed to get work were rounded up and sent to Eastern camps.[59]

A typical local order of 31 January 1930 by the chairman of the Kamyansk District Executive Committee called for the identification and dismissal of 'all former wealthy farmers' from jobs on the railway or in the three local factories.[60] Again, the head of the Krynychky District Executive Committee, Nelupenko, complained that village Soviets had issued 'wealthy farmers' with certificates of their property without stating that these were to be dispossessed. From these certificates it appeared that they were not 'subject to taxation', in fact not kulaks at all. 'Such certificates gave a false impression of the social status', and were used by wealthy farmers to 'penetrate' factories where workers were hired. 'This practice must stop immediately'.[61]

At the Kharkov Tractor Plant there were always large queues for jobs. But applicants had to answer routine questions. Were his parents of kulak stock? Had he left a collective farm? 'Most of them were turned away, particularly those from collectives'[62] – for not only kulaks but also ordinary peasants were appearing in the town in excessive numbers.

One thirteen-year-old boy tells of trying to get a job nearby but being denied it unless he obtained a birth certificate – which his village activists refused. A few days later, at a peat works, he was again denied a job on the same grounds.[63] Another boy who escaped describes getting jobs, but constantly having to flee when his class origins were discovered or suspected, ending up in Central Asia.[64]

Some kulaks, we are told, 'escaped from those places where they had been settled, wormed their way into Soviet institutions, into industrial enterprises, collective farms, sovkhozy, and MTS and undertook wrecking activities there, and pilfered property. Gradually these disorganizers of socialist production were discovered and received their deserved punishment'.[65]

In the same way, they were unable to join the armed forces. Special instructions were sent to check on recruits with the purpose of keeping out kulak elements who 'tried to penetrate the Red Army'.[66]

★

Thus the kulaks were expected to remain and await their fates in their villages. At the outset of the campaign *Pravda* warned against allowing them to sell up and disappear 'into the blue'.[67]

One Soviet analysis half way through the dekulakization is that by late 1930, 400,000 households had been dekulakized, 353,400 remained, and the rest (200–250,000) had in fact sold up and fled to the cities.[68] In general modern Soviet estimates are in this range – that 20–25% of the million odd officially kulak households were 'self-dekulakized' by fleeing from their villages over the period 1929–32.[69] This seems a likely enough proportion. And it affects our estimates of the numbers exiled: if we take the Politburo figure of five to six million persons 'dekulakized', this would mean that 1–1.2 million escaped, at least temporarily, and 4–4.8 million did not. As we have seen it is clear that by the extension of the kulak label, and by the 'subkulak' categorization, these figures must have been largely exceeded; but the proportions of exiles and escapers may yet be about right.

A Soviet scholar of the Khrushchev epoch quotes a total of 381,000 families deported up to October 1931.[70] The 1928 *Statistical Handbook USSR* gives an average of 6.5 persons per 'entrepreneurial' – i.e. kulak – family (5.4 for middle peasants, 3.9 for poor): this would mean, therefore, about 2.5 million souls.

As the Leninist dissident Roy Medvedev has pointed out, this is 'considerably understated',[71] for several reasons. First, mass deportation did not cease in October 1931, but went on, officially, until May 1933, when a decree signed by Stalin and Molotov ruled that in future only deportation by individual families would henceforth take place, at a rate of 12,000 such a year.[72] This decree stated that 100,000 families had in fact been scheduled for deportation in 1933, and it does not seem unreasonable to see this as the approximate rate for the eighteen months between October 1931 and May 1933 – a total of 150,000 households, or between three-quarters of a million and a million more souls, *after* the 'second wave'.

Meanwhile, it is reasonable to pay some attention to Stalin's remark to Churchill that dekulakization was a matter of 'ten millions', though we may disbelieve his comment that 'the great bulk were very unpopular and were wiped out by their labourers'.

Stalin in fact spoke in 1933 of 15% of pre-collectivization households as now belonging to the past, describing them as 'kulak and better off'.[73] Peasant households in June 1929 had numbered 25,838,080. 15% would mean about 3,875,000 households, or (at five members a household) 19,380,000 souls. From this we would have to subtract the numbers who in one way or another escaped deportation. We have noted Soviet calculations that 20–25% of the kulaks fled to the cities. A Ukrainian emigré estimate gives even higher figures of escapes – that about two-thirds of the dekulakized were exiled, and one-third escaped.[74] If we take a figure of this sort, it would leave approximately thirteen million actually deported.

Then, it was officially stated that fifteen million hectares of land taken from the kulaks had become the property of the kolkhozes in 1929–32. The average 'kulak' farm in 1928 had been 4.5 hectares, so this would imply 3.3 million *households*, or over fifteen million souls, with (if a third escaped) ten million exiled. (By the end of 1938, a figure of thirty million hectares of land confiscated from the kulaks is given, though this would include later seizure).[75] But the average size of dekulakized farms must now have been lower, for several obvious reasons, so on this approach ten million is an absolute minimum.

As Professor Moshe Lewin concludes, 'the number of deportees more or less admitted so far by Soviet sources already exceeds one million households or five million souls',[76] and this is for the RSFSR and the Ukraine alone, to which thousands of households from other republics (40,000 from Uzbekistan) must be added. He sums up that in fact 'ten million persons, or more, must have been deported'.[77] A similar estimate of ten to eleven million is reached by another prominent researcher, who concludes that about a third of them perished.[78]

Thus if we take ten million as a probable figure, with a possibility of fifteen million, we can hardly be exaggerating. For reasons which will appear in Chapter 16, ten to twelve million, with three million dying at this stage, appears to fit best with the numbers of peasant dead over the whole epoch.

At the same time, whatever figures we accept, we have to take account of those – mainly heads of families – actually arrested and shot or 'sent to Solovki'. We have noted the 200,000 arrested under category I in late 1929–early 1930. (And already it was by no means only 'kulaks' who were concerned: late in 1929 the authorities announced that in a single district 234 kulaks, 200 middle peasants and 400 poor peasants had been arrested in a single day).[79]

This continued: a Party organ of the present era tells us, for example, 'In the first half of 1931 the organs of Soviet power brought to responsibility (i.e. arrested) 96 thousand people. They were kulaks, White Guard officers, former policemen, gendarmes and other anti Soviet elements ...'[80] In Western Siberia, in the 1931–2 procurement campaign, 1,000 kulaks were sentenced, together with 4,700 other peasants described as 'close to them socio-economically'.[81]

Those who went to prison or labour camps suffered the fates that will be familiar to most readers. Their numbers cannot be accurately estimated (see Chapter 16). But it is known from a contemporary Soviet document that the numbers in places of detention in the RSFSR and the Ukraine alone was nearly two million in 1931–2. At this time, and until 1936–7, the great bulk of those imprisoned were peasants. The total of those imprisoned is generally estimated as going up to about five million in 1935, and at least four million of these were probably peasants, though not necessarily of the original kulak enrolment.

In the Komi camps alone there were already some 200,000 inmates in 1929, we are told by an ex-official of the camp, who adds that they were almost all peasants.[82] The Baltic-White Sea Canal camps also held 286,000 forced labourers in June 1934,[83] again mainly peasants.

In the summer of 1932 scores of thousands of prisoners, almost entirely peasants, were thrown ashore at Magadan in an ill-considered crash programme to exploit the newly discovered gold seams in the area. When the fearful winter of the coldest area in the Northern Hemisphere came, whole camps perished to a man, even including guards and guard dogs. Over the whole operation survivors estimate that not more than one in fifty of the prisoners, if that, survived; and the following year is reported as killing even more. As a fellow inmate remarks, (speaking of the Russians among them), 'they died, showing once again this national quality which Tyutchev has glorified, and which all politicians have abused – patience'.[84]

★

In *The History of the Communist Party* (Short Course) in use in the Stalin period, the events of 1930–31 were described as follows, somewhat in the vein of Stalin's own remarks to Churchill: 'the peasants chased the kulaks from the land, dekulakized them, took away their livestock and machinery, and requested the Soviet power to arrest and deport the kulaks'.

Needless to say, this is not an accurate account of what really went on in the villages. First, as a Soviet writer puts it, 'the province authorities sent the plan down to the district authorities – in the form of a total number of "kulaks". And the districts then assigned proportionate shares of the total number to the individual village Soviets, and it was in the village Soviets that the lists of specific names were drawn up. And it was on the basis of these lists that people were rounded up. And who made up these lists? A troika – three people'.[85] A recent Soviet study confirms the responsibility of these troikas, and their membership: the secretary of the Party committee, a member of the local Soviet, and a responsible officer of the OGPU.[86]

Groups of 'activists' were then ordered into action, supported by the leadership of the village Soviet, according to an organized plan. For instance, a large village of over a thousand households was divided into eleven sections, each with its 'staff' and 'brigade' of local Communists.[87]

There were indeed still village Soviets which resisted. In one village (an OGPU report relates) the chairman of the Soviet told the kolkhoz general meeting that they had been ordered to expel seven kulaks. The teacher (a Komsomol member) asked if this figure was obligatory, and was very angry at being told it was. The meeting then voted on seven supposed kulaks and all of them were reinstated, the chairman heartily agreeing and going off and drinking with one of them.[88]

The Ukrainian government organ quoted four village Soviet chairmen as saying there were no kulaks in their villages, so that they did not know how to conduct the class struggle. In one of them the chairman of the Soviet refused the help of outside 'brigades', while elsewhere the entire village Soviet, the leadership of the Committee of Unwealthy Peasants, and the executive committee of the kolkhoz were disbanded for sabotage. The periodical added that it could cite scores and hundreds of other examples of 'right opportunism' in the villages.[89]

A decree of the Central Executive Committee on 25 January 1930 said frankly that a village Soviet which did not satisfactorily take on the tasks of mass collectivization 'will in fact be a kulak–Soviet'. And sooner or later these were purged or replaced.

Among the activists, however, Stalin succeeded to a certain degree in his aim of inciting 'class struggle' in the villages, or at least struggle between friends of and victims of the regime. The necessary hatreds were inflamed; the activists who helped the GPU in the arrests and deportations

> were all people who knew one another well, and knew their victims, but in carrying out this task they became dazed, stupefied . . .
>
> They would threaten people with guns, as if they were under a spell, calling small children 'kulak bastards', screaming 'bloodsuckers!' . . . They had sold themselves on the idea that the so-called 'kulaks' were pariahs, untouchables, vermin. They would not sit down at a 'parasite's' table; the 'kulak' child was loathsome, the young 'kulak' girl was lower than a louse. They looked on the so-called 'kulaks' as cattle, swine, loathsome, repulsive: they had no souls; they stank; they all had venereal diseases; they were enemies of the people and exploited the labour of others . . . And there was no pity for them. They were not human beings; one had a hard time making out what they were – vermin, evidently.[90]

This last paragraph is from Vasily Grossman. Himself Jewish, and the Soviet Union's leading writer on Hitler's holocaust, he draws the analogy with the Nazis and the Jews. A woman activist explains, 'What I said to myself at the time was "they are not human beings, they are kulaks" . . . Who thought up this word "kulak" anyway? Was it really a term? What torture was meted out to them! In order to massacre them it was necessary to proclaim that kulaks are not human beings. Just as the Germans proclaimed that Jews are not human beings. Thus did Lenin and Stalin proclaim, kulaks are not human beings'.[91]

Not all activists could square their consciences in this way. One girl Komsomol is quoted in an OGPU confidential letter as saying that (contrary to the idea of the bestiality of the kulaks) it was the party activists who had excluded themselves from the human race by their brutality: 'We are no longer people, we are animals'.[92]

Sholokhov gives a dramatic account of the revulsion of some of them. The activist Andrei Razmiotnov suddenly says:

> 'I'm not going on'.

'What d'you mean? "Not going on"?' Nagulnov pushed the abacus to one side.

'I'm not going to do any more of this breaking up the kulaks. Well, what are you staring at? Do you want to send yourself into a fit?'

'Are you drunk?' Davidov asked, looking anxiously and attentively at Andrei's face, which was expressive of angry determination. 'What's the matter with you? What d'you mean by you're "not going on"?'

His calm tenor voice infuriated Andrei, and, stuttering with his agitation, he shouted:

'I've not been trained! I've not been trained to fight against children! At the front it was another matter. There you could cut down who you liked with your sword or what you liked . . . And you can all go to the devil! I'm not going on!' His voice rose higher and higher, like the note of a tautened violin string, and seemed about to snap. But, taking a hoarse breath, he unexpectedly lowered his tone to a whisper:

'Do you call it right? What am I? An executioner? Or is my heart of stone? I had enough in the war . . .' And he again began to shout: 'Gayev's got eleven children. How they howled when we arrived! You'd have clutched your head. It made my hair stand on end. We began to drive them out of the kitchen . . . I screwed up my eyes, stopped my ears, and ran into the yard. The women were all in a dead fright and pouring water over the daughter-in-law . . . The children – Oh, by God, you –'

But the other chief activist will not have it:

'Snake!' he gasped in a penetrating whisper, clenching his fists. 'How are you serving the revolution? Having pity on them? Yes . . . You could line up thousands of old men, women, and children and tell me they'd got to be crushed into the dust for the sake of the revolution, and I'd shoot them all down with a machine-gun'.

And 'Nagulnov's' example was on the whole followed. It is to an activist of this period that the well-known saying is attributed: 'Moscow does not believe in tears'.[93]

Not that Nagulnov's type of fanaticism was the only motive. One observer noted that 'envious neighbours, spies and informers looking for prey, arbitrary and corrupt officials, created kulaks by the legion'.[94] And a Soviet writer remarks: 'It was so easy to do a man in: you wrote a denunciation; you did not even have to sign it. All you had to say was that he had paid people to work for him as hired hands, or that he had owned three cows'.[95]

Activists sniffed out any departure from economic purity. Sholokhov tells of a middle peasant exiled on the demand of the chief local activist because he employed a girl 'for a month during the harvesting, and he hired her only because his son had been called up to the Red Army'.

A more recent Soviet novel has a character who is branded as a kulak although he has been prominent in organizing the extinguishing of a collective farm fire – or rather *because* of that. He is clearly a potential leader: 'At that time Chauzov, Stepan, went to extinguish the fire, but tomorrow he might destroy the collective farm, and some men are saving him for just that occasion. People like Chauzov have to be isolated from the masses forever, their influence has to be annihilated'.[96]

One teacher, the widow of a Communist killed in the Civil War, was dekulakized, according to a contemporary educational journal, 'essentially because she had more than once driven the local "activists" – the secretary of the village Soviet (a candidate member of the Party), the local cultural official (also a Party member) and the secretary of the local cooperative organization – out of the school where they intended to hold a drinking party'. As she had no means of production to confiscate, they took her clothes and cooking utensils and tore up her books.[97] Another woman teacher, dekulakized on the grounds that she was a priest's daughter, 'produced documents that showed that she was the daughter of a peasant', whereupon 'they declared that "her mother visited the priest, and therefore it is possible that she is the priest's daughter"'.[98]

This sort of thing illustrates Vasily Grossman's point that 'the most poisonous and vicious were those who managed to square their own accounts. They shouted about political awareness – and settled their grudges and stole. And they stole out of crass selfishness: some clothes, a pair of boots'.[99] Sholokhov, too, makes it clear that the activists steal food and clothing. Indeed, even official reports noted that the alleged kulak was regarded by his enemies as 'a source of boots, sheets, warm coats, etc'; *Pravda* itself denounced this 'division of the spoils'.[100] In the Western Province, of which we have the confidential GPU reports, kulaks were stripped of their shoes and clothing and left in underclothes. Rubber boots, women's knickers, tea, pokers, washtubs were simply seized by the village ne'er-do-wells.[101] A GPU report tells of 'certain members of the worker brigades and officials of the lower echelons of the Party Soviet apparatus' stealing clothes and shoes, even those actually being worn; eating the food they found, and drinking the alcohol. Even spectacles were stolen, and kasha eaten or smeared on ikons.[102] One kulak woman, though dispossessed, survived because she was a skilled dressmaker – and was much in demand from activist families who had looted kulak clothes, in order to have them remade.[103] Grossman sums up:

> There were bribes. Accounts were settled because of jealousy over some women or because of ancient feuds and quarrels . . . Now, however, I can see that the heart of the catastrophe did not lie in the fact that the lists happened to be drawn up by cheats and thieves. There were in any case more honest, sincere people among the Party activists than there were thieves. But the evil

done by the honest people was no less than that done by the dishonest ones.[104]

Moreover, the conduct of things at the local level was erratic. In a Ukrainian village, while one middle peasant was helping in the seizure of kulak property at one end of the village, others were expropriating his own property at the other end.[105]

Again, there were a number of cases, deplored as superficial, in which the class victory was reported in such terms as: 'During the period from 5 pm to 7 am the kulaks as a class were liquidated'.[106] It was even the case that enthusiastic dekulakizers (the OGPU complained) would start dekulakizing peasants outside their own area.[107]

In the spring of 1930 the Procuracy issued all sorts of orders with a view of bringing some legality and regularity into the system of arrest and trial.[108] But since such instructions were issued all through the period without apparent results, they clearly had no substantial support, or effect.[109] It was not until 8 May 1933 that the secret 'Stalin–Molotov letter' addressed to all Party and Soviet workers and to all organs of the OGPU, the courts and the procuracy, said that,

> The Central Committee and the Sovnarkom are informed that disorderly mass arrests in the countryside are still a part of the practice of our officials. Such arrests are made by chairmen of kolkhozes and members of kolkhoz administrations, by chairmen of village Soviets and secretaries of Party cells, raion and krai officials; arrests are made by all who desire to, and who, strictly speaking, have no right to make arrests. It is not surprising that in such a saturnalia of arrests, organs which do have the right to arrest, including the organs of the OGPU and especially the militia, lose all feeling of moderation and often perpetrate arrests without any basis, acting according to the rule 'First arrest, and then investigate'.[110]

By this time, of course, the kulak in any sense whatever had long since been eliminated. Nor did the concentration of the terror in the hands of the professionals of a by now vastly enlarged security police bring any notable improvement in the fate of future victims. In any case, Vyshinsky explained, revolutionary legality still did not exclude but rather incorporated 'revolutionary arbitrariness'.[111]

Meanwhile, police and activists, even in primitive and sometimes erroneous fashion, carried on with the destruction of the last enemy class. As we have said, they were usually able to whip themselves up into appropriate class hatred, but they had less success with the villagers as a whole.

Although *Pravda* asserted that 'every honest collective farmer avoids the kulak when he sees him in the distance',[112] this was, as before, an expression of what the party wanted rather than of the real situation. In the local documents we have, there are many references to chairmen of village Soviets, Party members, and peasants trying to help the 'kulaks'. An OGPU report makes it clear that many poor and middle peasants were against dekulakization, would not vote for it, hid kulak property and warned kulak friends of searches. 'In many cases' they would collect signatures for petitions in favour of kulaks.[113]

We know of scores of individual cases. One of the village poor, a Communist, showing grief at the shooting of a 'kulak' cousin who resisted expulsion, and even burying him, was expelled from the Party and exiled as a kulak supporter.[114] A modern Soviet writer recently recalled the common peasant sympathy for the kulaks, in this case being deported down one of the Siberian rivers: 'All the village came to the riverbank for the deportation; there was howling over the Yenisei; people brought to those deported an egg, or a loaf of bread, or a lump of sugar, or a shawl, or mittens'.[115]

Even at the time, official periodicals would tell such stories as of a peasant, defending another, who said that if his friend was to be dekulakized he should be too, as their farms were the same size. He was told to put this into writing, and was thereupon dekulakized,[116] In March 1930 *Pravda*, understandably understating the matter, nevertheless declared that 'far from all the middle peasantry were politically prepared, and able to recognize the need for the organization and development of collective farms, the need for the elimination of the kulaks as a class'.[117] The following year the Sixth Congress of Soviets, in March 1931, still had to deplore 'the poor and middle peasant who helps the kulak to combat the kolkhoz'. It was admitted that fear on the part of the middle peasants that they too might be dekulakized made them on occasion 'opponents of collectivization, Soviet power and the whole policy of the Party . . . and even abolished to some extent the isolation of the kulak'.[118]

But even the workers in the town are reported in OGPU secret letters as betraying 'negative attitudes' to the deportations.[119] The old connections still existed. Confidential Party reports speak of Communist workers in the factories who still keep their own land in the villages, and earn enough money in the factories to 'become kulaks'. At one factory 80% of the Party cell were connected with agriculture, and the cell therefore 'pursued a kulak policy'.[120]

As ever, the peasant grown prosperous by his work was on the whole admired more than he was envied. As a leading western scholar puts it of the peasant, 'his prosperous neighbour might be hated as a grasping kulak who exploited others, but primarily he was envied and respected as a successful farmer'.[121]

A friend of the regime, Maurice Hindus, describes a propaganda film of Eisenstein's about the collectivization:

> One of the villains was a *Koolack*, and what a monster he was – fat, lazy, gluttonous, brutal, as scummy a creature as ever trod this earth. Of course in real life one hardly finds such creatures, not even in Russia. The *Koolack* may at times have been cruel in his treatment of the poorer peasants, but he was never the fat, lazy, gluttonous monster that Eisenstein depicts him . . . In real life the *Koolack* was among the hardest working, the thriftiest and most progressive farmers in the village . . . He was a prodigious indefatigable worker'.[122]

An OGPU report quotes a kolkhoz bookkeeper, in 1931: 'The best and hardest workers of the land are being taken away' (with misfits and lazybones staying behind).[123] That the 'kulak' was not only the hardest worker, but also the most advanced farmer is also clear from Sholokhov, where the main enemy of the kolkhoz, starting in 1920 with 'a bare hut', has obtained better seed, used chemicals, followed the advice of agronomists. Time and again we hear of these pro-Soviet poor peasants who were given land and became 'kulaks' – indeed an expression sprang up, 'red kulaks'. Five are mentioned in three villages in the Chernihiv, Poltava and Vinnytsia provinces. Two had been shepherds, two others had also been completely landless, and the fifth had owned half a hectare. All were deported in 1930.[124] In the village of Rudkivtsi, in Podilia, twelve peasants who had taken the Bolshevik side in the Civil War, most of them former 'red partisans', died in one way or another as victims of the regime, including two suicides and seven dying in exile near Murmansk.[125]

A former activist quotes an agronomist friend in 1932:

> Some of them were even heroes of the Red Army, the same guys who took Perekop and near to took Warsaw. They settled down on the land and took root like oats. Got rich! Only the guy who didn't strain stayed a poor peasant. The kind of guy who couldn't grow anything but weeds in black soil, couldn't get milk from a prize cow. He's the one who made a big stink about the class enemy choking him, getting fat off his impoverished blood and sweat.[126]

A Red Guard, the son of a poor Cossack, wounded and decorated in the Civil War, is one of those in Sholokhov's novel who became a kulak. Under NEP 'he began to get rich, although we warned him. He worked day and night'. His line was, 'It isn't the likes of you who keep the Soviet government going. With my hands, I give it something to eat'. The outsider who is chairman of the kolkhoz sums up that these stories of his heroic past are meaningless: 'He's become a kulak, become an enemy. Crush him!'

★

The Party was acting without peasant support, and knew it. But its official line still had to be that the middle peasant was on its side in a class struggle against the kulak, and this doublethink had to be translated into class terror.

Sholokhov describes several expulsions of kulaks from their homes. The villagers that gather are sympathetic to the kulak. When an old man with his halfwitted son are thrown out of their hut, and he goes down on his knees to pray, the activists tell him to get going, but the crowd boos, and shouts 'let him say goodbye to his own farm at least' and the women start to cry – whereupon the old man is attacked for 'agitation' . . .

We have hundreds of first-hand accounts of what happened to the unfortunate kulaks.

A former landless peasant who had served in the Red Army had by 1929 thirty-five acres, two horses, a cow, a hog, five sheep and forty chickens, and a family of six. In 1928 the 'tax' on him was 2,500 roubles and 7,500 bushels of grain. He failed to meet this, and his house (worth 1,800–2,000 roubles) was forfeited and 'bought' for 250 roubles by an activist. The household goods were also 'sold' to activists, and the farm implements sent to the new kolkhoz.[127] He was arrested. In prison he was charged with being a kulak (though previously called only a subkulak); of having refused to pay taxes; of inciting against collectivization and the Soviet government; of belonging to a secret counter-revolutionary organization; of having owned 500 acres, five pairs of oxen, fifty head of cattle; of exploiting 'workers'; and so on. He was eventually sentenced to ten years forced labour.[128]

Another 'kulak' (with about eight acres of land) was sent with others to clean a railway line of snow on 5 February 1931, and on his return found that all his property had been removed except for a kettle, a saucer and a spoon. He was shortly afterwards arrested and sent to lumbering in the Far North.[129]

A Ukrainian 'kulak' – with twelve acres, a cow, a horse, ten sheep, a hog and about twenty chickens, on a farm which could support four people – was first ordered, in 1929, to sell to the state 619 bushels of wheat, an impossibility from his acreage. He sold possessions and bought some wheat at a high price to fulfil his requirement. However, on 26 February 1930 he was arrested and sent to Siberia. Another 'kulak' had all his property confiscated, including his children's clothes beyond what they had on. He was told to report regularly to district OGPU headquarters, eighteen kilometres away, and warned that if he fled his family would suffer. His children went out begging, but any food they got was usually seized by activists. On 14 December 1929 they were thrown out into the street, and soon afterwards deported. His wife, mother and six children all died in exile.[130]

A girl tells a fairly typical story, of her middle peasant family with a horse, a cow, a heifer, five sheep, some pigs and a barn in Pokrovna in the Ukraine. Her father did not want to join the kolkhoz. Demanding grain which he did not have, 'for a whole week they wouldn't let father sleep and they beat him with sticks and revolvers till he was black and blue and swollen all over'. When released, he felt obliged to slaughter a pig, leaving a little meat with the family, and selling the rest in the city to buy bread. Finally a GPU official, the chairman of the village Soviet and others came to the house, made an inventory, and confiscated everything including the remaining animals. Father, mother, the elder son, two small daughters and a baby brother were locked for the night in the village church, then marched to the station, and put in cattle trucks, part of a long train of them, which eventually moved off. Near Kharkov the train stopped, and a kind guard let the girls get off and try to get milk for the baby. In some nearby peasant huts they got a little food and milk, but when they returned the train had gone. The two girls wandered the countryside, learning the ways of the Homeless Ones, but were separated while being chased by a militiaman in a city market. The girl narrating this was eventually taken in by a peasant family.[131]

As these accounts indicate, the fate of the kulaks varied. The first category, designated as stubborn class enemies, were arrested in the winter of 1929–30. In Kiev jail they are reported at this time shooting 70–120 men a night.[132] A prisoner, arrested because of his church activities, mentions that in the GPU prison in Dnipropetrovsk, a cell for 25 held 140 – from which, however, one or two prisoners were taken each night to be shot.[133]

One 'kulak' sent to Poltava prison in 1930 tells typically of 36 prisoners in a cell built for seven, then of one for 20 holding 83. In prison, rations ranged from 100 grammes to 150 grammes of 'doughy black bread' a day, with about 30 dying every day out of the prison total of some 2,000. The doctor would always certify 'paralysis of the heart'.[134]

As to their families, a usual story is of the Ukrainian village of Velyki Solontsi where, after 52 men had been removed as kulaks, their women and children were taken in wagons, dumped on a sandy stretch along the Vorskla River and left there.[135] A former Communist official tells of how in one village in the Poltava Province, with a population of 2,000, 64 families were dekulakized in December 1929, and 20 more driven out of their homes, to live as best they could nearby. In March an order was issued forbidding villagers to help them, and 300 of them, including 36 children and 20 old people, were marched to some caves three miles away, and forbidden to return. Some escaped. But in April the 200 remaining were shipped to the Far North.[136]

★

The deportation of the kulaks was an event on so large a scale that it is often treated as a mass phenomenon merely, a move of millions. But each unit among these millions was a person, and suffered an individual fate.

Some destined for exile never reached it. One kulak, in Hrushka hamlet, Kiev Province, took a photo of his old home as he left it. He was arrested, and shot the same evening.[137]

Generally speaking, the really old were simply left behind to whatever life they could find. In one village an activist told an American that though forty kulak families had been deported, 'we leave the very old, ninety years or over, here, because they are not a danger to the Soviet Power'.[138]

A Soviet writer describes a typical scene:

> From our village . . . the 'kulaks' were driven out on foot. They took what they could carry on their backs: bedding, clothing. The mud was so deep it pulled the boots off their feet. It was terrible to watch them. They marched along in a column and looked back at their huts, and their bodies still held the warmth from their own stoves. What pain they must have suffered! After all, they had been born in those houses; they had given their daughters in marriage in those cabins. They had heated up their stoves, and the cabbage soup they had cooked was left there behind them. The milk had not been drunk, and smoke was still rising from their chimneys. The women were sobbing – but were afraid to scream. The Party activists didn't give a damn about them. We drove them off like geese. And behind came the cart, and on it were Pelageya the blind, and old Dmitri Ivanovich, who had not left his hut for ten whole years, and Marusya the Idiot, a paralytic, a kulak's daughter who had been kicked by a horse in childhood and had never been normal since.[139]

One 'kulak' describes a line of deportees in the Sumy Province stretching as far as the eye could see in both directions, with people from new villages continually joining, and later embarking on the train which, in eight days, took them to four 'special settlements' in the Urals.[140]

On 26 May 1931, a train of sixty-one cars, holding some 3,500 members of kulak families, left Yantsenovo, a small station in the Zaporizhia Province, arriving at their Siberian destination on 3 June.[141] Another train leaving Rostyh on 18 March 1931, consisted of forty-eight cars, carrying over 2,000 deportees.[142] Generally speaking, in fact, the wagons carried some forty to sixty people. They were locked in, with little air or light. On the train, typically, a loaf of bread (giving 300 grammes

137

each) and half a pail of tea or thin soup were provided for ten persons, though food did not arrive every day.[143] In some cases tea or soup was replaced by water.

Up to 15 and even 20%, especially young children, are reported dying in transit,[144] as was to be the case again in the 1940s, with the mass deportations of minority nationalities. Of course, the deportees were in every sort of physical condition, some of the women pregnant. A Cossack mother gave birth on a deportation train. The baby, as was usual, died. Two soldiers threw the body out while the train was on the move.[145]

Sometimes the deportees were taken more or less directly to their final destination. Sometimes, they remained in local towns, treated as transit points, till their next transports came – particularly in Vologda and Archangel in the North.

In Archangel all the churches were closed and used as transit prisons, in which many-tiered sleeping platforms were put up. The peasants could not wash, and were covered with sores. They roamed the town begging for help, but there were strict orders to locals not to help them. Even the dead could not be picked up. The residents, of course, dreaded arrest themselves.[146] In Vologda city too, forty-seven churches were taken over and filled with deportees.[147]

Elsewhere in the North, one of modern Russia's most distinguished writers describes how,

> In Vokhrovo, the district capital, in a little park by the station, dekulakized peasants from the Ukraine lay down and died. You got used to seeing corpses there in the morning; a wagon would pull up and the hospital stable-hand, Abram, would pile in the bodies. Not all died; many wandered through the dusty mean little streets, dragging bloodless blue legs, swollen from dropsy, feeling out each passer-by with doglike begging eyes . . . they got nothing; the residents themselves, to get bread on their ration cards, queued up the night before the store opened.[148]

Whether through such transit points or otherwise, the exiles finally reached their destinations in the taiga or the tundra.

Some of them – those being taken to the extreme north of Siberia – faced a further hazard, on the great rivers flowing down to the Arctic Ocean. A modern Soviet novelist describes kulaks being shipped down the Siberian river Ugryum on rafts, most of which are lost in the rapids.[149]

On the Siberian taiga, if there was a village, they were crammed in somehow; if there was not, 'they were simply set right there in the snow. The weakest died'; those who could, cut timber and built shacks: 'they worked almost without sleeping so that their families would not freeze to death'.[150]

Beyond Nadezhdinsk in Siberia, a column of kulaks was marched forty-three miles, in four days, to their new home. A GPU official stood on a stump and shouted: 'Your Ukraine is right here', pointing at the forest around. He added merely, 'Those who try to escape from here will be shot'.[151]

In a kulak destination near Krasnoyarsk there was, again, no shelter at all – but barbed wire fencing had been put up, and there were some guards. Of the 4,000 sent there, about half had died in two months.[152] In another camp on the Yenisei the kulaks lived in dugouts.[153] A German Communist describes how between Petropavlovsk and Lake Balkash in Kazakhstan, kulaks from the Ukraine and Central Russia were marched into empty country: 'There were just some pegs stuck in the ground with little notices on them saying: Settlement No. 5, No. 6, and so on. The peasants were brought here and told that now they had to look after themselves. So then they dug themselves holes in the ground. A great many died of cold and hunger in the early years'.[154]

A modern Soviet researcher confirms as a general thing that 'virtually all members of the newly arrived families capable of working were involved in the first months in the construction of living quarters'.[155]

Camp No. 205 in the Siberian taiga near Kopeisk, north of Severnoe, at first consisted of improvised shacks built by the inmates. About half the men were sent to saw timber, the rest to the mines; childless women and unmarried girls also worked in the mines. In November the old, the sick and those under 14 were sent to constructing wood-and-earth huts for the winter. The ration was now a pint of thin soup and ten half ounces of bread a day. Almost all the infants died.[156]

The system they lived under was known as 'special settlements'. These were not a form of imprisonment, but were under direct OGPU control, with no civil structure. On 16 August 1930 the Government issued a decree to collectivize the kulaks in their area of exile,[157] but this made no practical difference. We are told by a high official of the present day USSR that they did not have the right to vote for their leaders even in theory, and on the other hand 'at the head of the cooperatives stood the plenipotentiaries of Soviet organs, nominated by those organs',[158] which is to say OGPU men.

The inhabitants in fact had few rights, and were regarded both ideologically and civically as outcasts. If a girl or man from outside married a 'special settler' she or he passed into the serf class. A foreign Communist was told how even as the newcomers were erecting their mud huts, 'Party officials would often ride on horseback into the settlements . . . It wasn't so bad when they just bellowed at us or insulted and abused us, but sometimes they came with whips and anyone who was in the way

139

got a taste of them – they would even lash out at children at play'.[159]

At first the exiles depended on the OGPU for rations. In the northern special settlements, the full norm earned 600 grammes of bread a day, with 400 for those who fell short, and 200 as a punishment ration.[160] Such figures are rather lower than at the worst period in the forced labour camps proper.

The 'special settlements' were of course in areas no one had previously found useful, in the wilderness in fact.[161] A high proportion of them were in the Archangel, Vologda and Kotlas areas in the North and North East. On a 400 mile stretch in the far north between Gryazovets and Archangel, for a distance of thirty miles from the railway, there was a huge concentration of camps which was later moved deeper into the forest. One estimate is that up to two million kulaks – the largest single group – were in the area, Ukrainians predominating. Some half of them were children, though this proportion diminished as the younger children died off.[162]

Official figures give 70,000 exiled kulak *families* in the Northern Territory as early as February 1930[163] – that is, already, some 400,000 souls, with many more to come.

The 'urban' population of Karelia–Murmansk increased, in official figures, by 325,000, that of the North East by 478,000, that of Vyatka (Kirov) by 536,000 between 1926 and 1939. Most of this certainly represents kulak labour in camp or special settlement. (It can be shown that such labour, unless specifically agricultural, is listed in statistics as urban or industrial). If, as seems reasonable from the figures given on p. 141, deportees put into 'industrial' and agricultural work are roughly comparable, this would imply some 2.5 million in these regions alone.

In Siberia, Krasnoyarsk received 24,200 kulak families in 1930–31.[164] Another typical destination was Narym, in the Siberian far north. It is a territory frozen for much of the year, at other times a barren swampland. Solzhenitsyn tells of the arrival of kulaks in February 1931: 'the strings of carts rolled endlessly through the village of Kochenovo, Novosibirsk Province, flanked by convoy troops, emerging from the snow-bound steppe and vanishing into the snow-bound steppe again . . . they all shuffled off into the Narym marshes – and in those insatiable quagmires they all remained. Many of the children had already died a wretched death on the cruel journey'.[165]

A senior Soviet apparatchik, writing officially of this Narym movement, tells us that by the beginning of 1932, 196,000 'repressed kulaks from the central region of the country' had been exiled to Narym (where the local population only numbered 119,000).[166] These, we learn from another official source, formed 47,000 kulak families.[167] Even taking the average middle peasant family of five members this should have meant some

235,000 – so that a minimum of 40,000 may be taken as having perished even before reaching the Arctic, presumably children for the most part: that is, 17%.

Wherever they might be, the kulaks were expected to work. Kulaks not up to really heavy labour were sometimes given a loan and a ration until their first harvest, working under guards.[168] But sooner or later they had to feed themselves on whatever they could wring from the inhospitable soil of the north.

A decision of the Northern Territory Party Committee on 3 February 1932 to 'improve' the food supply of the exiles, laid down that it should be 'ensured that by 1934 the newcomers are supplied with bread, fodder, and vegetables through their own harvests'. To achieve this the settlers had to 'bring 90,000 hectares of forest into cultivation'[169] – that is, 900 square kilometres.

We are told that kulaks were the main labour force in 'newly created' state farms,[170] and many remained on the land. Others were used as a general labour force. About 60% of a group of more than a million peasant deportees were working in 'industrial' enterprises at the beginning of 1935.[171] In the far north, 'in spring of 1931 a decision was taken to put 10,000 kulak families at the disposal of Non-Ferrous Metals Industry and 8,000 for bringing into production the coal districts of Pechora'.[172]

At Magnitogorsk, the new industrial complex employed some 50,000 workers. About 18,000 of these are described as dekulakized peasants (together with 20–25,000 forced labourers working underground, and described as criminals, thieves, prostitutes and embezzlers).[173] In the northern Urals an engineer describes several trainloads of kulaks arriving in 1931. They were assigned to work in the mines; and he later came across similar groups at forced labour in gold, copper and zinc mines elsewhere in the country.[174] At Bachatskii on the Tom River, about 5,000 kulaks worked on building a harbour on seven ounces of bread a day, with instructions to procure additional food where they could.[175]

As to those who were kept at rural types of labour, their skill and hard work sometimes prevailed. In a recent work of Soviet fiction, the narrator tells of early dekulakization, in 1928, with all former kulaks deported to fell lumber. But they then worked so hard that they prospered, and had to be dekulakized and deported a second time.[176]

In general, without horses or ploughs, with a few axes and shovels, the toughest of the deported peasantry survived and created fairly prosperous settlements – from which they were again evicted when the authorities noticed their growth.[177] It is reported that one group of Old Believers even managed to set up a thriving settlement out of contact with the world until

141

1950, only to be discovered then and charged with sabotage.[178]

For control was difficult. The official literature holds that as many as a quarter of the deported kulaks of Siberia had in fact escaped by mid-1930, mainly the younger men.[179] They are described as the most irreconcilable enemies of the Soviet order.

There are many tales recounted like that of two young Ukrainians who managed to get hold of a station-master's shotgun, and with a frying pan and a few provisions struck out across the taiga living on deer and game.[180]

★

But though numbers escaped, and many others survived by sheer effort, it must be emphasized that many did not survive.

At Yemetsk there was a vast camp, mainly of families separated from their fathers, mostly children. 32,000 people lived in 97 barracks. There were outbreaks of measles and scarlet fever, but no medical care. Daily rations were 14 ounces of black bread, 3.5 ounces of millet seed, and 3.5 ounces of fish. The child mortality rate was great, with funerals all day. Passing through the area again in 1935, a former inmate noted that the cemetery, where endless crosses had stood, had now been levelled by the authorities.[181]

Of over fifty members of families in one village arrested and sent some hundred miles south of Sverdlovsk in Siberia, five returned with fake papers in 1942 to report that all the others had died of overwork and starvation.[182]

One Ukrainian peasant with his wife, nine children and two aged parents, were sent to the Solovki Islands. A nine-year-old son managed to escape, though shot in the legs. The others died.[183]

At an 'isolation camp' in Tomsk, 13,000 kulaks were held, on a diet of nine ounces of bread and a bowl of 'soup' a day. The death rate was eighteen to twenty a day.[184] Of 4,800 people who arrived in a Siberian forest 'camp' in October 1931, 2,500 had died by April 1932.[185] In the spring of 1932, food supplies ceased to be delivered to the Ukrainian special settlement of Medvezhoye in the Urals. Famine, as later in the Ukraine itself, killed off many.[186]

Solzhenitsyn tells of sixty to seventy thousand people going up the icebound Siberian stream of Vasyugan, to be marooned on patches of firm ground in the local marshes without food or tools. Later food was sent but did not reach them, and they all died. In this case there seems to have been an enquiry, and one of those responsible is reported shot.[187]

Considered estimates are that a quarter to a third of the deportees perished.[188] These, as we have said, were predominantly children. One deported kulak tells of how in the Yemetsk camp in the Far North, 'On 18 April my daughter died. The three-year-old "criminal" had paid for her parents' and grandparents' "crimes" '.[189]

The Party's reply, and rationale for everything done to the kulaks, is summarized with exceptional frankness in a novel published in Moscow in 1934: 'Not one of them was guilty of anything; but they belonged to a class that was guilty of everything'.[190]

★

7

Crash Collectivization and its Defeat, January–March 1930

I will not give thee the inheritance of my fathers

I. Kings

The peasant who was spared dekulakization was reserved for a different fate. He too was now subject to a forcible change in his condition. In Stalin's phrase, used more than once, the collectivization drive which now began was a 'revolution carried out *from above*', (though supposedly 'directly supported "from below" ' by the peasants).[1]

The crux of collectivization in fact lay in the decisions taken in 1929 by him and a group of his closest associates. These decisions were, of course, in a general strategic sense, rooted in the history of the Party and of the whole Marxist attitude. In the immediate tactical sense they arose as the result of manoeuvres in the Party leadership, in which the aims of dogma and of the struggle for power were inextricably entangled.

The plans and actions of the Communist Party at this stage have sometimes been interpreted by Western academics in terms appearing natural, or logical, or rational to Western academics. An orthodox Soviet reviewer notes approvingly that in contrast to the majority of his Western colleagues, one such writes of a 'broadly prepared programme of collectivization'.[2] No such programme existed. In fact, as we have seen, it was one of the conditions of the crash collectivization that Stalin and his closest associates hustled the party step by step into the full campaign without having any established plan on which argument might take place, (at the same time silencing the serious economic planners). The present official view is indeed as follows: collectivization of agriculture was absolutely necessary. The objective situation in the early 1920s had made concessions to private farms unavoidable. This had worked, but further advance was hindered by an 'outmoded mode of production in

144

agriculture'. A rapid development of industry and socialization of agriculture was now needed. Meanwhile the inefficiency of small peasant holdings was a major handicap; and kulaks were hostile. Only by a class war against the latter could the party mobilize the poor and middle peasants for collectivization and destroy the 'class enemy'. (And the grain crisis was thus solved, since socialist farming is more efficient than capitalist farming, etc. etc. but this need not detain us here).

Such a picture is almost entirely fantasy; especially the notion of the (virtually non-existent) class struggle, and the superior efficiency of collective farming. But even apart from its nature and results, the collectivization was not at all carried out in a rational and carefully planned manner.

The whole atmosphere of War Communism was recreated – the military jargon, the Utopian expectations, the brutal coercion of the peasantry, the lack of economic preparation. The Party was launched into an atmosphere of hysteria, with (as Adam Ulam puts it) 'the notion of demons and witches being on the loose'.

But what was the alternative from the point of view of the one-party dictatorship? The Right foresaw that a crash collectivization would be a grave crisis. On the other hand, the idea that gradual collectivization would attract the individual peasant, even over decades, seems highly sanguine. The choice, in fact, may well have been between a Communist regime which abandoned its schematics and performed an 'opening to the Right', with the ex-Mensheviks of Gosplan, and perhaps other parties (as in Budapest in 1956) emerging in a left-wing, but not universally hated, coalition; which could then have engineered a sort of people's socialism. Such, at least, is one view. But it was not the view of the Right. And their eschewing of any opening to forces outside the Party condemned them to impotence. Moreover, as Isaac Deutscher points out, 'from the moment the smallholder vanished, the right opposition had no ground to stand on'.[3]

Stalin's general attitude was not, or only to a small degree, a personal quirk. He had the support, for the collectivization revolution, of the bulk of the Party activists and, at a higher level, of the core of the old revolutionary underground, men like Kirov. Even the bulk of the 'Left' rallied to him once the battle was engaged, with reservations merely of the sort that they were more cultured and would have done things less crudely, but that one must rise above such petty considerations. And once the new revolution was launched, there was a strong feeling in the Party that, in the words of an official of the period long opposed to Stalin, 'any change in leadership would be extremely dangerous . . . the country must continue in its present course, since to stop now or attempt a retreat would

145

mean the loss of everything'.[4]

If there was no serious economic preparation for the crash collectivization, there was not much administrative preparation either. As in 1918, it was a matter of hastily constituted troikas of outsiders and other *ad hoc* bodies in the village acting with complete arbitrariness, while the old village soviets, cooperative societies, kolkhoz administrations just collapsed. On the official view, as given in a Party history published in 1960, the sending in of activists from the cities is represented in the following terms: the peasants

> saw that the Party and the government, overcoming difficulties, were building factories to make tractors and new farm machines. Numerous peasant delegations visited the new factories and construction sites, attended workers' meetings, and were inspired by their enthusiasm. Upon returning to their villages the advanced representatives of the working peasantry took the initiative in setting up new collective farms. The organized workers of industrial enterprises and building sites assumed patronage over rural areas, and sent numerous workers' teams to the countryside. That was how the mass movement for joining the collectives was prepared and begun, a movement which grew into solid collectivization.[5]

Although this way of looking at it is the merest romancing, it is true that, as in 1928 and 1929, emissaries from the town played a decisive role. This time, however, the effort was conceived on a more permanent basis than previous invasions of the countryside.

Pravda had noted that the plenipotentiaries sent out by the Party in 1928–9 to impose the 'social influence' method were known to the villagers as 'strolling players'. They dealt with a number of villages, and stayed only long enough in each to enforce the given collection figures, having no permanent power.[6]

Now a concerted effort was made. In the cities the '25-thousanders' – Communist workers – were mobilized to take over the villages. The final figure was in fact rather higher than 25,000 – 'more than twenty-seven thousand workers were selected and sent to the countryside'.[7] They were not just sent on an emergency basis like their predecessors. They were to remain in the villages, and run them. The 25-thousanders were given a two week course in January 1930 and then sent off to their assignations. Originally they were to stay a year; then this was extended to two years; finally, on 5 December 1930, the Central Committee made it permanent.[8]

The 25-thousanders were originally promised 120 roubles a month. They did not always get it: there is a letter from a group of them near Vyazma complaining of kolkhozes with no funds to pay them so that 'we must flee home'.[9] Official documents are full of their worries about salary, quotas and so on. The peasants' reaction is also described realistically in some official reports. They are quoted as saying that if a worker can manage a farm, send us to manage a factory; and that they are sending new bailiffs to exploit us: 'In some places this kulak propaganda is successful'.[10] But even the 25-thousanders were not always reliable, trying to gain 'cheap popularity' and 'giving in to the consumerist mood of the backward part of the village'.[11] The Collective Farm Centre complained of 25-thousanders who protested (rightly) that requisitioning of seed grain would lead to sowing failure: these were to be dismissed and expelled from the Party.[12] By mid-February 18,000 had been sent in to local work and 16,000 of these directly into the kolkhoz system. But about a third had been 'weeded out'.[13] Still, by May 1930, 19,581 were working in collective farms, mainly as chairmen or in other key posts.[14]

In addition to the 25-thousanders, 72,204 'workers' were sent to the countryside in the spring of 1930 on temporary assignment; 13,000 accountants – members of the Komsomol – were made available,[15] and 50,000 soldiers and junior officers about to be demobilized were given special training for the collectivization work. In the Ukraine alone 23,500 officials in addition to over 23,000 selected industrial workers had appeared in the villages by the end of February 1930.[16]

Once again, things did not go as smoothly as the bare figures imply. One official report tells of a typical district committee at Yelnaya in the RSFSR, ordered in August 1933 to mobilize fifty Communists for village work. Only twenty were actually mobilized and only four went to the villages – one a former individual farmer, the others totally ignorant of agriculture. In October another fifteen Komsomols were ordered in; four were actually sent, two of whom had to be fired for incompetence and drunkenness.[17]

But in spite of such failures, the numbers actually deployed constituted a powerful cadre. The way they were instructed and inspired over this period may be seen in a later account by an activist of a meeting of eighty picked organizers, addressed by M.M. Khatayevich. Their province had 'fallen behind'. They were to go into the country for a month or six weeks:

The local village authorities need an injection of Bolshevik iron. That's why we are sending you.

You must assume your duties with a feeling of the strictest Party responsibility, without whimpering, without any rotten liberalism. Throw your bourgeois humanitarianism out of the window and act like Bolsheviks worthy of Comrade Stalin. Beat down the kulak agent wherever he raises his head. It's war – it's them or us! The last decayed remnant of capitalist farming must be wiped out at any cost!

Secondly, comrades, it is absolutely necessary to fulfil the government's

147

plan for grain delivery. The kulaks, and even some middle and 'poor' peasants, are not giving up their grain. They are sabotaging the Party policy. And the local authorities sometimes waver and show weakness. Your job is to get the grain at any price. Pump it out of them, wherever it is hidden, in ovens, under beds, in cellars or buried away in back yards.

Through you, the Party brigades, the villages must learn the meaning of Bolshevik firmness. You must find the grain and you *will* find it. It's a challenge to the last shred of your initiative and to your Chekist spirit. *Don't be afraid of taking extreme measures.* The Party stands four-square behind you. Comrade Stalin expects it of you. It's a life-and-death struggle; better to do too much than not enough.

Your third important task is to complete the threshing of the grain, to repair the tools, ploughs, tractors, reapers and other equipment.

The class struggle in the village has taken the sharpest forms. This is no time for squeamishness or rotten sentimentality. Kulak agents are masking themselves and getting into the collective farms where they sabotage the work and kill the livestock. What's required from you is Bolshevik alertness, intransigence and courage. I am sure you will carry out the instructions of the Party and the directives of our beloved Leader.[18]

Another activist wrote years later, 'We were deceived because we wanted to be deceived. We believed so strongly in communism that we were prepared to accept any crime if it was glossed over with the least little bit of communist phraseology . . . Confronted by something unpleasant, we compelled ourselves to believe that it was an isolated phenomenon and that on the whole the country's state of affairs was just as the party described it . . . in other words, just as it was supposed to be according to communist theory'.[19]

Not all were of this ideologically motivated type. Stalin's favourite Mikhail Sholokhov well illustrates the nature of the motivations of the loyal Party activists. It is partly an enthusiastic belief in tractors; partly hatred of the present day kulak as an epitome of 'property' and representing the 'other side'; partly vengeance for the Civil War and economic exploitation; and partly devotion to the world revolution, based on things read in the papers about the class struggle in China and elsewhere ('He thinks he's killing a bullock, but in reality he's stabbing the world revolution in the back'). If we add the habit of accepting Party orders as the supreme criterion, this seems a full enough analysis.

Vasily Grossman sees the activist committees of the villages as including all kinds – 'those who believed the propaganda and who hated the parasites and were on the side of the poorest peasantry, and others who used the situation to their advantage. But most of them were merely anxious to carry out instructions. They would have killed their own fathers and mothers simply in order to carry out instructions'.[20]

As for the less devoted, we have already seen how mere greed and love of power raged in the villages. One recent Soviet reviewer says plainly that with collectivization 'new ideas and slogans became for some a guiding light, for others a lever to personal gain, and career advancement, for others still – demagogical promises covering up ulterior motives or ambitions'.[21]

Combining ideology and personal hatred, another modern Soviet writer has as the chief figure in a collective farm a dishonest and lazy character whose greatest dream is 'to heat up an enormous bath house, fill it with steam, drive all the priests and capitalists inside and set it on fire'.[22]

In the villages the Party's envoys organized their local supporters as best they could. Mikhail Sholokhov's Don Cossack village of 'Gremyachii Log' is collectivized by a 25-thousander who collects thirty-two 'poor Cossacks and active workers' who simply 'decide', in the absence of the village majority, to collectivize and dekulakize. Where available, Party members held the administrative posts. In one district, twenty-two of the thirty-six party members served as kolkhoz chairmen.[23] These would usually, and especially in the Ukraine, have included 25-thousanders, mainly Russians. But there were not enough Party members except for key posts, and Komsomols made up a high proportion of local 'activists'. In one district in Russia even in June 1933 there was not a single party cell, and only fourteen Party members in the seventy-five kolkhozes, but there were sixteen Komsomol cells with 157 members, and fifty-six more Komsomols were scattered through the remaining kolkhozes.[24] A local official noted that young people joined the Komsomols to escape fieldwork.[25] In addition, a larger 'non-party aktiv' was also organized, for political and state tasks in the village.[26]

Such locals, who had come to power in the villages under the regime, were often a lowgrade lot, though sometimes party veterans who still kept some of their illusions. In any case, those who did not revolt at their jobs, and fall with the rest of the victims, became hardened more and more. In the closing down of a Ukrainian village church, 'Kobzar, Belousov and the others undertook the jobs with relish. Slowly, imperceptibly, they had become antagonists of the population, enjoying most of the things other villagers disliked – precisely because they disliked them'.[27]

Yet, as we have seen, not all honest activists or Party members could accept the moral burden. In the Ukraine an official organ even complained that the 'Committees of Unwealthy Peasants', the Party's mainstay in the villages, were often directing sabotage of the collectivization.[28]

Pravda more than once denounced communists in the villages who 'deserted',[29] even citing a young agronomist who resigned from the Party after seven days in a village with a letter: 'I do not believe in collectivization. The pace . . . is too rapid. This is a wrong course taken by the Party. Let my words be a warning'.[30] In the then Central Black Earth Province 5,322 Party members were expelled, and 'several district committees were disbanded for Right opportunism'.[31] In the Drabove District in the Poltava Province of the Ukraine, thirty activists were arrested, (including the Secretary of the District Party Committee, Bodok), and were publically tried in July 1932 for such malpractices – allegedly the result of 'conspiring with the kulaks'. They received two to three year sentences.[32]

As for the official organs of local administration, they simply ceased to be effective, partly because the village soviets, in spite of all previous purging, still largely resisted collectivization. In one village, an OGPU report complains that the slaughter of livestock was started by the vice-chairman of the village soviet.[33] Such acts were general: 're-election' for 'those village soviets which were impregnated with alien elements . . . and of those district executive committees which failed to direct the village soviets to start work on the collectivization of agriculture' was ordered on 31 January 1930. In the Central Volga 'an overwhelming majority of village Soviets . . . have proved not to be at the level of their new tasks'.[34] In one area described as typical, 300 of the 370 chairmen of village soviets were removed between early 1929 and March 1930.[35] Overall, by March 1930, no fewer than 82% of the chairmen of village soviets had been replaced, only 16% of these resigning voluntarily.[36] In the Western Province out of 616 village soviet chairmen 306 had been removed and 102 'brought to trial'.[37] A confidential official document shows that in this Province there was no turn of the village soviets to the collective farm over 1929 even though 97 new ones had been elected. In 'a number of them' every possible form of dragging their heels on economic and political matters was to be found, up to 'clear connivance with the kulak'.[38] 'Self-abolition' of village soviets at the instance of the Party plenipotentiary was therefore introduced. And even at a higher level, there were some District Executive Committees which had *no* members elected by normal procedure.[39] The village soviets now began to be effectively superseded by appointed bureaus or troikas,[40] a governmental decision of 25 January 1930 confirming the system of plenipotentiaries and troikas,[41] with power to overrule the regular organs of state.

As to the village commune, even as late as May 1929, when the first Five Year Plan was adopted, it was seen as the 'cooperative sector' which would provide the greater part of grain procurements; and this – it was thought – would encourage the transformation of the villages into collectives.[42] But in the event, as a Western scholar remarks: 'the village organization which stood for all the collectivist objects of village life, and which had been rooted in the village for centuries, was given no part to play in the collectivization of the peasants'.[43] And, by decree of 10 July 1930 the ancient commune was finally abolished in areas of wholesale collectivization; it soon disappeared elsewhere.

The voluntary nature of the kolkhoz was in any case quite incompatible with the fact that local organizations were issued with orders from above on how many kolkhozes they were to have with how many members. One village Communist in the Kalinin Province was told to get over 100 families into his kolkhoz, could only persuade about a dozen, and reported this. He was told he was sabotaging collectivization and would face expulsion if he failed. He went back and told the villagers they would be expropriated and exiled if they did not sign up. 'They all agreed . . .' and the same night started to kill their livestock. When he reported this, the Party committee was not interested: it had fulfilled its plan.[44]

But the fictitiousness of the voluntary principle was even admitted, in the strange doublethink of the Politburo's own pronouncements, by Stalin's closest colleagues, as when Kaganovich (in January 1930) said that all guidance and activity in the development of the kolkhozes was being done 'directly and exclusively' by men of the party apparat.[45]

Modern official Soviet writers such as S.P. Trapeznikov often maintain, still, that collectivization was a majority choice of the peasantry. In fact, this line is nowadays increasingly found and the serious students who published in the 50s and 60s are silenced. But, as we have seen and shall see again, Soviet novelists published in Moscow in the period before 1982 are franker than the Party. One of them says flatly, 'the more widely and firmly collectivization was implemented, the more it met with hesitation, uncertainty, fear and resistance'.[46]

The claim, frequently made, is that the 'cultural level' of the peasantry was raised by incessant meetings and propaganda, so that they came to see the advantages of the kolkhoz. In fact the meetings were simply a vehicle of coercion. A normal procedure, often reported, was for the Party emissary to ask a village meeting 'who is against the collective farm and the Soviet government?',[47] or 'You must immediately enter the kolkhoz. Whoever does not is an enemy of the Soviet regime'.[48]

A Party official in the North Caucasus is quoted (from local archives) in a recent official Soviet work, as telling the peasants 'Karl Marx, our dear dead leader, wrote that peasants are potatoes in a sack. We have got you in our sack'.[49] Even the forms were observed only to a very limited extent. In one Volga village no more than a quarter to a third of the heads of households were counted at the village meetings, and committed the whole village to collectivization, and there are many such reports.[50]

At first stray voices were often raised against the activists. A peasant in Sholokhov's novel refuses to bring his seed grain into the communal granary, in spite of guarantees:

' "... it will be safer with me. If I give it to you, in the spring I shan't even get back the empty sacks. We've grown wiser now, you don't get around us that way."

Nagulnov raised his eyebrows and his face paled a little. "How dare you distrust the Soviet government!" he demanded. "So you don't believe what I say"?

"That's right. I don't believe it. We've heard that sort of yarn before".

"Who's told you yarns? And what about?" Nagulnov turned noticeably pale, and slowly rose to his feet.

But as though he had not noticed anything, Bannik continued to smile quietly, revealing his few firm teeth. Only his voice quivered with a note of grievance and burning anger as he said:

"You'll collect the grain, and then you'll load it into trains and send it abroad. You'll buy automobiles, so that Party men can ride around with their bobbed-hair women. We know what you want our grain for. We've lived to see equality, all right!" '

A poor peasant (in a village in the Poltava Province) is quoted as saying, 'my grandfather was a serf, but I, his grandson, will never become a serf'.[51] Indeed, it was now common peasant usage to refer to the VKP (initials of the All Union Communist Party) as 'second serfdom' (*vtoroe krepostnoe pravo*).[52] Official accounts, too, mention poor peasants saying 'you have turned us into worse than serfs'.[53] *Pravda* itself reported that in one Ukrainian village where collectivization had been put through a local meeting in silence, a crowd of women blocked the road when tractors arrived, shouting amongst other things, 'the Soviet government is bringing back serfdom'![54] And a recent Soviet account quotes the peasants as saying 'You want to drive us into collectives so that we would be your serfs', and perceiving local party leaders as 'landlords'.[55] Such attitudes prevailed among the peasantry. Large majorities often still refused to collectivize. Prominent objectors were then arrested, one by one, on other charges.[56] At Belosuvka, in the Chernukhi district, the peasants were summoned to a meeting and told to sign their names to a request to join the kolkhoz. One of them called on them to resist. He was arrested that night, and twenty others the following day, after which enrolment proceeded smoothly.[57]

We chance to have the (mostly unpublished) letters received by the Western Province peasant paper *Nasha Derevnya*. All from poor or middle peasants, they complain of forced entry to the kolkhoz, of excessive demands, of 'slavery' in the kolkhozes, of lack of nails, ...[58] In this area, even the rural Communists refused on a large scale to enter the kolkhozes.[59] In Sholokhov's Don village, even after immense pressure, and threats to consider opponents of the kolkhoz as 'enemies of the government' like those already deported, only 67 out of 217 present vote to join. The 25-thousanders 'could not understand the stubborn reluctance of the majority of the middle peasants'.

In the Ukraine, as the country's First Secretary Stanislav Kossior was to admit, 'administrative measures and the use of force, not only against middle peasants but also against poor peasants, became a systematic component of the work not only of district but also of provincial party committees'.[60]

A post-Stalin Soviet official scholar (himself a former activist in the collectivization drive) even writes that the strongest opposition came not from the wealthier peasants, but from those who had recently acquired land and 'poor peasants who had only recently become middle peasants'.[61]

But the pressures grew more and more intense:

Every form of pressure was applied to them – threats, slander, constraint. Hooligans loitered outside their homes, taunting them. Postmen were instructed not to deliver mail to such 'individualists'; at the District Medical Centre, they were told that only collective farmers and their families could be accepted as patients. Often, their children were expelled from school, and dismissed shamefully from the Detachment of Young Pioneers and the Komsomol. The corn-mills refused to grind their grain; the blacksmiths would do no work for them. The stigma of 'individualists', as applied by the authorities, was akin to classing a man as a criminal.[62]

For the borderline cases among the middle peasants facing the alternative of dekulakization, the choice was often a harsh one. As many joined the collective, and handed over their grain, one Communist noted: 'these people had apparently decided to face starvation at home rather than banishment to the unknown'.[63]

Village craftsmen were also eliminated. For example, against the opposition of the Krynychky village soviet all skins were confiscated from ten tanners working in it and the surrounding 24 villages, and they were fined 300 roubles each.[64]

Even the quasi-artisan activities traditionally practised by the peasants themselves were affected. For example, many of them used hand-mills to press the oil from sunflower seeds. This was prohibited under a decree of the Commissariat of Trade on 18 October 1930.[65]

★

Villages of any size were now required to have jails, which were only to be found in district capitals before the Revolution. They were needed not merely for peasants who had made verbal objections, or voted 'no' at village meetings. Resistance to collectivization often took violent form.

In 1929–30 a great effort had been made to prevent the peasantry possessing arms. Registration of hunting weapons had become compulsory in decrees of 1926, 1928 and 1929, and rules were also established to ensure that 'criminal and socially dangerous elements' should not be sold guns, this to be 'checked by the GPU authorities'. In August 1930, when various minor insurrections and individual acts of resistance had made it clear that this was not being obeyed, a massive arms search was ordered. By this time, however, few arms were left. Among the hundreds of search documents we find only the occasional discovery of 'one small-bore pistol', while the search was turned to the state's advantage by the seizure of 'silver money 30 roubles 75 kopeks; paper money 105 roubles; wedding rings-two' and so on in case after case.[66] In one village in the Kharkov Province, the GPU official complained to an activist that there were still people there who had already served sentences but been amnestied in 1927, and had weapons hidden.[67]

Adequately armed or not, the peasants resisted. There were many individual assassinations of officials. Party members were warned to 'stay away from open windows', and not to walk out after dark.[68] 'In the first half of 1930 the kulaks committed more than 150 murders and acts of arson in the Ukraine.'[69] Thereafter figures cease to be available, apparently because they became officially unacceptable. In the single village of Birky, in the Poltava Province, (population about 6,000), the local GPU chief was badly wounded in January 1930; in March the buildings of one of the village's four kolkhozes were burnt down, as were houses of dispossessed kulaks which had been taken over by communists. One of the leading local communists was attacked and injured.[70]

More serious were the widespread anti-kolkhoz demonstrations (some of them 'armed demonstrations') listed in Soviet sources, involving thousands of people, and committing large numbers of 'terrorist acts'. In the Sal'sk region of the North Caucasus it was admitted that one 'demonstration' could only be suppressed 'after five or six days' with the aid of 'cavalry and armoured cars'.[71] In fact, in some areas, a Soviet scholar of the Khrushchev period tells us, the demonstrations 'bore a semi-insurrectionary character ... people armed themselves with pitchforks, axes, staves, shotguns and hunting rifles ... in many cases they were headed by former Antonov bandits,'[72] that is, survivors (as minor participants) in the great peasant risings of the early 20s.

Armed demonstrations which can only be suppressed with army units are rather more than 'semi'-insurrectionary. And there were, indeed, large scale armed rebellions, recalling those of the first peasant war in 1918–22. But this time the peasants' armed resources were fewer, and above all the Party's control and power had enormously increased.

Some revolts were on a small scale, as with one confined to the village of Parbinsk; GPU units put it down, afterwards shooting a priest and his family of four.[73] In September 1930 a riot in the village of Rudkivtsi, in Podilia, drove off the police but three days later was suppressed by security forces. Two peasants were shot and twenty-six deported.[74] In June 1931, a cavalry regiment is reported sent to suppress a riot by peasants in Mykhaylivka, in the same area; artillery was used, and all the male population over fifteen arrested. Three hundred men and fifty women were sent to camps.[75]

Other revolts spread beyond individual villages, especially in the Ukraine. There was a real rebellion, put down by armed militia, in the villages of Hradenytsi and Troitsk in the Dniester valley, in the Odessa Province.[76] There was a rising in the Chernihiv Province in the spring of 1930 which spread to five districts and was put down by army troops.[77]

In another province, Dnipropetrovsk, an insurrection also spread over five districts. An infantry division stationed at Pavlograd failed to march against them, and entered into negotiations. The divisional commander was arrested. But the division was not used against the rebels, GPU troops and militia from outside being brought in. In one village alone, Dmytrivka, one hundred people were arrested, and the total ran into thousands. All were beaten, some shot, some sent to labour camp.[78]

In Moldavia, a group of villages rose, destroyed a mounted unit of militiamen, and defeated a GPU detachment, some villages even proclaiming a 'Soviet government without Communists'. Other rebellions broke out in two districts of the Kherson Province; in Kamianets–Podilsk and Vinnytsia provinces; and in three districts of Chernihiv Province, where locally raised troops supported the rebels, and major concentrations of regulars and GPU units had to be used; in Volhynia; and in three districts of the Dnipropetrovsk Province, where a Red Army lieutenant on leave led the ill-armed peasantry against army units supported by armour and planes and was killed in action. In such cases many executions took place, and families were exiled on a large scale.[79]

There are a number of reports of insurgent bands in which former anti-Soviet partisans of the Civil War period united with former 'red' partisans to form very effective groups.[80] On one estimate, there were as many as 40,000 Ukrainian rebels in 1930.[81]

155

In Siberia, the Civil War had never quite ended: Soviet sources speak of a continuation of 'political banditism'.[82] But between early 1927 and early 1929, the number of guerilla bands quadrupled, and thereafter grew at an even greater rate.[83] A typical rebellion in the Uch–Pristanski district in March 1930, was headed by the local head of militia, Dobytin, and armed with police weapons. GPU troops were used to suppress it, and an official analysis of its members showed that it was composed of 38% 'kulaks', 38% middle peasants and 24% poor peasants. Its political programme was a Constituent Assembly which would elect 'a tsar or a president.'[84] In general, the Siberian risings declared the Soviet government deposed and the Constituent Assembly remained a popular slogan.[85]

A recent work on the Siberian Military District's help in the collectivization gives an interesting picture of the soldiers getting true information from their families. In one batallion alone, in October 1931, 16% of the letters received were of 'anti-Soviet' character, in November 18.7%; in the first seventeen days of December 21.5%. Conversations between soldiers, as reported by informers, are full of such remarks as that the authorities 'rob everybody without distinction, and tell us they are liquidating the kulak'. Counter-revolutionary soldiers' groups were unmasked, for having tried to establish connections with the countryside through soldiers on leave, and in one case even issuing a leaflet.[86]

In some regions of the Ukraine and the North Caucasus, an OGPU officer tells us, military aircraft were used. In the North Caucasus one squadron refused to strafe the Cossack villages. It was disbanded and half its personnel executed. Elsewhere in the area, an OGPU regiment was annihilated. The notorious Frinovski, then Commander of the OGPU Border troops, who commanded the repression, reported to the Politburo that the rivers had carried thousands of bodies downstream. After these revolts some tens of thousands of peasants are reported shot, hundreds of thousands sent to camps and exile.[87]

In the Crimea, (where 35–40,000 Tatars were dekulakized), an uprising is reported in Alakat in December 1930, with thousands of sentences to death or labour camp. The President of the Crimea, Mehmet Kubay, complained of the plundering and starvation of the republic in 1931, and disappeared.[88]

Among the mountain nations of the North Caucasus, major rebellions continued for months, with large forces of regular troops engaged. In Armenia there were widespread peasant risings, with several districts in rebel hands for some weeks, in March–April 1930.[89] In Azerbaijan too, the collectivization produced risings: 'The Turkic peasants of Azerbaijan, including the wealthy, the medium and the poor, have all risen together' as Karayev, secretary of the Azerbaijan Party put it, explaining that clan relationships prevented class divisions. After severe fighting, some 15,000 escaped into Iran.[90] But even comparatively peaceful resistance was often crushed in a ruthless fashion. Isaac Deutscher, travelling in Russia, met a high OGPU officer who said to him, with tears in his eyes, 'I am an old Bolshevik. I worked in the underground against the Tsar and then I fought in the Civil War. Did I do all that in order that I should now surround villages with machine-guns and order my men to fire indiscriminately into crowds of peasants? Oh, no, no, no!'[91]

Arrests and executions in the case of real resistance were of course accompanied by a general terror against mere suspects. An arrested peasant is shown in a Soviet novel as falsely accused of trying to organize a military rebellion. In jail another peasant advises him to sign the required confession as all the others have had to. He replies that he is not guilty, but the answer is that neither are they. He objects,

> 'But then I shall be shot'.
> 'Yes, but at least you won't be tortured'.[92]

The more intelligent of those who opposed the regime, even by peaceful methods, knew the alternatives. In Sholokov's village an enemy of the regime is arrested. The OGPU man says,

> 'You wait: I'll talk to you in Rostov. You'll do a dance or two for me before you die.'
> 'Oh how terrible! How you frighten me! I'm trembling all over like an aspen, I'm trembling with terror!' Polovtsev said ironically, stopping to light a cheap cigarette. But from under his brows he looked up at the Cheka-man with sneering, hateful eyes.
> '. . . What do you think you can frighten me with? You're too naive! With tortures? That won't come off: I'm ready for anything'.

The most remarkable technique of resistance was, however, the astonishing *babski bunty* – 'women's rebellions', particularly in the Ukraine.

One of the reasons the women were particularly hostile to the kolkhozes seems to have been that they traditionally tended the farm animals, and relied on their cows for milk for the children, which now became a doubtful matter. The central Soviet press itself reported some of the women's revolts.[93] In village after village, official reports tell of such things as 'a great crowd of women came, armed with clubs and other things, and began demanding that the horses be returned. They also tried to beat up representatives of the District Executive Committee and the District Party Committee. The chief in this was Kanyashyna Nasta'

157

(described as a wife of a middle peasant).[94] In many cases, the women succeeded in retrieving the collectivized horses and sometimes grain was also taken and redistributed.[95]

The movement spread to Russia proper, if on a lesser scale. In the Western Province a riot of 200, 'mainly women', who attacked the kolkhoz is reported.[96] But most of our reports are from the Ukraine and North Caucasus, (as with armed rebellion when that was feasible). In three villages in the Odessa Province in February 1930 the women dispersed the local authorities and regained their property. GPU detachments suppressed the revolt with many arrests.[97] A women's revolt in Pleshky village, Poltava Province, in the spring of 1933 succeeded in breaking into the grain store and taking grain. They were fired on by police troops and a number were killed. All the survivors were deported.[98]

In general, thousands of women are reported arrested in such particular incidents.[99] But on the larger scale, the authorities were at somewhat of a loss, especially – as often – when the rebels' methods were careful, or their opponents unwilling to call in outside help.

For the 'women's rebellions', according to one activist observer, came to follow definite tactics. First the women would lead the attack on the kolkhoz; 'if the Communists, Komsomols and members of the village Soviets and Committees of Unwealthy Peasants attacked them, the men rallied to the women's defence. This tactic aimed at avoiding intervention by armed forces, and it was successful'. In the Southern Ukraine, the Don and the Kuban, the collective farm structure had virtually collapsed by March 1930.[100]

★

Yet the most devastating and widespread response of the peasantry to the new order was of a different nature: they slaughtered their cattle. At first, until this was suppressed, the peasants had merely sold their cattle and horses: *Pravda* complained in January 1930 that in Taganrog

> under kulak influence a mass sale of livestock is carried on by the middle and poor farmers before their entrance to the collective farms. During the last three months over 26,000 head of beef cattle were sold, 12,000 head of milch cows and 16,000 head of sheep. Buyers travel to different stations buying livestock at high prices, snatching them away from government markets, which are now at a standstill. Cattle, horses and sheep are criminally sold everywhere. This practice is most evident in regions where there is all-out collectivization.
>
> Before entering collective farming the middle, and even the poor farmers try to get rid of their livestock, hoarding the money from the sale.[101]

At the same time *Pravda* already noted that 'under the influence of kulak agitation to the effect that in collective farming their property will be taken away to make everyone equal, the farmers are not only slaughtering their beef cattle but even the milk cows and sheep'.[102]

A recent official history tells us that in Siberia 'kulak agitation to kill the cattle won over significant masses of the peasantry' and was far more difficult to prevent than sale.[103] As the meat could usually not be sold, it was eaten. Chernov, who was in charge of grain collection in the Ukraine, and later became People's Commissar of Agriculture, is reported as saying, 'for the first time in their sordid history the Russian peasants have eaten their fill of meat'.[104]

This constituted a vast economic disaster. At the Seventeenth Party Congress in 1934 it was announced that 26.6 million head of cattle (42.6% of all the cattle in the country) had been lost and 63.4 million sheep (65.1% of the total). (In the Ukraine 48% of the cattle, 63% of the pigs and 73% of the sheep and goats were slaughtered).[105] And even these official figures of cattle deaths are supposedly lower than the reality.[106]

Between January and March 1930, the Soviet countryside was thus reduced to ruin.

On the face of it, Party victory had been achieved. In June 1929, 1,003,000 holdings had been in collective farms. By January 1930 it was 4,393,100 and on 1 March 14,264,300.[107]

But the losses by slaughter; the resistance of the peasantry; the total lack of adequate planning – all the phenomena we have been recounting, amounted to a large and expensive débâcle.

In Khrushchev's time the Soviet scholar V.P. Danilov was even able to produce an article on collectivization in the *Soviet Historical Encyclopaedia* (vol. 7) – one much attacked in the post-Khrushchev period. In it he speaks of the 'mistakes' of the period: forcing the peasants into the kolkhoz; applying dekulakization to wide circles – up to 15% in some areas, including even poor peasants; setting up kolkhozes without consulting the peasants; and excessive 'socialization' in taking, for example, all the peasants' cattle.

Another Soviet scholar of the period (noting that 'a threat of disruption' of the supposed worker-peasant alliance had developed) goes to the length of saying that the kolkhoz movement 'was on the verge of being discredited.'[108] Yet another says that 'In the second half of February 1930 the dissatisfaction of the masses became very intense'.[109]

It was also a major Soviet journal of the Khrushchev epoch which declared that, 'on Stalin's orders, the press carried no reports of errors, abuses and other difficulties due to the lack of clear and consistent instructions'.[110]

Both the structure and the tradition of the Party were such that in the name of 'democratic centralism' orders from above were to be carried out without question. This quasi-military attitude largely prevented most of the phenomena which would have been found in any other type of political organization – disagreement, refusal to carry out central decisions, schism, resignation. Even Rightists like Bukharin made no attempt to break ranks. In fact, it is somewhat ironical that it was Bukharin who wrote the last major defence of the crash collectivization.[111]

But on 2 March 1930, Stalin published his crucial article 'Dizzy from Success' which attacked 'distortions' which had offended against 'the voluntary principle'.[112] In the future the peasant was to be allowed to leave the collective farm if he wished to do so. Like Lenin in 1921, Stalin in his turn had been fought to a standstill by the peasantry.

It appears that the retreat was due, at least in part, to the protests of a number of 'moderate Stalinist' Politburo members.[113] At any rate, as often before and afterwards, Stalin now launched a strong attack on the 'excesses' of those who had actually conducted his crash campaign. It was even widely admitted in high official statements, for example by Mikoyan, that these 'errors' had 'begun to undermine the peasants' loyalty to the worker–peasant alliance'.[114]

Stalin went on in various articles and speeches to denounce the 'coercive measures against the middle peasants'[115] as contrary to Leninism. A typical set-piece, in April, runs in part:

The Moscow Region, in its feverish pursuit of inflated collectivization figures, began to orientate its officials towards completing collectivization in the spring of 1930, although it had no less than three years at its disposal (to the end of 1932). The Central Black Earth Region, not desiring to 'lag behind the others' began to orientate its officials towards completing collectivization by the first half of 1930, although it had no less than two years at its disposal (to the end of 1931).

Naturally, with such a quick-fire 'tempo' of collectivization, the areas less prepared for the collective-farm movement, in their eagerness to 'outstrip' the better prepared areas, found themselves obliged to resort to strong administrative pressure, endeavouring to compensate the missing factors needed for a rapid rate of progress of the collective farm movement by their own administrative ardour. The consequences are known . . .

. . . They arose because of our rapid success in the collective farm movement. Success sometimes turns people's head. It not infrequently gives rise to extreme vanity and conceit. That may very easily happen to representatives of a party like ours, whose strength and prestige are almost immeasurable. Here, instances of Communist vainglory, which Lenin combatted so vehemently, are quite possible. Here, there is a real danger of the Party's revolutionary measures being converted into empty bureaucratic decreeing by individual representatives of the Party in one corner or another of our boundless country. I have in mind not only local officials, but also individual members of the Central Committee.[116]

Many local Communist activists, shaken by the retreat, even called Stalin's attitude incorrect – in fact occasionally even tried to suppress it. Apart from that they were reluctant to take the blame for 'excesses' which had been quite clearly approved from above.[117] As a later Soviet historian puts it 'Stalin shifted all the responsibility for the mistakes on to local officials and sweepingly accused them of bungling. The content and the tone of the article were unexpected for the Party, and caused some disarray in Party cadres'.[118]

A letter (published forty years later) from a Dnipropetrovsk Communist is cited by Roy Medvedev:

Comrade Stalin:
I, a rank-and-file worker and a reader of *Pravda* have all this time been following the newspapers closely. Is the person to blame who could not but hear the uproar about collectivization, about who should lead collective farms? All of us, the lower ranks and the press, messed up that crucial question of collective-farm leadership, while Comrade Stalin, it seems, at that time was sleeping like a god, hearing nothing, his eyes closed to our mistakes. Therefore you too should be reprimanded. But now Comrade Stalin throws all the blame on the local authorities, and defends himself and the top people.[119]

The party leaders nevertheless claimed that the Central Committee itself had not given any unrealistic targets[120] and from now on central and local papers are filled with accounts of the misdeeds of forcible collectivization, and the dismissal and trial of officials who had committed such acts – in one Ukrainian district, for example, the two leading figures in the District Party Committee, the Vice Chairman of the Executive Committee, the Komsomol Secretary, the Inspector of Schools and 16 others.[121]

The leading scapegoat was K.Ya. Bauman, Secretary of the Moscow Committee of the Party, blamed – as he still is – for his 'false theory' and 'gross breaches of the policy of the party'.[122] But Bauman, though removed from his higher posts, did not suffer greatly. He was transferred to the important position of Head of the Central Asian Bureau of the Party, where he oversaw the collectivization of the Turkic republics, winning much applause, for example at the Uzbek Party Congress in December 1933, for his successes.

One Soviet scholar, N.I. Nemakov, has flatly taken the view, (though in a work published in 1966 before the post-Khrushchev re-Stalinization had gathered force) that Stalin was indeed responsible for the 'excesses'. Nemakov was later heavily criticized for this in the Soviet press.[123] Post-Khrushchev historians in the USSR hold that Stalin's directives were correct but that the local and even some of the central agencies made serious errors in implementing them. However, these errors were universal, which makes the position hard to maintain.

Putting the blame on local officials was, in fact, a conventional farce. Even Politburo members privately objected,[124] among them Kossior. And Kalinin and Ordzhonikidze pointed out that *Pravda*, in effect Stalin's special mouthpiece, had incited these excesses.[125] Khrushchev goes to the length of asserting that 'the Central Committee actually found the courage to protest' against Stalin's putting the responsibility on them.[126] But nothing of this reached the public, (and Khrushchev's way of putting it seems a considerable exaggeration).

On the other flank, the Leninist principle of 'democratic centralism,' of submission to the decisions of the Centre, determined the action, or inaction, of the Right-wing leaders. They had been proved right. Forced collectivization had been a disaster; there was an alternative programme. The popularity of their view both in the country as a whole and in the rank-and-file of the Party was clear. In any other political order the Rightists would have made a bid for power. But Party-fetishism was too strong, except in the case of a handful of second-level apparatchiks.

So the political initiative remained in Stalin's hands, and he carried the offensive to the Rightists. In the *Theses* of the Sixteenth Party Congress in June–July 1930, the Right is described as 'objectively an agency of the kulak'. And the Congress, for the first time in Party history, saw no voices raised against official policy. Stalin's political victory was complete.

There were still some reservations among Communists never associated with the Right, and at fairly high Party levels – notably in the case of Sergei Syrtsov who had just been raised to candidate membership of the Politburo, and V.V. Lominadze. Both called, in effect, for some return to normality. They were dismissed from their posts in November and in December expelled from the Central Committee. It was something of an anti-climax when at the same time the last Rightist representative in high office, Rykov, lost the Premiership and was removed from the Politburo.

But meanwhile, neither the complaisance of the Right nor the qualms of some of his own followers affected Stalin's position as he faced the crisis of March 1930, produced entirely by his own policies. Again like Lenin in 1921, he retreated and regrouped in the face of disaster, but made the occasion one for tightening rather than loosening Party discipline. And even the refutation of his proclaimed aims of voluntary collectivization and a prosperous countryside had no effect on his resolve to carry out his true central purpose, the destruction of the independent peasantry.

★

8

The End of the Free Peasantry, 1930–32

Socialism is the feudalism of the future

Konstantin Leontiev (c. 1880)

With the Party's retreat from full compulsory collectivization in March 1930, the peasant had won a victory, though at immense cost.

The retreat included an improved model statute for the kolkhoz, which envisaged collectivized peasants being allowed to keep a cow, sheep and pigs, and implements to work their private plots.[1] Under the old commune, the peasant already had his household plot outside the commune's control, cultivating fruit and vegetables, and keeping his animals. Now the old arrangement was effectively revived.

At an All-Union Congress of kolkhoz 'shock-workers' a few years later, Stalin was to say that there was a 'kolkhoz economy . . . needed for the satisfaction of social needs, and that there exists along with this a small individual economy, needed for the satisfaction of the personal needs of the collective farmers'.[2] In fact, of course, the small private plot was and still is far the most productive agriculture of the country, not merely feeding the peasant who works it, but providing a good deal of the produce which feeds the cities.

The 'private plot' was a concession both to the peasant and to economic reality. But it was also an incentive to stay in and work for the kolkhoz. For it was to be taken away from any who did not put in the requisite number of 'labour-days' for the kolkhoz, and withdrawal from the kolkhoz naturally involved such forfeit. Thus underpaid labour on communal land was the condition of tenure – very much in the tradition of feudalism, in a stricter form.

In general, the peasants' victory was not comparable to their success nine years earlier in destroying War Communism. The Party now retreated from an impossible position, but only to regroup with a view to resuming the offensive as soon as possible, after months rather than years.

Even in the 'Dizzy from Success' article, Stalin took the line that the collectivization already achieved was a 'serious success' which guaranteed the turn to socialism in the countryside. In April *Pravda* laid down the line for the future accurately enough: 'Again we are dividing the land into individual farms for those who do not wish to farm collectively, and then once more we will socialize and rebuild until kulak resistance has been broken once for all'.[3]

★

First of all, depending on the state of mind of the local Communist plenipotentiary, it was made difficult by various measures for the peasant to withdraw from the kolkhoz. For it was not nearly as easy to leave as the mere decree indicated. The peasants' land had been consolidated into a single collective farm, and a 'seceder' could not just reclaim his portion. Instead he was allotted a supposedly equivalent acreage in the outskirts, on much poorer land. For example, in one North Caucasus *stanitsa*, fifty-two mainly poor peasant households were allocated only 110 hectares in place of their original 250, and those in the worst land, which they refused. In another, seven poor and middle peasant households were allocated land which they finally refused after breaking four ploughs on it in one day.[4]

Moreover, the allocation of both land and seed was delayed.[5] And the land might be, as the Commissariat for Agriculture noted, '10–15 kilometres away,' and hopeless from the peasants' point of view.[6] Another Commissariat of Agriculture report noted that a kolkhoz of a few houses 'very often' received all the best land, while poor and middle individual peasants 'retain only uncultivated land, marshes, shrubland, wasteland, etc.',[7] almost as if they were as yet undeported kulaks. Moreover, individual peasants were often not provided with access to pastureland or water, and lost their vegetable gardens and hayfields.[8]

In Sholokhov's village on the Don, the 25-thousander chairman also refuses to hand over the collectivized cattle to their late owners, on instructions from the District Committee. And, since all the land close to the village is now collectivized, individual peasants are, as elsewhere, offered only poor land further off:

' "Yakov Lukich, allot them land beyond the Rachy pond tomorrow morning," Davidov ordered.
"Is that virgin land?" they roared at him.

"It's fallow. How do you call it virgin land? It's been ploughed, only it was a long time ago, some fifteen years back," Yakov Lukich explained.

And at once a boiling, stormy shout arose:

"We don't want tough land!" '

This ends in a riot, the activists are beaten up, and then the 'inciters' are arrested and deported . . .

Apart from this, arrangements were, as usual, so muddled that, as an agricultural paper put it, 'neither the individual peasants nor the remaining collective farms know where to sow'.[9]

When permitted to leave the kolkhoz, the peasants were usually not allowed to reclaim their implements, and often (as in Sholokhov's case) not even their cattle.[10] In one village the activist finally returned cows to those who 'desperately' insisted, but simply refused to let the peasants leave the kolkhoz. A 'women's rebellion' chased him out, and things finally eased up a little even after order was restored.[11] The period saw, in fact, a great renewal of the technique of the 'women's rebellion', which was often able to retrieve implements or cattle when the local authorities tried to prevent this.

For even with all the disadvantages of bad soil and lack of cows and implements, the urge to leave was overwhelming and party officials took other measures to slow it up. Such measures usually failed as to the bulk of the peasantry, but they had some effect on those who had reason to fear trouble. In fact, those remaining in the kolkhoz were often formerly prosperous families who would certainly have been dekulakized if they became independent farmers again.[12]

But though the conditions for withdrawal were hard, it was only rarely that mere force prevailed in keeping the ordinary peasant in the collective farm. The local activists did not feel that they had the support of Moscow, while the peasants constantly quoted Stalin's article, and showed stiff resistance to pressure. Thus when attempts were made to prevent the peasants' withdrawal, there was often trouble. Typically, 'in Komariwka the collective farm guards were beaten up and all the machinery was taken away. In the village of Chernyawka all the village activists were held helpless in a schoolroom while the farm machinery was taken away'.[13]

Within a few weeks in March–April 1930 the figure of 50.3% collectivization shrank to 23% and continued to decline until the autumn. In all nine million households – forty or fifty million people – left the collective farms. The proportions varied with locality. In a Byelorussian village of seventy households, forty stayed and thirty left[14] but in the Ukraine the proportion of 'seceders' was far higher. More than half of those leaving the kolkhozes were in the Ukraine and the North Caucasus.

(In fact the Ukrainian authorities themselves were now accused of having swung from the Leftist error of coercion to the Rightist one of allowing resignation from kolkhozes without making efforts to dissuade it.)[15]

In general the débâcle appeared to be complete. Yet there were still some three million collectivized households. In every village in the main grain areas, and in most villages elsewhere, a collective farm occupied the best land, and held a good proportion of the surviving cattle.

Steps were now taken to use economic pressure. All the livestock of collective farmers, including their private cattle, were exempted from tax for two years; fines imposed before 1 April were cancelled in their cases, but not for individual farmers; and so on.

By September 1930 heavy pressure was again being put on the individual peasant, by large individual grain quotas and other methods. *Pravda* made it clear that the sure way to enforce collectivization was to make individual farming unprofitable, though in fact, even under the new unfavourable conditions, the individual farmers had been more successful than the kolkhozes in the 1930 harvest. *Pravda* finally asked, 'If the peasant can develop his individual economy, why should he join the kolkhoz'?[16]

The answer was to stop his developing his own farm. By such means, but also by a renewal of physical pressure, the last half of 1930 saw a reversal of the flow from the kolkhozes.

The second wave of dekulakization which now came struck mainly at those leading peasants who had headed the withdrawal from the kolkhoz, and in no intelligible sense kulak, except for their leadership of opposition to collectivization.

A typical story is of the village of Borysivka: a civil war hero had defended the peasants against forced collectivization. A Party official supported him in accusing his leading persecutors of excesses, in accord with Stalin's 'dizzy' line. (The original excesses had included the unpopular practice of applying hot frying pans to recalcitrant peasants.) But when the pressure resumed the same 'liberal' official joined in declaring him a kulak, so that he was expropriated, and some of his children died.[17] Such methods incidentally destroyed the great majority of the remaining 'hamlets' of individual farmers who had concentrated their land. For instance, in the Romanchuky khutir in the Poltava Province all the men of the 104 families there were arrested in the early spring of 1931,[18] and the land became collectivized.

By a continuation of force and economic pressure, the collective farms gradually prevailed. And on 2 August 1931, the Central Committee was able to pass a resolution noting that collectivization was fundamentally complete in the North Caucasus, in the Steppe and Left Bank regions of the Ukraine (though not in the beet-growing areas), in the Urals and in the Lower and Central Volga.

★

One of the rational arguments for collectivization was to assist industrialization, not merely in the Left's fashion of exploiting the peasantry to provide investment funds, but also to release the surplus population for factory work. But this was, of course, an argument not for the collectivization but for the modernization of agriculture, and the assumption that collectivization would in fact modernize, was, to say the least of it, premature.

All factions were agreed that rapid industrialization was necessary. This was in part for purely ideological reasons – the 'proletarian' state needed to increase the size of the class on which it was doctrinally supposed to rely; but the economic arguments also seemed compelling.

It is not the purpose of this book to follow the development of industry in the USSR under the First and Second Five Year Plans. But we should note that a variety of huge new projects were injected into the Plan in 1930.[19] Industrialization itself became a matter of crash programmes rather than the carefully planned growth envisaged by the Right, or even the original devisers of the Five Year Plan.

We are told, for instance, of a school for 'engineers' attached to the Kharkov Tractor Works. The pupils, picked for 'unusual ability or political reliability' were rushed through the courses, and sent at once to the factories. 'They would attempt at once to correct the work of foreign specialists, bringing untold confusion and wrecking the activities of really able technicians. Fine and expensive machinery was ruined . . .'[20]

The numbers transferred to industry grew beyond expectation (many cities had populations 'higher than the plan had envisaged' – at Dneprostrov, for example, 64,000 instead of 38,000).[21] As we have seen the labour made available by the dispossessed kulaks was discouraged, at least officially, from entering industry, except in the new areas of Siberia – though many other cases, such as lumbering and forced labour on the (as it turned out fairly useless) White Sea Canal might in abstract statistics represent a transfer from peasant to worker life. The bulk of the new industrial workers could nevertheless only come from the villages. Between 1929 and 1932, 12.5 million new hands entered industry and 8.5 million of them were from rural areas.[22]

This increase in the urban population meant, among other things, that more food was needed to supply them. 26 million urban persons were provisioned by the State in 1930. In 1931, this had risen to 33.2 million,

168

nearly 26%.[23] The increase in grain earmarked for their consumption was only some 6%.[24] The centralization of bread-distribution was complete by 1930–31, with strict rationing.[25] Soviet scholars (such as Moshkov and Nemakov) indeed put the case that this centralized rationing was caused less by procurement difficulties than by the theoretical aim of having non-commodity, non-market exchange.[26] It is certainly true that control of the grain at the kolkhoz level was at this point felt to be incompatible with marketing in any form.

The rations were low. And the system of wages was adjusted to the emerging Stalinist hierarchical state, being such that 'it was possible to pay a GPU man the same as a doctor, though in reality he received ten times as much and the great thing was that the doctor didn't know how much the GPU man could buy for his money. In the same way the worker in Moscow earned three times as much as the worker in Kharkov ... Workers in the provinces knew how much the Moscow worker earned, which was the same as they did, but they didn't know how much he could buy with it'.[27]

By 1932 the rouble on the free market had fallen to about one-fiftieth of its 1927 value.[28] That is, there was massive inflation. Workers' real wages were about a tenth in 1933 of what they had been in 1926–7.[29] Life in the towns was thus by no means idyllic, but, as a shrewd scholar notes, at the beginning of the 1930s it was impossible to improve the life of the average worker, but it was possible to make the life of the peasantry so unbearable that they would prefer even the factories.[30] This worked so well that, as we have seen, the problem was soon not one of recruiting labour for industry but of preventing the depopulation of the villages.

There were, indeed, still ties holding some of the new industrial hands to the land, and hence a counterflow from town to village. The conclusions of recent and earlier Soviet scholars have been summarized as follows: 'Seasonal labourers who had lost their land wanted to return to it to protect it from confiscation, those whose land had been collectivized dared not leave the collective farm for fear of losing their rights and their family home ...'[31] And even veteran factory workers in the small towns in fact often had long-standing connections with the villages (and are often quoted in the official documents as hostile to collectivization).[32]

Nevertheless, the urge to move from the collective farms was a powerful one, and generally speaking not to be countered by other influences. Administrative measures to prevent this were therefore introduced.

The old Bolshevik Rakovsky had written early in 1930, 'Finding themselves in a desperate position poor peasants and farm labourers will begin to flock to the city en masse, leaving the countryside without a work force. Can it really be that our proletarian government will issue a law attaching the rural poor to the collective farms'?[33]

Yes it could. The 'internal passport' was introduced in December 1932. Its practical application prevented not only kulaks, but any peasants who might wish to move to the cities from doing so without authorization. And a law of 17 March 1933 laid down that a peasant could not leave a collective farm without a contract from his future employers, ratified by the collective farm authorities. Moreover, these measures ran contrary to old peasant practice. As we have noted, a very high proportion of the peasantry were long accustomed to work in the cities, or to migrate annually (especially in the Ukraine) to different areas for work.

The introduction of internal passports, and the tying of the peasant to the land, was thus a major break with old practice, and implied a serfdom more constrained by law than that of the pre-Emancipation peasant. Moreover, the effect was to remove a major element in the peasants' economic life, and leave him at the mercy of local conditions. (The introduction of the internal passport, while denying the peasantry its old mobility, also tied down the workers, whose possession of the document, and of the 'labour book', was, with other measures, used to keep them in their jobs, or at least their cities).

Stalin, far from regarding the collectivization as helping provide labour for the cities, claimed that, precisely as a result of it, 'there is no longer any flight of the peasant from the village to the city, no waste of manpower';[34] which at least shows the direction of policy in the immediate post-collectivization years.

★

It has often been thought that collectivization, considered as a means of extracting grain and other products from the peasantry, was a source of the funds necessary for industrialization. This had indeed been the theme of party theoreticians since Preobrazhensky.

Nor is there any question that a peasantry can be so used to provide the surplus of industry, as we have noted in the case of Japan. Though the Stalinist method was understood to be more inefficient for such purposes, as well as more inhumane, it was long assumed that it had at least succeeded in squeezing funds for industrialization out of the agricultural sector. But recent research by a Soviet scholar (A.A. Barsov) magisterially analysed by a Western one (James Millar) seems to indicate that, wholly against expectation, there was a definite – though probably slight – input from the industrial into the agricultural sector over the years 1928–32, rather than the other way round; and that the intense and desperate

170

squeeze on the kolkhoz peasants was not quite enough to balance the inefficiencies and disruption due to the collectivization itself.[35]

Owing to the depression in the West, the world price of agricultural products in proportion to that of manufactured goods was low in 1932. It is clear that Soviet agricultural exports were nevertheless of use in obtaining foreign currency. But the average grain exports over the Five Year Plan were 2.7 million tons a year: they had been 2.6 million in 1926–7; and meanwhile export of other farm products had *declined* by nearly 65%.[36]

This is not to say, however, that the agricultural products were of no use in paying for the industrial side. But investment in farm machinery, to say nothing of the hugely increased cost of rural administration, outweighed this. Thus, though a quite significant part of the foreign currency required for modern machine purchases was after all provided by grain exports, the gross economic result was that the industrial sector was not, on balance, subsidized by the exploitation of the peasants.

★

The reasons for the continuing weakness of agriculture were various. First of all, we may consider the mere methods now employed to direct it. The real results of collectivization were clearly foreseen by Rakovsky early in 1930:

> Behind the fiction of collective farmer-proprietors, behind the fiction of elected managers, a system of compulsion is being erected that goes far beyond anything that already exists in the state farms. The fact of the matter is that collective farmers will not be working for themselves. And the only thing that will grow, blossom and flourish will be the new collective farm bureaucracy, bureaucracy of every kind, the creation of a bureaucratic nightmare . . . The collective farmers will suffer privation in everything, but extensive compensation will be provided for this in the form of officials and protectors, open and secret . . .[37]

The kolkhozes were incessantly denounced as inefficient, but the solution of putting them even more closely under the control of district and other Party Committees, incomparably more ignorant of agriculture, was a poor one. As a despatch from the British Embassy sensibly commented, 'there is small chance that Soviet agricultural production will respond favourably to the multiplication of elaborate paper ordinances such as these, any more than it does to open terror'.[38]

Each level of officialdom passed the blame on down to the lower level: 'certain managers of collective farms have shown a criminal attitude towards delivery of corn, a 'consumer's attitude', in particular Kachanov and Babansky, collective farm managers of the villages of Stepanivka and Novoselivka . . .'; and 'Kolomiyets, while chairman of the village soviet of Mikolaivka, behaved criminally and irresponsibly with regard to strengthening collective farms, ensuring a timely harvest and arrangements for deliveries of corn . . .'[39]

In 1930–32, throughout the USSR, there are stories of 'total disorganization and inefficiency'.[40] At the level of farm work the results are well illustrated in a typical account of a peasant on a Ukrainian State Farm (Yenakiyevo) who in 1931 showed a Communist friend the mismanagement and ignorance now prevailing and added, of the pigs, 'the miracle is that they are not dead yet. But they will be soon. And the director, the one responsible for this state of affairs, will not be penalized. "Kulak supporters" like me will be called enemies and there will be no way we can prove our innocence'.

When advised to leave the farm he said that they would then only arrest him earlier, while by staying on he could help his pigs, and try to resist the director. A few months later he was arrested, and later died in prison.[41]

A fairly typical OGPU report in 1932 runs:

In the kolkhoz 'Stalin,' Markovsk village soviet, Kransyi region, which includes more than 40 households, there exists the most complete negligence. Some members of the board of the kolkhoz systematically engage in drinking and abuses . . . The chairman of the board . . . a former middle peasant, systematically gets drunk and does not guide the work of the kolkhoz at all . . . about twenty hectares of oats lie cut down which, as a result of the fact that they were not harvested, almost completely rotted . . . There remained unmown one and a half hectares of oats, which were completely spoiled. The winter wheat, which was mowed on time, remained lying in the fields, thanks to which it rotted. Almost all the pulled flax is still lying in the field and is rotting, as a result of which the flaxseed is almost completely ruined. There are about 100 hectares of as yet unmown meadows, while the socialized livestock in the kolkhoz are not supplied with fodder for the winter, and according to calculations [feed] is about 4,000 poods short. With the funds of the kolkhoz four former kulak homes were bought for the construction of a cattle yard which the kolkhoz greatly needed, but these buildings are being pilfered by the kolkhozniks and burned as firewood. The equipment and harness of the kolkhoz are not repaired on time, as a result of which future use has been made impossible . . . Up to the present time *no income* [my italics] has been earned by the kolkhoz. At present, as a result of mismanagement and abuses on the part of the board of the kolkhoz, certain kolkhozniks . . . talk of leaving . . .[42]

The documents we have indicate a vast bureaucratic network, each making the others' task impossible, and creating so much organizational and reorganizational work that there was no time for essentials.[43] On the other hand, one scholar comments, 'it was the very inefficiency of the State machine which helped make it tolerable'.[44]

Extraordinary examples of unsuitable appointments were later given by Postyshev. Perhaps the oddest was that of the Odessa Provincial Committee sending as a Party organizer at a collective farm a Persian who spoke no Ukrainian and only broken Russian, and whose qualification was that his registration card showed that he had once worked as a watchman guarding grain.[45]

Only kolkhozes with exceptionally good natural resources and very capable chairmen could flourish in these conditions. Moreover, 'in a given district or province the top leader always saw to it that there was at least one "model" kolkhoz (which got the major share of the fertilizer and machinery allotments, and hence the awards and bonuses or premiums for exemplary output)'[46] – thus further exploiting the ordinary farm.

But, apart from these selected 'model' farms, successful kolkhozes were automatically victimized. As a peasant in one of them explained, there was little grain available from the others, so 'the local government filled its quotas with our grain and we were left with nothing'.[47] One of the few collective farms of the older dispensation which had flourished was that at Borysivka, in the Zaporizhia Province, founded in 1924. But when mass collectivization came, the issue of food products in return for 'labour days' ceased, so that the men tried to get outside jobs, sending the women and adolescents to work the fields.[48]

There were, especially in Siberia but also elsewhere, religious groups who had formed genuine and efficient communes – Evangelicals, Baptists, Mennonites prominent among them. They had been recognized as socialist by the Commissariat of Justice in the 1920s; but now it was alleged that they were 'facade' for kulak elements to carry out exploitation. When they attempted to have their farms recognized as kolkhozes, they were rebuffed and reorganized on Soviet lines, the more religiously active members being excluded and usually deported.[49]

The itch to organize on the grand scale also caused pointless trouble, as it had earlier. One of several now created in a single province was, on paper, a giant kolkhoz of 45,000 acres. It got nowhere. But it was replaced by an equally artificial system of squares of 2,500 acres each. This, we are told, 'frightened the peasants,' and took no account of their 'initiative'.[50] And so it was elsewhere, until finally, in 1933, the Party made some improvements on this point – breaking up the 5,873 hectare, 818 household Krassin kolkhoz at Chubarev in the Dnipropetrovsk Province, the 3,800 hectare Voroshilov kolkhoz at Pokrovsk in the Donetsk Province and others.[51]

173

But if arrangements on the farm were disorganized, the same applies to the handling of grain after its extraction from the peasants, 'Good data'[52] are available on losses of grain (at the level of procurement organizations alone): for 1928–9 to 1932–3 it totals about a million tons a year – about five million tons in all (four or five times the proportion of losses in 1926–7 to 1927–8). This may be compared with the amount of grain exports over 1928–9 to 1932–3, which was 13.5 million tons. And when we consider it in the context of the amount left to feed the peasantry, it may seem even more unacceptable. And while the amount of grain 'in transit' on 1 January 1928 was 255,000 tons, on 1 January 1930 it was 3,692,500 tons, 'mostly in stationary cars or ships or port storage, i.e. unheated buildings with a very low level of rat control'.[53]

★

But it was not the mere inefficiency, and costliness, of the new agrarian bureaucracy that was the main trouble. More profoundly, the whole principle that as much grain could be secured by orders from above as by the market process was at fault, when it came to long-term productivity.

Grain could indeed be secured, even if much of it was then wasted:

According to official data, the government's grain procurement rose from 10.8 million in 1928–29 to 16.1 in 1929–30, to 22.1 in 1930–31, to 22.8 million in 1931–2. That is, three years after the start of mass collectivization, the government had more than doubled the amount of grain it took from the countryside . . . .[54]

This extra procurement meant that little was left to the peasantry: and apart from the humanitarian objections, the economic ones of incentive are clearly very great. The *Soviet Historical Encyclopaedia* notes that at this time 'often all the grain in a collective farm was collected' including that meant to pay the kolkhozniks.[55]

Two prominent 'liberal' dissidents write of Stalin's idea being no more that that 'he thought that if a kolkhoz knew beforehand that the government demands would be large, then the kolkhozniks would work twice as hard to achieve a maximum harvest so that there would be something left for themselves'.[56]

The basic principle was that a certain amount of grain must be delivered to the state regardless, and that this demand must be satisfied before the needs of the peasantry could be taken into consideration. A law of 16 October 1931 forbade reserving grain for internal kolkhoz needs until the procurement plan was fulfilled.[57] Naturally this did not sit well even with local officials. In 1931, 'some lower level officials, limited in their political horizons, tried to place the interests of their village soviet or kolkhoz in the first place, and the needs of the entire country in the background'.[58]

In the last half of 1931 meat began to be procured by the same methods as grain: but, though heavily enforced, the results were unsatisfactory, being lower than in 1929.[59]

Not only was the state's demand for grain in excess of what the peasants could possibly spare, it was also paid for – on a system of 'contracts' with the collective farm – at arbitrarily low prices. A decree of 6 May 1932 indeed permitted private trade in grain by 'collective farms and collective farmers' *after* state quotas had been fulfilled. (Decrees of 22 August 1932 and 2 December 1932 provided sentences of up to ten years in concentration camp for those who did so before fulfilment.) And the degree to which the government was squeezing the peasantry then became obvious as (on official statistics) the free market prices were (in 1933) 20–25 times as high as those paid by the government for compulsory deliveries.[60] A lower figure, but still a startlingly inequitable one, is given by a Soviet scholar of the Khrushchev era, who notes that 'the prices for grain and many other products were symbolic (ten to twenty times lower than market prices). This system undermined the collective farmers' incentive to develop socialized production'.[61]

The State exacted grain deliveries from the farms not only in the form of compulsory deliveries, but also in the form of payments in kind made by the farms to the Machine Tractor Stations for work done on their fields, under a decree of 5 February 1933. This established that the MTS should receive 20% of the grain harvest in return for performing 'all the basic agricultural work on the fields of the kolkhoz'. A decree of 25 June 1933, said that legal proceedings would be started against any kolkhoz trying to avoid these payments in kind to the MTS. Moreover, as Roy and Zhores Medvedev put it, 'Charges of payment-in-kind for tractors, combines and other equipment were very high, while the prices the government paid to the kolkhoz were very low. Prices were in fact so low that they often did not cover even a fraction of the expenditure incurred in producing the crops'![62]

Yet another channel for compulsory grain deliveries was the exorbitant payments in kind for the grinding of grain: (it was not until 1954 that cash payments were substituted for this payment in kind).

A decree of 19 January 1933 substituted for the hitherto largely arbitrary assessments made in the guise of 'contracts', a new system of obligatory deliveries 'having the force of a tax', based on the farms' planned sown areas, and paid for at very low fixed State prices. According to the decree, fulfilment of these deliveries 'is the prior duty of every kolkhoz and individual peasant farm, and the first grain threshed must be used for carrying this out'. It permitted the farms to sell grain only after fulfilment of the grain deliveries plan by the whole republic, territory and province and the complete replenishing of the seed funds. Farms failing to complete their deliveries according to a fixed proportion of the total in each harvest month received proportionate monetary fines and were ordered to fulfil their entire annual deliveries ahead of schedule (Arts. 15, 16).

So, as Khrushchev writes in his memoirs,

> We were back to the food requisitioning, only now it was called a tax. Then there was something called 'overfulfilling the quota.' What did that mean? It meant that a Party secretary would go to a collective farm and determine how much grain the collective farmers would need for their own purposes and how much they had to turn over to the State. Often, not even the local Party committee would determine procurements; the State itself would set a quota for a whole district. As a result, all too frequently the peasants would have to turn everything over they produced – literally everything! Naturally, since they received no compensation whatsoever for their work, they lost interest in the collective farm and concentrated instead on their private plots to feed their families.[63]

The system for the obligatory delivery of meat, milk, butter, cheese, wool, etc. was altered in the same way as that for grain by decrees of 23 September and 19 December 1932, and was based on the supposed number of animals on a farm at a given time.

The agricultural decrees of 1932–3 meant that, after surrendering the grain quota to the state, kolkhozes had to 1) pay the Machine Tractor Station for use of machinery; 2) refund seed and other loans to the state; 3) form seed reserves of c.10–15% of the annual seed requirements, for forage funds in correspondence with the yearly requirements of collectivized livestock. Only then could the farm make any distribution to its members.

★

When we reach the level of the collectivized peasant himself, last and lowest of the farm's concerns, the method of paying him was by the 'labour-day'. This did *not* mean so much for a day's work. On the contrary the definition of a 'labour-day' was such that several days in the fields might be needed before the peasant could put one to his credit.

The 'labour-day' idea had been discussed in Communist academic circles in the 1920s. But Stalin's adoption of it seems to have been the first time its use had been considered as serious politics. What it amounted to was a piece-work method of securing the maximum effort from any peasant who did not want to end up empty-handed, and empty-stomached.

The 'labour-day' was formalized by a decree of 17 March 1931. A specific set of model work-norms, giving two 'labour-days' per diem to chairmen of kolkhozes, chief tractor drivers and so on, and half a 'labour-day' per diem to the lowest village group, were laid down on 28 February 1933. In practice the differentiation was greater still. In some kolkhozes, Postyshev was to admit in November 1933, management staff and overheads absorbed 30% of the 'labour-days'.[64]

A typical labour-day for the rank and file, as laid down in the Model Statutes published in February 1935, but evidently understood as a norm for some time previously, was the ploughing of a hectare of land or the threshing of a ton of grain. Several actual days' work might be required to fulfil it. In 1930–31 the 'labour-day' payment was 300 grammes of bread in some places, 100 grammes, or even none at all, elsewhere – starvation rations.[65]

Every week the 'brigadier' gave his calculation of a given peasant's 'labour-day' entitlement, and might make advances of cash or grain in proportion. But, in principle the cash payment was not made until the end of the year, and this was the more usual method in practice. Indeed, official documents mention that about 80% of the collective farmers 'postponed' payment of their members' 'labour-days' for one and a half to two years.[66] Even when this was not so, there was little to give the peasants when they had fulfilled their side of the bargain.

On one Ukrainian kolkhoz, quoted as typical, the peasants were paid for only 150 'labour days', at a rate of 2 pounds of bread and 56 kopeks a 'day'. The total *cash* for the whole year would scarcely buy a single pair of shoes. Per inhabitant the bread worked out as less than half a pound a day. As to private plots and cattle, each plot was taxed 122 roubles, and 64 quarts of milk and 64 pounds of butter were taken from each owner of a cow.[67] And a close observer noted, 'when, after the first collective harvest they received in return for a year's hard work perhaps a pair of sports shoes, instead of the heavy boots they needed, and perhaps a few low-quality cotton goods, they simply stopped working'.[68]

Thus, when one season had produced inadequate pay, the fact of this being a disincentive only declared itself when such things as a contraction in the area sown were reckoned up the following year; in the Ukraine, in spite of ever-increasing pressure, the sown acreage went down by 4–5% in 1931. In fact, the Party was being given a lesson in the old and simple point that excessive taxation destroys the sources of revenue.

When it comes to taxation proper, in the autumn of 1930 yet another impost was laid on the unfortunate population – a 'state loan.' This was entirely non-voluntary, the amounts being laid down at the centre. Indeed, the 111,620 roubles originally demanded of Krynychky District was simply increased to 173,000 roubles in October 'by order of the Council of People's Commissars'.[69] Some villages were condemned as 'scandalously behindhand'. The local authorities were urged to greater effort: 'chairmen of village soviets are responsible personally for collecting money from wealthy farmers, within forty-eight hours, otherwise it will be collected by force'.[70]

★

The collective farm was not, indeed, the only 'socialist' method of agriculture in use. On a far smaller scale, though doctrinally more in accord with Marxist aims, a small proportion of the land had long been operated by State Farms (Sovkhozy). In them, the worker got a wage, just as the idea of 'rural grain factories' implied. And in accordance with the factory principle, the State Farms handled single commodities – wheat, cattle or hogs (as they still do to a large extent).

In 1921 State Farms covered only 3.3 million hectares. Various attempts to make them more important failed, though between 1924 and 1933 area (not production) rose from 1.5 to 10.8% of the whole. By 1932, official decrees were speaking of the 'wastefulness and complete disorganization of the production processes' of State Farms.[71] A representative state farm is described in the official literature:

> The condition of Kamyshinskii grain sovkhoz (Lower Volga) can be considered a typical picture for many sovkhozy. 'Not one apartment had a water tap; there were no baths; in the workshops hands froze to metal; there were no taps or even drinking water. In the central house there was not one bathroom, nor a barn for firewood, nor a storage for food products. The cafeteria is cold, dirty, with always the same food of unsatisfactory quality . . . A number of families still live in underground mud-huts'.[72]

The grain deliveries from the state farms were, in fact, only one third of their plan, and other products worse still. At the Seventeenth Party Congress, 1934, Stalin spoke in a disillusioned fashion of their role; he noted their excessive size, a characteristic they retain to this day.

The state farms had had less tendency to party activism against their peasants. People with suspect pasts flocked to them, and since they needed workers they were reasonably tolerant. However, in 1933–4 OGPU representatives established themselves – getting rid of

100,000 'enemies' by April 1935. In one state farm, out of 577 employees, 49 turned out to be White Guards, 69 kulaks, four former white officers, six sons of otamans and priests. In another the director was the son of a trusted stableman of the Grand Duke Michael, the zoo-technician the son of a kulak, the agronomist an expelled Trotskyite with a kulak background, and a dozen brigade leaders and so on of similar origins.[73]

★

The idea that the tractor, replacing the horse, would transform agriculture into a modernized and prosperous sector of the economy was deeply rooted in the Party's mind.

Some extravagant accounts have been given in Soviet scholarship for the motives of collectivization. One very commonly met with is to the effect that 'successful industrialization of the country prepared the way for the successful launching of collective farms'.[74] It had indeed been generally thought in Party circles that the tractors produced by industrialization would ensure the success of collectivization; the tractor was seen as the technical basis for the modernization of the countryside.

As we have seen, Stalin realized that tractors would not in fact be ready in time for the first phase of collectivization. And he sanguinely repeated his thesis that the collective farms could at first be 'based on peasant farm implements', adding that 'the simple pooling of the peasant implements of production has produced results of which our practical workers never dreamed'.[75] The Commissar of Agriculture even called, in January 1930, for 'a doubling of the productivity of the horse and the plough'.[76]

But this calculation too was based on several misapprehensions, one of which was that the horse and plough would be available over the interim. In fact, the horses of the USSR met the same fate as the cattle. Over the same period, the number of horses went down from thirty-two to seventeen million, or by 47%.[77]

The reasons for the deaths of the horses were not quite the same as for those of the cattle. They were seldom eaten. When fodder gave out, the peasants often had pity on them and turned them loose instead, so that 'herds of starving horses ran wild throughout the Ukraine'.[78] Or they sold them. This was easier than with cattle, because party agencies were at first still under the delusion that the collective farm system would not need horses. *Pravda* complained that it was planned to slaughter 150,000 of them in Byelorussia alone for the use of a hide syndicate and the dairy-livestock cooperatives for their hides and meat, though 30% of those thus slaughtered were said to be fit for work.[79]

And apart from all this, they died off in the collective farms. When the peasants left the collective farms in March 1930, the horses were not returned to them. And in the collective, they were ill-cared for. A typical story is of one peasant showing an American traveller 'one of the worst kept and fed' horses the latter had ever seen, and telling him that this had been his own horse, well fed and cared for.[80]

An official who accompanied a Provincial Secretary of the Komsomol on a visit to kolkhozes, notes that in each of them from two to seven horses were dying nightly.[81] Moreover, by winter there was nothing to feed them on. (In some areas one of the typical quick fix schemes so often found in the Soviet Union was seen when it was discovered that in the current shortage of oats and grass, pine twigs were supposedly full of nourishment, and in some places these were collected and put in silos to produce an ensilage which the horses could not eat.)[82] Dead horses were seen all over the place, and a live one could now be bought for one and a half roubles.

The only backhanded benefit from the horses' death was that they no longer needed to be fed. The *entire* increase in marketed grain between 1928 and 1933, (even given the two good harvests of 1930 and 1931), amounts to the fodder no longer needed by no longer existing livestock.

A great effort was indeed put into the attempt to provide instead an adequate supply of tractors. By 1931 the production of farm machinery consumed 53.9% of the entire Soviet output of quality rolled steel. But for the time being there were simply not enough to begin to make up for the loss of horses, let alone bring on a new era. By the end of 1930, 88.5% of collective farms had no tractors of their own, while Machine Tractor Stations as yet served only 13.6% of all collective farms.[83]

To this shortage was added the even greater handicaps that the skills for tractor maintenance were inadequate, and that incentives to maintain public property in this as in other matters were not compelling – problems to this day, when the Soviet tractor parks have to be almost totally replaced every five years (in Britain, a small farm uses a tractor for an average of ten years, when it is still in condition for a profitable trade-in). It can well be imagined, then, that in the early 30s (in part because of the inefficiency of the cadre of engineers) the average Soviet-produced tractor had 'a very short life'.[84] One American, noting that identical tractors lasted less than a third of the time they did in the USA before needing an overhaul, blamed it on the inferior oil used.[85] Moreover, machinery could not be properly serviced. Another foreign observer saw 'an abandoned John Deere Combine of late model. It was rusted and out of order. A few more rains and it would probably be beyond repair'.[86] There are many similar stories.

★

And here we should describe the nature and significance of the Machine Tractor Station system, which was, with the collective farms and the State Farms, the third great element of socialization in the countryside. As the name implies, the main, or original, aim of these stations was the provision of tractors to the farms, though they also soon became agents of political control over the peasantry.

These 'stations' were centralized parks of the bulk of the country's farm machinery – though some tractors were in the hands of individual collective farms and the MTS did not establish total monopoly until 1934.

There had been some MTS-style tractor parks as early as 1928, when there was one in the Odessa Province, but they were set up on a major scale by a governmental decree of 5 June 1929. They began functioning in earnest in February 1930, though many had been formed in the interim – for example, eight in the Dnipropetrovsk Province.[87] In all, almost 2,500 MTS were established between 1929 and 1932. They were on a big scale – in fact often too big for efficiency. For example, one in the Kharkov Province with 68 tractors served 61 kolkhozes, some of them up to 40 kilometres away. In September 1933, 7,300 hours were wasted driving the tractors to work.[88]

The MTS' difficulties may be illustrated by two closely parallel accounts, one by an emigré, and one by a senior Soviet official of good standing.

The former tells of how, in February 1933 the whole administrative staff of the Machine Tractor Station in Polyvyanka was arrested, and tried for sabotage, in that the tractor and farm machinery were not in shape and the oxen and horses also in poor condition. The reason for the latter is obvious. For the former, there was no way to keep the machines in good shape. There were no spare parts available, and the forges were unable to obtain fuel, iron or even wood.[89]

The second, official, account does not mention sanctions inflicted, but adequately tells of the troubles of the Krasnovershk MTS in the Odessa Province. In 1933 it should have carried out medium repairs on twenty-five tractors and twenty-five threshing machines. But it had only three workers and a smith's forge and anvil borrowed from a neighbouring kolkhoz, besides having no spare parts at all.[90]

But the MTS was not merely technical, but also above all a method of politico-social control. It was seen as a node of proletarian consciousness,

181

headed by party officials and staffed by workers, and was given considerable powers over the kolkhozes it served. In June 1931 it was even laid down that the MTS should not only organize the work on the farms, but also deliver those farms' produce to the government. Indeed, this latter was called as the 'first, principal, basic problem' before the MTS.

MTS power in the villages was further strengthened and formalized by a decree of 11 January 1933 which established 'political departments' in the MTS (and less importantly in the State Farms).

OGPU personnel were appointed deputy chiefs of the political departments, subordinate to the chief *except* in their 'agent-operative work'.[91] The 'political department' of the MTS henceforth became a decisive power factor in the countryside, often overriding the official authorities, but also complicating and confusing the already unwieldy bureaucratic structure.

★

By the end of 1934 nine-tenths of the sown acreage of the USSR was concentrated in 240,000 collective farms which had replaced the twenty million odd family farms existing in 1929. The 'model statutes' of collective farms, revised and adopted in February 1935, show the main features of the new system:

(a) The kolkhoz undertook 'to conduct its collective economy according to the plan, adhering strictly to the plans for agricultural production established by the organs of the worker-peasant government and to its obligations to the State' (Art. 6);

(b) As the first charge on its production, it undertook 'to fulfil its obligations to the state for deliveries and for returning seed-loans, and paying the MTS in kind . . .' (Art. 11a); and, as the last priority, after fulfilling other obligations, such as building up seed-and fodder-reserves, 'it distributes all the remainder of the harvest and of the livestock products between the kolkhoz members . . .' (Art. 11d);

(c) Each peasant household was permitted to retain a small plot of land for its own use, limited to between a quarter and a half a hectare (0.62 to 1.24 acres) and exceptionally, in some areas, one hectare (2.47 acres) and a small amount of private livestock, the standard allowance being: one cow, up to two head of young cattle, one sow with offspring, up to ten sheep and/or goats, unlimited poultry and rabbits, up to 20 beehives (Arts. 2, 5);

(d) The distribution of the kolkhoz's income among members 'is carried out exclusively according to the number of labour-days worked by each member' (Art. 15);

(e) The 'highest organ' of the kolkhoz was declared to be the general meeting of its members, which elected the chairman and a board of five to nine members to run its affairs in the intervals between general meetings (Arts. 20, 21);

(f) The kolkhoz undertook to consider theft of kolkhoz property and a 'wrecking attitude' as 'treachery to the common cause of the kolkhoz and aid to the enemies of the people', and to hand over those 'guilty of such criminal undermining of the bases of the kolkhoz system' to the courts, 'for the infliction of punishment according to the full severity of the laws of the worker– peasant government' (Art. 18).

This confirms the real logic of the collective farm as that the peasant continued to perform the labour of agricultural production, but no longer had even temporary control of his output. It might be true that this led to a shrinkage in the crop. But this was more than made up for in Stalinist eyes by the establishment of State control over it. Moreover, any shortfall could be, at least to some degree, made up for by reduction in the share allotted to the peasant.

From now on we get Stalin himself, and his colleagues, warning against any 'idealization' of the kolkhoz and the kolkhoznik. Sheboldayev said bluntly that the kolkhozniks 'have too little goodwill towards the interests of the state'; and Kaganovich declared that not collectivization but procurement was 'the touchstone on which our strength and weakness and the strength and weakness of the enemy were tested'.[92] The 'enemy', in fact, was now to be found in the kolkhozes, and it was there, among the former poor and middle peasantry, that 'kulak' sabotage was to be fought.

Collectivization did not solve the peasant's problems, even apart from his loss of land. The collective farms were essentially a chosen mechanism for extracting grain and other products. In principle the entire kolkhoz output of cotton, sugar beet, and so on; most of their wool, hides and skins; and above all a high proportion of their grain, went to the State.[93]

One modern Soviet literary critic, granting the supposed economic advantages of collectivization and mechanization, nevertheless adds: 'but to some extent they weakened the feelings of deep bonds with the soil; they weakened the responsibility of the man who is master of his own land for his daily work on the land'.[94]

An activist who was sent to the large Ukrainian steppe village of Arkhanhelka, (pop. c. 2,000), in 1930 found eight men working on the harvest. The remainder did nothing, and when he said that the grain would perish they agreed with him. He comments 'I cannot believe that the loss of bread grains was of no consequence to the peasants. Their feelings must have been terribly strong for them to go to the extreme of leaving the grain in the fields . . . I am convinced that no one directed their action'. He managed to effect some improvement, though never feeling that he had converted anyone.[95]

But this sort of thing counted as sabotage, as did any attempt to divert the grain to the peasants' own use. The decree of 7 August 1932 'On the safeguarding of state property' (drafted by Stalin himself), laid down that all collective farm property, such as cattle, standing crops and agricultural produce should be so defined.[96] Offenders against such property were to be considered enemies of the people, and either be shot or, in extenuating circumstances, imprisoned for not less than ten years, with total confiscation of property. Official interpretations of the decree later included in it persons who falsified kolkhoz accounts, sabotaged agricultural work, 'wrecked' crops, and so on.

During 1932, 20% of *all* sentences in the USSR were under this decree, described by Stalin as 'the basis of revolutionary legality at the present moment'.[97] In Western Siberia alone, in a single month (October 1932) 2,000 households were charged with sabotage.[98]

It was not only the peasant who was blamed. A Central Committee resolution of 11 January 1933 runs:

Anti-Soviet elements, penetrating the kolkhozes in the capacity of accountants, managers, storekeepers, brigadiers and so on, and often in the capacity of leading officials of kolkhoz boards, are trying to organize wrecking, putting machines out of order, sowing badly, squandering kolkhoz property, undermining labour discipline, organizing the theft of seeds, secret granaries and the sabotage of the grain harvest; and sometimes they succeed in breaking the kolkhozes up.

The resolution demanded the expulsion of these 'anti-Soviet elements' from collective and State farms. It entrusted this task to the 'political departments' in Machine Tractor Stations and State farms – in particular to their deputy heads, the OGPU officials. In twenty-four Republics, territories and provinces, in 1933, 30% of the agronomists, 34% of the warehousemen, and similar proportions in other agrarian jobs were charged with wrecking.[99]

At a higher level yet, the planners and bureaucrats were made scapegoats. The better agricultural specialists were, in the nature of things, men who had had long training and experience, and so dated from before the revolution, few of them being Bolsheviks; as we have noted Chayanov was the best known among this group of senior scholars. A more ideological group, calling themselves Agrarian–Marxists, had as their main figure L.N. Kritsman. For some years the two schools had pursued somewhat different studies, without any great acrimony arising.

The 'Cultural Revolution' had naturally resulted in the dismissal of Chayanov and his followers in 1929; and Kritsman's group, which had taken too gradualist a view of peasant evolution, followed them in 1932, by

184

which time the agricultural academies were dominated by ill-educated intruders satisfactory to the Party for their Marxist orthodoxy but virtually illiterate in agricultural matters.

'Kulaks' and 'kulak-sympathizers' had, needless to say, infiltrated the People's Commissariat of Agriculture, Gosplan, agricultural research centres, the Agricultural Bank, the timber industry and so on. Twenty-one such were arrested by the GPU in the Ukraine in March 1930.[100]

On 22 September 1930, forty-eight members of the People's Commissariat of Trade, including the deputy chairman of the scientific and technical council for the food and agricultural industry, were indicted for sabotaging food supplies and *Pravda* printed two pages of their confessions. They were charged with being 'organizers of famine and agents of imperialism' – imperialism in this case being represented by a British cold storage firm which had plotted to disorganize refrigeration in Russia with a view to getting a contract. Three days later they were all shot.

On 3 September 1930, it was announced that nine prominent economists, including Groman, Chayanov, and other leading figures such as Makarov and Kondratiev, were under arrest as counter-revolutionary conspirators. All disappeared, though some were again given public mention as victims of a faked trial, the 'Menshevik Case' of 1931 in which Groman was the chief accused. They confessed to sabotage, and to working for foreign intervention: (we chance to have a good deal of evidence of how their 'confessions' were extracted). The economic side of the accusations against them were absurd:

> It was alleged that the defendants, several of whom had played an important part in preparing the Five-Year Plan, had tried to establish production targets far lower than the country's capability. In fact, the official Soviet figures prove that the accused planners had shown great prescience in forecasting the actual extent of fulfilment of the Plan. In almost every case they had actually tended to err slightly on the optimistic side. In steel, for example, they were accused of having criminally proposed the production in 1932 of 5.8 million tons. The Plan fixed the figure of 10.3 million; the defendants themselves confessed in court that 'much higher figures could and should have been fixed'. Actual production was 5.9 million tons. For pig-iron, they had envisaged a mere 7 million tons; the Plan demanded 17 million tons. Actual production in 1932 equalled 6.1 million tons.[101]

Kondratiev, former Minister of Food, appeared as a 'witness' in the Menshevik Trial. He was himself then indicted as leader of an alleged 'Toiling Peasant Party' which was supposed to include nine underground groups in Moscow, sabotaging agricultural cooperatives and credit unions, the Commissariats of Agriculture and Finance, the agrarian press, the research institutes in agrarian economics, the Timiryazev Agricultural Academy; and which had numerous groups in similar institutions in the countryside, with a membership of between 100,000 and 200,000.[102]

Such trials effectively silenced opponents, and made it clear that disagreement, or even failure to fulfil impossible plans, was a capital crime.

★

In some ways Stalin's tactics in the matter of the presentation of his actions were well suited to his purpose. He never spoke of an attack on the peasantry, but only the kulak, the class enemy. When the atrocities his policies made inevitable were being perpetrated in the villages, he would occasionally attack and punish a few officials in specific publicized instances. And the world of propaganda in which the Party, though also much of the urban population, moved, enabled loyalists to think that excesses were local merely, and the gross failure due to sabotage.

At the same time, the true situation in agriculture was carefully blurred. Ludicrous predictions of the expected increase in agricultural production had long heartened activists, and pleased foreign dupes. Butter consumption would soon overtake that of Denmark, because milch cows would increase in number by two to two and a half times, and their yield by three to four times.[103] (In fact, butter production in East Siberia, for which we chance to have figures, went down from 35,964 tons in 1928 to 20,901 tons in 1932).[104] Indeed, it was even officially predicted in 1929 that by 1932 grain yields would have risen by as much as 50%, and that a future 25% increase in marketable grain should be expected as the result of the introduction of tractors.[105]

It was clear that such results had not been attained, though the blame might be allocated to saboteurs, kulaks and incompetent junior officials. But the extent of the shortfall was not yet evident. One of the difficulties of estimating such things was that the monopolistic Soviet statistical methods gradually lost their connections with the facts.

First of all, a new way of estimating the grain crop – the 'biological yield' was introduced, estimating the crop as it stood in the fields rather than actually counting it in the farms. In 1953 Khrushchev revealed that it had produced an exaggeration of over 40%. The chief immediate advantage of the 'biological yield' method was that the 'crop' could be decreed in advance, by applying the maximum theoretical yield to the maximum utilizable area, while ignoring harvesting losses, moisture, etc. The share of the state and its agencies could then be made on that basis, leaving a minimal, or non-existent, residue to the peasant. There was even a decree to forbid collecting data on the quantity of grain actually threshed 'as distorting the picture of the actual condition of the crop.'[106]

The publication of price indexes ceased in April 1930. No price data appear in the latest statistical yearbook of the period, *Socialist Construction U.S.S.R. 1933–35*. And *Socialist Construction U.S.S.R. 1936* does not even contain the word 'prices' in its index, and not in any comprehensible form elsewhere. The publication of birth and death statistics ceased even earlier.[107]

What, in fact, had been achieved?

Not a superior agriculture. Not a contented peasantry. On the contrary, agricultural production had been drastically reduced, and the peasants driven off by the million to death and exile, with those who stayed reduced, in their own view, to serfs. But the State now controlled the grain production, however reduced in quantity. And collective farming had prevailed.

It is not to our purpose to consider whether Stalin was a better Marxist or Leninist than his rivals, a matter on which various views are arguable. But it may seem, indeed, that the Rightist notion of gradual collectivization by example was a chimera. Given anything like free competition between the private and public sectors in agriculture, the private sector would always have been more attractive to its traditional inheritors. The notion of setting up a limited number of collective farms to attract the individual peasant by their superiority could not have worked; wherever they had existed they had, with all advantages given them by the regime, done worse than the individual farm. Even in the future, with the advantages of unilateral modernization, the collective farms never flourished. In September 1953 and February 1954 Khrushchev reported officially to Central Committee plenums that mechanized Soviet agriculture was producing less grain *per capita* and fewer cattle absolutely than had been achieved by the muzhik with his wooden plough under Tsarism forty years earlier.

Not was it merely a matter of economics. A whole way of life had been destroyed and replaced by one felt to be vastly inferior. It is true that on a strictly Party view, Stalin may be thought right. The peasant would not join the collectives willingly. If collectives were needed, he must be forced into them. And as to the timing, since no amount of waiting would persuade him, it might as well be done straight away.

At any rate, Stalin's decisions were fully in accord with the Marxist–Leninist thesis that the individual peasantry was a class which a 'proletarian' regime intent on 'socialism' must defeat and subdue. His particular strategic attitude now dominated the party, and the considerations dealt with above were decisive in determining the Party views.

But there are other views possible besides those of the Party.

★

9

Central Asia and the Kazakh Tragedy

The old government, the landlords
and capitalists, have left us a
heritage of such browbeaten peoples
... these peoples were doomed to
incredible suffering

Stalin

Soviet Central Asia, the present republics of Uzbekistan, Turkmenistan, Tadzhikistan, Kirgizia and Kazakhstan, represent Islamic lands conquered by Tsarist armies in the 18th and 19th centuries, and reconquered from indigenous revolutionary and other governments by the Bolsheviks in the 20th century. There the collectivization campaign was, in a general sense, conducted in much the same way as in the European Soviet Union. But there were certain special characteristics.

In Uzbekistan, the declared policy was 'liquidation' of the kulaks in the cotton-growing areas, but only their 'limitation' in the cattle-rearing zones.[1] In 1930–33, a modern Soviet work tells us, 40,000 households were dekulakized – 5% of the total.[2] Similarly in Turkmenistan (on official figures) 2,211 kulak families were deported in 1930–31 alone;[3] In Kazakhstan 40,000 households were dekulakized, with a further 15,000 or more 'self-dekulakized' i.e. escaping;[4] and we can estimate the total dekulakization of the whole region as involving over half a million souls. Resistance was intense.

A recent Soviet study notes that 1929–31 saw a resurgence of the nationalist rebel movement, the Basmachi. Collective farms were one of their main targets. Bands of up to 500 came from Afghanistan into Tadzhikistan, picking up recruits on the way. In Turkmenistan too, 'the Basmachi movement, which had almost been liquidated in the preceding years, intensified again: a tense political situation developed in the

Republic'.[5] The rebels 'included not only obviously counter-revolutionary elements, but also a certain part of the toiling population',[6] and their political aims are described as anti-Soviet and anti-collectivization.[7]

In Uzbekistan even in 1931–2 the Uzbek Party Secretary Ikramov was reporting bands numbering 350; 164 cases of attempts to organize mass uprisings, with 13,000 people involved; 77,000 'anti-kolkhoz incidents'. One rebellion in the Syr Darya area lasted three weeks.[8] Bauman, Moscow's viceroy for the whole area (an attempt on whose life, with injuries to his wife, is reported) stated to the September 1934 plenum of the Uzbek CC that in 1931 risings had also taken place on the Turkmen steppe, in the Kirgiz cattle region, in Tadzhikistan.

As elsewhere, resistance also took the form of the slaughter of livestock. Bauman revealed at the September 1934 Uzbek plenum that in Central Asia (outside Kazakhstan) the number of horses decreased by a third, of cattle by a half, of sheep and goats by two-thirds.

In Kirgizia resistance took the form of 'mass destruction of cattle' but also of 'migration abroad . . .'; part of the frontier population 'migrated to China, driving with them 30,000 sheep and 15,000 head of cattle'.[9]

But all this, bad enough in all conscience, pales before the immense human tragedy of the Kazakhs.

The 1926 census showed 3,963,300 Kazakhs in the Soviet Union; the 1939 census (itself inflated) showed 3,100,900. Allowing for natural growth, the estimated population deficit from famine and general repression was about one and a half million out of a population of, by 1930, well over four million; and actual death (omitting the unborn and those escaping to China) must have been at least a million. In fact, more recently available figures imply that the loss was even larger. The number of Kazakh households declined from 1,233,000 in 1929 to 565,000 in 1936.[10] These terrible figures were matched by, indeed were caused by, a catastrophic decline in the livestock population. The number of cattle, which had been 7,442,000 in 1929, had shrunk to 1,600,000 in 1933; of sheep from 21,943,000 to 1,727,000.[11]

The causes, and the circumstances of this enormous human and economic disaster, impossible to match in the annals of any other colonial power, may seem to merit more attention than they have yet received among Western students of such matters.

★

Kazakhstan, conquered by the Russians in the 18th and 19th centuries, had at the time of the revolution set up its own government under the national Alash Orda party, but had succumbed to the Red Army. However, there was so little basis for a Communist movement in the area that many Alash Orda veterans had been taken into the new administration.

As the most northerly of the Central Asian peoples annexed to Russia in late Tsarist times, the Kazakhs' territory lay close to, and even athwart, the line of Russian colonization of Siberia and the Far East. Roughly speaking the northern part of the country, with many Russian settlers – over a million families between 1896 and 1916 – had developed a settled agriculture; the southern still consisted of steppe where the majority of Kazakhs pastured their flocks and herds.

The nature of the Kazakh economy presented the Bolsheviks with a special problem. In 1926 just under a quarter of the Kazakh population were engaged solely in agriculture; 38.5% depended on livestock alone; 33.2% on livestock and agriculture. Less than 10% were wholly nomadic, but two-thirds of the population were 'semi-nomadic', migrating with their herds in summer.[12]

The regime now undertook to turn a nomadic culture with centuries-old roots into a settled (and collectivized) agricultural society in a few years, against the deep-seated wishes of the population.

These matters had been debated several years earlier. Virtually all the country's experts had held the Kazakhs to be totally unready for collectivization in any sense. Most agronomists, pointing out that the Kazakh livestock economy was regulated by clan authority, agreed that the destruction of that authority would be economically dangerous. Experts on the region pointed out that grain growing was not suited to the area then used for animal husbandry.

And though a post-Stalin Soviet work[13] which concluded that the Kazakhs were not ready for collectivization at all has been much criticized in the USSR, most Soviet research today at least concedes that they were not ready for mass, or crash, or forced collectivization.

Settlement of the nomads was the crux. It had long been Party doctrine, seen as necessary in order to 'eradicate the economic and cultural anachronisms of the nationalities'. Or, more concretely, 'Settlement is the liquidation of the *bai* semi-feudalist. Settlement is the destruction of tribal attitudes . . .'[14]

A 'plan' for settling the nomads was included in the revised Five Year Plan, and a special Committee on Settlement set up in Alma Ata.

From an economic point of view the Kazakh territory appeared as a potential food-producing reserve for the whole of Soviet Siberia and the Far East. And the denomadization was intended to result in a vast grain production in Southern Kazakhstan.

191

One result of the November 1929 Central Committee plenum was a decision to confiscate the nomadic lands of Kazakhstan and build a number of giant grain farms. By 1932 these were to supply 1.6 million tons of grain.[15] This was economic nonsense. The territory was not suitable to grain production. Even today the gross value of livestock output is four times that of agriculture.[16]

★

Even under NEP, Kazakh society, still under its old leaders and arrangements, had irked the Soviet leadership. A campaign for the 'sovietization of the Kazakh *aul* ' (migrating village) in 1925–8 failed because the village Soviets which were formed fell without fuss into the hands of the traditional local leaders. Both clan organization and Muslim loyalties were highly resistant to Party penetration. Trotsky noted that Goloshchekin, the leading party official in Kazakhstan, 'preaches civil peace in the Russian village and civil war in the *aul*'. At the Fifteenth Congress in 1927 Molotov claimed that the 'feudal' clan chiefs or *bais* had 'massively deprived the state of bread'.

In January 1929 there were only 16,551 Kazakh Communists; and by 1931 there were 17,500 Communists, Russian and Kazakh, in the whole of rural Kazakhstan, only a quarter of these in predominantly Kazakh areas.[17]

A decree of 27 August 1928, made on the 'suggestion' of the All Union Central Committee, ordered the confiscation of landed property 'from those largest cattle raisers among the native population whose influence prevents sovietization of the *aul*', and the deportation of '*bai* and semi-feudal' families – though at this point only 696 of them – and the confiscation of their half million head of cattle.[18] But even this had little effect on Kazakh society. When it came to full dekulakization in 1930 55,000–60,000 households were labelled '*bai*'; 40,000 were 'dekulakized' and the remainder moved away and left their property.

★

A Kazakh Communist Party Central Committee plenum met on 11–16 December 1929, to pledge the carrying out of the Moscow plenum's decision of the previous month, and it added to the general line on collectivization the proviso that the 'settlement' of the nomads was a necessary prerequisite, (though it was not until 6 September 1930 that a formal decree was issued ordering the permanent settlement of all the nomads of the RSFSR). The Kazakh Central Committee now decided to begin planning for the settlement of the nomads, and in January 1930 the Kazakh Central Executive Committee decided that out of 566,000 nomadic and semi-nomadic households 544,000 should be settled by the end of the First Five Year Plan.[19]

In the case of the settlement of nomads, the Party did not even keep up the pretence that the population's voluntary assent was required or forthcoming, as it continued (and continues) to do in the case of collectivization. The Kazakhstan Communist authorities ruled that it was wrong to collectivize forcibly, but correct to settle forcibly.[20] And, of course, collectivization itself was put through as best it might regardless of any genuine voluntary principle. In the decree of 5 January 1930 the livestock areas of Kazakhstan were included in the category of regions which were to be completely collectivized by the end of 1933. As to the livestock itself, there seems to have been no clear policy on their collectivization. In some kolkhozes they were confiscated, and then returned: it was common for a confiscation order to be made, when the Kazakh would slaughter his livestock rather than give them up, only to have the authorities apologize and rescind the order.[21]

By 10 March 1930 56.6% of the population of the Republic was collectivized, though in the nomadic areas this was down to 20% or less. But Stalin's call for a relaxation of pressure on 2 March 1930 was not acted on in many areas until late April or early May.[22]

It is clear from all Soviet accounts that the collectives set up in the spring of 1930 were in chaotic state. There were few houses, sheds, agricultural implements; worse still, little arable land was made available, and many settlements were set up in desert and semi-desert locations without adequate water supplies, so that even livestock could not be maintained. Moreover, no fodder was provided, while 'driving the herds to the pasture was forbidden'.[23] Some kolkhozes had *no* seed, livestock or other capital at all. The Plan only called for the construction of 1,915 residences and seventy barns: but even of this, only 15% of the residences and 32% of the barns were actually completed! For the 320,000 settled in 1930–1932, 24,106 houses were provided, and 108 baths.[24]

Moreover, the normal kolkhozes now set up consisted of ten to twenty *auls* of ten to fifteen families each, settled several kilometres apart, and might have a territory of 200 square kilometres.[25] As to organization, some regions averaged one bookkeeper for twelve kolkhozes, one technical expert for fifty. In June 1930 there were only 416 agronomists and agricultural experts in the whole republic – four of them Kazakh.[26] Most kolkhozes in fact lacked any plan at all, and functioned at a subsistence level, if that.

One Soviet study[27] gives, though most others omit, evidence of the widespread resistance put up by the Kazakhs. Party activists met with armed opposition and many were killed: (in any case, of the 1,200 25-thousanders sent to the republic in the spring of 1930, fewer than 400 were deployed in the livestock-breeding regions).[28] Roving bands of Kazakhs attacked kolkhozes, and took away or killed the livestock. Groups of *auls* formed concerted plans against the authorities. Couriers were sent to warn Kazakhs against entering kolkhozes. Basmachi guerilla bands grew in numbers, battling against the OGPU troops. Many fled to other republics, or to China. Of 44,000 families who moved to Turkmenistan many joined the rebel bands of Basmachi.[29]

The Kazakh nationalist Alash Orda were naturally blamed for the toughness of the Kazakh response to crash collectivization. A 'plot' involving major nationalist figures was announced early in 1930, and the 'centres of resistance' it had formed were allegedly detected in all *auls* which had shown strong resistance.

The official view still taken about this national resistance is well illustrated by an article, over fifty years later, in which the early career of the late Konstantin Chernenko in the armed struggle against them by the OGPU frontier troops of the 'Eastern Border District' of Kazakhstan and Kirgizia in 1930–33 was warmly praised (and perhaps thought relevant to the similar struggle against Muslim guerillas in Afghanistan). The Basmachi are described as 'defeated' by 1933, with small bands still operating in 1936.[30]

As elsewhere, resistance included the slaughter of the livestock. In many areas 50% of the herd was destroyed in the first weeks of collectivization. One Soviet source speaks of a loss of 2.3 million beef cattle and ten million sheep in 1930; another says that 35% of the herd died in 1929–30.[31]

Much of the surviving collectivized livestock was taken to large state farms, but inadequate shelter was provided for the cattle and, on one account, of the 117,000 in the Gigant State Farm only 13,000 survived the winter.[32]

The economic, if not the human, disaster, was ill-received in Moscow, and local officials were purged on a big scale – by mid-1930 in two provinces alone five district committees were dissolved and a hundred officials arrested.[33] By the end of 1932 most of the Republican leadership had itself been purged.

In the early days the nomads were often forced into artel-type kolkhozes, but at the Sixteenth Party Congress in June–July 1930 it was belatedly decided that the more liberal TOZ was the correct form for the semi-nomadic areas.[34] 52.1% of the rural population were collectivized by 1 April 1930. It went down to 29.1% on 1 August, but was up to 60.8 on

1 September 1931,[35] in the usual pattern.

In June 1930 the local leadership decided to return farm implements and livestock to private hands in the nomadic and semi-nomadic areas; but in November 1930 they recollectivized the farm implements and in June 1931, the livestock too – upon which a new wave of slaughtering the cattle and sheep began.[36]

In the winter of 1931 it was admitted that the grandiose grain schemes of 1928 had failed. Only a quarter of the planned acreage was in use, and that most inefficiently.[37] Official documents speak of shortages of livestock, seed, implements, construction materials. People were shifted from one kolkhoz to another in the (usually vain) hope that more livestock or grain might be available. By February 1932 about 87% of all kolkhozes in Kazakhstan and 51.5% of non-collectivized households (the latter almost entirely nomad herders) were without livestock. In 1926 nearly 80% of the Kazakh population had earned their living through livestock; by the summer of 1930 this was down to 27.4%. But agriculture did not provide an alternative, for the area under cultivation only increased by 17%.[38] These figures give some idea of the extent and depth of this man-made disaster.

Kazakhs had of course taken their cattle back from the kolkhozes to the degree that this was permitted in mid-1930, and when the new collectivization drive started in 1931, they pastured them in distant ravines and woods. In the winter they had to slaughter them, and froze the meat and hid it, getting ample food until the thaws came. But by the spring of 1932, famine was raging.[39] This was only very slightly alleviated by a further limited restoration of private livestock late in 1932 – affecting 123,600 cattle and 211,400 sheep and goats:[40] small figures compared with the vast herds and flocks which had existed before 1930.

★

In the *auls*, the meat-and-milk consuming population now had nothing. Many surrendered and entered the collective and state farms. Even there, things were desperate. In one state farm 'the only meat they had had in six months was camel's udder'.[41]

The other alternative was attempted by some: migration elsewhere. Either way, the death toll was enormous. There was 'an enormous destruction of productive forces and the death of many people in the *auls*',[42] as a Soviet historian noted in the Khrushchev interlude.

The disaster was due to economic and political miscalculation in the narrow sense but even more profoundly to a misunderstanding of human cultures in the widest meaning of that term. The mechanical and

195

superficial nature of the Party's thought and practice shown in Kazakhstan is extraordinary, and extraordinarily revealing. (It is not surprising that Islam, as an official source tells us, became stronger than ever in southern Kazakhstan in these years).[43]

The famine in Kazakhstan was man-made, like the famine of 1921, in that it was the result of ideologically motivated policies recklessly applied. It was not, like the Ukrainian famine, deliberately inflicted for its own sake. Indeed in late 1932 two million pounds of grain were ear-marked for aid to Kazakhstan[44] – less than half a pound a person, but better than what the Ukraine was to get.

Nevertheless it has been suggested that the effectiveness of the unplanned Kazakh famine in destroying local resistance was a useful model for Stalin when it came to the Ukraine.

★

The situation was officially described by the local Party and Government in a report to the Central Committee on 19 November 1934 (though *not* published at the time) in terms of 'the famine that had assumed large proportions in the cattle-breeding districts in 1932 and early 1933 has been liquidated'; it added that migration abroad and the 'vagabondage of Kazakh cattle-raisers' had also stopped.[45]

As to the vagabondage, only 30% of the half million people who had been 'settled' in 1930–32 were regarded as fully settled, with land, barns and tools. Indeed, nearly 25% of those settled in 1930–32 had resumed migration, though without livestock, by the end of the latter year.[46] These movements were due to desperation and the effective breakdown or destruction of society and the economy. The new propertyless nomads still accounted for 22% of the Kazakh population in late 1933.[47] It is estimated that 15–20% of the Kazakh population left the Republic in 1930–31 – 300,000 to Uzbekistan, and others to areas elsewhere in Soviet Central Asia or to China. Official sources speak of the emigration as 'massive'.[48] Those remaining in Soviet Asia met the same fate as those who stayed home; and many in fact returned in despair.[49]

At the Seventeenth Party Conference in February 1934, the troubles of Kazakh collectivization were largely blamed on the failure actually to settle the nomads. But, by one means or another, a total of 400,000 households were 'settled' by 1936 (though only 38,000 new residences had been constructed for them!)[50]

This victory was accompanied by a withdrawal of the concession whereby the TOZes were the local form of collective and, they were converted into the usual cartel in 1935. By 1938 collectivization in its

Stalin (c. 1934)
Credit: John Hillelson Agency Ltd

Molotov, Stalin and Kaganovich, 1 May 1932
Credit: Popperfoto

The White Sea Canal under construction, with 'kulak' labour

Peasants handing in their applications to join a collective farm

Grain requisitioned in the Odessa area

Horses dying

Demolition of the Seminova
Monastery, 1930
Credit: Popperfoto

Near Kharkov: the child is the boy described on p 286

Famine victims

The 'homeless ones'

STARVATION OF PEASANT

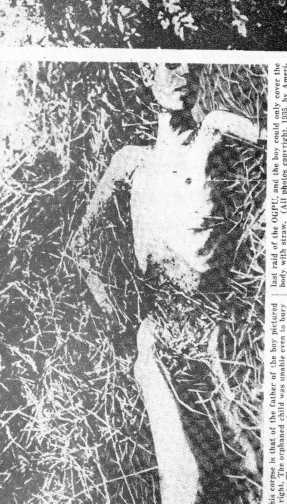

his corpse is that of the father of the boy pictured
right. The orphaned child was unable even to bury
arent. There were no shovels in the village since the

last raid of the OGPU, and the boy could only cover the
body with straw. (All photos copyright, 1935, by American Newspapers, Inc.)

llages Depopulated by Hunger in Ukraine
as Soviet Punish Their Opponents

Photograph of a victim in the Western Press (Chicago American, March 6 1935) orthodox form was complete.

*

Famine due to 'resettlement' of nomads also took a great toll in Kirgizia (where there were 82,000 nomad households out of 167,000: 44,000 households were settled, and 7,895 houses built for them with three baths);[51] and among the Tatar and Bashkir minorities in Western Siberia. A leading Party official in Chelyabinsk[52] told a foreign Communist that 'the famine has been of great benefit to us in the Urals, in Western Siberia and in the Trans-Volga. In these regions the losses from starvation have mostly affected the alien races. Their place is being taken by Russian refugees from the central provinces. We are, of course, not nationalists, but we cannot overlook this advantageous fact'. (That Stalin held the same view, not only in these areas but even more strongly vis-à-vis the Ukrainians, was to be demonstrated over the following year). The mortality of these Muslim and Asian peoples, such as the Bashkirs, the Chelyabinsk official attributed in large part to their failure to transfer from a nomad to a settled existence as the plan required.

Khrushchev tells us in his memoirs that he went to Samara in 1930 to a largely Chuvash collective farm and found them starving.[53] Further east at least fifty thousand Buryats and Khalkas fled to China and Mongolia.[54] In Kalmykia, with a similar economy, some 20,000 people – about 10% of the population – are estimated as dying – the nomad Kalmyks only increased by 1% between 1926 and 1939 (even on the dubious figures of the latter year's 'census'). A leading Kalmyk Communist, Arash Chapchaev, protested at a local Congress of Soviets in April 1933 that formerly prosperous villages had become derelict, with starving inhabitants. He called for the dissolution of the kolkhozes;[55] and soon disappeared. Kalmyk 'kulaks' are reported in large numbers in, for example, Severny prison camp in the Urals in the early 1930s, but by midsummer 1933 most had died.[56] Deported ex-nomads who had given little trouble were sent to work in the mines or forests. They did not thrive on their new meatless diet, and had even more difficulty than Russian peasants in mastering drills and other equipment.[57]

In Mongolia, technically beyond the Soviet borders, and not a Socialist but a 'People's' republic, though in fact under Moscow control, collectivization was also introduced. By early 1932, the Mongols had lost eight million head of livestock, a third of their total herds. In May 1932, they were instructed to reverse course and abandon collectivization.[58]

While dealing with Soviet Asian territories we may register the remarkable story of the Cossacks who had long been established behind the Amur and Ussuri frontiers, just as earlier on the Kuban and Don. In 1932 a Party official found their villages recently abandoned, in what was evidently a hurried departure, with some livestock and household goods left behind. It was explained that the entire population had crossed the frozen rivers *en masse* with most of their possessions to avoid dekulakization and imminent famine. Over the border were settlements of Cossacks who had fled earlier, and whose condition appeared far more attractive, so they went to join them.[59]

The fate of the Soviet Asian population under the collectivization and dekulakization policies in part matches that of the Soviet Europeans. But geographical and cultural differences add a number of special features. Above all, the application of party theory to the Kazakhs, and to a lesser extent to the other nomad peoples, amounted economically to the imposition by force of an untried stereotype on a functioning social order, with disastrous results. And in human terms it meant death and suffering proportionately even greater than in the Ukraine.

★

10

The Churches and the People

> But the end is not yet
>
> *St. Matthew*

One of the great focuses of village life was, of course, the churches: and moreover they represented an alternative view of life to the one presented by the regime.

That atheism was the official view of the Soviet government; that the Communist Party regarded religion as an enemy: these are, indeed, facts known to almost everybody and freely announced by the Communist authorities on numerous occasions. We will cite only one statement of the position, a particularly forceful and (given its author and its reappearance regularly to this day in his published works) authoritative one.

Lenin, in a famous passage in a letter of 13/14 November 1913 to Maxim Gorki had stated the Party position quite flatly:

> Every religious idea, every idea of God, even flirting with the idea of God, is unutterable vileness . . . of the most dangerous kind, 'contagion' of the most abominable kind. Millions of sins, filthy deeds, acts of violence and physical contagions . . . are far less dangerous than the subtle, spiritual idea of God decked out in the smartest 'ideological' costumes . . . Every defence or justification of God, even the most refined, the best intentioned, is a justification of reaction.

Given this basic attitude, various methods of action against the objectionable beliefs were available. The general tactic, throughout the life of the regime, has been to assert that religion will die out as the class nature of society which produced it disappears and that persuasion rather than force is theoretically the best approach, and to combine this in practice with State action. The difference between various periods in the Party's campaign have been in the extent and nature of the pressure thought suitable at a given moment.

For it was also wished to give as good an impression as feasible at home, but also most importantly abroad, as was likely to gain the support, or at least not provoke the enmity, of at least a section of possible sympathizers who nourished 'religious prejudices'. This involved, as in other fields, the usual indirection and, (depending on the policy requirements of the moment), an appearance of toleration, with control and humiliation of the churches rather than overt suppression as the usual procedure.

There are various views about the strength, or the nature, of religious belief among the peasantry. Some hold that the peasants held more strongly to ancient, semi-pagan superstitions: but this is true even in the countryside of Western Europe and, though formally un christian, has not in practice been found incompatible with loyal Christian belief, such being the eclectic minds of men.

Others see the peasants as devoted to the ceremonies of the Church, but more or less anti-clerical as regards the established priesthood: but even on this view greatly resenting attempts to close the churches they thought of as their own and the centres of their ritual life. But in any case, as the priesthood became a persecuted minority, and some of the weaker clergy submitted or abandoned religion altogether, the mass of the peasants are almost universally reported as rallying to and protecting the majority of priests who tried to defend their way of life and belief.

Moreover, even if the Marxist view of religion were correct, and it represented no more than a fantasy consolation where real consolation was not forthcoming, the conditions for seeking this were strongly present from 1929 on. A fairly sceptical peasant is quoted as saying 'It is too soon to abolish religion . . . if things were different, if someone made it up to you in full when something had happened to you, then you would feel better and you wouldn't need religion'.[1]

This chapter will not deal with the whole question of religion in the USSR, in all its breadth and complexity, but only in its connection with the dekulakization and collectivization on the one hand, and the campaign against Ukrainianization on the other.

*

Before the Revolution, the Orthodox Church had a nominal membership of about 100 million, with 67 dioceses and 54,457 churches served by 57,105 priests and deacons; and also 1,498 monastic institutions with 94,629 monks, nuns and novices.

The first Soviet Constitution of 10 July 1918 guaranteed 'freedom of religious and anti-religious propaganda'.

200

The 'rights' of propaganda were thus at this stage theoretically equal, though it is clear that the side enjoying the use of presses, the support of the state machine and all the other advantages accruing, was in a better position than its opponents.

Various legal restrictions were in any case placed on the Churches. Their property was nationalized without compensation, with local authorities being given the right to let them have 'buildings and objects needed for religious services' though the buildings could also be used for secular purposes by other groups. They were subjected to the same regulations as other associations, and were forbidden to 'levy obligatory collections or imposts', or to 'coerce or punish' their members – phrases open to broad interpretations.

Priests and clerics were declared, under another article (65) of the 1918 Constitution, to be 'servants of the bourgeoisie' and disfranchised. This involved their receiving no ration cards, or those of the lowest category; their children were barred from school above the elementary grade; and so on.

A decree of 28 January 1918 forbade religious instruction in schools, though it was permitted to 'study or teach religious subjects privately'. This last was further restricted by a decree of 13 June 1921 which forbade the religious instruction anywhere of groups of persons below the age of eighteen.

Church land was confiscated along with that of the landlords, and in so far as it was land supporting the central church and its magnates this was welcomed by the peasantry. However the greater part of the 'church land' was in fact owned by the individual parishes, whose priests ploughed it themselves, or hired labour, or rented it to the villagers.

The monasteries were almost all closed, and their property was confiscated. The peasants are reported as especially reluctant to turn out nuns,[2] (and there were more than three times as many nuns as monks).

The struggle was, of course, not confined to legal and constitutional measures, and by 1923 twenty-eight bishops and over a thousand priests had been killed, and many churches had been shut or destroyed.

In February 1922 a decree ordered all religious objects of gold, silver or precious stones to be handed over for famine relief. Stalin was later to praise Lenin's acuteness in using the famine to confiscate Church valuables in the name of the starving masses, the measures being otherwise difficult to put through.[3] However, there was much resistance from the peasants, and some 1,400 fights around churches are reported.[4] In April and May 1922 fifty-four orthodox priests and laymen were tried on charges of counter-revolution in connection with these riots and five were executed. Three months later the Metropolitan of Petrograd and

201

three co-defendants were executed on similar grounds.

Patriarch Tikon was arrested, and a new 'Living Church' set up which took over control. 84 bishops and over a thousand priests were expelled from their sees and parishes. But the 'Living Church' got almost no support, and the following year the Party, after accusing the Patriarch of 'dealings with foreign powers, counter-revolutionary work' and so on, released him and came to terms with him.

With NEP, logically or at least understandably enough, there came a parallel relaxation of the attack on religion. Here, as in other spheres, the period up to 1928 was, comparatively, a halcyon one. The census of 1926 shows that there were still over 60,000 full-time priests and other religious functionaries of various creeds in the countryside – one in almost every village; while at the end of 1929 there were still about 65,000 churches of all denominations in the RSFSR alone.

On the other hand the NEP period was an occasion for the development of more peaceful types of pressure. In 1925 the League of the Godless was formed, 'to assist the Party by uniting all anti-religious propaganda work under the general directions of the Party'. It produced a number of journals, organized forty anti-religious museums, ran sixty-eight anti-religious seminaries, and so on. At the same time other organizations, such as the Trade Unions and the Red Army, were ordered to conduct anti-religious propaganda among their members.

After Patriarch Tikon's death in April 1925, the temporary head of the church, Metropolitan Peter, was arrested and sent to Siberia. His successor, Metropolitan Sergey, was also arrested, released, and rearrested. Of the eleven hierarchs named as locum tenens ten were soon in prison. But this stubborn resistance impressed the Government with the need for compromise and in 1927 Sergey negotiated another *modus vivendi* and was released.

*

With the beginning of the new struggle against the peasantry, the decision seems to have been taken to resume the attack on the Church, and especially in the countryside.

The anti-religious campaign became more intense in the summer of 1928 and over the next year the few remaining monasteries were almost all closed and the monks exiled.

A law of 8 April 1929 forbade religious organizations to establish mutual assistance funds; to extend material aid to their members; 'to organize special prayer or other meetings for children, youths or women, or to organize general bible, literary, handicraft, working, religious study or other meetings, groups, circles or branches, to organize excursions or children's playgrounds, or to open libraries or reading rooms, or to organize sanatoria or medical aid'. In fact, as an official comment put it, church activity was reduced to the performance of religious services.[5]

On 22 May 1929, Article 18 of the Constitution was amended: instead of 'freedom of religious and anti-religious propaganda' it now read 'freedom of religious worship and anti-religious propaganda'; at the same time the Commissariat of Education replaced a policy of non-religious teaching in schools by orders for definitely anti-religious instruction.

Nevertheless, religion thrived. OGPU reports in 1929 show an increase in religious feeling even among industrial workers; 'even those workers who did not accept priests last year accepted them this year'.[6]

The Central Committee held a conference specifically on anti-religious matters in the summer of 1929.[7] In June 1929 came the All-Union Congress of Militant Atheists. And through the next year, all over the USSR, the attack on religion sharpened from month to month.

The natural instincts of the party activists, the true Leninist view of religion, came to the fore in place of tactical restraint. A major concerted assault on the churches began in late 1929, and came to a climax in the first three months of 1930.

★

Dekulakization was the occasion for attacks on the church and the individual priests. A party view was that 'The church is the kulak's agitprop'.[8] There were official attacks on peasants 'who sing the refrain, "we are all God's children" and protest that there are no kulaks among them'.[9]

Priests were commonly deported along with the first wave of kulak exiles.[10] The definition of a kulak farm issued by the government in May 1929 had in fact included any whose members had income not derived from work; and the priests were specified as such. (Party agitators, in a comparable position, were on the other hand 'workers'!).

The connection of priests with the supposed 'kulak organizations' was especially ill-regarded: 'This had particularly dangerous consequences, since along with the obvious enemies of the Soviet Government a significant portion of religious people – middle and poor peasants – was frequently involved in such organizations – having been fooled by the priests'.[11] In one officially reported case in 1929, when the priest and a group of kulaks disrupted the grain collection, and were then supported by the middle peasants, only the priest was shot, and the kulaks merely imprisoned.[12]

203

One arrested priest, being marched thirty-five or forty miles to Uman town from the village of Pidvoyska (with a man who had murdered his wife and another who had stolen a cow), tells of how the escort reviled him – 'according to him, clergymen were greater criminals than robbers and murderers'.[13] Another typical story (from the Zaporizhia Province): the seventy-three-year-old priest was arrested and died in Melitopil prison; the church was turned into a club. The village teacher, son of another arrested priest, was also arrested and disappeared.[14]

In 1931 the Theological Seminary in Maryupil was turned into a workers' barracks. But close by was a large barbed wire enclosure in which 4,000 priests and a few other prisoners were held at hard labour on miserable rations, with some deaths every day.[15]

Not only priests, but all those prominently associated with the church were in danger. In a typical village, (Mykhailiwka, Poltava Province), when the church was destroyed in 1929, the head of the Church Council and six of his associates were sentenced to ten years in prison camps.[16]

And peasants would be disfranchised and eventually dekulakized because the father had earlier been a church elder.[17] The children of one Church Council president who had been sentenced to ten years imprisonment in 1929 were variously persecuted. They were refused documents enabling them to leave the village; they were seldom given work on the kolkhoz, and then the most menial. Eventually they too were jailed.[18]

★

The OGPU complained that in a village in the Western Province 'the local priest . . . came out openly against the closing of the church'(!).[19] But it was not only the priests who tried to save the churches. It was also true that 'Many peasants, by no means the most prosperous in the village, tried to prevent the destruction of their churches, and they too were arrested and deported. The sufferings of hundreds of thousands during collectivization was not the result of their social status but of their religious beliefs'.[20]

For in general the villagers resisted the persecution, and the closing of churches, as best they could. The Soviet press reported such incidents as a priest in the village Markycha being assessed for 200 bushels of grain, and being given it all by peasants within half an hour.[21]

For the churches were undermined – like, indeed the prosperous peasants – by an accumulation of taxes, a new one being demanded soon after the last had, barely, been met.[22] An atheist journal was glad to claim that 'the taxation policy of the Soviet regime is hitting the pockets of the servitors of religious cults especially painfully'.[23]

In the village of Piski (Starobelsk Province) the first move was to lay a huge tax on the church. The villagers paid it. Then the village administrator was told by the district headquarters to liquidate the church. They imposed a heavy tax in meat on the priest. Again the village paid it. But a second tax (in meat) was then imposed which they could not pay. He was convicted of subversive activity in resisting Soviet tax measures, being sentenced to five years' imprisonment, which he served in the Kuzbas mines in Siberia, never returning; and the church was closed.[24]

Sometimes a church already closed in the first Communist attacks of 1918–21 was never reopened. In one such case, the villagers still valued it and prevented attempts to wreck it which started in 1929. Finally, in February 1930, with the help of the fire brigade from the local town, it was broken into and destroyed.[25]

Collectivization 'usually involved the closure of the local church as well'. Icons were confiscated as a matter of routine and burned along with other objects of religious worship.[26] A confidential letter from the Western Provincial Committee on 20 February 1930 speaks of drunken soldiers and Komsomols who 'without mass preparation' were 'arbitrarily closing village churches, breaking ikons, and threatening the peasants'.[27]

The closures applied to all religions. For example, an official periodical reports:

> In Kharkov it has been decided to shut down St. Dymytri Church and give it to the motorists' association for their headquarters.
>
> In Zaporizhia, it was decided to close the synagogue on Moscow Street and give the Lutheran Church to the German workers club.
>
> In the Vinnytsia region, it was decided to close the Nemyriv Convent and the adjoining churches.
>
> In the Stalino region it was decided to close the Roman Catholic Church and give the Armenian–Gregorian Church in the town of Stalino to the Workers of the East Club.
>
> In Luhansk St Michael's Cathedral is closed, and St Peter and Paul Church and the Church of the Saviour. All are used for cultural-educational purposes.[28]

Moreover when churches were closed, this did not mean that religious work was permitted outside them. The closure of nine major churches in Kharkov was accompanied by a decision 'to take proper steps to prevent prayer meetings in private homes now that the churches are closed'.[29]

In the countryside we are typically told, 'the village (Vilshana, Sumy Province) had two churches. One was stone, and its blocks were used to pave a road. The other was wood and was torn down and burned'.[30] Churches were sometimes closed after pressure as the result of a 'decision' of the village Soviet. But this often did not work even after a cycle of arrests and other measures were taken. As with collectivization itself, the 'village meetings' were often spurious – consisting of no more than the local activists. Or mere 'activist' assaults without the pretence of constitutional procedures were undertaken. In a typical account, first the elders were arrested, then the 'activists' removed the cross and bells, and finally, in an 'anti-religious carnival' the church was broken into and its ikons, books and archives burnt, while the rings and vestments were stolen. The church became a granary.[31]

In another village, the Party plenipotentiary simply received orders to turn the church into a storehouse for grain within forty-eight hours:

> The news spread like wildfire through the fields. Scores of peasants dropped their implements and rushed to the village. They cursed and pleaded and wept as they saw their sacred objects removed. The sacrilege was only part of what hurt them – in the whole business they sensed a direct insult to their dignity as human beings.
>
> 'They've taken everything from us', I heard one elderly peasant say. 'They've left us nothing. Now they are removing our last comfort. Where shall we christen our children and bury our dead? Where shall we turn for comfort in our sorrows? The scoundrels! The infidels!' . . .

On the following Sunday,

> the secretary of the local komsomol, a stupid, pimply-faced youth named Chizh, suddenly appeared on the street, playing a balalaika, his girl friend by his side, and singing popular anti-religious songs. That was a familiar enough scene. What caused the trouble was their attire. Both Chizh and the girl were wearing bright-red silk shirts, caught at the waist with gold ropes and silk tassels. The villagers immediately recognized their church hangings. Quickly their indignation flared into a lynching mood. Only the fact that they outran the older peasants and took refuge in the cooperative shop saved the two komsomols from harm at the hands of an infuriated mob.[32]

For the resistance was often fierce, and was of course linked by the Party to the struggle with the kulaks. A typical official tells us:

> Around this affair, however, a cruel and stubborn class struggle is waged. Kulaks and their fellow-travellers are using all means possible to hinder anti-religious propaganda and to halt the mass movement for closing the churches and taking down the bells . . . The 'popes' and their defenders, the kulaks, are using every means to halt the anti-religious current. Through agitation of the backward sections, especially the women, they are endeavouring to put up a struggle against the mass anti-religious movement.

For instance, in the village of Beryukha, when the Komsomols, the poor villagers and the local activists began taking the church bells down without first preparing the public for it the kulaks, who had prepared beforehand, beat up the youngsters, then with whoops and yells moved up to the village Soviet and set the building on fire.

At present a trial is taking place in Beryukha in connection with this event . . .[33]

The 'women's rebellions' were also strongly linked with the religious struggle. *Pravda* spoke of 'illegal meetings and demonstrations by peasant women carried out under religious slogans', including one in the Tatar Republic which forcibly returned church bells which had been removed by the authorities.[34] Another Party publication complained in 1930 about 'outbreaks of religious hysteria among kolkhoz women following on a number of divine manifestations'. In the village of Synyushin Brod, 'on the morning of 6 November, the day set for removing the bells, several hundred women gathered at the church and, agitated by the kulaks and their henchmen, interfered with the planned work. Thirty of them locked themselves inside the belfry and rang the alarm for a day and two nights, terrifying the whole village.

'The women would not allow anyone near the church, threatening to stone those who tried to get by them. When the head of the village Soviet arrived with a police officer and ordered the women to stop ringing the alarm and to go home they started to throw rocks at them. The mischief-makers were later joined by a group of drunken men.

'Later, it was discovered that the local psalmist with several kulaks and their friends, had gone from house to house asking the people to come to the church and not permit the bells to be taken down. This agitation influenced some of the simple-minded women'.[35]

*

The issue of the church bells, so often found in these accounts, is an interesting tactical point. The party sometimes demanded the bells, as necessary for the industrialization fund, before making further moves; a thin end of the wedge calculated – often wrongly – not to arouse too much immediate opposition.

But sometimes bell-seizure and church-closure went hand in hand. The local papers quoted scores of decisions by village meetings to close all churches, and to donate the bells to industrialization funds.[36] 'The workers and peasants' of a district in the Odessa Province sent two carloads of church bells to a factory. In fact a campaign (or, as *Pravda* put it, 'drive') to 'remove church bells for industrial needs' was 'spreading'.[37]

Sixty-seven villages had done so, and the total of 'atheist villages' was said to be over a hundred.[38] By 1 January 1930 bells had been removed from 148 churches in the Pervomaysk district alone.[39]

A report on 11 January 1930 from the enormous Gigant kolkhoz in the Urals boasted that all the church bells in the area had been sent off as scrap, and that over Christmas a large number of ikons had been burnt.[40]

On 2 March 1930, Stalin criticized the removal of church bells as excessive. For the attack on forced collectivization which the change to the 'Dizzy from Success' policy involved was also applied in the religious front. In mid-March 1930 – a couple of weeks after Stalin's article – the Central Committee resolution on 'distortion' in the struggle for the kolkhozes included a condemnation of the 'administrative closing of churches without the consent of the majority of the village, which generally leads to the strengthening of religious prejudices', and party committees were told to cease closures 'fictitiously disguised as the public and voluntary wish of the population'.[41]

Over the period that followed, as with the collectivization in itself, there was a short interlude of greater restraint, but the pressures were then tightened in a better organized and more inexorable way. 80% of the country's village churches were closed by the end of 1930.

★

The actual destruction of the churches was often of irreplaceable cultural monuments.

The Holy Trinity Monastery, in the village of Demydivka (Poltava Province) dated to 1755. In 1928 it was turned into a library and in 1930 it was demolished and the material used to build barns and a tobacco store on the local 'Petrovsky' collective farm. In the process, the bells, ikons and other treasures were looted by activists. Villagers who objected were among those arrested and sent to the large new penal encampment at Yayva in the Urals in 1930.[42] At the village church level we are told typically that in Tovkachivka (Chernihiv Province) the church records, going back to the 16th century, were destroyed with everything else.[43]

The Academy of Science in Moscow was forced to withdraw protected status from almost all the country's historic monuments with religious associations. Churches and monasteries were demolished – even within the Kremlin. We are told that when the Iversky Gates and Chapel on the Red Square were destroyed, all the architects objected, but Kaganovich, then head of the Moscow Party Organization, said 'My aesthetic conception demands columns of demonstrators from the six districts of Moscow pouring into the Red Square simultaneously'.[44]

208

Before the revolution Moscow had 460 Orthodox churches. On 1 January 1930 this was down to 224, and by 1 January 1933 to about 100.

The Kazan Cathedral in Leningrad was turned into an anti-religious museum. The 10th century Desyatynna church in Kiev, and the ancient Mykhaylivsky and Bratsky Monasteries were destroyed, together with a dozen other buildings of the 12th to 18th centuries. And similarly elsewhere. But even the old cathedrals kept to serve as museums were allowed to become dilapidated, and their paintings were covered with lime.

The St Sophia Cathedral and other churches in Kiev were turned into museums or anti-religious centres (Anyone wishing to get a vivid idea of the destruction is recommended to look at the photographs in *The Lost Architecture of Kiev*, by Titus D. Hewryk, New York, 1982.) In Kharkov, St. Andrey's was turned into a cinema; another into a radio station; another into a machine-parts store. In Poltava, two were turned into granaries, another into a machine repair shop.

In a slightly different vein, a recent Soviet novel rates the destruction of cemeteries, of the link between the living and the dead, as one of the worst signs of thoughtless modernization.[45] And (for example) many of the Volga German letters from Evangelicals (see p. 281) speak of it being hard to die without a pastor or a church or Christian burial.

The new Constitution of 1936 caused trouble with its guarantee of freedom of religion. Peasant elders, of the Old Believer or Evangelical sects especially, would try to register at the village Soviet, be told to collect fifty signatures, collect them, and then all fifty would be arrested as members of a secret counter-revolutionary organization.[46]

★

These measures applied to all religions. 'Churches and synagogues' is often the phrasing in official decrees in the European part of the USSR. Elsewhere Islam was equally persecuted, and with the Buddhists in Buryatia a major attack also coincided with collectivization.[47]

Protestants, originally favoured up to a point as disruptive of the other churches, were soon found to be dangerous. The Evangelicals had 3,219 congregations with some four million members in 1928. The following year saw the beginning of a continuous attack. Their Theological College (founded in December 1927) was closed. In February a band of twenty-five 'Baptist spies' for Poland was unmasked in Minsk, and at about the same time a similar group was arrested in the Ukraine. In the collectivization evangelical leaders in the villages were excluded from the kolkhozes and denounced as kulaks; and most of them were deported.[48]

In 1931 the Evangelical Church as such was denounced as 'a masked counter-revolutionary kulak organization receiving financial support from abroad'.[49]

But though all were crushed and reduced to remnants no churches were actually made illegal and totally destroyed except for the two national churches of the Ukraine – the Ukrainian Autocephalous Orthodox Church, and the Ukrainian Catholic Church (Uniats of the Eastern rite): the latter's main strength being in the Western Ukraine, then part of Poland, it was not driven underground until the annexation of that area.

★

The Ukrainian Orthodox Church, headed by the 'Metropolitan of Kiev and all Rus', whose traditional ties were with the Patriarch of Constantinople was, without consultation or consent, transferred to be subordinate to the Moscow Patriarchate in 1685–6, though retaining its autonomy and the right to elect its own Metropolitan. In 1721 even the rank of Metropolitan was reduced to Archbishop. Later in the century the Ukrainian rite was Russianized, the Church Slavonic liturgy ordered to be spoken in the Russian manner, and Russian vestments introduced.

The resentment at this continued throughout the period which followed, and with the rise of the Ukrainian nationalist movement, the Ukrainian orthodox seminaries at Kiev and Poltava were reported to have become hotbeds of nationalist agitation well before the revolution.

In 1917–18, a large element in Ukrainian Orthodoxy, supported by the Ukrainian Rada government, seceded from the Moscow Patriarchate and re-established a Ukrainian Autocephalous Church, holding services in Ukrainian.

In October 1921 it held its first Council (*Sobor*) in Kiev, with delegates both clerical and lay, the latter including some of the country's most prominent academicians, professors, writers, composers and others. At first it was no more persecuted than other religious bodies and indeed, was to some degree encouraged, with the idea of weakening the Russian Church. But things soon began to change.

A secret OGPU instruction of October 1924 draws attention to the 'constantly growing influence' of the Ukrainian Autocephalous Orthodox Church, and says that its Metropolitan Vasyl Lypkivsky and his colleagues 'have long been known' as 'secret propagators of Ukrainian separatism'. The local OGPU officers are warned that this is 'particularly dangerous for the Soviet regime', and told to take measures, including 'to increase the number of secret informers among the faithful and to recruit priests themselves for secret service work in the OGPU'.[50]

Attempts were made to split it, but these had failed by 1926, and by the end of that year the Autocephalous Church had thirty-two bishops, about 3,000 priests, and some six million members.

But the first blow was now struck. Metropolitan Lypkivsky was arrested early in August 1926. His removal was obtained by bringing him under guard to a Church *Sobor* in October 1927: on his refusal to resign, and a refusal of the majority of delegates to make him do so, many were arrested. Even then no vote for his resignation was obtained, but the minutes were faked with a decision that he should be 'unburdened' of the post 'owing to his advanced age'.

His successor, Mykola Boretsky, was forced to sign a document dissolving the church at a special meeting called by the GPU on 28–29 January 1930. But protests from abroad seem to have had some effect in postponing implementation, and at another Sobor on 9–12 December 1930, Ivan Pavlivsky became Metropolitan, though thereafter little organized action was possible. A remnant of 300 parishes was allowed to reconstitute itself as the 'Ukrainian Orthodox Church' but the last parish was extinguished by 1936.

At the trial of the 'Union for the Liberation of the Ukraine' in 1930 it was specifically charged that conspirators had organized cells in the Ukrainian Autocephalous Orthodox Church, and its hierarchy was accused of involvement.[51] Over twenty of the forty-five named at the trial were in fact priests or sons of priests, and one of the most prominent was Volodymyr Chekhivsky, former member of the Central Committee of the Ukrainian Social-Democratic Party, and Head of the Government of the Ukrainian Republic, who had given up politics for theology, and become prominent in the Autocephalous Church, though refusing appointment as bishop.

The 'Church group' in the conspiracy had allegedly ordered priests to agitate against the regime among the peasants; and it had also involved the church in plans for an armed rising, many of its priests being qualified ex-officers of the Petliura regime.

One of many reports from the countryside gives the tone: 'In the village of Kyslomut, Rzhyshchiv district, the GPU has uncovered a counter-revolutionary organization of churchgoers and kulaks. Its activities were directed by representatives of the Ukrainian Autocephalous Church. All the leaders have been arrested'.[52]

At the parish level, some 2,400 priests are reported arrested. A fairly typical account is that in October 1929–February 1930, twenty-eight Ukrainian priests were in Poltava jails: five were shot, one became insane, and the others were sent to prison camps.[53]

By 1934–6 the last remnants of the church's activity were finally

211

suppressed. The successive Metropolitans of the Ukrainian Autocephalous Church all perished in the hands of the NKVD. Metropolitan Lypkivsky was re-arrested and disappeared in February 1938, aged seventy-four; Metropolitan Boretsky was arrested in 1930, sent to the 'isolator' prison of Yaroslavl and later to the notorious Solovetsk camp on the White Sea, but was brought back to psychiatric prison in Leningrad in 1935, dying there in 1936 or 1937. Metropolitan Pavlivsky was arrested in May 1936 and disappeared.

In addition, thirteen archbishops and bishops are reported dead in Soviet prisons between 1928 and 1938,[54] while in all 1,150 priests and some 20,000 members of parish and district church councils perished then or later in camps. Of the Autocephalous bishops only two survived – eventually to become respectively Metropolitan of their church in the USA and its Bishop of Chicago.

But the transfer of the Ukrainian Church to Moscow control did not merely lead to a different priesthood. It was accompanied by a virtual destruction of the rural church both Autocephalous and 'Russian' in the Ukraine.

The Russian Orthodox Church had in 1918, under the pressure of Ukrainian national feeling, granted a good deal of autonomy to its branch in the Ukraine, now put under an Exarch. And it remained the larger church, comprehending the Russian minority in the republic, but also many of its traditional parishes in the countryside – in 1928 having 4,900 parishes in all. But it too suffered the usual fate. In 1937 the Exarch Constantine was arrested, and by 1941 only five parishes survived.

All in all, by the end of 1932, just over a thousand churches are estimated as having been closed in the Ukraine. (The major offensive of 1933–4 was yet to come, and in 1934–6 about 75–80% of the remaining churches in the Ukraine were destroyed).[55] In Kiev, with its hundreds of churches, only two small ones were still active in 1935.

As to the Ukrainian Catholics, Tsarist repression of these Uniats had been fairly thorough (in spite of various treaty guarantees). By 1839 the church had been crushed in the Russian Empire – though an Act of Toleration in 1905 permitted the reemergence of non-Uniat Catholics. In the first phase of the Soviet regime they were regarded with special suspicion and in 1926 there were a number of trials of Catholic priests as 'Polish spies'. Meanwhile the Uniats had flourished in that part of the Ukraine under Austrian rule and when the territory became Polish in 1918 this continued to be the case. The establishment of Soviet rule in the course of World War Two resulted in a forced 'return' of the Ukrainian Uniat church to the orthodox fold.

The archbishop and bishops were all arrested and some 500 priests joined them in April 1945. In March 1946 several bishops were tried, in camera, as Nazi collaborators, and sent to labour camps. The professors of the three Uniat seminaries and members of the Orders (including the nuns) were almost all arrested. Their institutions were closed, as were 9,900 primary and 380 secondary schools; seventy-three publications were suppressed.[56]

A fake congress of the Church which then took place could only raise a handful of venal priests to claim a secession from Rome and acceptance of Orthodoxy. The Catholics went underground, and still maintain a desperate existence 'in the catacombs'. There have been many stories in the Soviet press of continuing underground Catholic work with a secret priesthood – even of an underground nunnery in Lviv in November 1963[57] – and protests, illegal publications and arrests continue up to the present, and are increasing rather than diminishing.

The various Russo–Polish wars always involved massacres of Catholics by Orthodox and vice versa in the Ukraine. One of the remarkable things of the 19th, and even more of the 20th century, is the toleration between the two Ukrainian churches – the Autocephalous Orthodox Church of the East Ukraine, and the Catholic Uniat Church of the West Ukraine – each in turn destroyed by the Communist regime, neither dead past the possibility, even the probability, of eventual revival.

The Sovietization and collectivization of the countryside thus entailed at the very least repression and restriction of the churches which had ministered to the peasant for a thousand years, and, where a church was also a direct exemplar of nationhood, to its actual destruction, in so far as that lay in the regime's power. The sufferings inflicted on the peasantry and on the Ukrainian nation were not merely physical.

★

PART III

The Terror-Famine

A Tsar rules the world,
A Tsar without mercy,
And his name is Hunger

(traditional)

11

Assault on the Ukraine, 1930–32

This land of ours that is not ours

Shevchenko

At the same time that Stalin made his move to crush the peasantry in 1929–30, he resumed the attack on the Ukraine and its national culture which had been suspended in the early 1920s.

Academician Sakharov writes of 'the Ukrainophobia characteristic of Stalin'; but it was not, from a Communist point of view, an irrational Ukrainophobia. A great nation lay under Communist control. But not only was its population unreconciled to the system: it was also true that the representatives of the national culture, and even many Communists, only accepted Moscow's rule conditionally. This was, from the Party's point of view, both deplorable in itself and pregnant with danger for the future.

In 1929–30, having crushed the Right, and having embarked on a collectivization and dekulakization policy which hit the Ukraine with especial severity and met the strongest resistance there, Stalin was at last nearly ready to give effect to his hostility to all such centrifugal tendencies.

As early as April 1929, the OGPU was bringing charges of Ukrainian nationalist plotting against small groups. During the year there were public attacks on the most distinguished Ukrainian academics. In July mass arrests took place of some 5,000 members of an alleged underground organization, the Union for the Liberation of the Ukraine (SVU), of which we have spoken earlier.

From 9 March to 20 April 1930, a whole cycle of faked cases against Ukrainian personalities began with the set-piece public trial in the Kharkov Opera House of forty-five alleged members of this organization. They were mostly former political figures of extinct parties, now engaged in work as scholars, critics, writers, linguists, with some students, lawyers,

217

and especially priests, thrown in.

Their leading figure was Academician Serhii Yefremov, a linguistic scholar and lexicographer, one of the group which had maintained the Ukrainian identity in the last years of Tsardom. He had been vice-president of the All-Ukrainian Congress called by the Rada in April 1917 and head of the Socialist–Federalists.

Another former Socialist–Federalist was Zinoviy Margoulis, Jewish lawyer and member of the Ukrainian Academy of Science. The bulk of the other leading figures were academics or writers of the same background, or former members of the Social–Democratic and Social–Revolutionary Parties, or non-party men who had supported the independent Ukrainian Republic: such as the historian Yosyp Hermayze, the writers Mikhaylo Ivchenko and Lyudmila Starytska-Cherniakhivska, the linguist Hrihory Holoskevych, and others.

Confessions had been obtained, by the usual methods, and the accused were sentenced to long jail terms. It was announced in connection with the trial that the linguistic institutes of the Ukrainian Academy had been closed down and a number of scholars arrested.[1] The charges in the SVU trial included, in addition to conspiring to seize power, that of working to make Ukrainian as distinct as possible from Russian. This was, in fact, much the same linguistic aim of that of Skrypnyk and other Ukrainian Communists. And it is notable that Skrypnyk, while perforce condemning the SVU linguists, did so on the grounds that they had used their work to 'cover up' wrecking – making no reference to the alleged linguistic sabotage.[2]

The sweep of this purge was wide. Students from Kiev and elsewhere in the Ukraine are reported in the Solovki prison camp after the trial, sentenced as part of that faked conspiracy.[3] And it is noteworthy that many 'cells' of the conspiracy were discovered in the villages; while it is reported that in March 1930 Ukrainians serving in the First Siberian Cavalry Corps were imprisoned on charges of treason or anti-Soviet propaganda.[4]

In February 1931, a further series of arrests of leading intellectuals took place – mainly prominent figures who had returned from exile in 1924 or 1925. They had supposedly formed a 'Ukrainian National Centre' with the country's most distinguished figure, the historian Hrushevsky, as leader, and Holubovych, former Premier of the independent Ukraine, among the major plotters. Hrushevsky had been under attack for over a year; in fact we are told that in the mid-20s, when his *History of the Ukraine* was merely being *considered* for banning, an OGPU circular instructed agents to take note of all who took an interest in the book.[5]

Most of the members of this 'Ukrainian National Centre' were former Social–Revolutionaries. They too were alleged to have 'numerous' rank and file accomplices. This time no public trial took place. Most of the accused were sent to penal camps, though Hrushevsky himself was merely removed from the Ukraine under house arrest.

These moves were crucial in the assault on Ukrainianization. They amounted to the crushing of that old intelligentsia which had become reconciled to the Soviet regime on a programme of Ukrainian cultural identity. In 1931 the Ukrainian Communist intelligentsia in turn came under attack, in the beginning of a new phase in the destruction of all that had flourished in the late 20s (and to which we shall revert in Chapter 13).

★

This first assault on the Ukrainian intelligentsia preceded the general attack on the peasantry. Stalin clearly understood that the essence of Ukrainian nationhood was contained in the intelligentsia who articulated it, but also in the peasant masses who had sustained it over the centuries. The 'decapitation' of the nation by removing its spokesmen was indeed essential – and was later evidently to be the motive for Katyn, and for the selective deportations from the Baltic States in 1940. But Stalin seems to have realized that only a mass terror throughout the body of the nation – that is, the peasantry – could really reduce the country to submission. His ideas about the connection between nationality and the peasantry are clearly put:

The nationality problem is, in its very essence, a problem of the peasantry.[6]

And in fact one of the aims of collectivization in the Ukraine had been officially stated as 'the destruction of Ukrainian nationalism's social base – the individual land-holdings'.[7]

The SVU 'plot' was, as we have seen, extended to the villages. Many village teachers are reported shot in connection with it.[8] In one district the head of the Executive Committee, the District's chief doctor, and others including peasants were shot as SVU conspirators.[9] And there are scores of such reports.

Kossior was to sum up after the struggle: 'the nationalist deviation in the Communist Party of the Ukraine . . . played an exceptional role in causing and deepening the crisis in agriculture'.[10] Or, as his Police Chief Balitsky is quoted as saying, 'In 1933 the fist of the OGPU hit out in two directions. First at the kulak and Petliuraist elements in the villages and secondly at the leading centres of nationalism'.[11]

Thus the kulak was blamed as a bearer of nationalist ideas, the nationalist as a sponsor of kulak attitudes. But in whichever capacity the Ukrainian peasant was considered, he had certainly proved particularly troublesome to the regime. Resistance to collectivization is always reported as stronger, or rather more militant, in the Ukraine than in Russia proper.[12] The view is taken, by General Grigorenko for example, that since the defeat of the first collectivization drive was largely the result of mass action in the Ukraine and the North Caucasus, Stalin concluded that these were especially recalcitrant areas, and must be crushed.[13] (One observer thought that among the various other reasons for the special hostility of the Ukrainians to collectivization was the fact that the Ukrainian kolkhozes were on the whole much larger, and so even more impersonal and bureaucratized, than in Russia).[14]

Moreover, in the Ukraine collectivization was more complete than in the RSFSR. By mid-1932 70% of Ukrainian peasants were in kolkhozes, to 59.3% in Russia.

Stalin warned several times against 'idealization of the collective farms'. Their mere existence, he argued, did not mean that the class enemy had disappeared. On the contrary, the class struggle was now to be waged within the collective farms.

By now everyone who could possibly be called a kulak under any rational analysis whatever had already been removed. The famine-terror was to be inflicted wholly on the collectivized ordinary peasant and the surviving individual peasants, usually even poorer. That is, it was not part of the collectivization drive, which was already virtually complete. Yet, incredibly, the 'kulak' still remained, no longer openly opposing the collective farms: 'Today's anti-Soviet elements' Stalin said, 'are mostly people who are "quiet", "sweet", and almost "holy"'. The kulak, he added, had been 'defeated but not completely exterminated'.[15]

★

But it was not only the peasants who were inadequately subdued. The Ukrainian Communists, too, presented obstacles to Stalin. Even in 1929 the Ukrainian Party and Soviet organizations had been particularly stubborn in arguing against unrealistic grain targets, and particularly remiss in discovering kulaks. In the Kaharlyk District, Kiev Province, 'all the directors, up to the District Party Committee Secretary, encouraged the kulak line "we have no kulaks. We only have peasants" '.[16] Not merely District officials, but the Ukrainian Party as such was attacked in *Pravda* in September 1929 for objecting to its plan for next year 'especially for food crops'; and over the autumn the papers printed protests from various local organizations to the effect that nothing would be left for consumption. The Zaporizhia bureau complained that 70–75% of the quota would have to come from middle and poor peasants, leaving 'not a single kilogramme' for sale to the local population. As a result the Provincial secretary was removed.[17]

But the replacements of those purged were in the same difficulties. Only the most rigorous exercise of Party discipline could force the various revolutionary changes in the countryside. And when it came to the levels of grain requisition the Ukrainian Politburo and Central Committee themselves had little choice but to try to have them reduced. The problem was that, under the Communist system, according to the rules of 'democratic centralism' which had already ruined the Right, if Moscow insisted they were bound to obey.

As we have seen, grain plans were made on the basis of reckoning the total numbers of hectares available in theory, and applying to that the maximum possible yield per hectare. And Khrushchev, in retirement, was to blame the system whereby a Party official, or the State itself, 'set a quota for the whole district'.[18]

Ways to counter such arguments had already been devised; and in the Party the view prevailed that the strategy of the peasantry was to withhold grain in order to starve the towns, or, (later), to fail to reap or sow, relying on his reserves for food: so that the correct class reaction was, as in 1918–21, to seize the grain and let the peasant starve instead. As early as the summer of 1930 one of the Ukrainian Central Committee's activists tells of a meeting where Kossior told them:

> the peasant is adopting a new tactic. He refuses to reap the harvest. He wants the bread grain to die in order to choke the Soviet government with the bony hand of famine. But the enemy miscalculates. We will show him what famine is. Your task is to stop the kulak sabotage of the harvest. You must bring it in to the last grain and immediately send it off to the delivery point. The peasants are not working. They are counting on previously harvested grain they have hidden in pits. We must force them to open their pits.[19]

The activist, himself from the countryside, knew 'very well that pits full of grain are a myth. They did exist in the early twenties, but they've long since disappeared'.[20] But more generally, Kossior's threat already puts the Stalinist analysis and the future Stalinist programme in stark perspective.

In normal circumstances, the Ukraine and the North Caucasus had provided half of the total marketable grain. In 1926, the best harvest before collectivization, 3.3 million tons of grain (21% of the harvest) was taken from the Ukraine. In the good harvest of 1930 it was 7.7 million tons (33% of the harvest); and although the Ukraine only accounted for 27% of the total Soviet grain harvest, it had to supply 38% of grain deliveries.

In 1931 the same 7.7 million tons was demanded of the Ukraine, out of a harvest of only 18.3 million tons; that is, 42% (about 30% of the grain had been lost in the inefficiencies of collective harvesting). The Ukrainian leadership is reported as trying to persuade Moscow to bring it down, but without success.[21] Individual Moscow leaders were also approached; Mikoyan is reported visiting the southern Ukraine in 1931, and being told that no more grain could possibly be obtained.[22]

Only 7 million tons was actually collected. But this already meant that what amounted, by earlier standards, to a famine was afflicting the Ukraine in the late spring of 1932: for only an average of c. 250 pounds of grain per capita was left for the Ukrainian rural population.

Needless to say, the lapses produced further Party purges: these were announced in a whole series of districts in January 1932, invariably for poor agricultural work or Right opportunism. Complaints about the whole Ukrainian position, as 'disgracefully behind' and so on, became endemic in the central Moscow press. I note fifteen in *Pravda* alone between January and July 1932.

In July the vital decisions were taken which were to lead to the holocaust of the next eight months. Stalin had again ordered a delivery target of 7.7 million tons – out of a harvest which the conditions of collectivization had reduced to two-thirds of that of 1930 (14.7 million tons) though poorish weather in some provinces also had an effect; there was drought in some areas, but the leading Soviet authority on drought[23] notes that it was not as bad as that of the non-famine year of 1936, and was centred outside the Ukraine. Even this is generally described as a fairly good harvest in itself, (higher, for example, than that of 1928), had it not been subject to arbitrary seizure; but it was obvious to the Ukrainian leaders that the proposed levels of requisition were not merely excessive, but quite impossible. After considerable argument, the Ukrainians finally managed to get the figure reduced to 6.6 million tons – but this too was still far beyond the feasible.

This took place on 6–9 July 1932, at the 'Third All-Ukrainian Conference' of the Ukrainian Communist Party, with Molotov and Kaganovich representing Moscow. Kossior opened the Conference. Some areas, he said, were already 'seriously short of food'. And he noted that 'some comrades are inclined to explain the difficulties in the spring sowing campaign by the magnitude of the plans for grain deliveries, which they consider unrealistic . . . Many say that our pace and our plans are too strenuous'. He added, significantly, that such criticism came from the districts, but also from the Ukrainian Central Committee itself.[24] Moreover, it must have been clear to all that if the grain was indeed needed by the State, it could have been made up by a more equitable distribution of the burden, since production for the USSR as a whole was slightly higher than in the previous year (for example, see *Narodnoe Khozyaystvo SSSR 1958*, Moscow 1959).

Skrypnyk told the Conference frankly that peasants had told him that 'we had everything taken from us'.[25] And Kossior, Chubar, and others also argued that the grain targets were excessive.[26] Chubar, as Head of the Ukrainian Soviet Government, is reported in *Pravda* as saying that part of the trouble was that kolkhozes accepted unrealistic plans. He added, and the suggestion obviously applied to much higher levels, 'It is wrong to accept an order regardless of its practicability, and then try to distort Party policy, to destroy revolutionary law and order, to ruin the economy of the kolkhozes, justifying all this by orders from above'.[27]

However, Molotov called attempts to blame unrealistic plans for the failures 'anti-Bolshevik', and concluded by saying 'There will be no concessions or vacillations in the problem of fulfilment of the task set by the party and the Soviet government'.[28]

The 6.6 million tons was in fact never collected, in spite of resort to all the measures foreseen by Chubar. The only relief, and that minor, was when the Ukrainian Economic Council reduced the butter target for the Ukraine from 16,400 to 11,214 tons on 14 July 1932 – apparently by unilateral decision.[29]

★

So, on Stalin's insistence, a decree went out which, if enforced, could only lead to starvation of the Ukrainian peasantry. This had been made clear to Moscow by the Ukrainian Communist authorities themselves. All through the next months it was, indeed, enforced with the utmost rigour, and local attempts to evade or soften it were sooner or later crushed.

Things were already bad in July 1932, and they got worse. Some slight ameliorations were from time to time attempted by the Ukrainian authorities – for example, if only to keep a work force operating, in July the Ukrainian Central Committee ordered bread and fish to regions already suffering from famine, to be given only to those actually working in the fields. Some village officials gave the food to anyone who was starving – described in an official report as 'a waste of bread and fish'.[30]

To enforce the decree on 'the protection of socialist property' (see p. 184), watchtowers were now erected in the fields.[31] 'If the field was plain and clear, the tower consisted of four tall posts with a small hut of wood or straw on top. The top was reached by a high ladder. If there was a tall tree in the field, then a couple of posts would be dug in under the tree to support a hut built among the branches of the tree. Similar towers were built on the fringes of woods. An old oak or other big tree would support the hut without any props. The towers were manned by guards armed, as a rule, with shotguns'.[32]

The first procurements were carried out in August, and in many areas by great effort the norms were met. But this virtually exhausted the countryside. From now on in the twenty thousand villages of the Ukraine the inhabitants awaited an uncertain, but even more menacing future. A Soviet novel of the Khrushchev period describes the first outward signs:

> The early autumn of 1932 in Kokhanivka was not the same as other autumns. There were no pumpkins hanging their weary heads down the wattle fences to the street. There were no fallen pears and apples scattered on the paths. There were no wheat and ripe ears left on the stubbles for the hens. The reeking smoke of home-distilled vodka did not belch from the chimneys of the huts. Nor were other signs visible that normally betokened the quiet flow of peasant life and the calm expectation of winter that comes with prosperity.[33]

On 12 October 1932 two senior Russian apparatchiks were sent from Moscow to strengthen the local Party: A. Akulov, who had been Deputy Head of the OGPU, and M.M. Khatayevich, earlier prominent in Stalin's collectivization on the Volga – a portent of more to come.

At the same time a second procurement was announced, though there was now almost nothing available. By 1 November, the delivery plan had only been fulfilled to the level of 41%.

People were already dying. But Moscow, far from relaxing its demands, now launched into a veritable crescendo of terror by hunger.

★

12

The Famine Rages

The decree required that the peasants of
the Ukraine, the Don and the Kuban be put
to death by starvation, put to death along
with their little children

Vasily Grossman

Ukrainian peasants had seen the kulak deportation: 'and we thought, fools
that we were, that there could be no fate worse than that of the kulaks'.[1]
Now, two years later, they faced the deadliest yet of the regime's blows.

The July decree laying down the grain procurement targets for the
Ukraine and North Caucasus was supported by another, of 7 August
1932, which provided the legal sanctions to back the confiscation of the
peasants' grain.

As we noted in Chapter 8, this decree ordered that all collective farm
property such as cattle and grain should henceforth be considered state
property, 'sacred and inviolable'. Those guilty of offences against it were
to be considered enemies of the people, to be shot unless there were
extenuating circumstances, when the penalty must be imprisonment for
not less than ten years with confiscation of property. Peasant women
gleaning a few grains of wheat in the collective field were given the lesser
sentence. The decree also ordered that kulaks who tried to 'force'
peasants to leave kolkhozes should be jailed in 'concentration camps' for
from five to ten years. Stalin, as we have seen, described it in January 1933
as 'the basis of revolutionary legality at the present moment' and had
drafted it himself.[2]

As usual, the activists thus encouraged to a maximum of terror were
later rebuked for excesses. Vyshinsky announced with indignation that it
had been taken by 'some local officials' as a signal to 'shoot or roll into

concentration camps as many people as possible'. He quoted cases where death sentences had been imposed for the theft of two sheaves of corn; and amused his audience with an account of a young man sentenced to ten years for 'frolicking in a barn with some girls at night, thus disturbing the kolkhoz pigs'.[3]

Even before the issuing of the August decree, one often reads in the Ukrainian press such announcements as 'The alert eye of the GPU has uncovered and sent for trial the fascist saboteur who hid bread in a hole under a pile of clover'.[4] From now on, however, we see a great increase in both the extent and the severity of the law and its enforcement. 1,500 death sentences are reported in one month from the Kharkov court alone.[5]

The Ukrainian press carried story after story of executions of 'kulaks' who 'systematically pilfered grain'. In the Kharkov province five courts tried fifty such cases, and there was similar activity in the Odessa Province, where three cases are described in detail, mostly matters of stealing stooks of wheat, though one married couple was shot for unspecified 'pilfering'. At Kopani village in the Dnipropetrovsk Province, a band of kulaks and subkulaks bored a hole in the granary floor and pilfered much wheat: two were shot, the rest jailed. At Verbka in the same province the chairman of the village Soviet and his deputy, plus the chairmen of two kolkhozes, were tried with a group of eight kulaks, though only three kulaks were shot.[6] One peasant in the village of Novoselytsya (Zhytomyr Province) was shot for possession of twenty-five pounds of wheat gleaned in the fields by his ten-year-old daughter.[7]

Ten years was given for the 'theft' of potatoes.[8] A woman was sentenced to ten years for cutting a hundred ears of ripening corn, from her own plot, two weeks after her husband had died of starvation. A father of four got ten years for the same offence.[9] Another woman was sentenced to ten years for picking ten onions from collective land.[10] A Soviet scholar quotes a sentence of ten years forced labour without the right to amnesty, and confiscation of all property, for gathering seventy pounds of wheat stalk to feed the family.[11]

Those convicted of minor offences were sometimes sent to 'prisoner corps' state farms where they got a very small bread ration but had the opportunity to steal such things as tomatoes, and for such reasons usually did not try to escape.[12] But generally speaking, only occasional muddle, incompetence, and the turning of a blind eye eased the rigours of the new law. For example, in one district in Chernihiv Province, arrests only seem to have been made for hoarding five kilogrammes or more of grain. And a peasant member of the collective farm 'The Third Decisive Year' in Pushkarivka in the Dnipropetrovsk Province was sentenced to only five years (evidently by making the prosecution under a different law) when a bottle full of his own corn was found in his house.[13]

One woman, arrested with one of her children for attempting to cut some of her own rye, managed to escape from jail, gather her other son and some sheets, matches and pots, and live in a nearby forest for almost a month and a half, stealing potatoes or grain from the fields at night. She finally returned to find that in the busy harvesting now afoot her crime was forgotten.[14]

We also hear of a number of cases evidently dealt with under different, though no less rigorous decrees. In the village of Mala Lepetykha, near Zaporizhia, a number of peasants were shot for eating a buried horse. This seems to have been because the horse had glanders. The GPU feared some sort of epidemic.[15] There are a number of such accounts.

★

To enforce these decrees, once more the local activists in the village were sent into action, once more supported by a mobilization of Party and Komsomol members from the towns.

And once more, as with the exiling of the kulaks, activists with inadequately disciplined consciences were faced with a repugnant task in inflicting the Party's will on innocent men, women and children. But in 1930 it had been, as far as they themselves were concerned in it, a matter of dispossession and eviction. This time it was a matter of death.

Some activists, even ones with bad personal records, tried to get fair treatment for the peasantry.[16] Occasionally a decent-minded Party activist, especially one who had lost any illusions about the Party's intentions, could do something to help a village – working within the narrow margin of not stirring up his superiors nor, even harder, giving the more virulent of his subordinates a handle against him. Occasionally one of the latter would grossly exceed the level of violence (or corruption) condoned by the authorities, and might be removed. A little more often, the illegal diversion of some food back to the peasants might go undiscovered until the harvest which, if it proved good, would induce the Provincial authorities to pass over the fault.

Some activists were provoked into more overt defiance. One young Communist sent to the village of Murafa, Kharkov Province, reported by telephone that he could make the meat deliveries, but only with human corpses. He then escaped from the area.[17] In another village which had had Bolshevik sympathies in the revolution, and had been a base for Struk's 'Red Partisans', a group of young activists became disillusioned, and in 1933 cut off the head of the leading village Communist.[18]

★

Some kolkhoz chairmen and local party officials were likewise to be found, even in 1932 after the series of purges of the past few years, who had reached the sticking point. In August 1932, when it became plain that the grain plan was impossible, there was trouble at the village of Mykhailivka, Sumy Province. The chairman of the collective farm, a Party member and ex-partisan called Chuyenko, announced the plan, and then said he had no intention of giving their grain away without their consent. That night he left the village, but was captured by the OGPU, and imprisoned together with the head of the village Soviet. Next day there was a 'women's rebellion' which demanded their release, a tax reduction, the peasants' back pay, and a reduction of the grain quota. Sixty-seven people were sentenced, some – including Chuyenko – to be shot.[19]

Through the second half of the year there are continual official attacks on collective farm directors and local Communists who 'joined the kulaks and the Petliurists and became not warriors for grain but agents of the class enemy'.[20] They were, among other things, distributing grain for workdays.[21] We are even told by a modern Soviet scholar that in 1932, 'some collective farms of the North Caucasus and the Ukraine escaped from the organizing influences of the Party and the state'.[22]

Through the autumn the Ukrainian Party again complained of kolkhozes which distributed 'all the grain . . . the entire harvest' to the local peasants.[23] This sort of thing was branded by Khatayevich as action 'directed against the state'.[24] A Ukrainian Party organ complained in November of the secretaries of the local party cells in the villages of Katerynovtsi and Ushakivtsi refusing to accept the orders for grain collection; and these were not isolated actions.[25]

There were other cases in which kolkhoz leaders were attacked for evading rather than defying orders – for example some kept grain by filing it under various misleading guises.[26] The central Party organs continued to attack 'passive-hypocritical relations between some party organizations and the kulak opportunists' in the Ukraine.[27] More generally, the struggle was now linked to the last attempt within the Party to block Stalin – 'the counter-revolutionary Ryutin group'; for 'the Rightist agents of kulakdom have not as yet been unmasked and expelled from the Party'.[28]

A Ukrainian decree spoke of 'groups of rural Communists who literally became leaders of sabotage'.[29] The Komsomol organ denounced 'Communists and Komsomols' who 'stole grain . . . and acted as organizers of sabotage . . .'[30] The Kharkov provincial committee sent out top secret circulars to the effect that the grain results must improve or

228

those concerned would be 'brought to responsibility immediately before the district section of the GPU'.[31]

In five months of 1932, 25–30% of the agricultural middle management were arrested.[32] The Ukrainian Communist press gave many instances in the winter 1932–3 of numbers of individual Ukrainian Party members and District Party officials being expelled and sometimes arrested.[33] A typical story, and typically reprehensible, is of one kolkhoz chairman who organized a wholesale search, found nothing, and then claimed, 'There is no grain. Nobody pilfered it or received it illegally. Therefore there is nothing with which to fulfil the plan'. As a result he was accused of himself having organized the 'real thieves'.[34]

★

In spite of such aberrations the campaign proceeded, unsatisfactory Communists being liquidated and replaced by more reliable men.

By this time, at the lower level the rank-and-file activist 'brigades', called in the Ukraine *'Buksyr* (or *tow*) brigades', were often little more than thugs. Their technique consisted of beating people up and of using specially issued tools – steel rods about five-eighths of an inch in diameter and from three to ten feet long, with a handle at one end and a sharp point – or a sort of drill – at the other, to probe for grain.[35]

One villager's description applies universally:

These brigades consisted of the following persons: one member from the presidium of the village soviet, or simply any member for the village Soviet; two or three Komsomols; one Communist; and the local schoolteacher. Sometimes the head or another member from the co-operative administration was included and, during summer vacations, several students.

Every brigade had a so-called 'specialist' for searching out grain. He was equipped with a long iron crow-bar with which he probed for hidden grain.

The brigade went from house to house. At first they entered homes and asked, 'How much grain have you got for the government?' 'I haven't any. If you don't believe me search for yourselves,' was the usual laconic answer.

And so the 'search' began. They searched in the house, in the attic, shed, pantry and the cellar. Then they went outside and searched in the barn, pig pen, granary and the straw pile. They measured the oven and calculated if it was large enough to hold hidden grain behind the brickwork. They broke beams in the attic, pounded on the floor of the house, tramped the whole yard and garden. If they found a suspicious-looking spot, in went the crow-bar.

In 1931 there were still a few instances of hidden grain being discovered, usually about 100 pounds, sometimes 200. In 1932, however, there was none. The most that could be found was about ten to twenty pounds kept for chicken feed. Even this 'surplus' was taken away.[36]

An activist told Alexander Weissberg, the physicist, 'the struggle against the kulaks was a very difficult period. On two occasions I was fired at in the village and once I was wounded. I shall never forget 1932 no matter how long I live. The peasants lay helpless in their huts with swollen limbs. Every day new corpses were taken out. And yet we had to get bread out of the villages somehow, and fulfil the plan. I had a friend with me. His nerves weren't strong enough to stand it. "Petya" he said, one day, "if this is the result of Stalin's policy can it be right?" I let him have it hot and strong and the next day he came to me and apologized . . .'[37]

For even here, some were worse than others. In one Ukrainian village an activist describes operations. 'In some cases they would be merciful and leave some potatoes, peas, corn for feeding the family. But the stricter ones would make a clean sweep. They would take not only the food and livestock, but also "all valuables and surpluses of clothing", including ikons in their frames, samovars, painted carpets and even metal kitchen utensils which might be silver. And any money they found stashed away'.[38]

★

The agents of State and Party did not, of course, suffer the famine, but got good rations. The better of them sometimes gave food to peasants, but one attitude was 'You won't be any good if you let pity get the whip-hand. You must learn to feed yourself even if others are dying of hunger. Otherwise there will be nobody to bring home the harvest. Whenever your feelings get the better of your judgement, just think to yourself: "The only way to end the famine is to make sure of the new harvest" '.[39] The result, in any case, was (as a wife wrote her husband in the army), 'almost all the people in our village are swollen with hunger except for the head of the collective, the brigadiers and the activists'.[40]

Village teachers might get eighteen kilogrammes of meal, two kilogrammes of groats and a kilogramme of fat a month. They were expected to work after hours as 'activists', so that children in their daytime classes saw them bursting into their houses at night with the rest of the gang.[41]

In the early stages of hunger, in the larger villages where such things could be better concealed, women would be procured for the Party officials by their need for food.[42] At the district level, there was even luxury. A dining hall for Party officials in Pohrebyshcha is described:

Day and night it was guarded by militia keeping the starving peasants and their children away from the restaurant . . . In the dining room, at very low prices, white bread, meat, poultry, canned fruit and delicacies, wines and sweets were served to the district bosses. At the same time, the employees of the dining hall were issued the so-called Mikoyan ration, which contained twenty different articles of food.

Around these oases famine and death were raging.[43]

And when it came to the cities, in May 1933 two of the local Party secretaries and all the leading figures of Zaporizhia had a luxurious orgy – which became known later when they were all arrested under the Yezhov terror, and these misdeeds were thrown into the accusation.[44]

★

In both town and village officially encouraged, or ideologized, brutality flourished. One observer of the Kharkov Tractor Works saw an old applicant for a job being turned away: 'Go away, old man . . . go to the field and die'![45]

A woman seven months pregnant in Kharsyn village, Poltava Province, was caught plucking spring wheat, and beaten with a board, dying soon afterwards.[46] In Bil'ske (in the same Province), Nastia Slipenko, a mother with three young children whose husband had been arrested, was shot by an armed guard while digging up kolkhoz potatoes by night. The three children then starved to death.[47] In another village in that Province the son of a dispossessed peasant gleaning ears of corn in the kolkhoz field was beaten to death by the watchman 'activist'.[48]

In Mala Berezhanka, Kiev Province, the head of the village Soviet shot seven people in the act of plucking grain, three of them children of fourteen and fifteen (two boys and a girl). He was, however, arrested, and sentenced to five years hard labour.[49]

Brigades would now make complete formal searches every couple of weeks.[50] Even peas, potatoes and beetroots were finally taken.[51] It aroused suspicion not to be in a starving state. The activists would then make an especially careful search, assuming that some food had been hidden. One activist, after searching the house of a peasant who had failed to swell up, finally found a small bag of flour mixed with ground bark and leaves, which he then poured into the village pond.[52]

There are a number of reports of brutal brigadiers who insisted on carrying the dying as well as the dead to the cemetery, to avoid the extra trip, and of children and old people lying in the mass graves still alive for several days.[53] One head of a village Soviet (at Hermanivka, Kiev Province) saw the body of an individual peasant with the other corpses in a mass grave, and ordered it to be thrown out. It lay unburied for about a week, when he permitted its interment.[54]

231

That methods of terror and humiliation were common is made clear by Mikhail Sholokhov, who wrote to Stalin on 16 April 1933 of brutal excesses in the Don country.

Countless such examples could be cited. *These are not legalized cases of going it too strong, but a legalized 'method,' on a district scale*, of conducting grain procurement. I have heard about these facts either from communists or from collective farmers themselves, who came to me asking 'to have this printed in the papers' after having been subjected to all these 'methods' . . .

The cases not only of those who have committed outrages against collective farmers and Soviet power, but also those whose hand directed them should be investigated . . .

If everything I have described merits the attention of the central committee, send to the Veshenskaya district real Communists who will have enough courage to expose, irrespective of the person concerned, all those responsible for the mortal blow delivered to the collective farm economy of the district, who will investigate properly and show up not only all those who have applied loathsome 'methods' of torture, beating up, and humiliation to collective farmers, but also those who inspired them.[55]

Stalin replied to Sholokhov that his words gave 'a somewhat one-sided impression' but nevertheless revealed

A sore in our Party-Soviet work and show how our workers, wishing to curb the enemy, sometimes unwittingly hit friends and descend to sadism. But this does not mean that I agree with you *on all points* . . . You see only *one* side, though you see it quite well. But this in only *one* side of the matter . . . And the *other* side is that the esteemed grain-growers of your district (and not only of your district alone) carried on an 'Italian strike' (sabotage!) and were not loath to leave the workers and the Red Army without bread. That the sabotage was quiet and outwardly harmless (without bloodshed) does not change the fact that the esteemed grain-growers waged what was virtually a 'quiet' war against Soviet power. A war of starvation, dear Comrade Sholokhov . . .

This, of course, can in no way justify the outrages which, as you assure me, have been committed by our workers . . . And those guilty of those outrages must be duly punished. Nevertheless, it is clear as day that the esteemed grain-growers are not so harmless as they could appear to be from afar.[56]

★

An activist recalls,

I heard the children . . . choking, coughing with screams. And I saw the looks of the men: frightened, pleading, hateful, dully impassive, extinguished with despair or flaring up with half-mad, daring ferocity.

'Take it. Take everything away. There's still a pot of borscht on the stove.

It's plain, got no meat. But still it's got beets, taters 'n' cabbage. And it's salted! Better take it, comrade citizens! Here, hang on. I'll take off my shoes. They're patched and repatched, but maybe they'll have some use for the proletariat, for our dear Soviet power'.

It was excruciating to see and hear all this. And even worse to take part in it . . . And I persuaded myself, explained to myself. I musn't give in to debilitating pity. We were realizing historical necessity. We were performing our revolutionary duty. We were obtaining grain for the socialist fatherland. For the Five Year Plan.[57]

He adds,

With the rest of my generation I firmly believed that the ends justified the means. Our great goal was the universal triumph of Communism, and for the sake of that goal everything was permissible – to lie, to steal, to destroy hundreds of thousands and even millions of people, all those who were hindering our work or could hinder it, everyone who stood in the way. And to hesitate or doubt about all this was to give in to 'intellectual squeamishness' and 'stupid liberalism,' the attribute of people who 'could not see the forest for the trees'.

That was how I had reasoned, and everyone like me, even when . . . I saw what 'total collectivization' meant – how they 'kulakized' and 'dekulakized,' how they mercilessly stripped the peasants in the winter of 1932–3. I took part in this myself, scouring the countryside, searching for hidden grain, testing the earth with an iron rod for loose spots that might lead to buried grain. With the others, I emptied out the old folks' storage chests, stopping my ears to the children's crying and the women's wails. For I was convinced that I was accomplishing the great and necessary transformation of the countryside; that in the days to come the people who lived there would be better off for it; that their distress and suffering were a result of their own ignorance or the machinations of the class enemy; that those who sent me – and I myself – knew better than the peasants how they should live, what they should sow and when they should plough.

In the terrible spring of 1933 I saw people dying from hunger. I saw women and children with distended bellies, turning blue, still breathing but with vacant, lifeless eyes. And corpses – corpses in ragged sheepskin coats and cheap felt boots; corpses in peasant huts, in the melting snow of the old Vologda, under the bridges of Kharkov . . . I saw all this and did not go out of mind or commit suicide. Nor did I curse those who had sent me out to take away the peasants' grain in the winter, and in the spring to persuade the barely walking, skeleton-thin or sickly-swollen people to go into the fields in order to 'fulfil the bolshevik sowing plan in shock-worker style'.

Nor did I lose my faith. As before, I believed because I wanted to believe.[58]

Another activist tells of how he had been able in his own mind, following Stalin's lead, to blame 'excesses' on particular bad

Communists, but 'the suspicion that the horrors were not accidental, but planned and sanctioned by the highest authorities had been sprouting in my mind. This night it flowered into certainty that left me, for the moment, emptied of hope. The shame of it had been easier to bear as long as I could blame . . . individuals'.[59]

But even the better communists such as the one quoted became habituated to it all. 'Already I was becoming accustomed to this climate of horror; I was developing an inner resistance against realities which only yesterday had left me limp', he later noted of himself.[60]

Such men either succeeded in silencing their consciences, or they too went to the camps. As Bukharin foresaw, this led to 'dehumanization' of the Party, for whose members 'terror was henceforth a normal method of administration, and obedience to any order from above a high virtue'.[61]

Lenin's view of an earlier famine – that of 1891–2 on the Volga, where he then lived – may serve to indicate a whole Party attitude to individual, or mass, death and suffering, when considered against the claims of the revolution. While all classes, including the liberal intelligentsia, threw themselves into relief work Lenin refused on the grounds that famine would radicalize the masses, and commented: 'Psychologically, this talk of feeding the starving is nothing but an expression of the saccharine-sweet sentimentality so characteristic of our intelligentsia'.[62]

As the brigades of thugs and idealists probed their houses and yards for grain in the later months of 1932, the peasants tried to preserve, or find, something to eat. The hiding of grain in the straw by inadequate threshing was publicly attacked as the practice in a number of collective farms, and was a genuine though inadequate resource, at least where the collective farm leaders were sympathetic.[63] One peasant describes a few other methods by which a small quantity of grain could be hidden – in bottles sealed with tar and hidden in wells or ponds, for example.[64]

If the peasant took this grain to the local nationalized mill, it would go to the government. So local artisans constructed 'hand mills'. When these were found the constructor and user were arrested.[65] Also described as 'domestic millstones', they are reported in the Ukrainian Party press as discovered by the hundred – 200 in one district, 755 in one month in another.[66]

With or without such implements, extraordinary 'bread' was made – for example sunflower oil cake soaked in water, but with millet and buckwheat chaff, and a little rye flour to hold it together. A Soviet novelist gives us a scene in which the peasant chops up a cask which had formerly held fat and boils it to get any residue which may be in the wood. As a result, the family have the best meal they can remember.[67]

Another tells of how 'babki', a game with cattlebones, played by children from time immemorial, died out when all the old bones were 'steamed in cauldrons, ground up and eaten'.[68]

Yet another tells of a village (not in the Ukraine), that 'cattle died for lack of fodder, people ate bread made from nettles, biscuits made from one weed, porridge made from another'.[69] Horse manure was eaten, partly because it often contained whole grains of wheat.[70] Over the early winter they ate all the remaining chickens and other animals. Then they turned to dogs, and later, cats. 'It was hard to catch them too. The animals had become afraid of people and their eyes were wild. People boiled them. All there was were tough veins and muscles. And from their heads they made a meat jelly'.[71]

In one village acorns were collected from under the snow, and baked into a sort of bread, sometimes with a little bran or potato peelings. A Party official said to the village Soviet, 'Look at the parasites! They went digging for acorns in the snow with their bare hands – They'll do anything to get out of working'.[72]

★

Even as late as November 1932 cases are quoted in the Ukraine of peasant rebellion and the temporary dissolution of kolkhozes.[73] Leonid Plyushch's grandfather saw a pile of corpses in one village, and was told by his chief 'that was a kulak demonstration'.[74]

The peasants were usually infuriated into revolt by the fact that there was grain available to feed them, often within miles of where they starved. In Tsarist times, when lesser famines raged, every effort had been made to help. As a Soviet novelist writes of 1932–3, 'Old people recalled what the famine had been like under Czar Nicholas. They had been helped then. They had been lent food. The peasants went to the cities to beg "in the name of Christ". Soup kitchens were opened to feed them, and students collected donations. And here, under the government of workers and peasants, not even one kernel of grain was given them'.[75]

For not all the grain was exported or sent to the cities or the army. Local granaries held stocks of 'State reserves'. These were for emergencies, such as war: the famine itself was not a sufficient occasion for their release.[76] For example, the warehouses in the Poltava Province are described as 'almost bursting' with grain.[77]

The peasant's milk too was often processed into butter, in plants not far from the villages concerned. Only officials were admitted. One reports being shown, by a gloomy manager, the butter being sliced into bars and packed in paper bearing the imprint, in English: USSR BUTTER FOR EXPORT.[78]

When food was thus available on the spot, but simply denied to the starving, it constituted an unbearable anomaly and provocation.

This was particularly true when the grain was piled up in the open and left to rot. Large heaps of grain lay at Reshetylivka Station, Poltava Province, starting to rot, but still guarded by OGPU men.[79] From the train, an American correspondent 'saw huge pyramids of grain, piled high, and smoking from internal combustion'.[80]

Potatoes, too, were often piled up to rot. Several thousand tons are reported in a field in the Lubotino area surrounded by barbed wire. They began to go bad, and were then transferred from the Potato Trust to the Alcohol Trust, but were left in the fields until they were useless even for that.[81]

Such things were naturally explained in official reports by allegations that the crop was being 'sabotaged' not only on the steppe, but in the grain elevators and stores.[82] One accountant at a grain elevator was sentenced to death for paying workers in flour, but later released, himself in a starving condition, after two months, dying the following day.[83]

There are numerous reports of riots, with the sole aim of getting at grain in granaries, or potatoes in distilleries. Some failed even in this, but in the village of Pustovarivka the Party Secretary was killed, and the potatoes seized. About 100 peasants were then shot.[84] At Khmeliv, a 'women's revolt' stormed the granary, and three were later sentenced. As a witness of these events notes, 'It happened at a time when people were hungry but still had strength'.[85]

And there were other acts of desperation. In some areas peasants set fire to the crop.[86] But as against 1930 these acts were now always spontaneous and uncoordinated, partly because of physical weakness. Moreover, the OGPU had meanwhile been able to build up a network of *seksoty* – 'secret collaborators' – in the larger villages, by all the methods of blackmail and the threats in which they had become expert.[87]

Yet riots occurred even at the height of the famine in 1933. Near the end of April the peasants of Novovoznesenske, Mikolaiv Province, attacked a grain dump (already rotting in the open) and were machine-gunned by the OGPU guards. At Sahaydak, Poltava Province, hungry villagers looted a grain warehouse in May 1933, but some, too weak to carry the corn home, died on the way back, and the rest were arrested next day – many shot, the rest given five to ten year sentences. Peasants from several nearby villages attacked a grain warehouse at Hoholeve Station (Poltava Province) in the spring of 1933, and filled their sacks with the maize it happened to contain. However, only five were later arrested.[88]

★

Such actions were a last extremity. Even before the grip of the famine grew tighter in the autumn and winter, many peasants started instead to leave the villages, as 'kulaks' had done two years previously.

The Ukrainian peasant was indeed prevented by border guards from entering Russia proper; and if he evaded these and returned with bread, which was at least obtainable there, the bread was seized at the border, and the owner often arrested – as we shall develop in more detail in Chapter 18.

There also was some attempt by the GPU to prevent the starving from entering the zone near the Polish and Rumanian borders;[89] while hundreds of peasants inhabiting the frontier areas were reported shot down trying to cross the Dniester into Rumania.[90] (On the other hand, it does not seem to have been until later, and then not so systematically enforced, that Ukrainian peasants were prevented from going to the North Caucasus, where food might be sought in the distant areas of Daghestan, on the Caspian.)[91]

One estimate is that as early as mid-1932, almost three million people were on the move, crowding the stations, trying to get to the towns, seeking for more prosperous areas.[92] A foreign Communist describes the scene:

> Filthy crowds fill the stations; men, women and children in heaps, waiting for God knows what trains. They are chased out, and they return without money or tickets. They board any train they can and stay on it until they are put off. They are silent and passive. Where are they going? Just in search of bread, potatoes, or work in the factories where the workers are less badly fed . . . Bread is the great mover of these crowds. What can I say of the thefts? People steal everywhere, everywhere . . .[93]

But until the final climax of famine struck in the spring, the majority still tried to eke out their makeshift edibles, in the hope of lasting into the next harvest, in the hope too of government relief which was never to come.

Meanwhile, they naturally turned to the last resource of selling any personal property which might bring them bread.

As we have seen, it was hard for a peasant to move legally even to a Ukrainian city. But at this stage, the ban was not effectively enforced (indeed was to prove hard to impose even in the later and more desperate phase). Many were able to reach Kiev and other big cities. The wives of officials, who had large rations, would attend the Kiev bazaars and market their surplus food for the peasants' valuables, at bargain prices. A richly embroidered tablecloth would go for a 4 pound loaf of bread, a good carpet for a few such loaves. Or 'beautifully embroidered shirts of wool or linen . . . were exchanged for one or two loaves of bread'.[94]

But the state had foreseen ways to extract the peasant's family valuables in a more systematic fashion, and even in small neighbourhood towns or the larger villages he would find, and be able to use, the stores of Torgsin ('Trade with Foreigners'). These accepted in payment only foreign currency and precious metal or stones, and freely sold for them goods including food.

Many peasants had the odd gold ornament or coin which would bring them a little bread (though visits to such stores were dangerous, in that the GPU, acting contrary to the stores' whole rationale, would later often try to extract valuables supposedly not yet declared from Torgsin customers). The project was, of course, part of the Soviet Government's efforts to find any resources usable in the international market. At Torgsins, golden crosses or earrings would go for a few kilogrammes of flour or fat.[95] A teacher got '50 grammes of sugar, or a cake of soap, and 200 grammes of rice' for a silver dollar.[96]

In a village in Zhytomyr Province, the landlords and other richer pre-revolutionary inhabitants had been Roman Catholics. In the Catholic cemetery they had often been buried with gold rings and other jewellery. In 1932–3 villagers secretly opened the graves and these were used to buy food at Torgsin, so that proportionately deaths were fewer than elsewhere in the neighbourhood.[97]

★

As the winter wore on, things got worse and worse. On 20 November 1932 a decree of the Ukrainian government halted the remittance of any grain at all to the kolkhoz peasants in payment of their 'labour days' until the grain delivery quota had been met.

On 6 December 1932 a further decree of the Ukrainian Soviet Government and the Central Committee of the Ukrainian Communist Party named six villages (two each in Dnipropetrovsk, Kharkov and Odessa Provinces) as sabotaging grain deliveries. The sanctions imposed were:

> Halt the supply of goods immediately, halt the local cooperative and state trading, and remove all visible supplies from the cooperative and state stores.
>
> Prohibit completely all collective farm trading, equally for collective farms, members of collective farms and individual holders.
>
> Terminate the advancing of credits, arrange foreclosures of credits and other financial obligations.

> Examination and purging of all foreign and hostile elements from cooperative and state apparatus to be carried out by the organs of the Workers and Peasants Inspection.
>
> Examination and purging of collective farms of the above villages, of all counter-revolutionary elements . . .[98]

Many more followed; and Ukrainian villages that could not meet their quotas were literally blockaded, to prevent city products from reaching them.[99]

On 15 December 1932, a list was even published of whole *districts* 'to which supplies of commercial products have been halted until they achieve a decisive improvement in fulfilment of grain collective plans'. There were eighty-eight of these (out of 358 in the whole Ukraine), in the Dnipropetrovsk, Donets, Chernihiv, Odessa and Kharkov Provinces. Inhabitants of these 'blockaded' districts were deported *en masse* to the North.[100]

★

In spite of all the Party's efforts, at the end of 1932 only 4.7 million tons of grain had been delivered – only 71.8% of the plan.

An official list from the Krynychky district, of 'peasants with a high fixed tax in kind and their deliveries of corn up to 1 January 1933' covers eleven villages and seventy names. Only nine delivered their quota, most of the others finding only half, or a quarter, of the necessary grain. The one case of high over-delivery from an individual is explained: 'all his corn has been taken out of his pits: sentenced'. In all six had been 'sentenced' (plus a wife and a son in the absence of the two 'guilty' peasants) or arrested; thirty-nine had their property sold off; and twenty-one had 'escaped from the village'.[101] And so it was throughout the Ukraine.

So, at the beginning of 1933, a third procurement levy was announced, and a further assault on the now non-existent reserves of the Ukrainian peasantry took place, in the most horrible conditions.[102]

★

For Stalin and his associates had not looked kindly on the failure of the Ukraine to deliver grain which did not exist, and once again they exerted extreme pressure on the Ukrainian authorities.

At a joint sitting of the Moscow Politburo and Central Executive Committee on 27 November 1932, Stalin said that the difficulties encountered in the procurement of bread in the past year had been due to first, 'the penetration of the kolkhozes and sovkhozes by anti-Soviet elements who organized sabotage and wrecking'; and, secondly, 'the incorrect, unMarxist approach of a significant part of our village communists towards the kolkhozes and sovkhozes . . .' He went on to say that these 'village and district communists idealize too much the kolkhozes', thinking that once one had been formed, nothing anti-Soviet or of a sabotage nature could arise, 'and if they have facts about sabotage and anti-Soviet phenomena, they pass these facts by . . . nothing tells them that such a view of the kolkhoz has nothing in common with Leninism!'[103]

Pravda on 4 and 8 December 1932 called for a resolute struggle against the kulaks, especially in the Ukraine; and on 7 January 1933 it editorialized to the effect that the Ukraine was behind in its grain deliveries because the Ukrainian Communist Party permitted a situation in which 'the class enemy in the Ukraine is organizing itself'.

At a plenum of the All-Union Central Committee and the Central Executive Committee in January 1933, Stalin said that the 'causes of the difficulties connected with the grain collection' must be sought in the Party itself. The Kharkov first secretary, Terekhov, told him flatly that famine raged in the Ukraine. Stalin sneered at him as a romancer (see p. 325), and all attempts even to discuss the matter were simply dismissed out of hand.[104]

Kaganovich made a report, insisting again that 'in the village there are still representatives of kulakdom . . . kulaks who had not been deported, well-off peasants inclining to kulakdom, and kulaks who had escaped from exile and were being hidden by relatives, and occasionally by "tenderhearted" members of the party . . . in fact showing themselves traitors to the interests of the toilers'. And then there were 'representatives of the bourgeois-whiteguard, Petliuraist, cossack, SR-intelligentsia'.[105] The rural 'intelligentsia' at this time consisted of teachers, agronomists, doctors and so on, and the naming of their groups as the targets of a purge of anti-Soviet elements is significant.

Once more the call was for war on the 'class enemy'. 'What,' Kaganovich asked, 'are the basic manifestations of the class struggle in the countryside? Above all, the organizing role of the kulak in sabotaging the collection of grain deliveries and of sowing'. He went on to blame sabotage at every stage, including 'some central agricultural organs'. He attacked breakdowns in labour discipline; he said that the kulak had made use of the petty bourgeois tendencies of 'yesterday's individual peasant'; and he accused these elements of 'terrorizing' the honest kolkhoz workers.[106]

On 24 January 1933, the All-Union Central Committee adopted a special resolution on the Ukrainian Party organization (later described as 'a turning point in the history of the CP(b)U, opening a new chapter in the victorious battle of the Bolsheviks in the Ukraine').[107] It flatly charged the Ukrainian Party with failure in the grain collection; in particular the 'key provinces' of Kharkov (under Terekhov), Odessa and Dnipropetrovsk were singled out for 'lack of class vigilance'. The Plenum decreed the appointment of Pavel Postyshev, Secretary of the All-Union Central Committee, to be Second Secretary of the Ukrainian Party and First Secretary of the Kharkov Provincial Committee, (Khatayevich, remaining a Secretary of the Ukrainian Central Committee was made First Secretary in Dnipropetrovsk; and Veger First Secretary in Odessa). The three previous secretaries of these provinces were removed.

'The blunting of Bolshevik vigilance' had been largely responsible for the lag in agriculture, Postyshev later announced, and was 'one of the most serious accusations made by the Central Committee of the CPSU against the Bolsheviks of the Ukraine'.[108]

*

Postyshev was, in fact, Stalin's effective plenipotentiary in the task of 'Bolshevizing' the Ukrainian Party and extracting further grain from the starving Ukrainian villages.

On his arrival in the Ukraine, he spoke of the remnants of the kulaks and nationalists infiltrating the Party and the kolkhozes and sabotaging production.[109] He explicitly ruled out sending food to the villages; at the same time he announced that there was no question of the state helping with seed corn, which must be found by the peasants themselves.[110] (In fact a Moscow decree 'On Aid in Seeding to Collective Farms of the Ukraine and the North Caucasus', issued on 25 February 1933, released 325,000 tons for the Ukraine and 230,000 for the North Caucasus.[111] Even Postyshev, even Moscow, now knew that no future harvest would be possible otherwise. But this aid was not in fact made available till later).

There was still some Party resistance. Village managements in general were accused of trying to 'blur' and 'nullify' the planned grain deliveries of the All-Union Central Committee; while the Kharkov Committee 'tried to interpret' the replacement of Terekhov by Postyshev as a mere personnel matter, and at its local plenum did not even mention the All-Union Central Committee's main points.[112]

It was at a February plenum of the Ukrainian Central Committee that the new, even harder line was formalized. On the grain deliveries, Kossior, still First Secretary though thrown into the shade by Postyshev, gave a speech which makes clear the clash between Party demands and reality.

> We now have new forms of struggle with the class enemy as regards the grain supplies . . . When you come to the district to talk about the grain supply, the officials there begin to show you statistics and tables on the low harvest which are compiled everywhere by enemy elements in the kolkhozes, agricultural branches and MTS's. But these statistics say nothing about the grain in the fields or that which was stolen or hidden. But our comrades, including various plenipotentiaries, not being able to understand the false figures thrust upon them, often become champions of the kulaks and defenders of these figures. In countless cases it has been proven that this arithmetic is purely *kulak* arithmetic; according to it we would not even get half the estimated amount. False figures and blown-up statements also serve, in the hands of enemy elements, as covers for thefts, for the wholesale stealing of bread.[113]

He attacked many districts in the Odessa and Dnipropetrovsk provinces which had made various excuses to postpone sending in their grain; and said there was 'incessant talk of the need to revise the plan'. In various districts there and elsewhere, he claimed there was 'organized sabotage tolerated by the highest levels' of the local Party organization.[114]

★

Postyshev, who was accompanied by a new Head of the Ukrainian OGPU, V.A. Balitsky, had soon replaced 237 secretaries of Party district committees and 249 Chairmen of District Executive Committees.[115] Certain districts were made public scapegoats – in particular the Orekhov District in Dnipropetrovsk Province, 'the leadership of which was found to consist of traitors to the cause of the working class and the collective farm peasants'.[116]

The OGPU also found employment in a severe purge of veterinarians for livestock mortality,[117] a method of coping with animal death which became traditional: about 100 are reported shot in Vinnytsia Province alone in 1933–7, many because horses died of a fungus in the barley straw.[118]

Among other such scapegoats, the entire staff of the Meteorological Office had been arrested on a charge of falsifying weather forecasts in order to damage the harvest.[119] At a different level, thirty-five civil servants from the Commissariats of Agriculture and State Farms were shot in March 1933, for various types of sabotage such as damaging tractors, deliberate weed infestation, and arson. Forty more got terms of imprisonment.[120] They had used their authority, it was alleged, to 'create a famine in the country'[121] – a rare admission that any such thing could have happened.

At the same time, 10,000 fresh activists were sent for permanent employment in the villages, including 3,000 named chairmen of collective farms, or party secretaries or organizers.[122] In 1933 in the Odessa Province, '49.2% of all collective farm chairmen', and in the Donets Province 44.1%, were removed (and as many as 32.3 and 33.8% even of the lowly 'brigadiers', and similarly with other kolkhoz officials).[123] Two representative Communist collective farm chiefs in the Bohuslav region had twice succeeded in getting their quotas reduced, but did not succeed in fulfilling even those. They were now accused of sabotage and allying themselves with 'kulak-Petliuraist stragglers', and sent for trial.[124] In the majority of the villages from which we have reports, the leading party figures by 1933 were Russians.

17,000 workers were also sent to the MTS Political Departments, and 8,000 to those of the State Farms. In all, at least 40,000–50,000 people were sent to strengthen the rural Party. In a single district (Pavlohrad, Dnipropetrovsk Province) of thirty-seven villages and eighty-seven collective farms, 200 special collectors were sent down in 1933 from the provincial Party committee and almost as many from the provincial Komsomol committee.[125]

The much purged Party was again thrown into the struggle against the starving peasantry.

There was what amounts to a frank, or fairly frank, statement of the issue by A. Yakovlev, All-Union Commissar of Agriculture, at a Congress of Collective Shock Workers in February 1933: the Ukrainian collective farmers had, he said, fallen short in sowing grain in 1932; 'thus, they brought harm to the government, and to themselves'. Then, failing to harvest it properly, they 'occupied the last place in all the regions of our land in doing their duty to the government . . . By their poor work they punished themselves and the government. Then let us, comrade Ukrainian collective workers, conclude from this: now is the time of reckoning for the bad work of the past'.[126]

The hysterical brutality which followed Postyshev's intervention can have obtained very little grain. By now the supply was exhausted, and there was almost nothing to eat.

★

People had been dying all winter. But all reports make it clear that death on a mass scale really began in early March 1933.[127]

When the snow melted true starvation began. People had swollen faces and legs and stomachs. They could not contain their urine . . . And now they ate anything at all. They caught mice, rats, sparrows, ants, earthworms. They ground up bones into flour, and did the same with leather and shoe soles; they cut up old skins and furs to make noodles of a kind, and they cooked glue. And when the grass came up, they began to dig up the roots and eat the leaves and the buds; they used everything there was: dandelions, and burdock, and bluebells, and willowroot, and sedums and nettles . . .'[128]

The linden, acacia, sorrel, nettles and so forth now much eaten do not contain protein. Snails, only common in some districts, were boiled, and the juices consumed, while the gristly meat was chopped fine, mixed with green leaves and 'eaten, or rather, bolted'. This helped prevent the swelling up of the body, and promoted survival.[129] In the southern regions of the Ukraine, and in the Kuban, it was sometimes possible to survive by catching marmots and other small animals.[130] In other areas fish could be caught, though families could be sentenced for catching fish in a river near their village.[131] The swill from a local distillery at Melnyky, discarded as unfit for livestock, was eaten by neighbouring peasants.[132]

Even late the following year foreign correspondents brought horrifying first-hand reports. One American, in a village twenty miles south of Kiev, found every cat and dog had been eaten: 'In one hut they were cooking a mess that defied analysis. There were bones, pigweed, skin and what looked like a boot top in the pot. The way the remaining half-dozen inhabitants (of a former population of forty) eagerly watched this slimy mess showed their state of hunger'.[133]

At a Ukrainian village school the teacher reports that in addition to a pseudo-borshch made of nettles, beet tops, sorrel and salt (when available) the children were eventually also given a spoonful of beans – except for the children of 'kulaks'.[134]

In a village in the Vinnytsia Province, an agronomist recalls, when the weeds came up in April the peasants 'started to eat cooked orrach, sorrel, nettles . . . But after consuming such wild plants, people suffered from dropsy and died from starvation in great numbers. In the second half of May the death rate was so great that a kolkhoz wagon was specially set aside for the purpose of carrying the dead each day to the cemetery' (the bodies were thrown into a common grave, without ceremonies).[135] Another activist describes going with a sled-driver whose job was to ask at each house, or each house still with inhabitants, if they had any dead to be carted off.[136]

We have witnesses' reports of a variety of types, including that of victims, former activists, and Soviet authors who witnessed these events when young and wrote of them when it became possible years later. We have already quoted one such who was able under Khrushchev to tell how 'in 1933 there was a terrible famine. Whole families died, houses fell to pieces, village streets grew empty'.[137]

Another of the same period writes:

> Hunger: a terrible soul-chilling word of darkness. Those who have never experienced it cannot imagine what suffering hunger causes. There is nothing worse for the man – the head of the family – than the sense of his own helplessness in the face of his wife's prayers, when she cannot find food for her hungry children. There is nothing more terrible for the mother than the sign of her emaciated, enfeebled children who through hunger have forgotten to smile.
>
> If it were only for a week or a month, but it is for many months that most of the local families have nothing to put on the table. All the cellars were swept clean, not a single hen remained in the village: even the beetroot seeds have been consumed . . .
>
> The first who died from hunger were the men. Later on the children. And last of all, the women. But before they died, people often lost their senses and ceased to be human beings.[138]

A former activist comments:

> On a battlefield men die quickly, they fight back, they are sustained by fellowship and a sense of duty. Here I saw people dying in solitude by slow degrees, dying hideously, without the excuse of sacrifice for a cause. They had been trapped and left to starve, each in his home, by a political decision made in a far-off capital around conference and banquet tables. There was not even the consolation of inevitability to relieve the horror.
>
> The most terrifying sights were the little children with skeleton limbs dangling from balloon-like abdomens. Starvation had wiped every trace of youth from their faces, turning them into tortured gargoyles; only in their eyes still lingered the reminder of childhood. Everywhere we found men and women lying prone, their faces and bellies bloated, their eyes utterly expressionless.[139]

In May 1933 one traveller noted six dead bodies on a twelve kilometre stretch between two villages in the Dnipropetrovsk Province.[140] A foreign journalist, on an afternoon's walk in the country, came across nine dead bodies, including two boys of about eight and a girl of about ten.[141]

A soldier reports that as his train pulled into the Ukraine he and his comrades were horrified. They passed food out to the begging peasants and were reported by the train commandant. However, the corps commander (Timoshenko) took very mild disciplinary action. When the units deployed, 'men, women, girls, children came to the road that led into the camp. They stood silently. Stood and starved. They were driven away

but they reappeared in a different place. And again – stood and starved.'
The political instructors had to work hard to bring the soldiers out of a
state of gloom. When the manoeuvres started, the field kitchens were
followed by the famished peasantry, and when meals were served, the
soldiers handed over their rations. The officers and political commissars
went away and pretended not to have noticed.[142]

Meanwhile, in the village 'the poor begged from the poor, the starving
begged from the starving', and those with children from those without.[143]
In early 1933 in the centre of one large Ukrainian village, 'close by the
ruins of the church, which had been dynamited, is the village bazaar. All
the people one sees have swollen faces. They are silent, and when they
talk they can hardly whisper. Their movements are slow and weak because
of swollen legs and arms. They trade in cornstalks, bare cobs, dried roots,
bark of trees and roots of waterplants . . .'[144]

One young girl in a village in Poltava Province which had not suffered
as much as most describes her Easter in 1933. Her father had gone to
trade 'the very last shirts in the family' (the linen and embroidery having
gone already) 'for food for the holy day'. On his way back with ten pounds
of corn and four of screenings, he was arrested for speculation (though
released two weeks later), and the food confiscated. When he did not
arrive, 'Mother made soup for us from two glassfuls of dried, crushed
potato peelings and eight not very large potatoes'. The 'brigadier' then
came in and ordered them out to work in the fields.[145]

A woman in the village Fediivka, in the Poltava Province, whose
husband had been given five years in camp as a member of the SVU,
managed to keep her family fed in various ways until April 1933. Then her
four-year-old son died. Even then the brigades did not leave her alone,
and suspected that the grave she had dug for the boy was really a grain pit.
They dug it up again, found the body, and left her to rebury it.[146]

Everything ground to a halt.

> At school the upper grades continued to attend classes until nearly spring. But
> the lower grades stopped during the winter. And in the spring the school shut
> down. The teacher went off to the city. And the medical assistant left too. He
> had nothing to eat. Anyway, you can't cure starvation with medicines. And all
> the various representatives stopped coming from the city too. Why come?
> There was nothing to be had from the starving . . . Once things reached the
> point where the state could not squeeze anything more out of a human being,
> he became useless. Why teach him? Why cure him?[147]

★

It was in spring that the regulations against unlicensed movement began
to be enforced rigorously. An order to the North Donets Railway of 15

March is preserved, which instructs all railwaymen not to allow peasants, except on assignment from the director of their collective farms, to travel.[148]

The ban on employment in industry applied, at least in theory, to local industry as well as the cities. One brick tile works was typically ordered in 1933 not to take on locals.[149] But work was occasionally available, as with the rebuilding of a railway track to a sugar refinery, where people who had not seen bread for six months were to be paid 500 grammes a day plus thirty grammes of sugar. But to get this much, a norm was set of digging eight cubic metres of earth a day, which was beyond their powers, and the bread in any case arrived the day after the working day: people died at work, or during the night.[150] At a state farm near Vinnytsia, some thousands of workers were needed for truck-farming tomatoes, cucumbers, celery and so on; and an offer went round the nearby villages offering jobs at a kilogramme of bread, a hot meal and two roubles a day. Many came, over half of them incapable of work. Every day a number would die after their first meal – always dangerous to a starved stomach.[151]

When the end of bread rationing came in April, and stores were again opened in the towns where people could buy each a kilogramme per person – even if at a high price – the peasant was not legally in a position to take advantage of it.

But now, driven by desperation, large numbers of those who could still move left the village. If they could not reach the cities they hung around the railway stations. These small Ukrainian stations usually had little orchards. To these 'railwaymen, themselves swaying from hunger, took the corpses of the dead'.[152] Outside Poltava, near a railway signal, the bodies found along the tracks were brought for dumping into a number of deep ditches already dug.[153] If unable to, or prevented from, reaching the stations, the peasants went to the railway lines, and begged bread from the passing trains: a few crusts would sometimes be thrown out. But later many had not the strength even for this.[154]

At the small town of Khartsyzsk in the Donbas, a railwayman reports families begging round the station and being chased off, until in the spring they arrived in ever-increasing numbers, and 'lived, slept, died in streets or squares', in April 1933 overrunning the whole town.[155]

Things were more difficult when it came to the big cities. In Kiev there was no famine for those who had jobs and ration cards, but only a kilogramme of bread could be bought at a time, and supplies were poor.[156] One observer remarked: 'The supplies in the shops barely sufficed for the needs of the privileged classes'.[157] For them, goods were also often available in the 'closed stores' open to state employees, members of leading Party committees, OGPU officers, senior military officers, factory managers, engineers and so on, which are still a feature of Soviet life.

Nominally, incomes in the cities were fairly egalitarian, but the privileged rationing and purchasing system made nonsense of this. A teacher might be paid about half what an equivalently senior OGPU man got: but the latter's special ration card for consumer goods at low prices in such special shops made his real income some twelve times the former's.[158]

Even skilled workers in the Ukrainian cities earned no more than 250 to 300 roubles a month, lived on black bread, potatoes and salt fish, and lacked clothing and footwear.[159] As early as the summer of 1932 office workers' rations in Kiev were cut from one pound to half a pound of bread a day, industrial workers from two to one-and-a-half pounds.[160] Students at the Kiev Institute of Animal Husbandry got a ration of 200 grammes of ersatz bread a day, plus a plate of fish broth, sauerkraut, two spoonfuls of kasha or cabbage, and fifty grammes of horsemeat.[161]

In Kiev there were queues half a kilometre long at the stores. These were hardly able to stand, each holding on to the belt of the person in front.[163] They would each get 200–400 grammes of bread, the last few hundred getting nothing but tickets or chalked numbers on their hands to present the next day.[163]

To join these queues, or to buy from those who had managed to get bread there, or simply under vaguely understood compulsion, the peasants flocked to the cities. Although road blocks and controls were set up to stop this, many managed to get through, but usually found little help. Dnipropetrovsk was 'overrun' with starving peasants.[164] One railway worker estimates that perhaps over half of the peasants who reached the Donbas in search of food 'were living their last days, hours, and minutes'.[165]

To get to Kiev, avoiding the roadblocks, 'they would crawl through the swamps, through the woods . . . The ones who had managed to crawl there were the more fortunate, one out of ten thousand. And even when they got there, they found no salvation. They lay starving on the ground . . .'[166]

In the towns eerie scenes took place. People hurried about their affairs in normal fashion – and 'there were starving children, old men, girls, crawling about among them on all fours', hardly able to beg, mainly ignored.[167]

–But not entirely: there are many reports of townsmen in Kiev helping peasants avoid the police.[168] In Kharkov as well, people gave them bread.[169] In Kharkov too, 'I saw a woman swollen with hunger, lying in the Horse Market (Kinna Ploshcha). Worms were literally eating her alive. Along the sidewalk went people who placed small pieces of bread next to her, but the poor lady was already too close to death to eat them. She cried and asked for medical assistance, which no one gave.'[170] (A doctor reports that at a meeting of medical staff in Kiev an order had been given banning any medical assistance to peasants illegally in the city.)[171]

In Kiev, Kharkov, Dnipropetrovsk, and Odessa it became routine for the local authorities to go round the town in the early morning, clearing up the corpses. In 1933, about 150 dead bodies a day were gleaned in the streets of Poltava.[172] In Kiev too,

> In the morning horses pulled flattop carts through the city, and the corpses of those who had died in the night were collected. I saw one such flattop cart with children lying on it. They were just as I have described them, thin, elongated faces, like those of dead birds, with sharp beaks. These tiny birds had flown into Kiev and what good had it done them? Some of them were still muttering, and their heads still turning. I asked the driver about them, and he just waved his hands and said: 'By the time they get where they are being taken they will be silent too'.[173]

Those who lived were also removed from time to time and expelled. In Kharkov, special operations to round up the starving peasants took place every week or so, mounted by the police with the help of specially mobilized squads of Party members.[174] This was often done in a most heartless way, as with all the operations against the peasant. One eyewitness, a worker, describes a police raid in Kharkov on 27 May 1933 on several thousand peasants who had joined breadlines: they were put in railway wagons and transported to a pit near Lisove station, being left there to starve. A few escaped, and managed to inform a dying peasant in nearby Zidky village, whose wife had gone with her child to buy bread in town, that they were in the Lisove pit; but the father died at home and the other two in the pit the following day.[175]

Such victims, driven by starvation, won no advantage, at most a few days' respite, compared with those who died at home. But the compulsion to move was strong. A starving man, Grossman says, 'is tormented and driven as though by fire and torn both in the guts and in the soul'. At first he escapes and wanders but finally 'crawls back into his house. And the meaning of this is that famine, starvation, has won'.

★

Whether they returned to their village, or had never left it, most of the victims met their deaths at home.

Of a Ukrainian farm population of between twenty and twenty-five million, about five million died – a quarter to a fifth. The casualty rate varied considerably by area and even village, from 10% to 100%.

The highest death rates were in the grain-growing provinces of Poltava, Dnipropetrovsk, Kirovohrad and Odessa, usually with from 20–25%, though even higher in many villages. In the Kamianets–Podilsky, Vinnytsia, Zhytomyr, Donets, Kharkov and Kiev provinces, it was lower – usually some 15–20%. In the far north of the Ukraine, in the beet-growing area, it was lowest – partly because the forests, rivers and lakes held animal and vegetable life which could be used as food.

Doctors, who were state employees, put down all sorts of diseases as the causes of death, including 'sudden illness' and so on. By the winter of 1932–3 death certificates no longer appear. In the fairly favourably situated village of Romankovo, which is only six kilometres from the large metallurgical works at Kamyansk with members of the local families working there and receiving rations at the place of work, five months of 1933 saw 588 deaths in a population of 4,000–5,000. The death certificates (they include a high proportion of workers) of August to mid-October are available; except for older people ('senile weakness') the cause of death is almost always 'exhaustion' or 'flux'.[176]

In spite of the later suppression of death certificates, lists were preserved by responsible individuals of all those dying in various villages; and in others careful counts were kept, some by officials.

Report after report is available, short accounts by survivors: 'The Fate of the Village of Yareski'; 'Hurske Loses 44 Per Cent of its Population'; 'Famine Devastates the Village of Pleshkany'; '430 Famine Deaths in Zhornoklovy'; 'The Devastation by Famine of the Village of Strizhivka'; and so on. Outside the villages and even the small towns in Kiev and Vinnytsia Provinces, piles of human bodies to the number of several thousand lay on the frozen ground, with no one strong enough to dig the graves.[177]

The village of Matkivtsi, Vinnytsia Province, had 312 households and a population of 1,293. Three men and two women were shot for cutting ears of corn in their own garden plots, and twenty-four families were deported to Siberia. In the spring of 1933 many died. And the rest fled. The empty village was cordoned off, with a black flag hung up to indicate that it had an epidemic, and in the registers the notation made that typhus had struck it.[178] A Russian friend of the author similarly tells of his father in the Komsomol, who belonged to a squad which went to villages with the whole population dead, supposedly of disease, to put 'no entry' signs around them for health reasons – there being no possibility of burial of the many corpses. They only saw this part of the picture, and for the rest accepted indoctrination.

Time after time, officials tell of entering villages with few or no survivors, and seeing the dead in their houses. In villages of 3,000–4,000 people (Orlivka, Smolanka, Hrabivka), only 45–80 were left.[179] The village of Machukhy, in the Poltava Province, with 2,000 homes, lost about half its population. In the same area smaller settlements, more likely to be of advanced individual farmers, were wiped out: for example, the fifty family Soroky; the five family Lebedi; the five family Tverdokhliby; the seven family Malolitka.[180] An agronomist gives an approximate figure of 75% dead for another group of these last surviving *khutirs*.[181]

In some villages the death roll was small. 'In the spring of 1933, 138 persons died in the village of Kharkiwtsi. In comparison with other places this was very good'.[182] And, generally speaking, our reports vary over the range between annihilation and lowish casualties.

As a general guide, an American Communist employed in a Soviet factory says that of the fifteen state and collective farms he visited in September 1933, none had lost *less* than 10% of their workers through starvation.[183] In Ordzherdovo he was actually shown the books. The population had fallen from 527 in September 1932 to 420 in April 1934 (cows had dropped from 353 to 177, pigs from 156 to 103).[184]

The village of Yareski had often served as a location for Soviet films because of its beautiful scenery along the river Vorskla: its population of 1,500 went down by 700.[185] In a village of 1,532 inhabitants in the Zhitomir Province, 813 died in the famine.[186] In another village of 3,500 inhabitants, 800 died in 1933 alone, while one child, the son of an activist, was born.[187] A former Soviet journalist testified that in his home village about 700 of the 2,011 inhabitants had died in 1932–3 (Chairman: 'How old was your daughter when she died of starvation?' Mr. Derevyanko: 'Five years old').[188] In the village of Riaske (Poltava Province) a careful count showed that of a population of about 9,000, 3,441 had died in the famine.[189] In Verbky in the Dnipropetrovsk Province, more than half the houses were empty in September 1933.[190]

The correspondent of the *Christian Science Monitor* went to the Ukraine after the ban on foreign correspondents was lifted in the autumn of 1933. He visited two areas, one near Poltava, the other near Kiev. As with the American Communist quoted earlier, the local Soviets told him of a death rate nowhere lower than 10%. One secretary of a village Soviet said that out of 2,072 inhabitants, 634 had died. In the past year there had been one marriage. Six children had been born, of whom one had survived. In four named families, seven children, and one wife, remained: eight adults and eleven children had died.[191]

He describes, more impressionistically, the village of Cherkass, seven or eight miles to the south of Bila Tserkva, where

251

The 'normal' mortality of 10% had been far exceeded. On the road to the village, former ikons with the face of Christ had been removed; but the crown of thorns had been allowed to remain – an appropriate symbol for what the village had experienced. Coming into the village, we found one deserted house after another, with window-panes fallen in, crops growing mixed with weeds in gardens with no one to harvest them. A boy in the dusty village street called the death roll among the peasants in the face of the catastrophe of the preceding winter and spring.[192]

In Shylivka, there had already been very large casualties in the dekulakization campaign. In the famine, death was such that two calls a day were made by the corpse-cart. On a single day sixteen bodies were found round the cooperative.[193]

Korostyshiv, not far from Kiev, was a Jewish village. A former resident found it in 1933 'a mere corpse of the village I had known'. The synagogue was now a rope factory. Children were dying of hunger. (Resettlement of the 'depopulated Jewish kolkhozes of the Ukraine' was later made the subject of special measures.)[194]

There was a Protestant village, Ozaryntsi, in the Kamianets–Podilsky Province. Most of the inhabitants died.[195] A German Protestant village, Halbshtadt, in the Zaporizhia Province, had been settled by Mennonites in Catherine the Great's time. Some help came to the Mennonites from German co-religionists, and they did not die on a mass scale in 1933, but in 1937–8 they were all sent into exile as spies for having had this contact with the outside world.[196]

In one village (Budionivka, Poltava Province), an analysis is available of the social status of 92 of those dying. 57 were kolkhozniks, 33 individual peasants; and under the class scheme 31 were poor peasants, 53 middle and eight 'well-off', including two who had been expelled from the kolkhoz.[197]

In fact, it is reported more generally that those the Communists had categorized as 'poor peasants', or at any rate those in this category who had not been able or willing to join the new rural elite, were the main victims.[198] One report on corn confiscated in the town of Zaporizhe–Kamyansk and the surrounding villages shows nine cases of 'concealment'. All are identified as 'workers' (two) or poor or medium peasants (seven).[199]

We have some casualty figures for entire districts, which were, of course, partly urban. In the Chornukhy district, confidential official reports show that between January 1932 and January 1934, a population of 53,672 had lost 7,387 people, nearly half of them children.[200] In another Ukrainian district, where the total population was about 60,000, 11,680 people had died in 1932–3 (about one-fifth) while only twenty births had been registered.[201]

★

So far we have largely dealt with villages and figures. We cannot but also look at the individuals who suffered and died. A survivor gives a clear picture of the physical signs:

> The clinical picture of famine is well-known. It ruins the energy-producing resources of the human system, advancing as the necessary fats and sugars are withheld. The body withers. The skin assumes a dust-grey tinge and folds into many creases. The person ages visibly. Even small children and infants have an old look. Their eyes become large, bulging and immobile. The process of distrophy sometimes affects all the tissues and the sufferer resembles a skeleton covered with tightly-drawn skin. But a swelling of the tissues is more common, especially those of the hands, feet and face. Skin erupts over the swelling and festering sores persist. Motive power is lost, the slightest motion producing complete fatigue. The essential functions of life – breathing and circulation – consume the body's own tissue and albumen, the body consumes itself. Respiration and heartbeat become accelerated. The pupils dilate, Starvation diarrhea sets in. This condition is already dangerous because the slightest physical exertion induces heart failure. It often takes place while the sufferer is walking, climbing the stairs, or attempting to run. General weakness spreads. The patient now cannot get up, nor move in bed. In a condition of semi-conscious sleep he might last about a week, whereupon the heart stops beating.[202]

Scurvy and boils would also disfigure the bodies.

A less clinical account of a suffering peasant is given by a former neighbour: 'Under his eyes were two pocket-like swellings, and the skin on them had a peculiar glossy tinge. His hands were swollen too. On his fingers the swelling had burst, and the wounds exuded a transparent fluid with an extremely repulsive smell'.[203] There were also huge blisters on the feet and ankles. Peasants would 'sit down on the ground to prick their blisters, and then get up to drag themselves about their begging';[204] or again, 'her feet were dreadfully swollen. She sat down and pricked her swollen feet with a sharp stick, to let the water out of the huge blisters. There was a large hole in the top of her foot from continuous piercing of the skin'.[205]

'Death by starvation is a monotonous subject. Monotonous and repetitious', one observer comments.[206] And if we only give a handful of individual accounts, it must be remembered that such was the fate of millions.

Survivors record the deaths of their neighbours in simple, unemotional terms. The village of Fediivka, in the Poltava Province, had a population of 550 at the beginning of 1932:

> The first family to die was the Rafalyks – father, mother and a child. Later on the Fediy family of five also perished of starvation. Then followed the families of Prokhor Lytvyn (four persons), Fedir Hontowy (three persons), Samson Fediy (three persons). The second child of the latter family was beaten to death on somebody's onion patch. Mykola and Larion Fediy died, followed by Andrew Fediy and his wife; Stefan Fediy; Anton Fediy, his wife and four children (his two other little girls survived); Boris Fediy, his wife and three children; Olanviy Fediy and his wife; Taras Fediy and his wife; Theodore Fesenko; Constantine Fesenko; Melania Fediy; Lawrenty Fediy; Peter Fediy; Eulysis Fediy and his brother Fred; Isidore Fediy, his wife and two children; Ivan Hontowy, his wife and two children; Vasyl Perch, his wife and child; Makar Fediy; Prokip Fesenko; Abraham Fediy; Ivan Skaska, his wife and eight children.
>
> Some of these people were buried in a cemetery plot; others were left lying wherever they died. For instance, Elizabeth Lukashenko died on the meadow; her remains were eaten by ravens. Others were simply dumped into any handy excavation. The remains of Lawrenty Fediy lay on the hearth of his dwelling until devoured by rats.[207]

Again:

> In the village of Lisnyaky, in the Yahotyn district of the Poltava region, there lived a family named Dvirko, the parents and four children, two grown up and two adolescents.
>
> This family was dekulakized and evicted from their house which was demolished.
>
> During the famine of 1932–3, this whole family, with the exception of the mother, died of starvation.
>
> One day the chairman of the collective farm, Samokysh, came to this old woman and 'mobilized' her for work in the collective farm fields. The frail old woman took her hoe and, gathering the last reserves of her failing energy, went to the collective farm centre, but did not quite get there. Her energy failed, and she dropped dead at the very door of the collective farm centre.[208]

The fate of two families in another village: 'Anton Samchenko died with his wife and sister; three children were left ... In Nikita Samchenko's family the father and two children were left ... And Sidor Odnorog died with his wife and two daughters; one girl was left. Yura Odnorog died with his wife and three children; one girl was left alive'.[209]

In the small village of Horikhove, near Zhytomyr, only ten of the thirty households were still inhabited in 1933. Whole families died out. A typical example given is of the Viytovyches: 'Their youngest son, sixteen years old, was returning one day from school at Shakhvorivka . . . when he died on his way home by the roadside . . . The elder daughter Palazhka died in the kolkhoz field. The old mother died in the street on her way to work . . . The father's body was found in the Korostyshiv forest, half devoured by beasts.' Only the elder son, on service with the OGPU in the Far East, survived.[210]

Another survivor recounts that some of the tragic events in Viknyna (situated where the provinces of Kiev, Vinnytsia and Odessa meet) made an indelible impression on his memory.

> Among the first victims of famine towards the end of 1932 was the Taranyuk family: father, mother and three sons. Two of the latter were members of the Komsomol and actively assisted in 'grain collection'. The father and mother died in their cottage and the sons under neighbours' fences.
>
> At this time six persons died in the Zverkhanowsky family. By some miracle a son, Volodymyr, and a daughter, Tatyana, survived.
>
> The swollen blacksmith, Ilarion Shevchuk, who, in January 1933 came to the village soviet to ask for help, was lured to the fire hall and murdered with staves. The murderers were: Y. Konofalsky, chairman of the village soviet, his assistant I. Antonyuk and the secretary V. Lyubomsky.
>
> The poor widow Danylyuk and her sons had a very tragic end. Her dead body was eaten by maggots and the two sons, Pavlo and Oleska, fell dead begging for food. Only the third son Trokhym survived, by being able to find some food in the city.
>
> Porfir Neterebchuk, one of the most industrious farmers, lamed by hard work, was found dead by the church fence.
>
> An old man, Ivan Antonyuk, died when his daughter Hanya fed him with 'bread' made from green ears of grain which she had secretly cut in the fields, in spite of the watchfulness of the village soviet authorities.
>
> Oleska Voytrykhovsky saved his and his family's (wife and two little children) lives by consuming the meat of horses which had died in the collective of glanders and other diseases. He dug them up at night and brought the meat home in a sack. His older brother Yakiw, and his sister-in-law died earlier from hunger.[211]

A worker visiting his old village learnt how

> My father-in-law, Pavlo Husar, swollen with hunger, had started out to Russia to seek bread and died in a thicket in the village of Lyman, three and a half miles from home. The people in Lyman helped to bury him. They also told us how my wife's other sister had eaten chaff and roots and died the following day; how my oldest brother's widow had been intercepted at least five times on her way to Russia to get bread, and how she had exchanged all her clothes for food and tried to take care of her three children and my old mother, but finally died of hunger herself. Then two of her children died, Yakiv, six, and Petro, eight.[212]

Two Americans originating in the area were able to visit their native village late in 1934. They found their parents dead, and their sister's face so distorted as to be unrecognizable.[213] In one Ukrainian household where some lay just breathing, others not breathing at all, 'the daughter of the owner, whom I knew, lay on the floor in some kind of insane fit, gnawing on the leg of a stool . . . When she heard us come in, she did not turn around, but growled, just as a dog growls, if you come near him when he is gnawing on a bone'.[214]

The Associated Press correspondent describes being shown by a *Pravda* staff writer specializing in editorials about capitalist lies, a letter from his Jewish father in the Ukraine:

MY BELOVED SON,
   This is to let you know that your mother is dead. She died from starvation after months of pain. I, too, am on the way, like many others in our town. Occasionally we manage to snatch some crumbs, but not enough to keep us alive much longer, unless they send in food from the centre. There is none for hundreds of miles around here. Your mother's last wish was that you, our only son, say *Kadish* for her. Like your mother I, too, hope and pray that you may forget your atheism now when the godless have brought down heaven's wrath on Russia. Would it be too much to hope for a letter from you, telling me that you have said *Kadish* for your mother – at least once – and that you will do the same for me? That would make it so much easier to die.[215]

An American correspondent went to the village of Zhuky, Poltava Province, accompanied by the chairman of the local collective farm and an agronomist. They took him to various houses, all occupied by fairly contented brigadiers or Communists. Then he chose a hut at random and went in, his companions following. The only occupant was a girl of fifteen, and they had this conversation: 'Where is your mother?' 'She died of hunger last winter.' 'Have you any brothers or sisters?' 'I had four, they all died too.' 'When?' 'Last winter and spring.' 'And your father?' 'He's working in the fields.' As they left, the officials found nothing to say.[216]

Of a group of displaced persons in a camp in Germany in 1947–8, forty-one (mainly townsmen with relations in the village) were asked if anyone in their families had died in the famine. Fifteen said no and twenty-six yes.[217]

Peasant families, gradually starving in their empty huts, met their fates in various ways:

In one hut there would be something like a war. Everyone would keep close watch over everyone else. People would take crumbs from each other. The wife turned against her husband and the husband against his wife. The mother hated the children. And in some other hut love would be inviolable to the very last. I knew one woman with four children. She would tell them fairy stories and legends so that they would forget their hunger. Her own tongue could hardly move, but she would take them into her arms even though she had hardly the strength to lift her arms when they were empty. Love lived on within her. And people noticed that where there was hate people died off more swiftly. Yet love, for that matter, saved no one. The whole village perished, one and all. No life remained in it.[218]

For though some were capable of overcoming them, starvation produced psychological as well as physical symptoms. Poison pen letters would denounce one or another peasant for hoarding, sometimes accurately.[219] Murder was common, with such stories as the following:

In the village Bilka, Denys Ischenko killed his sister, brother-in-law, and their sixteen year old daughter in order to obtain thirty pounds of flour which they had. The same man murdered a friend of his, Petro Korobeynyk, when he was carrying four loaves of bread, which he had somehow obtained in the city. For a few pounds of flour, and a few loaves of bread, hungry people took the lives of others.[220]

There are innumerable reports, too, of suicide, almost invariably by hanging. And, in the same way, mothers not seldom put their children out of their misery. But the most horrifying symptom was different:

Some went insane . . . There were people who cut up and cooked corpses, who killed their own children and ate them. I saw one. She had been brought to the district centre under convoy. Her face was human, but her eyes were those of a wolf. These are cannibals, they said, and must be shot. But they themselves, who drove the mother to the madness of eating her own children, are evidently not guilty at all! . . . Just go and ask, and they will all tell you that they did it for the sake of virtue, for everybody's good. That's why they drove mothers to cannibalism.[221]

There was in fact no law against cannibalism (as is probably true in the West as well). A confidential instruction to OGPU and prosecution chiefs in the Ukrainian provinces from K.M. Karlson, Deputy Head of the Ukrainian OGPU, dated 22 May 1933, tells them that since cannibalism is not covered in the criminal code, 'all cases of those accused of cannibalism must immediately be transferred to the local branches of the OGPU'. He added that if preceded by murder (covered by Article 142 of the Penal Code), such cases should nevertheless be withdrawn from the courts and transferred to the Security Police.[222] Not all were shot. 325 cannibals from the Ukraine – 75 men and 250 women – are reported still serving life sentences in Baltic–White Sea Canal prison camps in the late 30s.[223]

There are scores of stories of particular acts of cannibalism, some eating their own families, others trapping children or ambushing strangers. Or (as at Kalmazorka, Odessa Province, in this case in connection with the theft of a pig) a search of the whole village might result in the discovery of children's corpses being cooked.[224]

Not all cannibalism, or ideas of cannibalism, were based on despair alone. One activist who had been working on the collectivization campaign in Siberia came back to the Ukraine in 1933 to find the population of his village 'almost extinct'. His younger brother told him that they were living on bark, grass and hares, but that when these gave out, 'Mother says we should eat her if she dies'.[225]

These examples of people driven by hunger beyond normal human behaviour are matched, in a different sense, by what may appear to a non-Communist as, in some ways, even less understandable derangements of normal values – as with the treatment now given the loyal local activists.

The true local elite – Party officials, GPU and so on – survived the famine comfortably fed. But this was not the case with the rank and file.

The 'Committees of Unwealthy Peasants' had 'fought mercilessly the manoeuvres of kulaks and counter-revolutionaries to undermine grain procurements'.[226] In the final phase of 'collection', activists were switched to other villages, and any food they themselves had hoarded was taken in their absence.[227] And on 8 March 1933, their task completed, the Committees were abolished, and their members left to starve with the rest of the villagers.[228]

They were not popular. A typical story is of one village where the 'Committee of Unwealthy Peasants' had picked Christmas Eve to order the population to transport the harvest to the nearest town, where they had to spend two or three days in line to deliver their own grain.[229]

So when they too died, they received little sympathy. A local activist in Stepanivka, Vinnytsia Province, a member of the grain confiscation groups, was always singing the Internationale, starting 'Arise! . . .' In the spring villagers found him lying by the roadside, and sardonically called, 'Eh, Matvey, arise!', but he died almost at once.[230]

In village after village activists are reported dying of starvation in the spring of 1933.[231] In a typical case in the Kiev Province, half of them died, one after sinking into cannibalism.[232]

★

An even more striking, or at least more important, aspect of the psychopathy of Stalinism may be seen in the fact that no word about the famine was allowed to appear in the press or elsewhere. People who referred to it were subject to arrest for anti-Soviet propaganda, usually getting 5 or more years in labour camps.

A lecturer at an agricultural school in Molochansk, near Melitopil, remarks how she was forbidden to use the word 'famine' – though food was insufficient even in town, and in one neighbouring village no one was left at all.[233]

At the Nizhyn Lyceum (Chernihiv Province), where Gogal was educated, students living on inadequate food were told, if they said they were hungry, 'You are spreading Hitler's propaganda!' When the old librarian and some girl servants died and the word 'hunger' was used, a party activist cried 'Counter-revolution!'[234]

A soldier serving in 1933 in Fedosiya in the Crimea received a letter from his wife, describing the deaths of neighbours and the miserable condition of herself and their child. The political officer seized the letter, and next day had the soldier denounce it as a forgery. The wife and son did not survive.[235]

A doctor is reported sentenced to ten years 'without the right of correspondence' (a common euphemism for the death penalty) for saying that his sister had died of hunger, and that the cause was the forcible seizure of food.[236]

Even the officials who could see death all around were not permitted – did not permit themselves – to see 'starvation'. One agronomist sent an old man with his routine report to the local MTS, but the messenger died on the way. The agronomist was then bullied for sending a sick messenger, and replied that the whole village was starving. The response was 'there is no starvation in the Soviet Union – you are listening to kulak rumours', followed, however, by a mutter of 'keep your mouth shut'.[237]

This refusal to countenance the truth or allow the faintest reference to reality was certainly part of Stalin's general plan. As we shall see in Chapter 17, it was to be applied on a world scale.

★

13

A Land Laid Waste

It happened in the Ukraine, not long ago
Shevchenko

In the early summer of 1933, Malcolm Muggeridge reported,

> On a recent visit to the Northern Caucasus and the Ukraine, I saw something
> of the battle that is going on between the government and the peasants. The
> battlefield is as desolate as in any war and stretches wider; stretches over a large
> part of Russia. On the one side, millions of starving peasants, their bodies often
> swollen from lack of food; on the other, soldier members of the GPU carrying
> out the instructions of the dictatorship of the proletariat. They had gone over
> the country like a swarm of locusts and taken away everything edible; they had
> shot or exiled thousands of peasants, sometimes whole villages; they had
> reduced some of the most fertile land in the world to a melancholy desert.[1]

Another Englishman saw,

> The fertile fields of Soviet Ukraine – field after field covered with ungarnered
> grain, that had been allowed to rot. There were districts where it was possible
> to travel for a whole day between these fields of blackening wheat, seeing only
> here and there a tiny oasis where the harvest had been got safely in.[2]

An observer from the city describes the worst land: 'Mile after mile we
walked through uncultivated ground. Maxim said it hadn't been
cultivated for over two years . . . Another hour's walk and we came to a
wheat field, or I should say a weed and wheat field. Maxim pulled at the
wheat and showed me a few undeveloped kernels'.[3] The matter of weeds
had even reached Politburo level earlier in the year, but was blamed on the
peasantry: 'In a number of places we have many weeds. We are pulling
them up and burning them. But why did they come up? Because of poor
tillage of the land', Kaganovich reported to a conference of 'village shock-

260

workers' in February 1933.[4]

If 1921 had been a desperate victory and 1930 an unfavourable draw, 1932–3 saw a disastrous defeat of the Ukrainian peasantry.

What gave the regime its advantage both in 1930–31 and even more in 1932–3 was that it was now organized and centralized as it had not been in 1921. Herzen, back in the 1860s, had said that what he most feared was a 'Genghis Khan with the telegraph'. This is a true description of what was now happening in the lands the Mongols had laid waste so many centuries before, and which were now seeing a repetition of that horror.

The celebrated German Communist writer, Theodor Plivier, long in the USSR, has a character in his *Moscow* speak of 'one man' who could 'make famine his ally so as to achieve his aim that the peasant should be at his feet like a worm'. And at the time, in a crucial analysis from the Communist point of view, M.M. Khatayevich told an activist: 'A ruthless struggle is going on between the peasantry and our regime. It's a struggle to the death. This year was a test of our strength and their endurance. It took a famine to show them who is master here. It has cost millions of lives, but the collective farm system is here to stay. We've won the war'.[5]

Any 'difficulties', as with Kaganovich's view of the weed-infested fields, were blamed on the peasants themselves. In June Kalinin told a congress of collective farm workers, 'Every farmer knows that people who are in trouble because of lack of bread, are in that predicament not as the result of a poor harvest, but because they were lazy and refused to do an honest day's work'.[6] Indeed, this line is still taken by some Soviet scholars, one of whom remarks that 'the events of 1932 were a great lesson for the collective farmers', adding that kulak sabotage of the harvest had led to food shortages.[7]

But with the 'victory' won, the disastrous agricultural situation could hardly be allowed to go on indefinitely, and this had been understood in Moscow.

★

The authorities had in fact, as we have seen, already been preparing for a reversion to normal methods at the very time when the starving Ukraine was being denied help.

On 19 January 1933 a new law laid down a simple grain tax (from 'land actually under cultivation') instead of the grain collections, though this did not come into effect until later. On 18 February, the Council of People's Commissars permitted the introduction of trading in grain in the Kiev and Vinnytsia provinces, and some other areas of the USSR: (by this time there was no grain to trade in the two provinces named). Finally, on

25 February, as we noted earlier, the authorities authorized a 'seed subsidy' for the *next* harvest – with 325,000 tons to go to the Ukraine.

The grain collection in the Ukraine was at last officially halted on 15 March 1933.[8] Up to the last grain requisition had been encouraged – allegedly to get back necessary 'seed grain stolen or illegally distributed', as Postyshev put it.[9] However, by April Mikoyan is reported in Kiev, ordering the release of some of the army grain reserves to the villages.[10] There are many stories of peasants being given bread in the late spring of 1933, and eating too much too quickly, sometimes with fatal results. In May, further attempts were made to save the survivors' lives: clinics were set up in some areas, in abandoned peasant houses, and the starving were fed with milk and buckwheat porridge, to bring them back to health. Many of those far gone enough to get the treatment did not survive but some did, women and girls doing better than men and boys,[11] but one official saw, at one of these emergency clinics, a father, still a young man, himself in a desperate state, watching as his wife and two sons – one eight years old, one six – were carried off to the cellar used for corpses. The man, unusually, survived.[12]

But by the end of May observers noted a virtual end of the deaths by famine on a mass scale, though the death rate remained abnormally high.[13]

★

The debilitated peasantry were now launched on a new harvest campaign. Neither they nor their surviving horses were capable of hard labour. The death and emaciation of the latter is widely reported in the Ukrainian press. As a result, it was laid down that milch-cows could be used to help.[14] – Needless to say 'kulaks' were blamed for the horses' condition: (one criticism of poor and middle peasants was the strange one that they showed a 'kulak incompetence in the care and use of draught animals').[15] One student drafted to the countryside describes a kolkhoz where most of the horses had to be 'kept upright with ropes, for if they lay down they would never rise': their food was straw from the thatch, cut and steamed. Only four of the thirty-nine horses which started for one of the fields reached it, (and only fourteen of the thirty collective farmers). The horses were not strong enough to pull harrows, and had to be helped, and the men could only carry the seed sacks for a short time, and then had to be relieved. They somehow pulled through until four in the afternoon, when the horses gave in. The kolkhoz head then called off work for the day, but 'something had been accomplished'.[16]

The Ukrainian government called for harder work, instancing a collective farm where the peasants were only actually working for seven and a half hours instead of the sixteen hours they pretended to put in.[17]

Zatonsky is reported visiting a village in June 1933, and being approached by a crowd of exhausted peasants, whom the District Party Secretary introduced to him as shirkers. Zatonsky replied, 'if they die it will be a lesson to the others'.[18]

With this physical inability of the peasants to do more than part of the work, and the great depletion of the work force, the sowing of 1933 was accomplished in various ways. Fodder was finally made available to the kolkhoz horses, with instructions that it should not be used for other purposes on pain of prosecution under the 7 August 1932 law.[19] And from May on, every possible human hand was brought in to help. This included the peasant women. In one beet kolkhoz a brigade of twenty-five or thirty women would start on the rows of beet; but by the time they reached the end of the field half of them were lying exhausted among the beets. Yet even now, when the envoy of the MTS Political Department (i.e. the local GPU officer) went to the field when rations – barley and oats mush – were being issued, and attacked the women as lazy 'fine ladies', they shouted him down, threw dishes of groats at him, threw hot soup over him and beat him up. The woman ringleader hid in the woods next day, but it then appeared that the officer had preferred not to report the matter.[20]

The inadequate local work force was supplemented from outside. Students and others from the towns were 'mobilized' to reap the harvest;[21] and army squads were also sent to help. In one village where the whole population had died or left, troops were kept in tents away from the village and told, as others had been, that there had been an epidemic.[22]

More important, and permanent, was the moving of Russian peasants into empty or half-empty villages.[23] An unpublished decree signed by Molotov is quoted, which speaks of meeting the wishes of inhabitants of the central districts of the USSR to settle in 'the free lands of the Ukraine and North Caucasus'.[24] Nearly one hundred Russian families are reported sent to a village in the Dnipropetrovsk Province; others to places in Zaporizhia Province, Poltava Province, and so on – though some could not stand living in houses still smelling of death, and 'returned to Orel'.[25] In Voroshilovgrad Province, deserted villages overrun with weeds, with winter wheat standing unharvested in early 1933, were now occupied by Russians.[26] Their presence, reported by many of our sources, is confirmed in the official press.[27] They were given special rations of about fifty pounds of wheat a month.[28]

In a village in the Kharkov Province (Murafa) some children were living as orphans in the care of surviving activists. When the Russians came in 1933 and took over these children's former houses, the orphans attacked the Russian children, calling them thieves and murderers. As a result the village school teacher was sentenced to twelve years hard labour.[29]

Of course, and as before, not only the peasantry but also the less effective members of the Party were blamed for 'mistakes'. An instruction dated 17 June 1933, signed by Stalin and addressed to Kossior, with copies to secretaries of Provincial, City and District Committees is quoted:

> For the last time you are reminded that any repetition of the mistakes of last year will compel the Central Committee to take even more drastic measures. And then, if you will pardon my saying so, even their old party beards will not save these comrades.[30]

This was clearly a threat to the old cadres, the leadership, in the Ukraine – even though the Ukrainian Central Committee was itself attacking its own subordinate organizations. Once more the Odessa Provincial Committee was singled out. It had, the Ukrainian Party organ complained, 'decided that the wheat of the first hectare should be used for the needs of local, or rather public, alimentation. It is incorrect and false because the decision puts at second remove the yielding of bread to the state, and puts the problem of public alimentation in the first place. It proves that some of our provincial committees have been under the influence of the interests of collective farmers, and have therefore served the interests of the enemies of our proletarian state'.[31] – The last a remarkably frank formulation.

Similarly, the paper attacked the chairman of one collective who had had bread baked for the peasants from their own wheat on three separate occasions. He was sent for trial, as was the chairman of the village soviet, who had also distributed wheat.[32] By 15 October 1933, 120,000 Ukrainian party members had been screened, and 27,500 'class enemies and unstable and demoralized elements' expelled.[33]

In the Resolution of the Third Ukrainian Party Conference in January 1934, failures were ingeniously accounted for. The distribution of the plan's grain requirements had been made 'mechanically', without taking local circumstances into account, so that 'in a number of districts' by no means with harvest failure, there had been a 'very severe supply situation, and there was damage to the economy of a section of the kolkhozes in these districts'.[34] As with other attempts to blame the local authorities, these points are not without some substance. But they only deal with superficial aspects of the campaign. The central fact is that the USSR's total grain crop of 1932, no worse than that of 1931, was only 12% below the 1926–30 average, and far from famine level. But procurements were up by 44%. There was no way in which local re-adjustments could have prevented the crisis and the famine; and it can be blamed quite unequivocally on Stalin and the Moscow leadership.

*

Kossior had revealed the true procurement situation when he said at the February 1933 plenum that if the Party had based itself on estimates from the grain-growing areas it would not have been able to collect *half* of what it had. It is estimated that the total collection, as actually secured, included at least two million tons originally destined to feed the peasantry.[35]

Such figures, and indeed most figures in the field of Soviet agriculture, depend on the skills of Western analysts, for the Soviet official figures are either misleading or non-existent. Until 1928, districts would estimate crops from actual trial threshings, and the method was reliable. But it was revealed in 1933 that the published 'yield' was now obtained by deducting 10% from the estimate of what the crop would have been if it had been brought from field to granary without loss. Since the writer (in *Izvestiya*) added that 'in most cases the threshings proved to be 30, 40 or 50% lower' than the estimated 'biological crop'[36] this was obviously quite fraudulent. And since, as we have seen, the State's requirements were the first to be allotted, it followed that much of the residue left to the peasants was imaginary.

A leading Western student of Soviet agriculture estimated that the true yield of the USSR in 1933 was 68.2 million tons, of which only 0.8 million tons were exported[37] (though this latter figure is officially given as 1.75 million tons). In 1930–31 five million tons a year had been exported. None of these figures are sufficient to cause famine in themselves. The main culprit was less the exports than the grain held in 'reserves'. Stalin himself stressed their importance in the circular quoted earlier in this chapter, accusing 'naive comrades' of allowing 'tens of thousands of poods of valuable grain' in the Ukraine to be 'thrown away' the previous year, owing to under-estimating the importance of the Grain Stock Project. These 'reserves', he added, should never be allowed to run low.[38]

Moreover, much of the grain seized at such cost from the peasantry was never available as a reserve either. As before, (and as is common even today in the Soviet Union), the wastage was stupendous. Postyshev noted in November 1933 that 'quite a considerable amount of grain has been lost through careless handling'.[39] There were scores of press reports of how this happened: At the Kiev-Petrovka Station a huge pile of wheat simply rotted away;[40] at the Traktorski collecting point, twenty railway wagons of grain were flooded;[41] at Krasnograd the wheat rotted in bales;[42] in Bakhmach it was piled on the ground and rotted there.[43] The pro-Soviet *New York Times* correspondent Walter Duranty noted, (but did not publish in his paper), that 'large quantities of grain were in evidence at the railway stations, of which a large proportion was lying in the open air'.[44] In the autumn of 1933 a freight train loaded with grain was wrecked near Chelyabinsk. The grain lay in the open for a whole month. It was almost at once surrounded by barbed wire, and guards were set. Every night there were attempts to take the grain. Some gleaners were killed, and the wounded taken to hospital and later arrested. But when the grain was finally removed, it was found that it had entirely rotted in the rain and was no longer even fit for 'technical' use in industry.[45] This was, indeed, the result of an accident, but a similar fate is often reported of grain routinely stacked. All in all, the British Embassy reports a German agricultural expert's view that 'up to 30% of the (1933) harvest may be lost'.[46] Even a considerably lower figure would have been enough to make a great difference to the peasant.

For meanwhile the cowed survivors were reduced to a subsistence level. Stalin's June circular laid down that only 10% of the total threshed grain could remain in the kolkhozes 'for subsistence, after the fulfilment of deliveries, payment to the Machine Tractor Stations, and seed and forage'.[47] Famine had been an emergency method of struggle. But the Ukrainian peasant now faced deprivation and exploitation made permanent.

At the same time the attack on his national heritage continued. The popular and patriotic culture of the Ukraine had long been sustained in the countryside by the blind bards – the Kobzars, celebrated by Shevchenko – who wandered from village to village, earning their keep by singing the old national songs and reciting the national ballads. Thus the peasantry were constantly reminded of their free and heroic past. This undesirable phenomenon was now suppressed. The bards were invited to a congress, and when they assembled they were arrested. Most of them are reported shot[48] – logically enough, for they would have been little use at forced labour in the camps.

★

In the cities the campaign against the defenders of Ukrainianization had also continued unabated. During the height of the famine, most of the 'saboteurs' in official places were linked with the agrarian disaster. The seventy-five senior agricultural officials denounced on 5 March had been especially linked with sabotage in the Ukraine, the North Caucasus and Byelorussia.[49]

But in the Ukraine the attack soon developed into a specifically anti-national campaign. The old intelligentsia, who represented the whole breadth of the country's culture, had been dealt with. Now it was the turn of the nationalist element in the Communist Party itself.

A link was of course provided between Communist 'nationalist' plotters and the earlier non-Communist victims. Matvii Yavorsky, the chief Party 'ideological watchdog' over Ukrainian historians in the 1920s had been denounced for his hitherto orthodox 'nationalist-kulakist' system of ideas in 1930.[50] He was now (March 1933) arrested, charged with belonging to a 'Ukrainian Military Organization'. He seems to have been sent to camp, and to have been shot there in 1937. And among those charged as fellow-conspirators, allegedly financed by 'Polish landlords and German Fascists',[51] were Shumsky, the original leader of the Ukrainian Party's 'national deviation', and a number of other figures, including Skrypnyk's secretary, Esternyuk. Soon a 'Polish Military Organization' with nationalist as well as Polish associations was exposed, with a former Secretary of the Chernihiv Provincial Committee at its head. And a little later a 'Union of the Kuban and the Ukraine' was brought to trial, though without publicity.[52]

On 1 March 1933, various governmental changes were announced, the most crucial being the removal of Skrypnyk from his long tenure of the Ukrainian Commissariat of Education, (and his appointment instead as Chairman of the State Planning Commission, a post of little influence).[53]

The Ukrainian Language Institute of the Ukrainian Academy of Science had been a main centre of the national renaissance under Shumsky and Skrypnyk. On 27 April 1933, *Pravda* attacked it as a hive of bourgeois nationalists, who plotted to alienate the Ukrainian language from the 'fraternal Russian tongue'. Soon afterwards seven leading philologists and scores of lesser figures were arrested.[54]

On 12 May came the arrest of Mykhaylo Yalovy, chief political editor of the Ukrainian State Publishing House. On 13 May his close colleague, Mykola Khvylovy, 'the most colourful personality in Ukrainian literary life' shot himself, leaving a letter to the Ukrainian Central Committee attacking the new terror.[55] Over the next weeks and months there were other suicides, and scores of arrests among the literary intelligentsia.

On 10 June 1933 Postyshev spoke to the Ukrainian Central Committee of cultural figures who had turned out to be enemy agents, and who had been 'hiding behind the broad back of the Bolshevik Skrypnyk'. In philosophy, literature, economics, linguistics, agronomy and political theory, they had developed ideas aimed at abolishing the Soviet Government – and had been responsible for difficulties in grain procurement. Skrypnyk, Postyshev added, had sometimes openly defended them.[56]

Skrypnyk is reported as having defiantly attacked Postyshev before the

Central Committee, accusing him of betraying the principles of internationalism. He seems to have repeated this at a meeting of the Ukrainian Politburo. Over June and July Postyshev and other leaders attacked him, and on 7 July he again defended himself to the Politburo. They demanded his unconditional surrender. That afternoon, instead, he shot himself.

The official obituary did not directly name him as a criminal, but rather a 'victim of bourgeois-nationalist elements who . . . gained his confidence'. He had then committed 'a series of political errors' which he had not had the courage to overcome, and so committed suicide – 'an act of faintheartedness particularly unworthy of a member of the Central Committee of the All-Union Communist Party'.[57]

By November he had become a 'nationalist degenerate . . . close to the counter-revolutionaries working for the cause of intervention'.[58] His crimes included his stubborn attempts to prevent Russification of the Ukrainian language. He had continued the struggle in his last year of activity, even mildly criticizing Kaganovich for saying on a visit to Kiev, in accordance with new Stalinist line, that the syntax of Ukrainian should be brought closer to Russian.[59] He was now accused of actually working 'towards the maximum separation of the Ukrainian language from the Russian language'.[60] As he fell, one of the most vehemently pressed charges against him was that he had helped introduce a soft 'L' and a new symbol for a hard 'G' into Ukrainian orthography. These were criticized as bourgeois in 1932, but in 1933 were equated with counter-revolution, Postyshev saying that the hard 'G' had aided 'nationalist wreckers'. It was also held to be – 'objectively' – assistance to the annexationist plans of the Polish landlords.[61]

Skrypnyk's later views were not unfairly summarized (from the Stalinist point of view) by Kossior, when condemning him in November 1933: 'Skrypnyk severely overestimated and exaggerated the national question; he made it the cornerstone, talked of it as an end in itself, and even went so far as to deny that the national question plays a subordinate role in the class struggle and proletarian dictatorship'. Indeed, as he pointed out, Skrypnyk had actually written, 'It is not true to say that the national question is subordinate to the general theory of class struggle'.[62]

★

A massive attack on the country's cultural institutions was foreshadowed early in June by Stalin's henchman Manuilsky (described by Trotsky as 'the most repulsive renegade of Ukrainian Communism'), speaking before the Kiev Party organization on the cultural problem: 'Here in the

Ukraine there are a number of institutions which have the elevated titles of academies, institutes, and learned societies, which frequently harbour not socialist science but class-enemy ideology. The national problem has been leased out to former members of nationalist parties who failed to join organically with the Party'.[63] These last were later defined (by Kossior) as 'many members of petty-bourgeois nationalist parties, of conciliationist parties, who later joined the ranks of our Party . . . Ukrainian Social-Democrats, and Borotbists' and others.[64]

Every conceivable cultural, academic and scientific organization was now purged. As Kossior put it, 'Whole counter-revolutionary nests were formed in the People's Commissariats of Education, of Agriculture, of Justice; in the Ukrainian Institute of Marxist-Leninism, the Agricultural Academy, the Shevchenko Institute etc'.[65]

The Agricultural Academy was (naturally) purged, the Director, his deputy and other leading figures dying in camps. The Shevchenko Research Institute of Literary Scholarship was more heavily penalized: fourteen of its research assistants were given long camp sentences, and its Director and five other leading figures were shot.[66]

Other victims included most of the staffs of the Ukrainian Institute of Eastern Studies, the Editorial Board of the *Soviet Ukrainian Encyclopaedia*, the Ukrainian Chamber of Weights and Measures, the Ukrainian Film Company (VUFKU), the Ukrainian Conference for the Establishment of a New Ukrainian Orthography.[67] The 'whole of' the Karl Marx State Institution in Kharkov was denounced as 'actually in the hands of counter-revolutionaries'.[68]

But enemies of the people were everywhere – editing the main literary journal *Chervony Shlyakh*, in State Transport, in the Geodesic Board, in the publishing houses (four of which had to be dissolved).[69] The Ukrainian Institute of Philosophy was purged, and its leading figures Professors Yurynets and Nyrchuk were later arrested, the latter as head of a fictitious 'Trotskyite-Nationalist Terrorist Centre'.[70]

At the Ukrainian Central Committee's November 1933 plenum, Kossior was able to quote a number of confessions from 'nationalist' professors, to the effect that they had planned to partition the Ukraine between Germany and Poland. From now on, lists were posted daily in the Academy of Science, bearing the names of those dismissed, with reasons for dismissal – usually 'wrecking' or 'hostile ideology' or 'maintaining contact with enemies of the people'. Over the next months almost all had gone.

The Ukrainian theatre had never been wholly suppressed and was seen as a monument of national continuity. In October 1933, the leading director, Les Kurbas, founder of the Berezil Theatre, was attacked as a nationalist and dismissed. Postyshev is reported to have tried to win him over, being staunchly rebuffed. He was arrested in November, and died in labour camp, his theatre becoming a venue of 'socialist realism'.[71] A group of five artists who painted the frescoes in the Chervono-Zavodsk Theatre in Kharkov were arrested, and three of them shot; the frescoes were destroyed as having a 'nationalist' content immediately after their unveiling.[72]

While crushing the 'nationalist' deviation, and all the independent elements of national culture, the Postyshev regime nevertheless made no attempt to destroy the formal side of Ukrainianization, as the earlier Russian Communist intruders had wished to do. The capital was transferred from Kharkov to the traditional site of Kiev on 24 June 1933, and a partial Russification rather than an elimination of the language was put in train. What was attacked was 'mechanical' Ukrainianization,[73] and this meant any autonomous development whatever.

Postyshev summed up the cultural purge on 19 November, to the effect that 'The discovery of Skrypnyk's nationalist deviation gave us the opportunity to rid the structure of socialism, and in particular the structure of Ukrainian socialist culture, of all Petliuraist, Makhnoist and other nationalist elements. A great job has been done. It is enough to say that during this period we cleaned out 2,000 men of the nationalist element, about 300 of them scientists and writers, from the People's Commissariat of Education. Eight central Soviet institutions were purged of more than 200 nationalists, who had been occupying positions as department chiefs and the like. Two systems, those of the co-operatives and grain reserves, have been purged of over 2,000 nationalists and white-guardists to my personal knowledge'.[74]

★

But the purge of Ukrainian nationalism was not over, indeed would never be over as far as the Soviet regime was concerned. Balitsky, the OGPU chief, announced to the Twelfth Congress of the Ukrainian Party in January 1934 that yet another conspiracy – a 'Bloc of Ukrainian Nationalist Parties' – had been uncovered;[75] (it was later alleged by Postyshev to have included Skrypnyk's group).[76] At the same Congress Postyshev named twenty-six Professors of the All-Ukrainian Association of Marxist-Leninist Institutes as enemies of the State;[77] and the Association was later dissolved as a nest of 'counter-revolutionaries, Trotskyites and nationalists'.[78]

A month later, Postyshev boasted to the Seventeenth All-Union Party Congress, 'we have annihilated the nationalist counter-revolution during the past year; we have exposed and destroyed the nationalist deviation'. This was, in Soviet historical terms, premature, for there were to be Ukrainian nationalists purged both in the country as a whole, and in the Party itself, right up to the present time. Even on the same occasion, Kossior made it clear that – still – the 'class enemy are attempting to do their work of destruction under the flag of Ukrainianization'.[79]

When, after the Kirov murder in December 1934, large groups of alleged underground terrorists were shot in Moscow, Leningrad and the Ukraine, the names given in the two Russian cities were of unknown victims apparently selected at random. In Kiev, twenty-eight members of a 'White Guard Terrorist Centre' were shot on charges of infiltrating from abroad with revolvers and hand-grenades for terrorist purposes.[80] In fact, only two of them had travelled abroad, though seven were West Ukrainians long settled in the USSR. Some were figures of the Rada regime, but most were literary men like Dmytro Falkivsky, Hrihory Kosynka, and the young deaf-and-dumb poet Oleksa Vlyzko – whose 'confession' was quoted by Postyshev the following year: he had, in 1929, 'joined a Ukrainian fascist nationalist organization . . . I fully subscribed to all the terrorist precepts of the fascist platform'.[81]

A 'Borotbist plot' was uncovered in 1935, with a leadership which included famous writers such as the country's leading dramatist, Mikola Kulish – who also confessed to 'terrorism', though only since April 1933.[82] Then, in January 1936, a group headed by the celebrated literary critic, poet, and professor of literature Mikola Zerov was secretly tried in Kiev, on charges of espionage and terrorism. Zerov, who had been mentor to virtually the whole literary revival of the 20s, was said to have attended a requiem for those shot in December 1934, and to have decided to avenge them. He and his 'gang' were mostly his fellow neo-classical poets, students of language, and members of the Higher Literary Seminar at Kiev University.[83]

Trotskyism was already among the charges, and as the purge progressed the connection became even more lethal than that of nationalism, with which it was often associated. From 1935, Trotskyites were found in Kiev, Kharkov and Dnipropetrovsk Universities, the Publishing House of the already much purged *Soviet Ukrainian Encyclopaedia*, the Institute of People's Education at Luhansk. In 1937 it was stated that Trotskyite groups existed in all the Ukrainian cities.[84]

The extent of the blow at Ukrainian culture can be seen in the mere numbers. One estimate is that about 200 of 240 authors writing in the Ukraine (another estimate is 204 out of 246) disappeared: their names are all listed, and amount to a panorama of the country's culture (one escaped abroad, and there were seven natural deaths, which left thirty-two or thirty-four to Stalinism or silence). Of about eighty-four leaders in the field of linguistics, sixty-two were liquidated.[85]

So the Ukraine now lay crushed: its Church destroyed, its intellectuals shot or dying in labour camp, its peasants – the mass of the nation – slaughtered or subdued. Even Trotsky was to remark that, 'nowhere do repression, purges, subjection and all types of bureaucratic hooliganism in general assume such deadly proportions as in the Ukraine in the struggle against powerful subterranean strivings among the Ukrainian masses towards greater freedom and independence'.[86]

Stalin's measures must have seemed to him to be adequate to his purpose. If they were not, it was because he underestimated the power of national feeling to take these blows and, after all, survive.

*

Nowadays the term 'genocide' is often used rhetorically. It may be worth recalling the text of the United Nations Convention on the Prevention and Punishment of Genocide, adopted by the General Assembly on 9 December 1948, which came into effect in 1950 and was ratified by the USSR in 1954:

Article I

The contracting parties confirm that genocide, whether committed in time of peace or in time of war, is a crime under international law which they undertake to prevent and punish.

Article II

In the present Convention genocide means any of the following acts committed with intent to destroy, in whole or in part, a national, ethnic, racial or religious group, as such:
a) Killing members of the group;
b) Causing grievous bodily or mental harm to members of the group;
c) Deliberately inflicting on the group conditions of life calculated to bring about its physical destruction in whole or in part;
d) Imposing measures intended to prevent births within the group;
e) Forcibly transferring children of the group to another group.

It certainly appears that a charge of genocide lies against the Soviet Union for its actions in the Ukraine. Such, at least, was the view of Professor Rafael Lemkin who drafted the Convention.[87]

But whether these events are to be formally defined as genocide is scarcely the point. It would hardly be denied that a crime has been committed against the Ukrainian nation; and, whether in the execution cellars, the forced labour camps, or the starving villages, crime after crime

272

against the millions of individuals forming that nation.

The *Large Soviet Encyclopaedia* has an article on 'Genocide', which it characterizes as an 'offshoot of decaying imperialism'.

★

14

Kuban, Don, and Volga

Wherefore should we die before thine eyes,
both we and our land?

Genesis

East of the borders of the Ukraine, on the lower reaches of the Don, and across the Sea of Azov over the lowlands stretching out to the Kalmyk country, were territories in large part inhabited by Cossacks and Ukrainian peasants. Of the former the Don Cossacks were of Russian origin, but had developed their own dialect. Indeed, a special 'Don Dictionary' was published by the North Caucasus section of the Academy of Sciences in Rostov for the use of 25-thousanders who could not otherwise make themselves understood.[1]

But the Kuban Cossacks were of Ukrainian origin, being direct descendants of the Zaporozhe Cossacks, who fled to Turkish territories after the Russian attack on the Sich in 1775, but later returned and moved to the Kuban as the nucleus of the Kuban Cossack Host, which was thus the legitimate descendant of the old republic on the waterfalls.

The Kuban Cossacks, and the Ukrainian peasantry which followed them to the area, together with others in the North Caucasus, are estimated at the beginning of the 20th century as 1,305,000;[2] while just before the revolution the Kuban had a population of 2.89 million, of whom 1.37 were Cossacks.[3]

There is, in the West, a certain misunderstanding of the Cossacks. As warrior 'Hosts' they were at the disposal of the pre-Revolutionary governments both in war and in putting down riots and revolutionary demonstrations. And their role in that different and worse phenomenon the pogroms is, of course, well known. Even though the word Cossack was frequently used indiscriminately of all mounted troops and police, the true Cossacks were too often the effective instruments of the regime or its local officials.

They had, observers noted, the virtues and the faults of a comparatively privileged and comparatively free military-agricultural community. Their pre-revolutionary standard of education is described (by Prince Kropotkin in the Encyclopaedia Britannica, XIth edition) as higher than the Russian average.

The Cossacks declared independent states in the chaos of 1917–18. In general, they inclined to the White armies, to which many of their leaders rallied. But this was by no means unanimous, as Mikhail Sholokhov shows (from his own experience) in *And Quiet Flows the Don*. He also makes it clear that many Cossacks previously favourable to the Reds, or neutral, were thrown into resistance by terror tactics, without which Bolshevik victory would have met far less opposition.

In the Kuban and the Don the Communists were even weaker than in the Ukraine. The Cossacks, moreover, presented a tougher problem for other reasons. Unlike the Ukrainian peasantry their tradition, even their organization, was military. And their 'stanitsas' were, typically, not small villages which could be put down by a handful of police soldiers, but large settlements of up to 40,000 inhabitants or over.

There were Cossack risings in 1922–3 and 1928. The collectivization struggle was intense, and the authorities took early steps to anticipate trouble.

Already in November 1929, army deployment was made with a view to coping with the most dangerous areas. In addition to Police units the 14th Moscow Rifle Division was deployed on the Don, and two other divisions sent to reinforce the North Caucasus Military District.[4]

We shall not revert here with the dekulakization and collectivization of these areas, except to note the stubbornness of resistance, and the main-tenance of an anomalously high proportion of individual farms right up to 1933, in spite of particularly harsh measures. Many adults were deported; many youths, mobilized for road labour, died.[5] In the Kuban and the Don the collectivization struggle never ceased, and merged directly into the terror-famine of 1932–3.

★

Cossack resistance held off the effective implementation of the famine until later than elsewhere. As the local First Secretary Sheboldayev was to put it, 'the kulaks again in 1932, this time from the base of the collective farms, tried to fight us about bread . . . But we did not understand it'; so that the Central Committee had to send in 'a group of Central Committee members under Comrade Kaganovich to us, to help us correct the situation'.[6]

This special Commission of the Central Committee appeared in Rostov at the beginning of November 1932. It met with the North Caucasus Territorial Committee on 2 November, and named special plenipotentiaries for each district.[7]

On 4 November Stalin's notorious terror operative Shkiryatov was appointed by a decision of the Central Committee to be chairman of a Commission to purge the Party in the North Caucasus, and especially the Kuban, of 'people hostile to Communism conducting a kulak policy'; and two days later a similar purge was ordered of Komsomol 'organizers of kulak resistance'.[8]

Sheboldayev spoke on 12 November of kulak bands running kolkhozes: for example, of a former red partisan with the Order of the Red Star as head of a kolkhoz concealing half its bread: indeed there were 'tens and hundreds' of instances of kolkhozes headed by communists which 'plundered' the grain. He added that this crime was prevalent 'especially in the Kuban', where he spoke of 'huge' White Guard cadres, and attacked several stanitsas, especially the celebrated Poltavskaya, where two-thirds of the peasants were still individual farmers, and which had been known in its time for 'actively fighting against Soviet forces'.[9]

Breach of the plan had led to 'shameful failure' in ten districts, and grave faults in eleven others. Seven District secretaries were censured on 24 November, and court sentences called for against the director of a state farm and others. One kolkhoz was attacked for distributing the paltry amount of 2 kg of grain a head to its members, when in need. Even in the great State Farm 'Kuban', of 35,000 acres, which had been a Communist model for years, a third of the workers and administrators had to be fired and 100 odd of the 150 odd Party members purged for such offences.[10]

Sir John Maynard, who visited the area and generally denied that there was a famine, speaks of the deportations from the North Caucasus, but especially the Kuban, of Communists and high local officials who had made common cause with the peasants, and adds that the mortality here was 'very high'.[11]

The Don and the Kuban were now declared to be under special military emergency on the pretext of a cholera epidemic, (a traditional method – used also in the Novocherkassk riots in 1962).[12] And the whole North Caucasus seems, we are told by an observer sympathetic to the regime, to have been placed in January 1933 under a special commission empowered 'to exact compulsory labour, and to evict, deport and punish even with death, the resisters'.[13] In the Rostov prison cells now held fifty inmates.[14]

Sheboldayev's attack on the Poltavskaya stanitsa on 12 November had been no mere verbal threat. On 17 December a decree of the President of the Executive Committee of the North Caucasus Territory ordered the deportation of the whole 27,000 population of the stanitsa.

A partisan movement had existed in the Poltavskaya area until 1925 and scattered bands long afterwards. In 1929–30, 300 of the 5,600 households had been sent into exile, and 250 people tried for non-fulfilment of grain deliveries with about forty shot. The women's revolt in this area was led by Red partisan widows. In 1930–31 there were a number of arrests of alleged members of the 'Union for the Liberation of the Ukraine'.[15]

Now, in December 1932, there had indeed been a genuine rising, with killings of NKVD men and activists; the stanitsa had fallen into the hands of the rebels, who had sent out squadrons to raise the nearby settlements. They had, however, delayed this, and the authorities were able to concentrate overwhelming force and retake Poltavskaya after heavy fighting.

The NKVD Commandant, Kubayev, issued an order to the effect that the Poltavskaya stanitsa had fallen into the hands of kulaks, and that the entire population was to be exiled with the exception of a few loyal citizens. For this purpose a 'state of war' was declared, and the inhabitants were warned with posters that any breach of the orders given would be met with the 'highest measure of socialist defence, SHOOTING': this was to apply to those who 'conducted agitation, spread provocative rumours, caused panic or plundered property or production'.[16] Russian settlers took over the stanitsa and it was renamed *Krasnoarmeiskaya* ('Red Army').

The Poltavskaya operation was given most publicity, as an example, but similar acts were committed in Umanskaya (population 30,000) Urupskaya, Medveditskaya, Myshativskaya, and elsewhere.[17] Rebels at the large Labinskaya Stanitsa were tried in Armavir, with many death sentences, though the whole population was not removed.[18] We are told by Roy Medvedev[19] that sixteen stanitsas in all were deported to the Far North, and that their total population must have been something like 200,000. Some stanitsas (e.g. Ivanivska) had only half the population exiled, yet still contributed to these figures.[20]

A soldier tells of arriving at the Cossack stanitsa Briukhovetska, in the Armavir area, which had had 20,000 inhabitants. As elsewhere, some months earlier an attempted uprising had been put down, and all the survivors, men and women, children and invalids, had been deported,

except for the odd old couple. In the street, the weeds were jungle-height, with wrecked and abandoned houses barely visible.[21]
He went into a house:

> In the half a minute that I spent there I saw two human corpses. An old woman sat on the floor, her gray unkempt head on her chest. She was leaning against the bed, her legs were wide spread. Her dead arms were crossed on her chest. She died just like that, gave up her soul to God without uncrossing them. An old yellow arm extended from the bed and rested on the grey head of the woman. On the bed I could see a body of an old man in a home-woven shirt and pants. The bare soles of the feet stuck over the edge of the bed and I could see that these old feet had walked far on earth. I could not see the face of the old man, it was turned to the wall. To my shame I have to confess I was really frightened. For some reason that hand resting on the head of the dead woman, especially shook me. Perhaps in a last effort the old man lowered his hand on the head of his dead wife and that is how they had both expired. When did they die – a week ago or two?

But there was, after all, one live inhabitant. A naked man with long hair and beard was fighting with some cats under an acacia, for possession of a dead pigeon. He had gone mad, but the soldier was able to piece together his story. He had been a Communist, and was Chairman of the local Soviet; but when collectivization came he had torn up his Party card and joined the rebels. Most of them had been killed but he had managed to hide in the malarial swamps among the Kuban's clouds of mosquitoes. His wife and children had been among the deported. He had somehow lived through the winter, and then returned to his old home – the last inhabitant of what had once been a large and flourishing settlement.[22]

★

Moreover, as in the Ukraine itself but more completely, the Ukrainian nationality and culture was strongly attacked.

In 1926 there were 1,412,276 Ukrainians in the Kuban alone, and 3,107,000 in the whole North Caucasus Territory. Many Ukrainian schools were established in the 1920s, coming under the administration of Skrypnyk as Ukrainian Commissar of Education. There was a Ukrainian Pedagogical Institute in Krasnodar and a Ukrainian Pedagogical Technical School in Poltavskaya.

In December 1929, a number of Ukrainian academics of Kuban descent had been arrested, as part of the general purge of Ukrainian culture then being launched.[23]

In 1932–3 accusations of 'local nationalism' were freely made, (as in the Ukraine), in the local paper *Molot*.[24] And early in 1933 a number of cultural and political figures in the Kuban were arrested, including most of the professors at the two Ukrainian Institutes. Russian replaced Ukrainian as the language of instruction. And between 1933 and 1937 all the 746 Ukrainian primary schools in the Kuban were turned into Russian schools.[25]

Crushed, decimated and more than decimated by deportation, denationalized, the area had probably suffered more greatly than any. Soviet victory over the inhabitants had finally been achieved.

★

But meanwhile among those not deported the famine took hold. The methods used were those we have described elsewhere. We have quoted the testimony of Mikhail Sholokhov, a devoted adherent of the regime: it refers to the Don Cossack region where he lived.

One inhabitant wrote 'Here in the Kuban is such a famine that the dead can no longer be buried'.[26] Another that 'The children sit huddled together in a corner, trembling with hunger and cold'.[27] Other letters run, 'My dear husband and I and the children worked very hard last summer. We had bread for a whole year . . . they left us helpless and without means';[28] 'In December we had to deliver all our corn, and other products including vegetables to the government';[29] 'On the steppe or in the fields, if one goes there, whole families are lying'.[30] Two peasants in their sixties were given ten year sentences for having 2 kilogrammes of raw corn pods.[31]

On one occasion two of a truckload of dead children being taken to the cemetery were found to be alive. However, in this case the doctor concerned was shot.[32]

An engineer who worked on the railroads in the Northern Caucasus describes the following:

Early in 1933 from Kavkaz station in the Northern Caucasus, every morning at a fixed hour before dawn two mysterious trains would leave in the direction of Mineralni Vody and Rostov. The trains were empty and consisted of five to ten freight cars each. Between two and four hours later the trains would return, stop for a certain time at a small way station, and then proceed on a dead-end spur towards a former ballast quarry. While the trains stopped in Kavkazka, or on a side track, all cars were locked, appeared loaded and were closely guarded by the NKVD. Nobody paid any attention to the mysterious trains at first, I did not either. I worked there temporarily, being still a student of the Moscow Institute of Transportation. But one day, conductor Kh., who was a communist, called me quietly and took me to the trains, saying: 'I want to show you what is in the cars'. He opened the door of one car slightly, I looked in and almost swooned at the sight I saw. It was full of corpses, piled at random. The conductor later told me this story: 'The station master had secret orders from his superiors to comply with the request of the local and railroad NKVD and to have ready every dawn two trains of empty freight cars. The crew of the trains was guarded by the NKVD. The trains went out to collect the corpses of peasants who had died from famine, and had been brought to railroad stations from nearby villages. The corpses were buried in the remote section beyond the quarries. The whole section was guarded by the NKVD and no strangers were permitted nearby'.[33]

As we have said, even in the big stanitsas which were not deported en bloc the losses by famine were huge – 14,000 out of the 24,000 remaining in Labinskaya, and so on.[34] They are often reported as almost empty of all except the old and sick.

At the Starokorsunska stanitsa a detachment of GPU cavalry sent there in 1930 was always kept on battle alert. There were several mass arrests of fifty to one hundred people. After the famine only about 1,000 of the 14,000 inhabitants remained; and the position was similar in the neighbouring stanitsas of Voronizka and Dinska.[35]

By late 1933, a despatch from the British Embassy summed this up: 'the Cossack element has been largely eliminated, whether from death or deportation'.[36]

Non-Cossack Ukrainian villages were also badly hit: at Pashkivske, in the Krasnodar region, the population of 7,000 was reduced to 3,500.[37]

Unlike the Ukraine the cities of the North Caucasus were not spared and also had a high death rate: 50,000 is the figure reported in Stavropol, (population 140,000), 40,000 in Krasnodar (population 140,000).[38] There are occasional stories with happier endings. In the Salsk region on the Don thousands survived by moving out into the steppe and trapping marmots. One village of a thousand householders – Zavitne – lived on them for six months and even built up reserves of fat.[39]

But in general, we can say that the Kuban and the Don suffered the extremes of the terror-famine.

A foreign visitor reports: 'The first thing that struck me when I began to walk about in the Cossack villages in the neighbourhood of Kropotkin was the extraordinary deterioration in the physical condition of what had once been an extremely fertile region. Enormous weeds, of striking height and toughness, filled up many of the gardens and could be seen waving in the fields of wheat, corn, and sunflower seeds. Gone were the wheaten loaves, the succulent slices of lamb that had been offered for sale everywhere when I visited the Kuban Valley in 1924'.[40]

280

In the Kuban, moreover, there were no draught animals left, so that cultivation would anyhow have been almost impossible.[41]

A Party official, back in his native North Caucasus for the first time since the Revolution, comments, 'I had known this land when it was all prosperity . . . Now I found the countryside reduced to utter desolation and misery. Fences, hedges and gates had disappeared for fuel. Streets were overgrown with weed and bracken, houses were falling to pieces . . . Even the once enthusiastic Party activists had lost faith . . .'[42]

An English visitor to the area told the British Embassy that it resembled 'an armed camp in a desert – no work, no grain, no cattle, no draught horses, only idle peasants and soldiers';[43] another that it was 'a semi-devastated region which would almost have to be recolonized'.[44]

★

Further north and west, the famine struck the Lower Volga area, partly Ukrainian and Russian by nationality, but centring on the Volga Germans. We have quoted various accounts by modern Russian Soviet writers of the horrors of their famine childhood, and several of these are from the Volga. One tells of 'the four coffins our family carried to the village cemetery in that terrible year', though adding that (unlike the Ukraine) some minimal rations were issued 'to long queues', which were just enough to survive on between issues.[45] Another says 'whole families died out. In our village, Monastyrskoe, of the 600 households 150 remained, and the place had not been touched by any wars!'.[46]

But most of our information comes from the Volga German Republic, which seems to have been a main target. The German Evangelical Churches received about 100,000 letters from Russian Germans about the famine, mainly appeals for help.[47] These letters, to co-religionists, with whom contact had always been maintained, are almost all strongly religious in tone.

A number of the letters are from the North Caucasus or the Ukraine and they tell the familiar story. But most are from the Volga German Republic itself – there too famine conditions prevailed, and for the same reason: 'We had to give it all to the State'. (February 1933).[48] Letter after letter speaks of no bread for four, five, six months. On the State farms, indeed, 'Those who work for the State get 150 grammes of bread a day, to neither die nor live'.[49]

But in the ordinary villages – 'Four of Brother Martin's children have died of hunger, and the rest are not far from it' (March 1933); 'the big village (of about 8,000 inhabitants) is half empty' (March 1933); 'We have had no bread, meat or fat for five months already . . . Many are dying';

281

'dogs are no longer to be found, nor cats' (April 1933); 'So many are dying that there is no time to dig graves' (April 1933); 'In the village all is dead. Days pass when one does not see a soul . . . we have shut ourselves in our house to prepare for death'[50] (February 1933). One starving evangelical writes 'When I look into the future, I see a picture before me, as of a mountain which I cannot climb'.[51]

Occasional letters note the arrival of parcels from the West.[52] For this, and perhaps for other reasons, the death roll seems not to have been as great as in the Kuban. Nevertheless, the German dead in the famine are reported as 140,000.[53] And it is estimated that by now some 60,000 further Germans were in prison camp.[54]

The survivors were, of course, to be deported *en masse* in 1941, and though rehabilitated, have not yet been permitted to return to their home territory.

It has seemed worthwhile to quote the letters from the German peasantry, (settled in the area since the 18th century), as virtually the only absolutely contemporary first-hand testimony from those actually suffering the famine as they wrote. It does not indeed differ greatly from what we are told by observers in the Ukraine and the Kuban, nor what we learn from survivors testifying later to their experiences.

★

15

Children

Pianger senti' fra il sonno i miei figliuoli
Ch' eran con meco, e domandar del pane

Dante

A whole generation of rural children, in the USSR as a whole but especially in the Ukraine, was destroyed or maimed. And, clearly the significance of this to the Soviet future cannot be overstated. From a humanitarian point of view, it need hardly be said that the fate of children in this great disaster seizes the mind most strongly; but it is also true that in the perspective of the country's future, both the shrinkage of a generation and the experiences of the survivors have effects which are still felt.

The photographs we have of children, even infants, with limbs like sticks and skull-like heads, are heartrending, as always in such circumstances. And this time, unlike even the Soviet famine of 1921, there are no accompanying pictures of relief workers trying, however much against the odds, to save them.

One observer notes of a survivor 'The poor youngster had seen so many deaths and so much suffering that he seemed to think it all part of life. There was no other life for him. The children always accepted the horrors of their environment as a matter of course'.[1]

★

The war on children was justified by the necessities of history, and absence of 'bourgeois' sentimentalism in enforcing the Party's decision was made the test of a true Communist.

In 1929 already, an educational paper noted how 'some comrades

283

coming in for grain procurements recommend doing everything to encourage the incidents of persecution of kulaks' children that occur in school, using this persecution as a means of putting pressure on the kulak parents who are maliciously holding back grain. Following their advice, one has to observe how the class tensions among the children became acute, beginning with teasing the little children and usually ending in a fight'.[2]

When a district committee secretary said that enough seed should be left to kulaks to sow and feed their children, he was attacked: 'don't think of the kulak's hungry children; in the class struggle philanthropy is evil'.[3] Up in Archangel, in 1932–3, the destitute children of deported 'kulaks' were not given school lunches or clothing vouchers available to others.[4]

There was logic in this attitude. An economic class, such as the 'kulaks', which the regime was concerned to crush, consists of children as well as adults. Moreover, Marx's idea that economics determines consciousness was applied in a very direct fashion – for example, the surviving children of kulaks, even if separated from their families, carried their social stigma in their identity documents, and on that basis were denied education and jobs, and were always liable to arrest in periods of vigilance.

The involvement of children in their family's offences was traditional. From the shooting of the fourteen year old Tsarevich in 1918, to that of the fourteen year old son of the old Bolshevik Lakoba in 1937, is a logical step. In the 1930s children, like wives, were often sentenced under the rubric ChSIR – Member of the Family of a Traitor to the Fatherland – a charge impossible to disprove.

Kulak children were often left abandoned when both their parents were arrested. As Lenin's widow Krupskaya wrote in an educational publication, 'A young child's parents are arrested. He goes along the street crying . . . Everyone is sorry for him, but no one can make up his mind to adopt him, to take him into his home: "After all, he is the son of a kulak . . . There might be unpleasant consequences" '.[5] Krupskaya herself pleaded against this, on the grounds that the class-war was between adults, but her voice had long ceased to count.

Yet there were many occasions when adults were braver or more decent than Krupskaya feared. We hear of cases where (for example) the father gone, the mother simply dying of fatigue in the fields, some fellow workers took in her child.[6] A typical story of such kindness is of a small Ukrainian peasant refusing to join the kolkhoz and being arrested, beaten up and deported. His wife then hanged herself in their barn and a childless family took in their little boy. He spent his time haunting his deserted home, coming back to them only to sleep on the oven, never speaking.[7] Time and again we have such stories of 'orphans of collectivization' being taken in by peasants.

Sometimes a man's foresight and ingenuity saved his family, at least for a time. One survivor tells of arriving home from school at the age of ten, and finding the house empty and locked. His father had been arrested and his mother and the younger children were being put up by a poor peasant family. To save these, she told him and his twelve year old brother to shift for themselves. The father, however, escaped and travelled working as a shoemaker, telling those he served to send food to his family instead of paying him. He had also taken the precaution of burying food on the property of a local activist, where it would not normally be searched for. The boys managed with this, and also fished, when able to evade the patrols which now prevented this where possible.[8]

But such help – or any help – might not be available, for obvious reasons. One boy who escaped from a deportation train, some months later visited his native *khutir*. It was deserted, the roof torn off, weeds man-high, polecats nesting in the ruined cottages.[9]

Young children, as we have noted, formed a high proportion of the 15–20% dying on the train in the deportations of 1930–32, and many more died in exile.[10] In March, April and May 1930 nearly 25,000 children are reported dying in the churches of Vologda,[11] the way-stations to exile of which we spoke in Chapter 6.

Children of those simply expelled from their homes, or escaping from exile, lived at the margin of existence, and many died. As with the adults, it is impossible to say exactly how many were victims of the deportation, how many of the famine; but the indications are that famine was the greater killer.

When it struck in 1932, the Ukrainian peasant children led a dreadful life. Not only was there the ever increasing hunger, but the mental strain on the family which sometimes led to the breakdown of its mutual love. We have already quoted Vasily Grossman's remark that mothers sometimes came to hate their children, though in other cases 'love was unbreakable . . .' In one family the husband refused to let the wife feed the children, and when he found a neighbour giving them some milk reported him for hoarding, though without result. However, he did not survive and the children did . . .[12]

In other cases, the lunacy of starvation led, as we have seen, to cannibalism, and many of the accounts we have are of children being eaten by a parent.

More generally, there was simple starvation. Sometimes this led to heartrending choices. One woman, congratulated in the spring of 1934 on her three fine children said that she had had six, but decided to save the 'three strongest and cleverest' and let the others die, burying them behind the house.[13]

An agronomist describes finding, on a walk with another official between two villages, a young woman dead, with a living baby at her breast. He saw from her passport that she was twenty-two years old and had walked about thirteen miles from her own village. They handed the baby – a girl – in to the nutrition centre at their destination, and wondered if anyone would ever tell her what became of her mother.[14]

Arthur Koestler saw from his train starving children who 'looked like embryos out of alcohol bottles';[15] or, as he puts it elsewhere: 'the stations were lined with begging peasants with swollen hands and feet, the women holding up to the carriage windows horrible infants with enormous wobbling heads, stick-like limbs and swollen, pointed bellies . . .'[16] And this was of families with at least the strength to reach the railway line.

There are many such descriptions of the physical condition of the children. Grossman gives one of the fullest descriptions of how they looked, and how it got worse as the famine closed in: 'And the peasant children! Have you ever seen the newspaper photographs of the children in the German camps? They were just like that: their heads like heavy balls on thin little necks, like storks, and one could see each bone of their arms and legs protruding from beneath the skin, how bones joined, and the entire skeleton was stretched over with skin that was like yellow gauze. And the children's faces were aged, tormented, just as if they were seventy years old. And by spring they no longer had faces at all. Instead, they had birdlike heads with beaks, or frog heads – thin, wide lips – and some of them resembled fish, mouths open. Not human faces'. He compares this directly with the Jewish children in the gas chambers and comments, 'these were Soviet children and those who were putting them to death were Soviet people'.[17]

In many cases the children simply died at home with the whole family. The last survivors might be the children, with no real idea of what to do. A foreign journalist describes a cabin in a village near Kharkov where only a fourteen year old girl and a two and a half year old brother survived. 'This younger child crawled about the floor like a frog, and its poor little body was so deformed that it did not resemble a human being . . . [It] had never tasted milk or butter, and had only once in its life tasted meat. Black bread and potatoes in very rare quantities had been the sole nourishment of this infant that had been on the point of death many times in the past winter'. At the time of his arrival they had not eaten for two days.[18] Others might wander off with no special hope: 'By the roadside between Kryzhivka Budyscha, in the orrach near Budyshcha pond, at the end of June were found the bodies of two children – one about seven years old and the other perhaps ten. Who knows whose children they were? Nobody seemed to have missed them, no one asked for them, they perished like kittens . . .'[19]

★

In a desperate situation, parents would send their children off, in the hope that they would have a chance to survive in the world of begging and petty theft which would not be theirs if they remained with their families.

A former Red partisan and activist in Chornukhy, Poltava Province, had joined the collective farm in 1930 with his wife and five children and been a loyal kolkhoznik. When death by starvation was imminent he took his four surviving children (one had been knocked dead while stealing vegetables) to the district chief, asked for help, but could get no definite promise. He then left the children with the official, who put them in a children's home, where two of them soon died. A few days later the father hanged himself on a tree outside the district office.[20]

A boy of seven said that after his father had died and his mother swelled up and could not get up, she told him 'go and find food for yourself'; a boy of eight left when both parents died; a boy of nine, whose mother had died, became frightened of his father's inexplicable movements and left home; another boy of nine was told by his mother to save himself, both of them crying as he left; a boy of eight saw his parents lying swollen and helpless and left.[21]

Sometimes the mother would wander off with her last baby. There are many stories of mother and infant lying dead on the road or in a city street; others of a dead woman with a still living infant at her breast.[22] Some would abandon a small child at a door, or simply anywhere, on the mere chance that someone might help it as she could not. 'A peasant woman dressed in something like patched sacks appeared from a side path. She was dragging a child of three or four years old by the collar of a torn coat, the way one drags a heavy bag-load. The woman pulled the child into the main street. Here she dropped it in the mud . . . The child's little face was bloated and blue. There was foam round the little lips. The hands and tiny body were swollen. Here was a bundle of human parts, all deathly sick, yet still held together by the breath of life. The mother left the child on the road, in the hope that someone might do something to save it. My escort endeavoured to hearten me. Thousands and thousands of such children, he told me, had met a similar fate in the Ukraine that year'.[23]

Another account tells us 'In Kharkov I saw a boy, wasted to a skeleton, lying in the middle of the street. A second boy was sitting near a keg of garbage picking eggshells out of it . . . When the famine began to mount, the parents in the villages used to take their children into the towns, where they left them in the hope that someone would have pity on them'.[24] They often died in the first day or two: they were usually in poor condition anyway. One seen dying in a gutter in Kharkov is described as having a 'skin covered with an unhealthy whitish down like fungus'.[25]

There were other dangers. Criminals even set up a regular slaughterhouse for children in Poltava, eventually discovered by the GPU, (and this was not a unique case, at least two similar ones being reported).[26]

If the children survived, it would be because they fell in with established groups. At the Kharkov Tractor Plant, all the unfinished buildings were occupied by homeless children. They trapped birds, rummaged through garbage for fishheads or potato peelings, caught and cooked any surviving cats, and begged.[27]

Criminal children's gangs at railway stations are typically noted as sometimes consisting of twelve to fourteen year olds, sometimes even five to six year olds.[28] It was mainly a matter of petty larceny. In a poll taken (at an earlier date) in a reception centre for homeless boys in Leningrad, a questionnaire about 'hooligans' – i.e. petty criminals – given to seventy-five twelve to fifteen year olds, got the following typical answers:

> 'A hooligan is a homeless boy who because of the power of hunger has to be a hooligan'.
> A hooligan is 'a thief who escapes from an orphanage'.
> 'There was a family, they had a son. When mother and father died, the boy became a homeless one, so he became a hooligan'.
> 'Hooligans appear when parents die and they are left all alone . . .'
> 'A mother and a father die, a son remains, he is turned over to the orphanage, but he escapes and becomes a hooligan'.[29]

It was in fact the only life available to many.

There were other fates: of children who managed to find distant relatives, or of older children getting some sort of employment. But many were eventually assimilated into the old criminal element of the *urkas* which had flourished as a separate culture, with its own laws and dialect, since the early 17th century.

The *urkas* proper seem to have numbered between half a million and a million by the 1940s. The young element, of teenage boys whose personalities had never been 'socialized', are universally reported in labour camps and prisons as the most terrifying, with no compunction whatever about killing for the slightest motives.

But for the present most of the children kept in their own groups, and presented a problem for the authorities.

★

A great stream of orphans, the 'homeless ones' (*bezprizornye*), had flowed over the country following the famine of 1921–2. Relief organizations reported 'fugitive bands of a dozen or more, led by a child of ten or twelve and including now and then a baby in arms'.[30] This had all been admitted by the authorities. Even Soviet novelists of the time had taken it as a theme – as with Shishkov's *Children of Darkness*, describing a colony of children living under a large abandoned boat on the riverside, with robbery, sex, drug-taking, and finally murder.

The *Large Soviet Encyclopaedia*'s current (3rd) edition, says that the number of children needing direct help from the state was four to six million in 1921, and two and a half to four million in 1923. In 1921–2 five million had received help in the Volga region alone, and in 1923 more than a million. In 1921 940,000 had been in children's homes, in 1924 280,000, in 1926, 250,000, in 1927–8 159,000; no later figures or information are given except the bare statement that the problem was basically liquidated by the mid-1930s.

In spite of the *Encyclopaedia*'s view that homeless children were a phenomenon of the 20s, with nothing worth recording in later years, there are plenty of official accounts available from the period of the famine.

One ploy was to blame it on the kulaks:

Some difficulties in food-supply in certain areas of the country have been used with the purpose of raising the level of homelessness among children in the cities. 'Send the children to the cities, let the state take care of them in the orphanages . . .' Local leaders in public education have not always or everywhere understood this to be a kulak trick. And instead of combating this trick, the rural [education] workers felt compassion. For the rural workers the easiest way to get rid of the children was to send them to the city. And the kulak is using this. The District Executive Committees and especially the village soviets frequently themselves issued papers to a child and sent him to the city institutions responsible for the protection of childhood. The city accepted these children. As a result, the existing children's institutions were overcrowded; new ones were created, but the street orphans not only did not disappear but new contingents kept arriving . . . Homelessness grew, particularly in the North Caucasus.[31]

In 1935, it was announced that the placing of 'direct and immediate responsibility for the care of children on the village soviets and collective farms . . . finally creates the conditions for putting a stop to the appearance of homeless and unprovided-for children. This measure finally creates the possibility of stopping the flow of unprovided-for children from the countryside to the cities with the purpose of entering orphanages'.[32] At this time official figures were that 75% of the homeless children were from the countryside.[33]

One Soviet authority claims that owing to the success of industrialization and collectivization, the problem of homeless children was fully solved: 'This is one of the most remarkable testimonies to the fact that only the socialist regime can rescue the growing generation from starvation, pauperism, and homelessness – the inevitable companions of the bourgeois society'.[34]

Another comment on the superiority of Soviet treatment of these orphans should perhaps also be registered. At a meeting of the Commissariat of Education, the Deputy People's Commissar, M.S. Epstein, 'compared the care by our Party and its leaders for children with the horrifying status of children in the capitalist countries. The falling number of schools, the tremendous growth of homelessness – that is characteristic of all capitalist countries. There are over 200,000 homeless children and adolescents in the USA now. Juvenile courts, juvenile correction halls and shelters maim the children; the entire system of measures of the bourgeois states is geared toward the 'elimination from sight' of the homeless children by the way of their physical elimination'.[35]

Professor Robert C. Tucker has a theory that whatever the Soviet press accused an enemy of was exactly what the Soviet Government was doing itself. It is perhaps relevant that we are told in an official journal that in the North Caucasus, where the problem of homeless children was particularly acute, it was 'liquidated' in two months by measures taken, (which, however, are not described).[36] As we shall see, the solutions available were not limited by humanitarian considerations.

★

There were 'children's labour camps', that is prison camps, to which a child might be formally sentenced. After the arrest and deportation of one 'kulak', a brigade came to his house to check on grain, and tried to arrest his wife. Her young son, who had a bandaged hand from an abscess, held on to her. One of the brigade hit him on the hand and he fainted. The mother escaped in the confusion and got away to the woods. Thereupon the boy was arrested instead and two weeks later tried on a charge of attacking the brigade leader with a knife. Though one of the brigade, to the disgust of the court, told the true story, the boy was nevertheless sentenced to five years in a 'children's labour colony'.[37]

Children treated in such a way were not cooperative. A recent account by the former head of an NKVD children's 'labour colony' describes the young criminals as free in their irreverence about Soviet matters. In one revolt, they barricaded themselves in an office and shouted that they were

290

going to burn down 'the prison of the peoples', a parody of Lenin's description of Tsardom; and they went on to burn all the documents and personal files.[38]

Many more, however, landed in regular adult prisons or camps. One prisoner mentions a nine year old in his Kharkov prison cell along with all the adults.[39]

But even non-'criminal' homeless children were effectively penalized. In March 1933 at the Poltava railway station a special railway car was drawn into a siding and the children who swarmed round the station seeking food were put in it, under guard. There were about seventy-five of them, and they were given roasted grain coffee-substitute and a little bread. They died off quickly, and were buried in holes in the ground. A station worker comments, 'This procedure became so common at that time that nobody paid the slightest attention to it'.[40]

In Verkhnedniprovsk on the right bank of the Dnieper about 3,000 orphans aged from seven to twelve years old, children of executed or deported kulaks, were similarly held, starving to death in the spring and summer of 1933.[41]

A lecturer in botany writes of the child mortality he witnessed in Kirovohrad. In Kirovohrad there used to be a bazaar which was liquidated at the same time as private trade, and some of the buildings left vacant were turned into orphanages. Peasants would bring their children to town and leave them so that they would be taken in. During the famine the orphanage became so overcrowded that it could no longer hold all the children. Then the children were transferred to a 'children's town' where they could ostensibly live 'under the open sky'. They got nothing to eat and starved to death away from the public eye, their deaths being listed as caused by a weakness of the nervous system. A walled fence surrounded it, so that people could not see in, but they could hear 'frightening, inhuman cries . . . women crossed themselves and fled from the place'. To hide the extent of the deaths, trucks would haul off the bodies only at night. They fell off the truck so often that every morning each caretaker would look over his 'territory' to see if a child's body had fallen there. The burial pits would be filled so high and covered so poorly that dogs and wolves would partly dig the bodies up. Dr Chynchenko estimates that thousands of children died this way in Kirovohrad.[42]

Even less improvised 'orphanages' might be highly unpleasant. One official of the Commissariat of Education tells of being entertained at a privileged summer camp for children at Ulyanivka. After a fine meal another official approached him quietly and said he would show him another 'Children's Shelter' a quarter of a mile out of the village. Here was a barn built of stone, the floor covered with sand and in the semidarkness about 200 children from two to twelve years old in the condition of skeletons, dressed only in dirty shirts. They all cried for bread. When the education official asked who was looking after them he received the sardonic reply 'the Party and the Government' – the looking after consisting of the removal of the corpses each morning.[43]

One girl, taken in a bad condition to Chornukhy children's home, was loaded on to a truck of corpses, but the mass grave had not been dug, so she and the dead were just piled up, and she crawled off, being rescued and looked after by the wife of a Jewish doctor. This doctor, Moisei Feldman, saved numbers of starving people by getting them into his hospital under false diagnoses and feeding them; and was often in trouble because of this.[44]

Elsewhere one ten year old boy was taken with his six year old sister, after their parents' death, to a local orphanage – an old peasant house with broken windows, where food was insufficient. The nurse in charge had the older children dig the graves up at the cemetery and bury the dead inmates. He finally did this for his own sister.[45]

Some children's homes, in the actual villages of their birth, are described as well run. But the boys brought up in them were, we are told, the first to desert from the Soviet Army in 1941.[46]

Early in 1930, when the pressures were comparatively low, the orphanages were already in a poor state. One education periodical complained: 'Materially the children are exceedingly unprovided for; nutrition is insufficient, in many orphanages there is filth, lice-infestation, lack of discipline, lack of habits for collective life'.[47]

A Government decree on the liquidation of child homelessness on 31 May 1935,[48] noted that

> a) the majority of orphanages are managed unsatisfactorily as far as housekeeping and education are concerned;
>
> b) the organized struggle with juvenile hooliganism and criminal elements among the children and adolescents is utterly insufficient and in a number of places is completely non-existent;
>
> c) up till now conditions have not been created under which children, who for one reason or another ended up 'on the street' (loss of parents or running away, escape from orphanages, etc.), would be immediately placed in the proper juvenile institutions or returned to the parents;
>
> d) parents and guardians indifferent to their own children and allowing them to engage in hooliganism, stealing, sexual corruption, and vagabondage are not held responsible.

– This last, an accurate description of the homeless ones' life.

The decree established orphanages under the Commissariat of

Education, homes (for sick children) under the Commissariat of Health, and 'isolators, labour colonies and reception stations' – under the NKVD, which was now to take over all matters of juvenile delinquency.

Homeless children, as the decree notes, often escaped from these homes, which they usually reported as brutally run.[49] The Gorki Commune near Kharkov was noted for 'little food and plenty of discipline'.[50] An educational organ gave as an 'example' of inadequate work that at the orphanage at Nizhne Chirski 'the delivery of proper food was delayed for months'.[51]

A modern Soviet novelist lived with other homeless ones in an abandoned theatre, and reports tales of terrible orphanages.[52] But there were indeed exceptions. For example, the novelist himself, (V.P. Astafiev), was in an orphanage in Igarka in the far North. In his *Theft* he has a more or less autobiographical account of this: the head of the orphanage is a very decent man, much respected by the inmates, (though getting into trouble when it is discovered that he is a former Tsarist officer).

Most, though, seem to have been little more than children's prisons. Even so, many children passed through the police-run homes and went on to respectable careers. Others were recruited to crime. And others, by a horrible irony, became suitable material for entry into the ranks of the NKVD itself. Even the comparatively humane Cheka children's homes of the 1920s had already been recruiting ground for the Secret Police.[53]

At the Belovechensk 'children's colony' near Maikop in the North Caucasus, we are told that 'half of the boys who were inmates in the school were sent, on reaching the age of sixteen, to special NKVD schools to be trained as future Chekists'. These were often from the more unsocialized criminal element. One, who had earlier escaped on two occasions with some friends, once murdering a peasant, once setting fire to a church, was some years later recognized by a local resident under arrest in Baku, as one of his Secret Police interrogators.[54]

★

It is indeed a horrible moral irony that children whose parents had been killed by the regime should be indoctrinated and brutalized into becoming the most obnoxious of that regime's agents.

But there are many other points about the attitudes and actions of the regime towards children in this period which have been regarded by some as a spiritual destruction no less intolerable, perhaps even more intolerable, than the physical holocaust of the rural young.

We may find it disagreeable to hear a Komsomol's description of an indoctrination film he and his friends were shown of kulaks burying wheat, Komsomols discovering the wheat, and then being murdered by the kulaks.[55] We may not relish one observer noting at a round-up of starving peasants in Kharkov that 'the children of well-fed Communist officials, young Pioneers, stood by and parroted phrases of hate learned in school'.[56] We may be repelled by a 'pioneer brigade' arresting two women, (whose husbands had been killed and exiled respectively) for gleaning two or three ears of corn; (they were sent to concentration camps in the far North).[57] The Pioneers, (of the Communist organization for children between ten and fifteen) had many similar triumphs. In one kolkhoz four of them were praised for throwing a kulak woman to the ground and holding her till help arrived and the militia took her away to be sentenced under the decree of 7 August 1932. 'This was the first victory of the kolkhoz's Pioneers'.[58]

In a kolkhoz at Ust-Labinsk in the Kuban a contemporary official account tells approvingly of how 'the Pioneer detachment presented the Political Department with a whole list of people they suspected of thieving, based on the class principle: 'We, the children's "Camp" of the kolkhoz *Put' Khleboroba*, announce to the Political Department that so-and-so certainly steals, because he is a kulak and in the hamlet of Razdomny his mother-in-law was dekulakised'. They had learnt in the detachment to speak the class language'.[59]

Children were in fact mobilized to keep watch on the fields – Postyshev says that over half a million of them served thus, with ten thousand specifically 'combatting thieves' – that is, peasants trying to keep a little grain.[60] *Pravda* quoted a 'Song of the Kolkhoz Pioneer', by the Stalinist hack A. Bezymenski, which included such verses as

> We take the thieves to jail
> To intimidate the foe.
> We guard the village soil
> To let the harvest grow.
>
> We'll round up all the shirkers:
> To the fields we'll make them march,
> And then we'll man the checkpoints
> And keep a careful watch.[61]

As to the children and youths of 15 and over, we are told that in general 'the Komsomols took an active part in all economic-political campaigns and fought the kulak relentlessly'.[62] Indeed, in Krushchev's time it was stated that in Stalin's view, 'the very first task of all Komsomol education was the necessity to seek out and recognise the enemy, who was then to be

removed forcibly, by methods of economic pressure, organizational–
political isolation, and methods of physical destruction'.[63]

This general harnessing of the young to the brutalities and falsification
of the. class struggle will certainly be distasteful to most of those not
accustomed to such standards of conduct. Yet, there is, from our point of
view, an even baser phenomenon to be found.

Already at the Shakhty trial, a boy was publicly quoted as demanding
the death sentence for his father. And in the countryside, children who
had accepted the indoctrination of the 'Pioneer' were used against their
own families. The most famous was that of the celebrated Pavlik
Morozov, after whom the Palace of Culture of Young Pioneers in Moscow
is named. The fourteen year old Morozov 'unmasked' his father,
previously head of the village Soviet in the village of Gerasimovka. After
the trial and sentence on the father, Morozov was killed by a group of
peasants, including his uncle, and is regarded as a martyr. There is now a
Pavlik Morozov Museum in his village: 'in this timbered house was held
the court at which Pavlik unmasked his father who sheltered the kulaks.
Here are reliquaries dear to the heart of every inhabitant of
Gerasimovka'.[64] In 1965 the village was additionally adorned with his
statue. We are told by the current *Large Soviet Encyclopaedia* that Morozov,
with others in similar case (Kolya Myagotin, Kolya Yakovlev, Kychan
Dzhakylov), is entered in the Pioneer 'Book of Honour'.

A number of books and pamphlets about Morozov were published,
including several edifying novels, one of them (by V. Gubarev) with what
might be thought the inappropriate title of 'Son'.

In May 1934, another young hero, thirteen year old Pronya Kolibin,
reported his mother for stealing grain, and received much favourable
publicity.[65] Another, Pioneer Sorokin, in the North Caucasus, caught his
father filling his pockets with grain, and had him arrested.[66]

In a major speech at the celebration of the 20th Anniversary of the
Secret Police in December 1937, Mikoyan praised a number of named
citizens who had denounced their fellows, citing with particular pride the
fourteen year old Pioneer Kolya Schelgov of the village of Poryabushki in
the Pugachev District, who had exposed his father I.I. Schelgov: 'The
pioneer Kolya Schelgov knows what Soviet power is to him and to the
whole people. When he saw that his own father was stealing socialist
property, he told the NKVD'.[67]

These children may indeed deserve blame, but surely not so much as
those who inculcated such conduct into them. At any rate, the mother of a
boy whose son disappeared in the famine has told me that she would have
preferred, and would still prefer, his dying physically to his being
spiritually destroyed and transformed into what she described as

something lower than a human being, in this manner.

★

Physical elimination, straightforward killing, was indeed also a possibility. When the problem became too great for local officials *bezpeizornie* are reported shot in large numbers.[68] The decree legalizing the execution of children of twelve or over was not indeed to come into force until 7 April 1935. But this extending of all penalties down to the age of twelve may also seem to have certain implications when it comes to the Party's interpretation of Marxism. If economics determines consciousness, by the age of twelve the full class consciousness may reasonably be supposed to be established beyond eradication. However, the record of starving infants in 1933, or deporting them in 1930, certainly shows that at times of heightened 'class' struggle those a good deal younger had to take their chance. The point being perhaps, rather, that twelve years old was the limit the Party felt was overtly defensible.

Even in the comparatively tranquil circumstances of NKVD orphanages a few years later the authorities contrived to extend the age limit downwards, for example, by having doctors certify that two delinquent boys of eleven were physically older than their papers, assumed to be forged, showed.[69]

Meanwhile, we are told by a senior OGPU officer, as early as 1932 confidential orders were issued to shoot children stealing from railway cars in transit.[70] Such measures were also taken for various health reasons, as when in the Lebedyn Children's Centre seventy-six children are reported shot after getting glanders from horsemeat.[71]

It is certainly true that unwanted children were got rid of by inhumane or lethal practices, though mainly by starvation in various centres; and it is also reported, for example, that some were drowned in barges on the Dnieper, (a method also used with adults).[72] But most of the children perished from hunger. There is reasonably clear evidence of the numbers, if not the exact numbers, of the child victims.

The 'dissident' Soviet demographer M. Maksudov estimates that 'no fewer than three million children born between 1932 and 1934 died of hunger'.[73] It was above all the new-born who perished. A figure of two and a half million infants dying of starvation was given to Lev Kopelev by a Soviet researcher.[74] The 1970 Census shows 12.4 million people living who were born in 1929–31, and only 8.4 million born in 1932–4; though the natural rate of increase fell only slightly. In 1941 there were a million fewer seven year olds than eleven year olds in the schools – and this even though the eleven year old group had also suffered severely. Moreover when we come to the famine areas, this disproportion is greater still. In Kazakhstan the seven year old group was less than two-fifths the size of the eleven year old; while in Moldavia (most of which had not formed part of the USSR in the 1930s) the seven year old group was two-thirds as large again as the eleven year old.[75]

When we turn to the few local estimates we have the picture is much the same.

In one village it was noted that 'of the young boys not one in ten survived'.[76] (Young boys are elsewhere described as the most vulnerable category of all).

In one district in the Poltava Province, of a total death roll of 7,113, the respective numbers[77] are given as:

Children (under 18)	3,549
Men	2,163
Women	1,401

A teacher in the village of Novi Sanzhary, Dnipropetrovsk Province, reports that by 1934 there were no school children left for her; another, that only two were left of a class of thirty.[78] And as to younger children, in the Ukrainian village of Kharkivtsi, the 1940–41 school year found no beginners at all, as against an average of twenty-five previously.[79]

We may reasonably conclude that of the seven million dead in the famine some three million were children, and mostly young children. (We discuss the total casualties, including adults, in Chapter 16.) But it should be noted that registration of births was not kept up accurately in the villages during the famine, for obvious reasons – though in fact few births seem to have taken place in the worst period, for equally obvious reasons: so that an unknown number of new-born babies may have died without their birth having ever been recorded.

To this figure of three million or more children dead in 1932–4, we must add the victims of dekulakization. If, as we have estimated, some three million dead are to be reckoned in this operation (not counting the adults dying later in labour camp), all accounts agree that the proportion of child deaths was very high, and all in all it can scarcely have been less than another million, again mostly the very young. To these four million odd victims of actual infanticide we should perhaps append the number of children's lives ruined or deeply scarred in the various ways we have noted: but this is beyond quantification.

Meanwhile, when it comes to the famine, measures which could have been taken at any time were finally put into effect at the end of spring 1933. Some food was released to be given to the children at school – meal, groats, and fat. The children who had not died by the end of May generally did not die; though by now many were, of course, orphans.

★

16

The Death Roll

No one was keeping count

Khrushchev

There has been no official investigation of the rural terror of 1930–33; no statement on the loss of human life has ever been issued; nor have the archives been opened to independent researchers. Nevertheless, we are in a position to make reasonably sound estimates of the numbers who died.

First, we should consider the total loss for the whole cycle of events, both in the dekulakization and in the famine. In principle this is not difficult.

We need only apply to the population given in the Soviet census of 1926, the natural growth rate of the years which followed, and compare the result we obtain with that of an actual post-1933 census.

There are a few rather minor reservations. The 1926 census, like all censuses even in far more efficient conditions, cannot be totally accurate, and Soviet and Western estimates agree that it is too low by 1.2–1.5 million,[1] (about 800,000 of it attributed to the Ukraine). This would mean an increase of almost half a million in the death roll estimates. But the convenience of an official established base figure, that of the census, is such that we shall (conservatively) ignore this in our calculations. Then again, 'natural growth rate' is variously estimated, though within a fairly narrow range. More of an obstacle, at first sight, is the fact that the next census, taken in January 1937, is unfortunately not available. The preliminary results seem to have been before the authorities on about 10 February 1937. The census was then suppressed. The Head of the Census Board, O.A. Kvitkin, was arrested on 25 March.[2] It turned out that 'the glorious Soviet intelligence headed by the Stalinist Peoples'

Commissar N.I. Yezhov' had 'crushed the serpent's nest of traitors in the apparatus of Soviet statistics'.[3] The traitors had 'set themselves the task of distorting the actual numbers of the population', or (as *Pravda* put it later) 'had exerted themselves to diminish the numbers of the population of the USSR',[4] a rather unfair taunt, since it was, of course, not they who had done the diminishing.

The motive for suppressing the census and the census-takers is reasonably clear. A figure of about 170 million had featured in official speeches and estimates for several years, a symbolic representation of Molotov's boast in January 1935 that 'the gigantic growth of population shows the living forces of Soviet construction'.[5]

Another census was taken in January 1939, the only one in the period whose results were published, but in the circumstances it has always failed to carry much conviction. All the same, it is worth noting that even if the official 1939 figures are accepted, they show a huge population deficit, if not as large as the reality.

But on the matter of the total of unnatural deaths between 1926 and 1937, the 1937 census *totals* are decisive, and these (though no other details of that census) have been referred to a few times in post-Stalin Soviet demographic publications. The most specific gives a population for the USSR of 163,772,000,[6] others, a round 164 million.[7]

The total, in the lower projections made over previous years by Soviet statisticians, and on the estimates of modern demographers, should have been about 177,300,000.

Another, rougher approach is to take the estimated population of 1 January 1930 (157,600,000)[8] and add to it Stalin's statement in 1935 that 'the annual increase in population is about three million'.[9] This too gives a figure of 178,600,000, very near our other projection. The Second Five Year Plan had also provided for a population of 180.7 million for the beginning of 1938,[10] which also implies between 177 and 178 in 1937. Oddly enough, the Head of the Central Statistical Administration in Khrushchev's time, V.N. Starovsky, attributes Gosplan's 180.7 million to 1937, comparing it with the census figure of 164 million 'even after adjustment'[11] – a phrase which implies significant upward inflation: an 'adjustment' of 5% would mean as a base figure the 156 million given to the Soviet scholar Anton Antonov-Ovseenko by a more junior official.[12] But, in accord with our practice elsewhere, we will conservatively ignore the 'adjustment'. Without it Starovsky implies a deficiency of 16.7 million. The explanation may be that the Gosplan figure, like most other Gosplan figures, at the beginning of October 1937 – in which case the deficiency would be about 14.3 million. However, we shall here rely again on the most conservative interpretation (and ignore, too, even higher projections by

Soviet demographers of the period) and accept a deficiency of no more than 13.5 million.

Since at the beginning of 1937 no serious killing of other social categories – beyond the odd tens of thousands – had taken place, virtually the whole of this deficiency comes from the peasantry.

The 13.5 million does not in its entirety represent death. We have also to take into account those unborn because of the deaths or separation of their parents, and so on. A deficit here of 2.5 million would be about the equivalent of no births whatever for a year in the rural famine areas, and no births for two years among the 'kulak' deportees, and thus can hardly be an understatement. If we take this very high figure it leaves us with 11 million actually dying by 1937 in the dekulakization and the famine, and omitting those dying later in the labour camps.

Another approach is to note that in 1938 there were c. 19,900,000 peasant households. In 1929 it had been c. 25,900,000. At an average of 4.2 persons per peasant family, this means c. 108,700,000 peasants in 1929 and c. 83,600,000 in 1938. Natural increase should have produced a figure of 119,000,000 – a deficit of 36 million, from which we must subtract 24,300,000 people moving to towns, or in villages reclassified as urban – leaving 11,700,000 no longer accounted for at all.

To this eleven million odd we must add those peasants already sentenced, but dying in labour camp after January 1937 – that is, those arrested as a result of the assault on the peasantry of 1930–33 and not surviving their sentences (but *not* including the many peasants arrested in the more general terror of 1937–8). This gives, (as we shall estimate later), not less than another 3.5 million, which would make the total peasant dead as a result of the dekulakization and famine about 14.5 million.

*

We must next consider the way in which this fearful total is divided between the dekulakization and the famine. Here we are on less certain ground.

It seems to be felt in demographic circles that of the fourteen million plus odd peasant deaths due to the rural terror, the casualties fell about equally between the two causes: that is about seven million plus from dekulakization and about seven million plus in the famine. However, we can examine this proposition in more detail.

Of the 14.5 million, the 3.5 million odd dying in camps in the post-1937 period must be largely those sentenced before the decree of May 1933, though it certainly included an important component from the desperate villages of the Ukraine and the Kuban of the famine period. These last are not, however, specifically victims of the famine itself, and to discover the death roll from starvation we must go back to the eleven million dead before 1937, and attempt to divide that figure between deportation and famine victims.

We may start with the victims of the famine: and here we begin with the deficit in the Ukrainian population. (As we have said, this does not account for the whole of the famine victims, but unofficial figures imply that about 80% of the mortality was in the Ukraine and the largely Ukrainian areas of the North Caucasus).

For the deficit of Ukrainians we must first turn to the faked 1939 census, since, as we have said, no figures by nationality – indeed nothing but the gross population result – has been published even now from the genuine 1937 census on which we have hitherto relied.

The official figure for the Soviet population in the 'census' of January 1939 was 170,467,186. Western demographic work indicates that the real numbers were probably about 167.2 million. (Even this last figure indicates a sharp recovery from 1937, in spite of an estimated two to three million dead in camps or by execution in 1937 and 1938. It appears to be explained in part by natural and in part by legal factors. Recovery in the birthrate after disaster or famine is normal; the copulation and fertility rates which have gone down drastically in them improve later. On the official side, in 1936 abortion was made illegal, and contraceptives ceased to be sold; and other measures were taken).

Of the official figure of 170,467,186 the census gives Ukrainians as 28,070,404 (as against 31,194,976 in the 1926 census). There is no way of telling how the 3.4 million inflation in the 170.5 million is distributed, and it is normally assumed that each nationality group was proportionately exaggerated (though the better concealment tactics might imply a special attempt to give the Ukrainians an extra boost, considering their poor showing).

Given no more than equal exaggeration, the true Ukrainian figure in 1939 should have been about 27,540,000. But the 31.2 million of 1926 should have risen to about 38 million in 1939. The deficit is therefore about 10.5 million. Allowing about 1.5 million for unborn children, this gives a deficit of 9 million Ukrainians up to 1939.

This does not all represent death. By 1939 heavy pressures were being put on Ukrainians outside the Ukraine to register as Russian, and a significant transfer certainly took place. A Soviet demographer grants that between the 1926 and 1939 censuses 'the low rate of growth (!) in the number of Ukrainians is explained by the lowering of the natural growth as a result of a poor harvest in the Ukraine in 1932', but adds that 'people who formerly thought of themselves as Ukrainians, in 1939 declared themselves Russians'.[13] And we are told, for example, that people with forged documents often changed their nationality, as Ukrainians were always suspect to the police.[14]

This applied not in the Ukraine so much as among the Ukrainians elsewhere in the USSR. There were 8,536,000 of them in 1926, including 1,412,000 in the Kuban. The remnant of the Kuban Cossacks are definitely reported as being re-registered as Russian, but by now their numbers must have been very much lower than in 1926. Elsewhere it seems to have been a matter of pressure on individuals, and was doubtless a long-term process – even in the 1959 census there were over 5 million Ukrainians in the USSR outside the Ukraine. If we assume a transfer of as many as 2.5 million from the Ukrainian to the Russian listings, that leaves us with 9 minus 2.5 = 6.5 million actually dead.

Subtracting about 500,000 for the Ukrainian dead of the dekulakization of 1929–32, we are left with six million dead in the famine.

This would be divided into five million in the Ukraine and one million in the North Caucasus. The figure for non-Ukrainians may be as little as one million dead. Thus the total famine deaths would be approximately seven million, about three million of them children. As we have pointed out, these are conservative figures.

★

A further clue to the numbers dying in the famine, or in its worst period, may be found in the difference between the Census Board's estimate of the population made shortly before the 1937 census, and the actual figures of that census. The prediction is 168.9 million;[15] the actuality 163,772,000 – a difference of just over five million. This is believed to be accounted for by the non-registration of deaths in the Ukraine after late October 1932 (see p.250), which meant that such figures were not at the disposal of the estimators; and in consonant with the other figures we have for deaths in the famine as a whole.

We also have a number of less direct estimates of the famine deaths, including some based on official leaks.

A Russian-born American citizen who had a pre-revolutionary acquaintance with Skrypnyk visited him in 1933, and also met other Ukrainian leaders. Skrypnyk gave him a figure of 'at least' eight million dead in the Ukraine and North Caucasus.[16] He was also told by the Ukrainian GPU chief Balitsky that eight–nine million had perished: Balitsky added that this figure had been presented to Stalin, though only as an approximation.[17] Another security officer writes that, perhaps at an earlier stage, the GPU gave Stalin a figure of 3.3–3.5 million famine deaths.[18] A foreign Communist was given figures of ten million deaths for the USSR as a whole.[19]

Another foreign worker in a Kharkov factory, when the famine was still far from over, learnt from local officials that Petrovsky had admitted a death roll, so far, of five million.[20]

Walter Duranty told the British Embassy in September 1933 that 'the population of the North Caucasus and Lower Volga had decreased in the past year by three million, and the population of the Ukraine by four to five million', and that it seemed 'quite possible' that the total death roll was as high as ten million. It seems reasonable to suppose that Duranty's figures derive from the same source as those, also never printed, given one of his colleagues by another high official (see p. 310): or at any rate from similar official estimates circulating among authorities on the spot.

An American Communist working in Kharkov estimated a death roll of 4.5 million, from starvation alone, with millions more from the diseases of malnutrition.[21] Another American was told by a high Ukrainian official that six million had died in 1933.[22] A Ukrainian-Canadian Communist who attended the Higher Party School of the Ukrainian Central Committee was told that a secret report to this Committee gave a figure of ten million dead.[23]

As to other areas, decreases proportionally as high as the Ukraine, or nearly so, are reported in the Central Volga, Lower Volga and Don regions. The Director of the Chelyabinsk Tractor Plant, Lovin, told a foreign correspondent that more than a million had died in the Urals, Western Siberia and the Trans-Volga.[24]

These estimates, it should be noted, are not all necessarily comparable, since it is not always clear – though it sometimes is – if the total deaths in the Ukraine alone are referred to; or to what date the figures refer; or to whether deaths from famine-related diseases are included.

In any case, even the confidential official reports vary by several million. Nor need we assume that exact or even approximate figures were available (as, in fact, the report of Balitsky's estimate explicitly admits). As Leonid Plyushch says, 'party members cited a figure of five or six million . . . and others spoke of about ten million victims. The true figure probably lies in between'.[25]

★

While our figure of c. eleven million premature deaths in 1926–37 remains firm, the c. seven million share of it in famine deaths is best described as reasonable or probable. If it is correct it leaves c. four million of the deaths to dekulakization and collectivization (or those taking place before 1937).

Among this four million are included the dead of the Kazakh tragedy. Among the Kazakhs the population deficit between the 1926 and 1939 censuses (even accepting the latter's figures) was 3,968,300 minus 3,100,900: that is, 867,400. Correcting the 1939 figure by the national average (as we have done for the Ukrainians) gives us 948,000. But the 1926 population should have grown to 4,598,000 in 1939 – (on the very conservative assumption that the average USSR growth rate of 15.7% prevailed, whereas in fact other Soviet Muslim populations grew much faster). That is, the population should have been over 1.5 million higher than it was. If we allow 300,000 for unborn children and 200,000 for successful emigration from the areas closest to Sinkiang, we have a death roll of one million.

Thus we are left with three million as the 1926–37 deficit attributable to the deportation of the kulaks. We have already discussed the numbers deported, and the reported death rates. Three million is a figure which is consonant with our estimates (if 30% of deportees died, it would mean 9 million deported; if 25%, then twelve million would be the deportation total).

By 1935, in one approximate view,[26] a third of an estimated eleven million deportees were dead; a third in 'special settlement'; and a third in labour camp. Estimates of the total 1935 labour camp population run at around the five million level,[27] and up till the mass arrests of officials in 1936–8, these are always reported as 'overwhelmingly', 70–80%, peasant.[28]

Of the four million odd peasants probably in camp by 1935, most probably survived until 1937 or 1938, but thereafter the likelihood is that no more than ten percent ever saw release, and we must thus, as we have noted, probably add a minimum of another c. 3.5 million deaths to the peasant account.

★

Throughout, our conclusions are based either on exact and certain figures, or on reasonably conservative assumptions. So when we conclude that no fewer than fourteen million odd peasants lost their lives as a result of the events recounted in this book we may well be understating. In any case, the eleven million odd excess dead shown by the 1937 census is hardly subject to serious amendment. The famine figures seem both reasonable in themselves and consonant with the census's shortfall; as do the dekulakization figures.

Why we cannot be more exact is obvious. As Khrushchev says in his memoirs, 'I can't give an exact figure because no one was keeping count. All we knew was that people were dying in enormous numbers'.[29]

It is significant that statistics (even if unreliable) of the mortality of cattle were published, and those of human mortality were not – so that for fifty years we have had some account of what happened to the livestock but not what happened to the human beings. In a much published speech a couple of years later Stalin was to say that more care should be taken of people, giving as an example something that supposedly happened to him in exile in Siberia: by a river-crossing with some peasants, he saw that they made every effort to save horses from being swept away, but cared little for the loss of a man, an attitude he deplored at some length. Even for Stalin, whose words seldom revealed his true attitudes, this was – and particularly at this time – a complete reversal of truth. It was he and his followers for whom human life was lowest on the scale of values.

We may now conveniently sum up the estimated death toll roughly as follows:

Peasant dead: 1930–37	11 million
Arrested in this period dying in camps later	3.5 million
TOTAL	14.5 million

Of these:

Dead as a result of dekulakization	6.5 million	
Dead in the Kazakh catastrophe	1 million	
Dead in the 1932–3 famine:		
in the Ukraine	5 million	
in the N. Caucasus	1 million	7 million
elsewhere	1 million	

As we have said, these are enormous figures, comparable to the deaths in the major wars of our time. And when it comes to the genocidal element, to the Ukrainian figures alone, we should remember that five million constitutes about 18.8% of the total population of the Ukraine (and about a quarter of the rural population). In World War I less than 1% of the population of the countries at war died. In one Ukrainian village of 800 inhabitants (Pysarivka in Podilia), where 150 had died, a local peasant ironically noted that only seven villagers had been killed in World War I.[30]

In the events which we have been describing the 'casualties' in a general sense, the 'walking wounded', constitute whole populations. Our concern, in this chapter, has been to establish as closely as may be possible the actual dead. But we need not for a moment forget the dreadful effects suffered, and far into the future, by individuals and nations.

Moreover, further terrors, inflicting yet further death on much the same scale, faced the survivors.

Let us once more emphasize that the figures we have given are conservative estimates, and quite certainly do not overstate the truth. And if we cannot be more exact, it is because the Soviet regime will not let us. It is not only a matter of Stalin concealing the true facts back in the 1930s.

We owe a number of useful details to honest and courageous Soviet scholars and writers: but, even today, Moscow permits no real investigation of these monstrous events. Which is to say that to this degree the regime remains the accomplice, as well as the heir, of those who fifty years ago sent these innocent millions to their deaths.

★

17

The Record of the West

O grave keep shut, lest I be shamed
Masefield

A major element in Stalin's operations against the peasantry was what Pasternak calls 'the inhuman power of the lie'. Deception was practised on a giant scale. In particular every effort was made to persuade the West that no famine was taking place, and later that none had in fact taken place.

On the face of it, this might appear to have been an impossible undertaking. A great number of true accounts reached Western Europe and America, some of them from impeccable Western eyewitnesses. (It was not found feasible, at least in 1932, to keep all foreigners out of the famine areas).

But Stalin had a profound understanding of the possibilities of what Hitler approvingly calls the Big Lie. He knew that even though the truth may be readily available, the deceiver need not give up. He saw that flat denial on the one hand, and the injection into the pool of information of a corpus of positive falsehood on the other, were sufficient to confuse the issue for the passively uninstructed foreign audience, and to induce acceptance of the Stalinist version by those actively seeking to be deceived. The Famine was the first major instance of the exercise of this technique of influencing world opinion, but it was to be followed by a number of others such as the campaign over the Moscow Trials of 1936–8, the denial of the existence of the forced labour camp system, and so on. Indeed, it can hardly be said to be extinct even today.

★

Before discussing the operation of these schemes, let us first insist on the fact that the truth was indeed widely available in the West.

In spite of everything, full or adequate reports appeared in the *Manchester Guardian* and the *Daily Telegraph; Le Matin* and *Le Figaro;* the *Neue Zuericher Zeitung* and the *Gazette de Lausanne; La Stampa* in Italy, the *Reichpost* in Austria, and scores of other Western papers. In the United States, wide-circulation newspapers printed very full first hand accounts by Ukrainian-American and other visitors (though these were much discounted as, often, appearing in 'Right Wing' journals); and the *Christian Science Monitor*, the *New York Herald Tribune* (and the New York Jewish *Forwaerts*) gave broad coverage. We have quoted many of these reports in our text.

We should however, enter the reservation that in most cases journalists could not both keep their visas and report the facts, and were often forced, or lured, into what was at best compromise. It was only when they left the country for good that men like Chamberlin and Lyons were able to tell the full story. Moreover, their despatches had meanwhile to pass the censorship – though Muggeridge sent some of his reports *sub rosa* through the British diplomatic bag.

For the time being, fairly immediate reports were limited to despatches sent like Muggeridge's; to incomplete, though often informative pieces passing the censor; and to the evidence of recent visitors who had the language and had penetrated the famine area – some of them foreign Communists who had worked there, other foreign citizens with relatives in the villages, occasionally an eccentric Westerner merely bent on the truth.

One of these last was Gareth Jones, a former secretary of Lloyd George's, and a student of Russia and of Russian history. He got to the Ukraine from Moscow, like Muggeridge, without telling anyone. He went on foot through villages in the Kharkov Province, and on his return to the West reported the constant cry of 'There is no bread. We are dying'. He said, writing, like Muggeridge, in the *Manchester Guardian* (30 March 1933), he would never 'forget the swollen stomachs of the children in the cottages in which I slept'. Moreover, he added, 'four-fifths of the cattle and the horses had perished'. This honourable and honest report was subject to gross libel, not only by Soviet officialdom, but also by Walter Duranty, and by other correspondents wishing to stay on in order to cover the forthcoming 'Metro-Vic' faked trial, then major news.

Still, some of the much harassed foreign journalists did their best in the occasional despatch which passed the censorship with useful information. One (of 22 September 1933) by the Associated Press correspondent Stanley Richardson quoted the head of the MTS Political Departments for the Ukraine, the old Bolshevik Alexander Asatkin, former First Secretary of the Byelorussian Communist Party, on the famine. Asatkin had actually given him figures, and those were removed by the censor; but a reference to 'deaths in his area last spring from causes related to undernourishment' went through. (This confirmation by a Soviet official was not printed in most American papers: Marco Carynnyk writes that he could only find it in the *New York American*, the *Toronto Star* and the *Toronto Evening Telegram*).

In any case, in 1933, new regulations in effect excluded foreign correspondents from the Ukraine and North Caucasus.[1] The British Embassy reported to London as early as 5 March 1933 that 'all foreign correspondents have now been 'advised' by the Press department of the Commissariat for Foreign Affairs to remain in Moscow'. But it was only in August that W.H. Chamberlin felt able to inform his editors in the West that he and his colleagues had been *ordered* not to leave Moscow without submitting an itinerary and obtaining permission, and that he himself had just been refused permission to go to areas in the Ukraine and North Caucasus which he had previously visited. He added that the same applied to two American correspondents and to others.[2] The *New York Herald Tribune*'s correspondent P.B. Barnes put it that 'New censorship measures exclude accredited foreign correspondents from those regions of the USSR where conditions are unfavourable'.[3]

The more honest journalists could only be muzzled, not silenced. When such books as Chamberlin's came out, in 1934, there was no longer any real possibility of doubt about the famine, or any of the previous sufferings of the peasantry. Indeed, even western writers regarded by Communists and non-Communists alike as friends of the regime expressed reservations and told truths. Maurice Hindus, writing of collectivization, while favouring it in principle, told of the 'human tragedy' of the kulak deportations, of the 'callous insensitiveness' of the Party; described the peasant reaction in the slaughter of livestock and later lapse 'into apathy'; the incompetence of the kolkhoz management (with pigs and chickens dying of mismanagement, cows and horses of underfeeding).[4]

Enough information was already in existence to put the issue past all reasonable query, and the Western public had it available. Some acted: on 28 May 1934 a resolution was submitted to the US House of Representatives (73rd Congress, 2nd Session, House Resolution 39a) by Congressman Hamilton Fish Jr., registering the facts of the famine, recalling the American tradition of 'taking cognizance' of such invasions of human rights, expressing sympathy and the hope that the USSR would change its policies and meanwhile admit American relief. It was referred to the Committee on Foreign Affairs and ordered to be printed.

As in 1921, though on a lesser scale since the facts were not as fully available, an international humanitarian effort was made. In this case, however, it was ineffectual. An International Relief Committee was set up under the chairmanship of Cardinal Innitzer, Archbishop of Vienna. The Red Cross had to reply to appeals that it was constitutionally unable to operate without the consent of the government concerned. And that government continued to rebuff the reports as lies, and to print rejection by prosperous Soviet peasants of such impertinent offers of help. Collective farmers of the Volga-German Republic are similarly quoted by *Izvestiya*[5] as saying that they rejected the assistance of organizations created in Germany 'for rendering assistance to the Germans who are supposed to be starving in Russia'.

In the Western Ukraine, under Polish sovereignty, the facts were well known, and in July 1933 a Ukrainian Central Relief Committee was founded in Lviv which was able to give a certain amount of clandestine help with parcels.

The Ukrainian emigré organizations in the West fought in the most active manner to bring the facts to the attention of the Governments and the public. In Washington, for example, the files of the State Department are full of appeals to the US administration to intervene in some way, always answered with a statement that the absence of any American state interest made this impractical.

The files of the State Department are also full of letters from editors, professors, clergymen and others reporting that lecturers such as W.H. Chamberlin had given figures of deaths of from four to ten million people, the letters in almost every case casting doubt on the probability of such figures. The State Department sometimes answered that its policy was not to comment, sometimes it gave a list of sources which might be referred to.

The United States at this time had no diplomatic relations with the Soviet Union, (until November 1933), and the State Department was under instructions to work to establish such relations – a political move in which reports of the terror-famine were regarded by the Administration as unhelpful. The foreign diplomatic corps actually in Moscow was not deceived, the British Embassy, for example, reporting to London that conditions in the Kuban and the Ukraine were 'appalling'.[6]

Thus, in one way or another, the truth was available, was in some sense known in the West. The task of the Soviet Government was to destroy, distort, or blanket this knowledge.

In the first phase, then, the famine was ignored or denied. In the Soviet press itself, there was no reference to it. This was true even of the Ukrainian papers. The disjunction between reality and report was quite extraordinary.

311

Arthur Koestler, who was in Kharkov in 1932–3, writes that it gave him a most unreal feeling to read the local papers, full of young people smiling under banners, giant combines in the Urals, reports of awards to shock brigaders, but 'not one word about the local famine, epidemics, the dying out of whole villages; even the fact that there was no electricity in Kharkov was not once mentioned in the Kharkov papers. The enormous land was covered with a blanket of silence'.[7]

At an earlier period, during the collectivization, it had been difficult to discover what was going on. As an American correspondent wrote 'A resident in Moscow, Russian or foreigner, would in many cases only learn by accident, if indeed he learned at all, of such episodes of "class war" as the death from hunger of many exiled peasant children in remote Luza, in Northern Russia, in the summer of 1931; or the widespread scurvy among the forced labourers in the Karaganda coal mines, in Kazakhstan, as a result of inadequate diet; or the perishing of cold of kulak families which were driven out of their homes in winter near Akmolinsk, in Kazakhstan; or the development of diseases of the female organs among the women exiles in bleak Khibinogorsk, beyond the Arctic Circle, as a result of the complete absence of sanitary provision in the severe winter'.[8]   But when it came to the famine, even in Moscow, it was at first referred to fairly openly by Russians not only in their houses, but even in public places like hotels. It soon became, indeed, an offence carrying a three to five year sentence to use the word; but enough was now already known, even by foreigners, to make more active measures than mere denial necessary.

Meanwhile, the denials were hot and strong.

There were many attacks on 'slanders' which had appeared in the foreign press. The Austrian *Reichpost* was accused by *Pravda* (20 July 1933) of 'stating that millions of Soviet citizens in the Volga region, the Ukraine and the North Caucasus had died of starvation. This vulgar slander, dirty invention about famine in the USSR has been cooked up by the editors of *Reichpost* to divert the attention of their own workers from their hard and hopeless situation'. President Kalinin spoke of 'political cheats who offer to help the starving Ukraine' commenting: 'only the most decadent classes are capable of producing such cynical elements'.[9]

When the famine became widely reported in the USA and a Congressman, Herman Kopelmann of Connecticut, drew official Soviet attention to it, he received the following answer from Foreign Commissar Litvinov:

I am in receipt of your letter of the 14th instant and thank you for drawing my attention to the Ukrainian pamphlet. There is any amount of such pamphlets full of lies circulated by the counter-revolutionary organizations abroad who specialize in work of this kind. There is nothing left for them to do but spread false information and forge documents.[10]

The Soviet Embassy in Washington also claimed that the Ukraine's population had increased over the Five Year Plan period by 2% per annum, and that it had the lowest death rate of any Soviet republic![11]

From now on, all sorts of raw distortion were produced. For example, *Izvestiya* of 26 February 1935 published an interview with an American correspondent, Lindesay M Parrott, of the International News Service. In it he was quoted as saying that he had found well organized farms and plenty of bread in the Ukraine, and the Volga region. Parrott told his employer, and the American Embassy, that he had been thoroughly misquoted, having merely told the *Izvestiya* correspondent that he had not seen any 'famine conditions' on his trip, made in 1934, and that farm conditions seemed to be improving. From this, *Izvestiya* had invented the rest.[12]

★

However, the main methods of falsification were of a broader and more traditional type.

An American journalist in Moscow describes one of the deceptions of the dekulakization period:

> For the special purpose of appeasing American public opinion, an American 'commission' was despatched to the lumber area and in due time it attested truthfully that it had not seen forced labor. No one in the foreign colony was more amused by this clowning than the 'commissioners' themselves. They were: a salesman of American machinery, long resident in Moscow and dependent on official good-will for his business; a young American reporter without a steady job and therefore in the USSR by sufferance of the government; and the resident secretary of the American-Russian Chamber of Commerce, a paid employee of the organization whose usefulness depended on maintaining cordial relations with the Soviet authorities.
>
> I knew all three men intimately, and it is betraying no secret to record that each of them was as thoroughly convinced of the widespread employment of forced labor in the lumber industry as Hamilton Fish or Dr Deterding. They went to the North for the ride, or because it was difficult to refuse, and they placated their conscience by merely asserting ambiguously that they personally had seen no signs of forced labor; they did not indicate that they made no genuine effort to find it and that their official guides steered the 'investigation'.
>
> Their findings, published with all solemnity and transmitted obediently by the American correspondents to the United States, were a good deal along the line of a later 'commission' in search of forced labor in the Don Basin coal area.

One of the 'commissioners', the famous American photographer Jimmy Abbe, put it to me this way:

'Sure, we saw no forced labor. When we approached anything that looked like it, we all closed our eyes tight and kept them closed. We weren't going to lie about it.'[13]

Edouard Herriot, the French Radical leader, twice premier of his country, was in the USSR in August and September 1933. He spent five days in the Ukraine: half this time was devoted to official receptions and banquets, and the other half to a conducted tour. As a result he felt able to claim that no famine existed, and to blame reports of such on elements pursuing an anti-Soviet policy. *Pravda* (13 September 1933) was able to announce that 'he categorically denied the lies of the bourgeois press about a famine in the Soviet Union'.

Such comments, from a widely known statesman, had, we are told, a great effect on European opinion. The irresponsibility shown must have greatly encouraged Stalin in his view of the gullibility of the West, on which he was to play so effectively in later years.

A visitor to Kiev describes the preparations for Herriot. The day before his arrival the population was required to work from 2 a.m. cleaning the streets and decorating the houses. Food-distribution centres were closed. Queues were prohibited. Homeless children, beggars, and starving people disappeared.[14] A local inhabitant adds that shop windows were filled with food, but the police dispersed or arrested even local citizens who pressed too close, (and the purchase of the food was forbidden).[15] The streets were washed, the hotel he was to stay in was refurbished, with new carpets and furniture and new uniforms for the staff.[16] And similarly in Kharkov.[17]

Herriot's round of visits is illustrative. At Kharkov he was taken to a model children's settlement, the Shevchenko Museum and a tractor factory, together with meetings, or banquets, with the Ukrainian Party leaders.[18]

Certain villages were set aside to show to foreigners.[19] These were 'model' collectives – for example 'Red Star' in the Kharkov Province, where all the peasants were picked Communists and Komsomols. These were well housed and well fed. The cattle were in good condition. And tractors were always available.[20] Or a normal village might be reorganized for the occasion.

One witness describes the preparations made to receive Herriot at the collective farm 'October Revolution' in Brovary, near Kiev:

A special meeting of the regional party organization was held in Kiev for the purpose of transforming this collective farm into a 'Potemkin village'. An older communist, an inspector attached to the Commissariat of Agriculture, was appointed temporary chief and experienced agronomists were made into brigade members of the farm. It was thoroughly scrubbed and cleaned, all communists, komsomols and activists having been mobilized for the job. Furniture from the regional theatre in Brovary was brought, and the clubrooms beautifully appointed with it. Curtains and drapes were brought from Kiev, also tablecloths. One wing was turned into a dining-hall, the tables of which were covered with new cloths and decorated with flowers. The regional telephone exchange, and the switchboard operator, were transferred from Brovary to the farm. Some steers and hogs were slaughtered to provide plenty of meat. A supply of beer was also brought in. All the corpses and starving peasants were removed from the highways in the surrounding countryside and the peasants were forbidden to leave their houses. A mass meeting of collective farm workers was called, and they were told that a motion picture would be made of collective farm life, and for this purpose this particular farm had been chosen by a film-studio from Odessa. Only those who were chosen to play in the picture would turn out for work, the rest of the members must stay at home and not interfere. Those who were picked by a special committee were given new outfits brought from Kiev: shoes, socks, suits, hats, handkerchiefs. Women received new dresses. The whole masquerade was directed by a delegate of the Kiev party district organization, Sharapov, and a man named Denisenko was his deputy. The people were told that they were a movie director and his assistant. The organizers decided that it would be best for M. Herriot to meet the collective farm workers while they were seated at tables, eating a good meal. The next day, when Herriot was due to arrive, now well-dressed workers were seated in the dining-hall, and served a hearty meal. They were eating huge chunks of meat, washing it down with beer or lemonade, and were making short work of it. The director, who was nervous, called upon the people to eat slowly, so that the honoured guest, Herriot, would see them at their tables. Just then a telephone message came from Kiev: 'Visit cancelled, wind everything up'. Now another meeting was called. Sharapov thanked the workers for a good performance, and then Denisenko asked them to take off and return all the clothes that had been issued to them, with the exception of socks and handkerchiefs. The people begged to be allowed to keep the clothes and shoes, promising to work or pay for them, but to no avail. Everything had to be given back and returned to Kiev, to the stores from which it had been borrowed.[21]

It is evidently to Herriot that Vasily Grossman is referring when he writes of 'a Frenchman, a famous minister' visiting a kolkhoz nursery school and asking the children what they had had for lunch. They answered 'Chicken soup with pirozhki and rice cutlets'. Grossman comments 'Chicken soup! cutlets! And on our farm they had eaten all the earthworms'. He goes on to speak contemptuously of the 'theatre' being made of the situation by the authorities.[22]

315

Herriot's interpreter, Professor Seeberg of the Ukrainian College of Linguistic Education in Kiev, is later reported arrested and sentenced to five years in a Karelian camp for 'close connections' with the Frenchman.[23]

On another occasion a delegation of Americans, English and Germans came to Kharkov. A major round up of peasant beggars preceded it. They were taken off in lorries and simply dumped in barren fields some way out of town.[24] A Turkish mission, on its way home, was scheduled to eat at the junction of Lozova. In anticipation of their stay, the dead and dying were loaded in trucks, and removed to an unknown fate. The others were marched eighteen miles away and forbidden to return. The station was cleaned up, and smart 'waitresses' and 'public' were brought in.[25]

This Potemkin method thus proved useful with men of international reputation, though few of them went to the length of Bernard Shaw, who said 'I did not see a single under-nourished person in Russia, young or old. Were they padded? Were their hollow cheeks distended by pieces of india rubber inside?'[26] (Bernard Shaw had also felt able to say, – or is at any rate so quoted in the Soviet press – that 'in the USSR, unlike Britain, there was freedom of religion').[27]

In an interesting variant one Western sympathizer of the regime tells a striking tale (quoted at length by the Webbs as evidence against the existence of famine): his party of foreign visitors heard rumours that in a village called Gavrilovka all the men but one were said to have died of starvation. They 'went at once to investigate', visited the village registry office, the priest, the local soviet, the judge, the schoolmaster and 'every individual peasant we met'. They found that three out of 1,100 inhabitants had died of typhus, as a result of which immediate measures had stopped any epidemic, and that there had been no deaths from starvation.[28] The perspicacious reader will think of at least three different ways in which this result could have been a hoax. But even if it had been genuine how could it refute the first hand evidence from elsewhere of Muggeridge and all the others?

★

What is perhaps more reprehensible is that these methods worked, at first or second hand, with prominent scholars concerned to instruct the intellectual West.

Sir John Maynard, then a leading British expert on Soviet agriculture, takes a view of the casualties of collectivization: 'these pictures are distressing, but we shall get our perspective right only if we remember that the Bolsheviks conceived themselves to be fighting a war, a war against an enemy class instead of a war against an enemy nation, and to be applying

316

the methods of war'.[29] When it comes to 1933, he speaks flatly, as one who visited the areas in question: 'Any suggestion of a calamity comparable with the famine of 1921–2 is, in the opinion of the present writer, who travelled through Ukraine and North Caucasus in June and July 1933, unfounded'.[30]

More extraordinary still was the 'research' of the doyens of western social science, Sidney and Beatrice Webb, in the huge work in which they sum up the Soviet Union.[31]

They visited the country in 1932 and 1933, and put an immense amount of labour into producing a full, judicious and scholarly documentation of what was going on.

To start with, one finds in them the general hostility to the peasantry we have noted of the Bolsheviks. The Webbs speak of their 'characteristic vices of greed and cunning, varied by outbursts of drunkenness and recurrent periods of sloth'. They speak approvingly of turning these backward characters 'into public spirited co-operators working upon a prescribed plan for the common product to be equitably shared among themselves'.[32] They even speak of the ('partially enforced') collectivization representing the 'final stage' of the rural uprisings of 1917![33]

'The cost' of collectivization was 'driving out the universally hated kulaks and the recalcitrant Don Cossacks by tens or even hundreds of thousands of families'.[34] (They describe one piece of official propaganda on dekulakization as 'the artless recital of a peasant woman'.)[35]

The Webbs take it that the later phase of dekulakization was necessary because the kulaks would not work and were demoralizing the villages so had to be sent to far off areas where they could be put to labour or useful projects, as a 'rough and ready expedient of "famine relief" '. Their finding is that 'Candid students of the circumstances may not unwarrantably come to the conclusion that . . . the Soviet Government could hardly have acted otherwise than it did'.[36]

Their enthusiasm may be thought a little distasteful when, for example they conclude that the dekulakization was planned from the start to summarily eject from their homes 'something like a million families' and permit themselves the comment 'strong must have been the faith and resolute the will of the men who, in the interest of what seemed to them the public good, could take so momentous a decision'.[37] Words which might equally be applied, by any wishing to do so, to Hitler and the Final Solution.

However, these are at least in part matters of opinion. When it comes to the facts the Webbs ask themselves 'was there or was there not a famine in the USSR in 1931–2?'. They quote a 'retired high official of the Indian Government' (evidently Maynard) who had himself administered famine

317

districts, and who had visited localities in the USSR where conditions were reported worst, and who found no evidence of what he would describe as a famine.[38] Their conclusion, based also on official reports and conversations with unnamed British and American journalists, is that a 'partial failure of crops' was 'not in itself sufficiently serious to cause actual starvation, except possibly in the worst districts, relatively small in extent'. And they (quite falsely) attributed famine reports to 'people who have seldom had the opportunity of going to the suffering districts'![39]

The Webbs blame even these minor food shortages on 'a refusal of the agriculturalists to sow . . . or to gather up the wheat when it was cut'.[40] Indeed they speak of 'a population manifestly guilty of sabotage';[41] while in the Kuban 'whole villages sullenly abstained from sowing or harvesting.'[42] They even describe 'individual peasants' who 'out of spite' took to 'rubbing the grain from the ear, or even cutting off the whole ear, and carrying it off for individual hoarding, this shameless theft of communal property'![43]

They repeat, too, without comment, the confession of one of the alleged Ukrainian nationalists, as quoted by Postyshev, to the effect that they had worked by agitation and propaganda in the villages to sabotage the harvest.[44] And they describe Stalin's announcement at the January 1933 plenum of further steps to squeeze non-existent grain from the Ukraine, as 'a campaign which for boldness of conception and vigour in execution as well as the magnitude of its operations, appears to us unparalleled in the peace-time annals of any government'.[45]

When it comes to their sources, the Webbs often refer to, for example, 'competent observers'. One quoted claims that peasants no longer wish to own a house or a plough any more than a worker would wish to own a turbine, and would use the money to live better instead – a 'mental revolution'.[46]

On the collectivization, the Webbs approvingly quote the Communist Anna Louise Strong, as saying that far from the Western assumption that the exiling of kulaks was done by 'a mystically omnipotent GPU' it was carried out by 'village meetings' of poor peasants and farm-hands who listed kulaks impeding collectivization by force and violence and 'asked the Government to deport them . . . the meetings I personally attended were more seriously judicial, more balanced in their discussion, than any court trial I have attended in America'.[47]

But for the famine period itself their favourite source is the *New York Times* correspondent Walter Duranty, whose activities and influence deserve special treatment.

★

As the closest Western co-operator of all with the Soviet falsifications, Walter Duranty obtained all sorts of privileges, such as praise from, and interviews with, Stalin himself – while at the same time receiving unstinted adulation from important Western circles.

In November 1932 Duranty had reported that 'there is no famine or actual starvation nor is there likely to be'.

When the famine became widely known in the West, and reported in his own paper and by his own colleagues, playing down, rather than denial, became his method. Still denying famine he spoke of 'malnutrition', 'food shortages', 'lowered resistance'.

On 23 August 1933 he wrote that 'any report of a famine in Russia is today an exaggeration or malignant propaganda', going on to say that 'the food shortage which has affected almost the whole population in the last year, and particularly the grain-producing provinces – that is the Ukraine. the North Caucasus, the Lower Volga Region – has, however, caused heavy loss of life'. He estimated the death rate as nearly four times the usual rate. This usual rate would, in the regions named 'have been about 1,000,000' and this was now in all probability 'at least trebled'.

This admission of two million extra deaths was thus made to appear regrettable, but not overwhelmingly important and not amounting to 'famine'. (Moreover he blamed it in part on 'the flight of some peasants and the passive resistance of others').

In September 1933 he was the first correspondent to be admitted to the famine regions, and reported that 'the use of the word famine in connection with the North Caucasus is a sheer absurdity', adding that he now felt that for this area at least his earlier estimate of excess deaths had been 'exaggerated'. He also spoke of 'plump babies' and 'fat calves' as typical of the Kuban.[48] (Litvinov found it useful to cite these despatches in answering Congressman Kopelmann's letter of inquiry).

Duranty blamed famine stories on emigrés, encouraged by the rise of Hitler, and spoke of 'the famine stories then current in Berlin, Riga, Vienna and other places, where elements hostile to the Soviet Union were making an eleventh-hour attempt to avert American recognition by picturing the Soviet Union as a land of ruin and despair'.

The reputation Duranty had already acquired by the autumn of 1933 is dryly expressed in a despatch from the British Embassy about the visit Duranty (an Englishman) had now been permitted to make to the grain areas of the Ukraine: 'I have no doubt that . . . he will have no difficulty in obtaining sufficient quantitative experience in tour hours to enable him to say whatever he may wish to say on return'. It also described him as 'Mr Duranty, the *New York Times* Correspondent, whom the Soviet Union is probably more anxious to conciliate than any other'.[49]

Malcolm Muggeridge, Joseph Alsop and other experienced journalists held the plain opinion that Duranty was a liar – as Muggeridge later put it 'the greatest liar of any journalist I have met in fifty years of journalism'.

Duranty had personally told Eugene Lyons and others that he estimated the famine victims at around seven million. But an even clearer proof of the discrepancy between what he knew and what he reported is to be found in a despatch of 30 September 1933 from the British Chargé d'affaires in Moscow, which we quoted earlier: 'According to Mr Durranty the population of the North Caucasus and the Lower Volga had decreased in the past year by three million, and the population of the Ukraine by four to five million. The Ukraine had been bled white . . . Mr Duranty thinks it quite possible that as many as ten million people may have died directly or indirectly from lack of food in the Soviet Union during the past year'.

What the American public got was not this straight stuff, but the false reporting. Its influence was enormous and long-lasting.

The *New York Times* Company Annual Report of 1983 prints a list of the paper's Pulitzer Prizes, not omitting the one to Walter Duranty in 1932 for 'dispassionate, interpretive reporting of the news from Russia'.

The announcement of the prize had in fact added to this citation the points that Duranty's despatches were 'marked by scholarship, profundity, impartiality, sound judgement and exceptional clarity', being 'excellent examples of the best type of foreign correspondence'.

The Nation, in citing the *New York Times* and Walter Duranty in its annual 'honour roll', described his as 'the most enlightening, dispassionate and readable despatches from a great nation in the making which appeared in any newspaper in the world'.

At a banquet at the Waldorf Astoria to celebrate the recognition of the USSR by the United States, a list of names was read, each politely applauded by the guests until Walter Duranty's was reached; then, Alexander Woollcott wrote in the *New Yorker*, 'the one really prolonged pandemonium was evoked . . . Indeed, one got the impression that America, in a spasm of discernment, was recognizing both Russia and Walter Duranty'. Well, a spasm anyway.

The praise which went to Duranty was clearly not due to a desire to know the truth, but rather to a desire of many to be told what they wished to hear. Duranty's own motives need no explaining.[50]

★

This lobby of the blind and the blindfold could not actually prevent true accounts by those who were neither dupes nor liars from reaching the

West. But they could, and did, succeed in giving the impression that there was at least a genuine doubt about what was happening and insinuating that reports of starvation came only from those hostile to the Soviet government and hence of dubious reliability. Reporters of the truth like Muggeridge and Chamberlin were under continuous and violent attack by pro-Communist elements in the West over the next generation.

For the falsification was not temporary. It had entered the field of 'scholarship' with the Webbs and others. It continued to produce results – such as one scandalous piece of active, rather than merely conniving, falsification coming as late as in the 1940s, with the production in Hollywood of the film *North Star*, which represented a Soviet collective farm as a hygienic, well-fed village of happy peasants – a travesty greater than could have been shown on Soviet screens to audiences used to lies, but experienced in this particular matter to a degree requiring at least a minimum of restraint.

One Communist gave as the reason, or one of the reasons, for the suppression of truth, the fact that the USSR could only win the support of workers in the capitalist countries if the human cost of its policies was concealed.[51] It seems not in practice to have been so much a matter of the workers as of the intellectuals and formers of public opinion.

As George Orwell complained (of England) 'Huge events like the Ukraine famine of 1933, involving the deaths of millions of people, have actually escaped the attention of the majority of English russophiles'. But it was not only a matter of pure russophiles, but also of a large and influential body of Western thought.

The scandal is not that they justified the Soviet actions, but that they refused to hear about them, that they were not prepared to face the evidence.

★

18

Responsibilities

Where has that life gone? And what
has become of all that awful torment
and torture? Can it really be that
no one will ever answer for
everything that happened? That it
will all be forgotten without even
any words to commemorate it? That
the grass will grow over it?

Vasily Grossman

The historian, registering the facts beyond doubt, and in their context, cannot but also judge. *Die Weltgeschichte ist das Weltgericht* – World History is the World's Court of Judgement: Schiller's dictum may seem too grandiose today. Yet the establishment of the facts certainly includes the establishment of the responsibility.

In the case of the 'kulaks' dead or deported in 1930–32, there is no problem. They were the victims of conscious governmental action against 'class enemies'; Communist officials were discussing the necessity of 'destroying' five million people even before the measures had taken effect;[1] and Stalin himself, to all intents and purposes, later admitted the extent of the slaughter. When it comes to the great famine of 1932–3, however, a great effort was made at the time – and is still to some degree persisted in today – to obscure or obfuscate the truth.

The first line of defence was the plea that no famine had occurred. This was the official line of the Soviet Government. Abroad it was put about, as we saw in Chapter 17, by Soviet diplomats and Western journalists and others who had been deceived or corrupted by the Soviet authorities. Internally, on the whole the Soviet press simply ignored the famine, but occasionally printed a refutation or rejection of some insolent foreign slander. It became an offence (as anti-Soviet propaganda) to refer to famine – and this was enforced even in the famine areas themselves. And at the top Stalin simply laid it down that no famine existed.

This remained the official story for years. Indeed, even now references to the famine in Soviet scholarly and historical work are rare, and usually oblique – though some Soviet fiction has been franker.

In the West, it had its effect. Some people were able to believe the official line; others to think that there were two contradictory stories, with no clinching evidence on either side. So accounts of the famine could be rejected, or at least easily forgotten, by those so predisposed.

However, reports of the famine were hard to suppress entirely. The next line of defence is two-fold: that there was indeed malnutrition, and even an increase in the death rate, and that the responsibility for this was the recalcitrance of the peasants who had refused to sow or reap properly. The Soviet Government's need for grain was attributed to the requirements of the Army, a war with Japan being supposedly expected.

The admission of an increase in the death rate was permitted to journalists running a pro-Soviet line, who were, as we have seen, even able to say that there was no famine – only an excess of some two million deaths! This too confused the issue by its implication that such figures did not amount to much. The recalcitrance of the peasantry was, of course, in accord with the official line that kulaks were sabotaging the crop in various ways: it too was made good use of in the West.

Between them, these amounted to an admission that there was indeed something most people would call a famine, but that it was not the Soviet's fault, and was not as serious as malignant propaganda had reported.

And here, Stalin had a much better means of baffling criticism. For even if it was known that there was a famine, the mere existence of famine does not in itself prove the responsibility of Stalin and the Party leadership. There have been many famines, and the assumption would be that here was another, with natural causes, perhaps exacerbated by the policies of the Government, but with no reason to believe that the Government procured the famine of express malice, unless proven to the hilt.

It is in dealing with this not unreasonable presumption that we reach the crux of the matter.

★

But first, let us ask whether the leadership indeed knew of the famine.

We know, of course, that the leading Ukrainian Communists were well aware of the situation. Chubar, Khatayevich, Zatonsky, Demchenko, Terekhov, Petrovsky, had been in the countryside and seen with their own eyes how things were. They had always known that the grain quotas were too high, and now they saw the famine. Chubar is also reported at a conference in Kiev answering a question as to whether the Ukrainian Government knew about the famine with 'the government is aware of this, but cannot help it'.[2]

Petrovsky himself is reported by a peasant as walking through a village past all the dead and dying.[3] He also promised a crowd of starving peasants at Chornukhy that he would speak of it in Moscow, but perhaps did not do so.[4] When a factory official told Petrovsky that his employees were talking of five million people having already died and asked what he should tell them, he is quoted as answering, 'Tell them nothing! What they say is true. We know that millions are dying. That is unfortunate, but the glorious future of the Soviet Union will justify that. Tell them nothing!'[5]

But we know that the top Moscow Stalinists too knew of the famine. Molotov visited the Ukrainian countryside late in 1932 and is reported to have been approached by district officials who told him that there was no grain and that the population was starving.[6] Kaganovich is also reported in Poltava in the winter, receiving the same information from local Party veterans, who soon found themselves expelled.[7] As for the others in the Politburo, Khrushchev tells us that Mikoyan was approached by Demchenko, First Secretary of the Kiev Provincial Committee, who asked him if Stalin and the Politburo knew what was going on in the Ukraine. Demchenko went on to describe a train pulling into Kiev station loaded with corpses it had picked up all the way from Poltava.[8]

Khrushchev himself says that 'we knew . . . that people were dying in enormous numbers':[9] That is, the high party circles in Moscow among whom he moved were well aware of the facts. Indeed, when the veteran revolutionary Fedor Raskolnikov defected, when Soviet Ambassador to Bulgaria, his open letters to Stalin made it clear that the inner party knew perfectly well that the famine had been, as he put it, 'organized'.[10]

Finally, we know that Stalin himself was adequately informed.

Terekhov, First Secretary of the Kharkov Provincial Committee, told Stalin that famine was raging, and asked for grain to be sent in. By an odd anomaly, Terekhov was one of the few Ukrainian apparatchiks to survive the Yezhov terror a few years later, and was able to recount the story in *Pravda* in Khrushchev's time. Stalin's retort to his frank remarks was, 'We have been told that you, Comrade Terekhov, are a good speaker; it seems that you are a good storyteller, you've made up such a fable about famine, thinking to frighten us, but it won't work. Wouldn't it be better for you to leave the post of provincial committee secretary and the Ukrainian Central Committee and join the Writers' Union? Then you can write your fables and fools will read them'.[11]

(During the famine of 1946, a similar scene took place when, as Khrushchev tells us, Kosygin was sent to Moldavia by Stalin, and on returning reported widespread malnutrition and dystrophy. Stalin 'blew up and shouted at Kosygin', and 'for a long time afterwards' would call him in mocking vein 'Brother Dystrophic').[12]

Of course, in his retort to Terekhov Stalin could not have believed that a responsible Party official was simply fantasizing, risking his career and more into the bargain. What he was signalling was, in effect, that no reference to the famine would be allowed in the Party's discussions.

Terekhov's intervention seems, from the context, to have been at, or in connection with, the January 1933 plenum of the Central Committee. It seems almost certain that Terekhov took the initiative not in a lone outburst, but as a spokesman for the other Ukrainian leaders who, as we have seen, shared his view of the facts and of the desirability of some understanding of them in Moscow. Nor can Stalin's reply be accounted sincere, or attributed to a genuine if crazed belief that there really was no famine. For of course, his obvious reaction to such a report by a senior official of the Party, if he himself had for some reason not been in possession of the facts, must have been to investigate them, if necessary by a personal visit.

Terekhov's report to Stalin is authenticated far beyond any reasonable doubt. There are a number of other reports of approaches by Ukrainian figures.

We are told of Army Commander Iona Yakir, in command of the Ukrainian Military District, asking Stalin to provide grain for distribution to the peasantry and being rebuffed with advice to stick to military matters. The Commander of the Black Sea Fleet is also reported to have raised the issue, again unsuccessfully.[13]

There is another report that Chubar, as Chairman of the Ukrainian Council of People's Commissars, 'appealed to Stalin for food at least for the starving children' receiving the reply 'no remarks on that question' – (i.e. 'no comment').[14] Stalin's response was logical. To send in relief would be to admit the famine's existence, and so abandon the idea of kulak hoards of grain. Moreover, to feed the children and let the adults starve would present administrative problems . . .

Another of Stalin's informants was his wife, Nadezhda Alliluyeva.[15] Stalin had allowed her to go to a technical school, taking a course in textile production. Students who had been mobilized to help with the collectivization in the rural districts told her of the mass terror, in the hope that she could do something about it. They described the bands of orphaned children begging for bread, the famine in the Ukraine. When she told this to Stalin, thinking he had been badly informed, he dismissed it as Trotskyite rumours. Finally two students described cannibalism there, and how they themselves had taken part in the arrest of two brothers who were selling corpses.

When she told all this to Stalin, he reproached her for collecting 'Trotskyite gossip', had Pauker, head of his bodyguard, arrest the offending students, and ordered the OGPU and the Party Control Commission to institute a special purge of the students in all colleges who had taken part in the collectivization.[16] The quarrel which led to Nadezhda Alliluyeva's suicide on 5 November 1932 seems to have taken place on this very issue.

In addition to all this, as we have noted, Stalin got reports from the OGPU of millions dying in the famine.

★

Stalin could, at any time, have ordered the release of grain, and held off until the late spring in the clear knowledge that the famine was now doing its worst.

That Stalin was fully informed does not quite prove that he had planned the famine from the first. His continuing to employ the policies which had produced the famine after the famine had clearly declared itself, and indeed to demand their more rigorous application, does however show that he regarded the weapon of famine as acceptable, and used it against the kulak-nationalist enemy.

But the conscious nature of the operation is reasonably demonstrated before it took effect. When the Stalin regime moved into excessive requisition in late 1932, it had the experience of 1918–21 behind it. Then, excessive requisition had resulted in disastrous famine. If it was again to do so, this cannot have been for want of understanding in the Kremlin.

More conclusively, it had been made clear by the Ukrainian leaders when the quotas were fixed in 1932 that these were grossly excessive, to a degree which was not true of anywhere else (except the Don, Kuban, Lower Volga, and the other famine regions). So that Stalin was already informed of what they considered the certain result.

The fact that the seed grain for the next harvest was, for the first time, taken away in the Ukraine in the early autumn of 1932 and put in storage in the cities, clearly shows that the authorities understood that it would be eaten if left in the kolkhoz granaries: which is to say that they knew no other resource would be left.

326

Nor is it the case that the famine, or the excessive grain targets, were imposed on the most productive grain-producing areas as such, as a – mistaken or vicious – *economic* policy merely. There was no famine in the rich Russian 'Central Agricultural Region'; and on the other hand the grain-poor Ukrainian provinces of Volhynia and Podilia suffered along with the rest of the country.

But perhaps the most conclusive point in establishing the deliberate nature of the famine lies in the fact that the Ukrainian-Russian border was in effect blockaded to prevent the entry of grain into the Ukraine.[17] In fact 'Troops were stationed at the borders of the Ukraine to prevent them from leaving'.[18] On the trains and in the stations OGPU men would check travellers for travel permits.[19] The last station between Kiev and the border, Mikhaylivka, was surrounded by an armed OGPU detachment, and all without special passes were held, and loaded on freight trains back to Kiev next morning.[20] Of course, some nevertheless got through. People 'tried extraordinary tricks, used fictitious stories, merely to travel' to Russia, 'to buy a little of something edible in exchange for the last fur coats, for carpets and linen, to bring it home and so save their children from dying of hunger'.[21]

For over in Russia, as became widely known, things were different. 'One had only to cross the border and outside Ukraine the conditions were right away better'.[22] The then editor of the main Odessa daily newspaper, Ivan Maystrenko, later described two villages on either side of the Russo-Ukrainian border, where all the grain was taken from the Ukrainian, but only a reasonable delivery quota from the Russian villages.[23] So those who got through were able to get bread. But where possible they were searched, and the grain confiscated, on returning from the RSFSR.[24] One Ukrainian peasant who had earlier been recruited to work on the railway in the Moscow Province heard of the famine at home and left Moscow in April 1933 with seventy-nine pounds of bread. At Bakhmach on the Russo-Ukrainian border seventy pounds of it was confiscated. He was allowed to keep the rest as a registered Moscow worker, but two Ukrainian peasant women who were also trying to bring in bread had it all confiscated and were 'detained'.[25]

People with bread from Russia slipped into the empty wagons which were returning from delivering the Ukrainian grain, but these trains too were raided, both by officials effecting confiscation and arrest and also by train staff demanding blackmail.[26]

There were indeed other hurdles. The railways at this time were overcrowded. Those who had got to Orel, in the RSFSR, to buy bread had to change in the return journey at Lozova, where the wait was two weeks or longer. Waiting, they ate what they had bought, and then lay around the station starving.[27]

The essential is that, in fact, clear orders existed to stop Ukrainian peasants entering Russia where food was available and, when they had succeeded in evading these blocks, to confiscate any food they were carrying when intercepted on their return. This can only have been a decree from the highest level: and it can only have had one motive.

A subsidiary, but contributory, argument is of course that, as we have seen, the assault by famine on the Ukrainian peasant population was accompanied by a wide-ranging destruction of Ukrainian cultural and religious life and slaughter of the Ukrainian intelligentsia. Stalin, as we noted, saw the peasantry as the bulwark of nationalism; and common sense requires us to see this double blow at Ukrainian nationhood as no coincidence.

★

In a more general sense, the responsibility for the massacre of the 'class enemy' and the crushing of 'bourgeois nationalism', may be held to lie with the Marxist conceptions in the form given them by the Communist Party, as accepted by Stalin.

The motives of the actual executives of the Party's decisions were various. The acceptance of the idea of the 'class enemy' of course exempted them from human feeling. For those who felt qualms, the mystique of devotion to the 'Party line' often prevailed. It was reinforced by the knowledge that evasion of orders would result in the purge of the insufficiently inhumane. (Obedience to orders was held no defence at the Nuremburg Trial).

In the event, then, even those like Kossior or Chubar, who had expressed doubt, or rather certainty that Moscow's policies would lead to disaster, nevertheless enforced them.

As to Stalin's personal guilt (and that of Molotov, Kaganovich, Postyshev and the others) it is true that, as with Hitler's responsibility for the Jewish holocaust, we cannot document the responsibility in the sense that any decree exists in which Stalin orders the famine.

But the only possible defence, such as it is, would be to assume that Stalin merely ordered excessive requisitions out of ignorance of the true position, and had no *mens rea*; and this is contradicted by the powerful considerations which we have examined.

We may add that the banning of foreign reporters from the famine areas is, indeed, a further tacit admission by the authorities of what was going on.

★

We may sum the matter up as follows:

1. the cause of the famine was the setting of highly excessive grain requisition targets by Stalin and his associates.
2. Ukrainian party leaders made it clear at the start to Stalin and his associates that these targets were highly excessive.
3. the targets were nevertheless enforced until starvation began.
4. Ukrainian leaders pointed this out to Stalin and his associates and the truth was also made known to him and them by others.
5. the requisitions nevertheless continued.

Such are the major points. We may add as subsidiary evidence:

6. bread rations, even though low ones, were established in the cities, but no such minimum food allowance was made in the villages.
7. grain was available in store in the famine area, but was not released to the peasants in their extremity.
8. orders were given, and enforced as far as possible, to prevent peasants entering the towns, and to expel them when they did.
9. orders were given, and enforced, to prevent food, legally obtained, being brought over the republican borders from Russia to the Ukraine.
10. the fact of famine, and a particularly frightful famine at that, is fully established by witnesses – high Communist officials, local activists, foreign observers and the peasants themselves. Nevertheless, it was made illegal, within the USSR, to suggest that there was a famine; Soviet spokesmen abroad were instructed to deny that famine existed; and to this day the phenomenon is not admitted in the official literature, (though confirmed, fairly recently and fairly rarely, in certain Soviet fiction).

The only conceivable defence is that Stalin and his associates did not know about the famine. This appears impossible to maintain in the face of the above. The verdict must be that they knew that the decrees of 1932 would result in famine, that they knew in the course of the famine itself that this had indeed been the result, and that orders were issued to ensure that the famine was not alleviated, and to confine it to certain areas.

When it comes to motive, the special measures against the Ukraine and the Kuban were specifically linked with, and were contemporaneous with, a public campaign against their nationalism. In these, and the other areas affected, the apparent concern in the agrarian sphere proper was to break the spirit of the most recalcitrant regions of peasant resentment at collectivization. And when it comes to the Party itself the result, and presumable intention, was to eliminate those elements insufficiently disciplined in the suppression of bourgeois-humanitarian feelings.

329

Thus, the facts are established; the motives are consistent with all that is known of Stalinist attitudes; and the verdict of history cannot be other than one of criminal responsibility. Moreover, until there is a frank Soviet investigation of these actions, the silence must surely be seen as the silence of complicity, or justification.

★

EPILOGUE

The Aftermath

Unrespited, unpitied, unreprieved
Milton

The aftermath recorded here comprehends the whole fifty years of Soviet history which have since passed; and, in a sense, of world history too. '

The social and political order consolidated by the beginning of 1934, when the Seventeenth Party Congress was christened 'the Congress of Victors', has persisted ever since. The one-party Leninist state, the collectivized system of agriculture, have gone through various phases, but have not been replaced. But rather than rehearse, even briefly, the general history of the USSR in the years which follow, we may concentrate on certain key areas or events.

★

The events which followed most closely were those of the 'Great Terror' of 1936–8, of which the present author has written elsewhere.

Pasternak's view of this later terror, (in *Doctor Zhivago*), is doubtless over-simple, yet surely gives at least part of the truth: that 'Collectivization was an erroneous and unsuccessful measure and it was impossible to admit the error. To conceal the failure people had to be cured, by every means of terrorism, of the habit of thinking and judging for themselves, and forced to see what didn't exist, to assert the very opposite of what their eyes told them. This accounts for the unexampled cruelty of the Yezhov period'.[1]

Unlike the events of 1930–33 the new terror struck massively at the Party and Governmental leadership, and it is this aspect that has received the most attention. But in the context of this book we should rather stress the further sufferings of the peasantry.

Of course, kulaks in 'special settlement' were a prime target. In 1938 hundreds of them were in Sverdlovsk jail, mostly with ten year sentences on various charges from espionage and sabotage to plotting armed uprisings.[2] But the peasants in the villages also suffered severely. In particular, those who had been the victims of injustice earlier were hauled in, on the grounds that they were likely to be malcontents. In general, peasants provided most of the rank and file of those arrested. One prisoner notes that in the Kholodna Hora prison, in Kharkov, peasants dominated the picture from September 1937 to December 1938. They would be beaten up, then stool-pigeons in the cells would tell them what confessions were expected of them, after which they would be shipped off to the camps, from which few returned.[3] Peasants were also subject to execution. Of the over 9,000 bodies in the mass graves found at Vinnytsia, mostly shot in early 1938, about 60% were those of peasants.[4] These peasants were of course Ukrainian. And we may note that in addition to the usual charges 'members' of the SVU who had served short terms and been released were now arrested and shot.[5]

At this period peasants in general were expected to inculpate collective farm chairmen and other officials, as well as – or even before – their fellow peasants.[6] The chairman would inculpate his committee, and they the foremen or brigadiers.

Many of the arrests were, of course, on grounds of sabotage, and the charges show something of how the kolkhozes were working. In the second half of 1937, there were hundreds of 'trials' in the country districts, the accused being local Communists and rank-and-file kolkhozniks. Roy Medvedev tells us that 'Usually the same ranks of officials were put on trial everywhere, indicating a uniform scheme worked out at the centre'.[7] For example, the local party and administrative officials, the head of the local MTS, one or two kolkhoz chairmen, a senior agronomist, would be charged with anti-Soviet wrecking in general; livestock-wrecking would have the same personnel with the substitution of a veterinary surgeon and a livestock specialist for the agronomist and the MTS man; and so on. In a typical district in 1937 the victims included the senior agronomist, a veterinary surgeon, a forestry technician, the deputy director of the MTS political branch, and various peasants accused of such crimes as poisoning wells. The trials, held in public in the places with lowest output, would attribute all the normal kolkhoz faults such as loss of cattle, or late harvesting, to this sabotage. One trial in the Leningrad Province accused the local representatives of the first list above of bringing the kolkhozes to such a state that the members were generally paid nothing for a 'labour-day', and of failing to supply the state with their products.[8]

★

But, as we have said, unlike the arrests of 1930–33, this terror also struck heavily at the Party itself. It brought about the deaths of almost all the Party characters of whom we have written: Zinoviev, Pyatakov, Bukharin, Rykov and Hrynko shot after public trials and confessions, Tomsky committing suicide. Yakovlev, Bauman, Kaminsky, who had overseen the collectivization drive, were executed secretly. Chubar, Postyshev and Kossior too were shot (together) in prison. Other figures of the Ukrainian apparat like Khatayevich and Demchenko and Zatonsky were similarly disposed of, as was Sheboldayev, who had terrorized the North Caucasus. So were Balitsky and Karlson, the Ukraine's NKVD chiefs; while Liubchenko committed suicide, with his wife.

Stalin, Kaganovich and Molotov survived – the last two are still alive as I write. Petrovsky was removed from his post, but not arrested. And, by an odd irony, Terekhov, who had actually raised the issue of the famine, also survived into post-Stalin times.

Ukrainian Communists were killed off in the terror on a greater scale even than that prevailing elsewhere. At the Fourteenth Congress of the Ukrainian party in June 1938, the new Central Committee had among its eighty-six members and candidates only three survivors from the previous year, all honorary or non-political figures. Those purged were often charged with nationalism – in particular Liubchenko and Hrynko, and even Balitsky.

The republic's party and state virtually disintegrated with the arrest of all the members of the Ukrainian Government and their immediate replacements. All the provincial secretaries were replaced, and their successors replaced again in the early part of 1938. There was no longer a quorum of the Central Committee, nor a body capable of appointing a Council of Peoples' Commissars, and by late 1937 the Republic became little more than an NKVD fief.

★

Naturally there was no real 'nationalist' plot among the Stalinist cadres. But, going beyond the issues of the 1936–8 purge, we may consider whether Stalin succeeded by his actions since 1930 (though especially in 1932–3) in crushing Ukrainian nationalism. The answer seems to be a partial yes. Over the next decades, indeed, Ukrainian nationalism showed itself completely irreconcilable in the Western Ukraine, annexed from Poland in 1939, which had not undergone the terror-famine. The area was subjected to the normal extremes of terror both in 1939–41 and on the reoccupation from 1944. There were mass arrests, collectivization was imposed and so on. The population fought back. Large partisan movements, anti-German and anti-Soviet at the same time, took the field, and were not crushed until the 1950s, (leaders in exile being then assassinated by Soviet secret agents).

Thousands were shot, and many more sent to labour camps or deported – a figure of up to two million is usually given, which accords with the proportions deported from those other newly occupied areas, the Baltic States.

In the period 1945–56 Ukrainians constituted a very high proportion of labour camp inmates, and are invariably reported as the most 'difficult' prisoners from the police point of view. Their death roll, especially in the worst camps where they were most often sent, was very high. In the 1950s in the fearful arctic camps of Kolyma, girl villagers who had supported the rebels were to be found. A Polish prisoner unsympathetic to Ukrainian nationalism, nevertheless noted, 'But why had Soviet officers, interrogating seventeen year old girls, broken the girls' collar-bones and kicked in their ribs with heavy military boots, so that they lay spitting blood in the prison hospitals of Kolyma? Certainly such treatment had not convinced any of them that what they had done was evil. They died with tin medallions of the Virgin on their shattered chests, and with hatred in their eyes'.[9]

Some idea of the numbers of actual prisoners may be seen from an announcement on 17 March 1973 by the Lviv First Secretary, Kutsevol, reporting that since 1956 55,000 members of the Ukrainian anti-Communist OUN had returned to the Lviv Province alone (with about a quarter of the population of the West Ukraine) having served their sentences and survived.[10]

It is in this context that we may consider Khrushchev's remark on Stalin ordering the deportation of seven small nations in 1943–5, that he also wanted to deport 'the Ukrainians, but there were too many of them'; and Stalin later told Roosevelt that his position in the Ukraine was 'difficult and insecure'.[11]

★

It is certainly true that in that part of the Ukraine which had been within the USSR in the 1930s, national feeling had received a numbing blow in 1930–33, with the extirpation of so many of its natural leaders and adherents at every level. It still seems to be true that national feeling is rather stronger in the West Ukraine than the East, though broad sections of the intelligentsia in Kiev and elsewhere form something of an exception.

Yet it has been abundantly shown in more recent years that far from the effect being as decisive as Stalin would have wished, Ukrainian national feeling remains powerful, or has regained much of its power, in the East as well as the West Ukraine – and among the millions of Ukrainians now in Canada, in the USA and elsewhere.

Meanwhile, the Ukraine went through further sufferings in the post-war years. (It is significant that for thirty years, up to 1958, no economic statistics were published for the Ukraine as such).[12] In 1947 another famine struck the country, together with Byelorussia and adjoining areas. It was not directly planned, but with people dying of hunger, Stalin once again exported grain.[13] We have no way of estimating the casualties, but the land was saved from worse by United Nations Relief and Rehabilitation Administration aid, mainly American, which delivered nearly a hundred million dollars worth of food (288,000 metric tons) to the Ukraine alone by the end of January 1947.

On the cultural side came a further assault on the thin ranks of surviving Ukrainian writers. On 26 July 1946 the All-Union Central Committee adopted a resolution to the effect that in 'the fields of science, literature and art' there were attempts by 'hostile bourgeois ideology . . . to reinstate Ukrainian nationalist concepts'.

Through the following year, the literary press attacked writers and cultural figures in such terms as 'incorrigible bourgeois nationalists', 'a wretched and disgusting figure', 'a typical pseudo-scientist', 'incontinent books'.[14] Several thousand were sent to camps.

After this there came a period of comparative calm, followed again (in 1951–2) by further attacks on the Ukrainian cultural leaders. On the negative side, a minor indicator is the fact that no Lenin Prize was awarded to a member of the Ukrainian Academy of Science between 1950 and 1957, though in every year before and after that.[15]

It is not our purpose to relate the whole of the post-war history of the Ukraine. In brief, there have been periods when a looser rein on Ukrainian sensibilities has been used; others when measures were stricter. But the idea of independent Ukrainian statehood, and the free flourishing of Ukrainian culture without Moscow control, have always remained forbidden.

In considering the position as it is today, we should begin with the emergence of an ever-stronger stream of Ukrainian cultural nationalism, starting in the 1960s.

This manifested itself both in the new samizdat, (Ukrainian: *samvydav*), and in published literature. In 1966 alone there were at least twenty trials of writers of the former, with sentences of up to fifteen years for the odd essay or anthology of verse.[16] The latter are represented by such work as Oles Honchar's *The Cathedral*, in which the heroes try to save that building from destruction, pointing out that even Makhno, even the Nazis, had not destroyed it.

In the same period, a long essay by Ivan Dzyuba attacked the arrests of cultural figures, and called 'internationalism', as now applied, little different from Tsarist russification.

Significant events followed. The First Secretary of the Ukrainian Party, Petro Shelest, came to give open support to Dzyuba, and himself wrote in what was regarded by both nationalists and orthodox communists as a nationalist vein. He even departed from the traditional line so far as to describe Catherine the Great's annexation of the Ukraine in hostile terms.

The significant point is that a local leader clearly thought that there was political capital to be made in pursuing this line, that support would be forthcoming even within the Party. And when he was dismissed in 1973 a massive operation had to be undertaken against his sympathizers. At the Higher Party School of the Ukrainian Communist Party alone thirty-four instructors were fired, including the Head of the School. A quarter of the ideological secretaries at all party levels were removed. Books by nearly a hundred authors were banned. The scholarly institutes were purged, with dozens of dismissals. In the University of Lviv twenty lecturers and professors were dismissed, together with dozens of students. There were also expulsions from the University of Kiev. Dozens of well-known intellectuals were sent to labour camp or psychiatric prison over the next two years, and the total of arrests is believed to have been in the thousands.

What was revealed was that even in official party and academic circles, there had been ready cooperation in the attempt to Ukrainianize in the spirit of the 1920s – on which Dzyuba had specifically relied. (Dzyuba himself was later to recant, after much pressure).

In the decade which has followed, the official policy has been one of attacking 'the fiercest enemy of the Ukrainian people, Ukrainian nationalism' as the present Ukrainian First Secretary, Shcherbitsky, has put it. But every report makes it clear that the desire for a free expression of national feeling remains unquenched. In 1976 a Ukrainian 'Helsinki Monitoring Group' was formed in Kiev – to be effectively crushed by 1978, with ten to fifteen year sentences. Many other groups and individuals have suffered since; and we should note that in the workers' unrest in the Ukraine in the 1970s there was often a national component – as in the three days' riot in Dnipropetrovsk in May 1972; and it was in the Ukraine that the first 'free trade union' had its brief existence.

All in all, there is no doubt that, as a Ukrainian writer has put it, the issues raised by the national dissidents 'still dominate the agenda' in the Ukraine.

It is not for us to make predictions about the course of events. But in any future crisis in the USSR, it is clear that Ukrainian nationhood will be a factor and a vital one. It has not been destroyed by Stalin's methods, nor have any of the later tactical shifts of his successors disarmed it.

★

When we turn to the effects of the events of 1930–33 on Soviet agriculture, its mere inefficiency even today is common knowledge. Far from the collective farm system releasing new productive energies and possibilities, and outstripping the world, the USSR still employs twenty-five agricultural workers to produce what four do in the United States. Nor is this due, at least in recent years, to financial neglect. Huge sums have been poured into agriculture, but with little result. For the faults are in the system itself.

In January 1933 Stalin reported that the Five Year Plan had been carried out in four years and three months in its maximum form. This was wholly untrue: the main targets even for industry were nothing like reached. Only just over a third of the pig iron, just half of the steel, three-fifths of the electricity production; in consumer goods, just over half the cotton cloth, under a third of the woollen cloth, just over a quarter of the linen cloth. On the agricultural side it was even worse: a mere one-eighth of mineral fertilizers, less than a third of the tractors.[17]

By the beginning of 1935 it was possible to abolish bread rationing, and a rough supply-demand equilibrium was reached at prices a good deal higher than the old ration prices, but lower than previous prices on the legal and illegal market. The net effect was that the price to consumers had risen by about 10 times since 1928, while that paid to the agricultural producer had hardly risen. The difference was taken in 'turnover' tax.[18]

By the end of the 1930s the average Soviet citizen was worse off than before the revolution. He ate about the same amount of bread, but less meat, fat and dairy products, was ill-clad and had worse housing conditions.[19] In his *The Development of Capitalism in Russia* Lenin had calculated that an average agricultural worker in the reasonably typical Saratov region in the 1890s consumed 419.3 kilogrammes of cereal products a year. In 1935 the official economist Strumilin found the average Soviet citizen eating 261.6 kilogrammes of grain . . .[20]

As for the peasantry, rural life had sunk to an unprecedented level of misery. The actual value of the labour-day in terms of the cash and agricultural produce distributed to the kolkhozniks for their labour-days remained extremely low and quite insufficient to cover their minimum needs. In 1938, they received from this source only about three-quarters of their grain requirements, less than half their potatoes and negligible amounts of other foodstuffs. The daily 'pay' of a kolkhoz peasant in fact amounted to about six pounds of grain, a few pounds of potatoes and vegetables and a little straw, and the money equivalent of about a kilogramme of coarse bread or half a kilogramme of white bread.[21]

A decree of April 19 1938, admitted: 'In some provinces and Republics . . . there are kolkhozes in which the cash income in 1937 was not distributed at all for labour-days'. This was blamed on 'enemies of the people . . . [who] for provocative purposes – to undermine the kolkhozes – deliberately inspired the artificial inflation of their capital and production costs and the reduction of monetary income distributed for labour-days'. The decree ordered that not less than 60–70% of a kolkhoz's monetary income should be distributed for labour-days and that capital expenditure should not exceed 10% of this income. This was, however, rescinded in December of the same year.

A medium sized kolkhoz – the Stalin kolkhoz at Stepnaya in the Ordzhonikidze Territory – produced only corn. Its output was 74,240 hectolitres. After the State's share and seed reserves, investments, maintenance, and so on, were covered 12,480 hl were left for division among the workers – c. 20% of the total. The labour force was 1,420. First the administrative staff got their share. After that a 'Stakhanovite' with 280 labour-days to his credit got eight hl; a normal worker got four hl; and a widow got two hl. The worker had four children and a wife who also worked on the farm. The widow had three small children. In neither case was the corn adequate. She gleaned illegally. He simply stole from the kolkhoz itself.[22]

In the first decade of collectivization the draught power, horse and mechanical, was always lower than in 1929;[23] (Moreover, between one-fifth and one-third of the tractors were out of action at any given time, further worsening the formal situation).[24]

The officially permitted holdings of private livestock, though limited, were higher than many kolkhozniks ever achieved. By 1938, even though 55.7% of the country's cows were privately owned by kolkhozniks, this meant that there were only 12.1 million cows in a total of 18.5 million households.[25] More important was the total prohibition, except in some nomadic areas, of the private ownership of horses. The peasants, who had formerly relied on horses for a variety of tasks, could now only use one with the authority of the kolkhoz board, and on payment.

For most kolkhozniks the plot, tiny as it was, represented the last remnant of their traditional way of life. Despite difficulties such as lack of equipment, fodder and fertilizer, the kolkhoznik managed to secure a surprisingly large return from this land. In 1938 the private plots were responsible for no less than 21.5% of total Soviet agricultural produce, although they covered only 3.8% of the cultivated land.[26]

At the Communist Party of the Soviet Union's Eighteenth Congress in 1939 Andreev, Politburo member in charge of agriculture, admitted that 'in some places, the private plot economy of the kolkhoz household has begun to outgrow the communal economy of the kolkhoz, and is becoming the basic economy, while the kolkhoz economy, on the other hand, is becoming the subsidiary one'. He claimed that private plots were no longer necessary because the kolkhozes were strong enough to supply all the needs of the kolkhozniks, and insisted that 'the private economy of kolkhoz households must increasingly take on a strictly subordinate character while the communal-kolkhoz economy grows as the basic one'.

Soon after the Congress a decree of May 27 1939, said that the plots were being illegally extended at the expense of kolkhoz land, and 'to the advantage of private property and self-seeking elements who make use of the kolkhoz for speculation and private profit'. It complained that the plots were treated as 'private property ... which the kolkhoznik, and not the kolkhoz, disposes of at his own discretion', and that they were even leased out to other peasants. It also said that 'there is a fairly considerable proportion of pseudo-kolkhozniks who either do not work at all in the kolkhozes, or work only for show, spending most of their time on their private plot'. The decree provided for various measures to prevent such abuses, with a permanent corps of inspectors set up to enforce them.

The private plots were not merely designed for production for the market or state purchase. Taxes were also levied on them in cash or kind, eggs, meat, milk, fruit and so on. In 1940 the government was getting in this direct way from the private plot 37.25% of the meat, 34.5% of the milk and butter and 93.5% of the eggs that it got from the whole kolkhoz and sovkhoz system.[27] In spite of all hopes to abolish the anomaly, this source of products remained essential, as it has done ever since.

The 1940s saw the extension of the collective farm system to newly annexed territories – not only the Western Ukraine, but the Baltic States and elsewhere. In Estonia for example 'mass collectivization proceeded in conditions of a sharp aggravation of the class struggle', so that 'kulaks' had to be deprived of their property and equipment.[28] There were massive deportations.

★

339

During the war, ex-kulaks were allowed to move within the districts of settlement and often further movement was permitted.[29] But the last legal restrictions on surviving kulaks, or rather on those not in labour camps, were removed only in 1947.[30]

The end of the war saw another tightening up of the collective farm system. Fourteen million acres of collective fields which had been diverted to private use by the peasants were recollectivized in 1946–7.[31]

Over the following years various schemes were put forward to improve grain production, and at the Nineteenth Party Congress, in 1952, it was announced that the grain problem had been finally solved with a harvest of 130 million tons of grain. After Stalin's death it was revealed that this total had been reached by using the 'biological yield' method and that the actual crop was only 92 million tons.

In fact at the Central Committee plenum in September 1953 and February 1954, Khrushchev showed that grain production was, still, less per capita, and cattle figures less absolutely than in Tsarist times. On 1 January 1916 there were 58,400,000 cattle on the present territory of the USSR; on 1 January 1953, 56,600,000. The population had gone up from 160 million to an estimated nearly 190 million. Moreover, in spite of all investment and effort, the yield in 1965 of 950 kilogrammes per hectare was small improvement on the 1913 figure of 820 kilogrammes.[32]

★

Moreover, during the Stalin period and for a number of years afterwards, unscientific doctrines prevailed in Soviet agricultural science, in particular those of Vilyams and Lysenko, which resulted in disastrous crop decisions. And, as in the 1930s, quick-fix promises and schemes proliferated. In Khrushchev's time, A.N. Larionov, First Secretary of Ryazan Province promised to double his province's meat production in a year. He and his associates succeeded in this by slaughtering all the milch cows and breeding stock, buying (with illegally diverted funds) cattle from other provinces, and so on. Larionov, by now a Hero of Socialist Labour and holder of the Order of Lenin, had to commit suicide in 1960 when the truth came out. He had had many imitators in other provinces.

Comparable interventions continued in the post-Khrushchev era. One of dozens of examples was a great efficiency drive in the Kokchetav Province which took the form of enforced specialization, by which sheep, cattle and so forth were concentrated in the areas thought best for them. As a result, villages where sheep farming had been practised for centuries were left with no sheep, and dairy farms were suddenly filled with hordes

340

of them. Pigs were banned on all except a few specialized farms, the rest being slaughtered immediately. As a result, meat, milk and food production in the province fell drastically. The peasantry, for the first time, had to import food. The local meat factories refused to buy pigs except from the special farms, which had not got round to producing any, so the pigs left in private hands had to be marketed in provinces hundreds of miles away . . .

★

In the post-Stalin period improvements have been made but they have been of a marginal nature, and all in all the system retains all its main negative characteristics.

All the symptoms we noted in the 1930s remain – apathy due to lack of incentive, 'leadership' by incompetents, huge bureaucratic overheads, intensive intrusion by ignorant and distant central planners.

A class struggle of sorts did indeed emerge in the villages – between the collectivized peasantry and the 'New Class' of bureaucrats and administrators. One official organ complained:

> We have collective farmers who are careless about common property. Once I reproached one of them for squandering the collective farm harvest, and I reminded him that he was a part-owner of the common property. He grinned sarcastically and sneered: 'Nice lot of owners! It is all empty talk. They just call us owners to keep us quiet, but they fix everything themselves . . .'
>
> A real collective farmer won't say, when he sees the chairman drive past in his car, 'Here am I, part-owner of the collective farm, tramping along on foot, while he takes his ease in a Pobeda'. Any collective farmer who really cares for his collective farm will agitate to see that the chairman should have his own car! The collective farmer, like the Soviet workers, is interested in strengthening the management of his economy.[33]

A Soviet fictional character remarks,

> –'How are our collective farms organized? The same way they were in the nineteen-thirties. Brigadiers, controllers, guards, and God knows what were introduced then. What for? For Control . . . And yet nobody is responsible for anything'.
> –'Why is that?'
> –'Because land, and implements, and power – all is impersonal. As if you could not work in the same collective farm with horses and a plot of land assigned in your possession'.[34]

Or, as another author remarks, 'Always the same old story. It really was a vicious circle! In order to produce a decent return for a day's labour people would have to work – what other source of funds did the farm have? But in order to make people work there had to be a decent return for the day's labour'.[35]

One Soviet story of the Khrushchev era makes the point that a collective farm disaster – the death of a herd of cows through gorging on damp clover – could not have happened even under the landlords of Tsarist times. It took place at the week-end and the kolkhoz chairman was off duty: 'can anyone imagine a landlord keeping a bailiff who resided permanently in town and went off home like an office worker even when summer work was in full swing?'[36]

The extent of 'planning' and 'management' may be seen from a recent newspaper investigation of one collective farm, overwhelmed by 'a constant flow of paper': 773 directives had reached it within a year. When the reporter went to the office issuing the directives he was told that during the year it had received some 6,000 directives for this particular farm from the central authorities.[37]

The USSR in 1982 had only 65% of the harvesters it required; and at the beginning of July 100,000 of those it had were out of action.[38] And a confidential report by a Soviet commission on agriculture revealed that the Soviet tractor industry was producing about 550,000 tractors a year, but writing off about as many. In 1976 there were 2,400,000 tractors in use, in 1980 2,600,000 – but meanwhile nearly three million tractors had been produced.[39] And one reads in the Soviet press of 1982 of a State farm using forty horses, but with its stable in ruins and no hay or grain fodder for the winter.[40]

In all, in 1982 'a third of the fodder crop' was lost. Of this 40–45% was due to failure to harvest on time; 20% to failures of stacking, and the rest through shortages of storage facilities – the farms having only 25–30% of the storage they need.[41]

The system of calculation at present in use is, if not so scandalous as the 'biological yield', still a remarkably unsatisfactory one. Under it the crop is measured out on the ground, or in the bins of the combine harvesters, before transport, drying and the removal of dirt. It seems that a loss of up to 20% by weight is implied. But this is only one of the dubious methods by which an admittedly unsatisfactory situation is made to appear nearly tolerable.

Another fictional character remarks of a different aspect of the collective farmer's life, 'Marx said if you do not give all vital necessities to the producer he will obtain them in a different way. If you open the accounts of some of our collective farms and look, you'll see: from year to year collective farmers used to receive 200 grammes of bread plus a kopek in currency. Everybody understands that a man can't live on such earnings. Yet he survives. That means that he gets his means for existence in other ways. And these other ways cost the state, the collective farms, and the collective farmer himself dearly'.[42]

The mania for even larger kolkhozes persists. It involves the transfer of the inhabitants of small villages to large settlements. But as an article in the official *Sovetskaya Rossiya* points out, first of all this has poor economic side-effects, as the farm workers cannot reach the now distant fields: 'the rural worker needs to have daily access to his workplace, just as the old time peasant did. Yet . . . roads are poor, as we know, and in bad weather they often become completely unpassable. Cows go unfed in the livestock section because people cannot get to them'. Moreover, people did not like the new settlements: 'the population begins to move away and what had initially been bigger settlements just become smaller again, and finally they disappear entirely'.[43]

For there is a dimension to all this which goes far beyond the economic. Academician Sakharov has spoken of an 'almost irreversible' destruction of rural life as a whole. A modern Soviet author writes, 'the old village, with its millennium of history, decays into oblivion . . . its age-old foundations are collapsing, the age-old soil which nurtured all our national culture is disappearing. The village is the physical breast on which our national culture was weaned'.[44] Another sums up 'And now, when I hear people wondering: how come, why did the barbaric indifference to land come about? – I can say precisely: in my own village Ovsianka it began in the stormy days of the 1930s'.[45]

★

We have quoted Bukharin's view that the worst result of the events of 1930–33 was not so much the sufferings of the peasantry, frightful though these were: it was the 'deep changes in the psychological outlook of those Communists who participated in this campaign and, instead of going mad, became professional bureaucrats for whom terror was henceforth a normal method of administration and obedience to any order from above a high virtue', diagnosing 'a real dehumanization of the people working in the Soviet apparatus'.[46]

A Party official directly involved comments, 'In war, there is a palpable difference between those who have been in the front lines and the people at home. It is a difference that cannot be bridged by fuller information and a lively sympathy. It is a difference that resides in the nerves, not in the mind. Those of the Communists who had been directly immersed in the horrors of collectivization were thereafter marked men. We carried the scars. We had seen ghosts. We could almost be identified by our taciturnity, by the way we shrank from discussion of the 'peasant front'. We might consider the subject among ourselves, as Seryozha and I did after our return, but to talk of it to the uninitiated seemed futile. With them we had no common vocabulary of experience. I do not refer, of course, to the Arshinovs. Under any political system, they are the gendarmes and executioners. I refer to Communists whose feelings had not been wholly blunted by cynicism'.[47]

In her *Into the Whirlwind* Evgenia Ginzburg describes the evolution of the NKVD interrogators 'Pace by pace, as they followed one routine directive after another, they climbed down the steps from the human condition to that of beasts'. To a degree, this is clearly applicable to all those engaged in enforcing the terror regime. And it was precisely the 'Arshinovs' who survived and flourished. Nor can it be concealed that some of the leading figures of the present generation of Soviet leaders were of this age group and, at first-hand or otherwise, certainly experienced the brutalization of which we speak. Others were in the Komsomol in the mid-30s, many joining the party when it was reopened to recruitment after the Yezhov terror, in 1939–40.

Nor is it merely a matter of first-hand experience: the younger men were inducted into, and trained in, a Party which had been turned into an instrument for such action as the collectivization and the famine, and the cycle of terrors which followed.

★

The main lesson seems to be that the Communist ideology provided the motivation for an unprecedented massacre of men, women and children. And that this ideology, perhaps all set-piece theory, turned out to be a primitive and schematic approach to matters far too complex for it. The sacrifices were made, (of other people), and they were in vain.

The question whether the present leaders of the USSR would be willing to kill tens of millions of foreigners, or suffer a loss of millions of their own subjects, in a war is sometimes canvassed nowadays. The fact that the older leaders were direct accomplices in the actual killing of millions of Ukrainians and others, in order to establish the political and social order prescribed by their doctrine, and that the young leaders still justify the procedure, may perhaps be regarded as not without some relevance. Thus, as we have suggested earlier, the events described in this book cannot be shrugged off as part of the dead past, too remote to be of any current significance. On the contrary, until they can be freely and frankly investigated the present rulers of the USSR remain – and ostentatiously so – the heirs and accomplices of the dreadful history recounted in this book.

★

It is only in a limited range of fiction, (and by writers denied this type of expression since 1983), that human sentiments occur and true facts are registered on our theme in the USSR. If we apply to the Soviet regime the criterion of truth, in this major element of its past and present, we are on interesting ground.

During the Khrushchev interlude, though also to some extent for a few years afterwards, Soviet historians and experts were able to deploy facts and argue doctrinal points in a way which – though never explicitly opposing the policies of the 30s – did a great deal to make the facts available.

This produced sharp controversies and after Khrushchev's fall S.P. Trapeznikov, the 'neo-Stalinist' head of the Science and Culture Department of the Central Committee, attacked leading scholars like Danilov, for 'incorrect assessments of collectivization', 'emphasis on certain episodes';[48] for 'questioning the necessity of liquidating the kulaks as a class', and other errors.[49] Indeed, the Party's theoretical journal *Kommunist* (No. 11, 1967) specially denounced Danilov's article on collectivization in the *Soviet Historical Encyclopaedia*, a most useful source.

One neo-Stalinist scholar even felt that the official crop figure for 1938 (77.9 million tons) was too low, arguing, 'is it possible to think seriously that our large socialist agriculture, equipped with the most modern technology, gave less grain than the agriculture of Tsarist Russia, characterized by the prevalence of the wooden plough and the three-field system? If this gigantic effort of the party for the socialist reconstruction of the village was a meaningless undertaking, then the new technology represented money thrown to the winds. This would mean that the heroic labour of collective farmers, of mechanizers and specialists was all for nothing. Obviously there is not a grain of logic in this'.[50]

In the post-Khrushchev epoch moreover, not only are the Stalin policies defended, but Bukharin and his followers are publicly named as having 'openly' taken 'the side of the kulaks and all the reactionary forces in the country'.[51] And while controversy was at times possible, if muted, about the excesses of collectivization proper, at no time did the existence, let alone the cause, of the 1932–3 famine enter the textbooks, though at the height of Khrushchev's power he was able to refer briefly to 'a war of starvation'.[52] And at the same time, one novel, by Ivan Stadnyuk, dealing with the famine was permitted – and probably indicates an intention on Khrushchev's part to bring the issue into the open.

Since then there has been little of a veridical nature from the scholars. And until the late 70s there was not much in published fiction. Even in the period just before 1983, when such work ceased almost entirely, there were only a handful of writers and editors touching on 1930–33 briefly and occasionally – though several times with remarkable frankness, at least by implication.

Officially, the most that is said is that there were 'difficulties' and 'problems'. The current edition of the *Large Soviet Encyclopedia* in its article on Famine tells us that it is 'a social phenomenon accompanying antagonistic socioeconomic formations', with 'tens of millions' suffering from malnutrition in the USA and elsewhere since 'hunger can only be overcome as a result of the socialist reconstruction of society'; as to the USSR, 'Thanks to the effective measures taken by the Soviet state, the catastrophic drought of 1921 did not result in the usual grave consequences', with nothing said of 1933. A typical admission of 'grave difficulties in regard to food supplies' in that year, published (in English) in 1970, attributes these to inexperience, kulak sabotage and 'other reasons'; and adds that they were 'overcome' with the aid of the government.[53] More recently drought (see p. 222) has begun to be mentioned as the 'major' cause of shortages, as in a News Release Communiqué from the Soviet Embassy in Ottawa dated 28 April 1983, 'On the so-called "Famine" in the Ukraine', though 'wealthy farmers called "kulaks" ' played an important role by sabotage and 'terror and murder'; (however, any 'alleged decrease in the Ukrainian population' was a myth, and the period, far from being a 'tragedy', was one of 'vigorous work and unparalled enthusiasm).

The position is, therefore, that there have been breaches in the monolithic suppression of the truth about the period, but that there is little sign of the regime coming to grips with its past, and permitting or sponsoring the full reality.

For those who hope for an evolution of the Soviet system into something less committed to the attitudes which have emerged in this book, the first step to be looked for might be a frank examination of the past, or at least a recognition of what actually happened in 1930–33. This applies, of course, to other as yet unadmitted massacres and falsifications. Yet admission of the truth, and restitution to the victims, in the agrarian sphere is not merely a moral or intellectual test. For, until the facts are faced, the USSR continues to work ruin in its rural economy.

Indeed, on one view, it would be possible to check whether the Soviet leadership were in a general way evolving out of the constrictions of their doctrines by the test of their agricultural policies. If they were to abandon, after so many years of failure, an erroneous dogma, then we might hope that the burden of their other ideological convictions, and in particular that of irremediable hostility to other ideas, and in the international field to states founded on different principles, might also have begun to lift.

Meanwhile, in the USSR itself, we seem to find – after fifty years – a demonstration of the point made by Burke two centuries ago: 'it is the degenerate fondness for tricking short cuts, and little fallacious facilities, that has in so many parts of the world created governments with arbitrary powers . . . with them defects in wisdom are to be supplied by the plenitude of force. They get nothing by it . . . the difficulties, which they rather had eluded than escaped, meet them again in their course; they multiply and thicken on them'.

For it is clear that the terrors inflicted on the peasantry have failed to produce the agricultural results promised by theory. At the same time, the crushing of Ukrainian nationhood was only temporary. Nor is that a local matter merely – if the word local can be used of a nation of nearly fifty million members. Even the true spokesmen of Russia itself, Andrei Sakharov and Alexander Solzhenitsyn, insist that the Ukraine must be free to choose its own future. And beyond that, Ukrainian liberty is, or should be, a key moral and political issue for the world as a whole.

It is not the concern of this book to speculate about that future. To record, as fully as may be possible, the events of a period – such is the sufficient duty of the historian. But still, so long as these events cannot be seriously investigated or discussed in the country where they took place, it is clear that they are in no sense part of the past but, on the contrary, a living issue very much to be taken into account when we consider the Soviet Union as it is today, and the world as it is today.

★

Notes

Where readily found dated decrees, speeches at and reports of congresses, plenums etc. are addressed in the text, references are normally not provided.

Introduction

1. Janusz Radziejowski has written a most useful paper on Soviet sources of the period: *Journal of Ukrainian Studies* no. 9, 1980, pp. 3–17.
2. *Pravda* 8 October 1965; *Selskaya zhizn* 29 December 1965, 25 February 1966; *Kommunist* no. 11, 1967.
3. Mikhail Alekseev, 'Khleb – imya sushchestvitelnoe,' *Zvezda* no. 1, 1964, p. 37.
4. M. Alekseev, 'Seyatel i khranitel,' *Nash sovremennik* no. 9, 1972, p. 96.
5. Quoted by Roy Medvedev in Robert C. Tucker, ed., *Stalinism*, New York, 1977, p. 212.
6. Alekseev, 'Seyatel i khranitel,' p. 96.

Part I: The Protagonists: Party, Peasants and Nation

Chapter 1. *The Peasants and the Party*

1. P.A. Zayonchkovsky, *Krizis samoderzhaviya na rubezhe 1870–1880-ykh godov*, Moscow, 1964, p. 10.
2. Naum Jasny, *The Socialized Agriculture of the USSR. Plans and Performance*, Stanford, 1949, p. 137. [Unless otherwise stated, 'Jasny' henceforth refers to *The Socialized Agriculture*.]
3. I am indebted to Professor Michael Confino for these figures.

4. 'Marxism and Russian Rural Development: Problems and Evidence, Experience, and Culture,' *American Historical Review* vol. 86, 1981, p. 752.
5. Ibid., pp. 732–5.
6. Ibid.
7. R.W. Davies, *The Socialist Offensive. The Collectivization of Soviet Agriculture 1929–30*, Cambridge, Mass., 1980, p. 10. [Unless otherwise stated, 'Davies' henceforth refers to this work.]
8. V.I. Lenin, *Polnoe sobranie sochineniy*, 5th edition, Moscow, 1958–1965, v. 16, p. 219. [Unless otherwise stated, 'Lenin' henceforth refers to this edition of his collected works.]
9. Dorothy Atkinson, *The End of the Russian Land Commune: 1905–1930*, Stanford, 1984, p. 79.
10. Atkinson, *The End of the Russian Land Commune*, p. 95.
11. E.K. Mann, 'Marxism and Russian Rural Development,' p. 751.
12. Maxim Gorky, *Lenin et le Paysan Russe*, Paris, 1925, pp. 140–41, quoted in Moshe Lewin, *Russian Peasants and Soviet Power: A Study of Collectivization*, London, 1968, p. 22. [Unless otherwise stated, 'Lewin' refers to this work.]
13. Maxim Gorky, *O russkom krestyanstve*, Berlin, 1922, pp. 43–4.
14. G.V. Plekhanov, *Sochineniya*, Moscow, 1920–27, v. 10, p. 128.
15. Lenin, 'Karl Marx,' in v. 26, p. 74.
16. See Harry Willets, 'Lenin and the Peasant,' in Leonard Schapiro and Peter Reddaway, eds., *Lenin: the Man, the Theorist, the Leader*, New York, 1967, pp. 211–33.
17. *Khrushchev Remembers: The Last Testament*, New York, 1976, p. 124.
18. *The Eighteenth Brumaire of Louis Bonaparte*, ch. 7.
19. David Mitrany, *Marx Against the Peasant*, Chapel Hill, 1951, p. 6.
20. KPSS, *VIII syezd*, Moscow, 1959, p. 348; Lenin, v. 41, p. 6.
21. Lenin, v. 16, p. 406.
22. Ibid., v. 17, pp. 29–32.
23. e.g. Lenin, v. 17, p. 66 and v. 23, p. 437.
24. Lenin, v. 11, pp. 44, 77.
25. Schapiro and Reddaway, *Lenin*, p. 215.
26. Lenin, v. 3, pp. 177–8.
27. Quoted by Alec Nove in Schapiro and Reddaway, p. 204.
28. R. Abramovich, *The Soviet Revolution*, New York, 1962, p. 312; idem, *In Tsvei Revoluties*, New York, 1944, v. 2, p. 148.
29. *Severnaya Kommuna*, 19 September, 1918.

Chapter 2. *The Ukrainian Nationality and Leninism*

1. *Kolokol* no. 34, p. 274.
2. Petro Grigorenko, *Memoirs*, London, 1983, p. 345.
3. Mykola Kovalevsky, *Pry dzerelakh borotby*, Innsbruck, 1960, p. 101.
4. Lenin, v. 27, p. 256.
5. Ibid., v. 25, p. 258.
6. Ibid., v. 25, p. 269.
7. Ibid., v. 30, p. 56.
8. Ibid., v. 30, pp. 38–9, 43.
9. See Karl Marx, *The Revolution of 1848*, London, 1973, p. 231.
10. Marx, 'Democratic Panslavism,' *Neue Rheinische Zeitung*, February, 1849.
11. Friedrich Engels, letter to Karl Kautsky, 7 February 1882, Marx and Engels, *Collected Works*, New York, 1973, v. 10, p. 393.
12. I.V. Stalin, *Works*, Moscow, 1953–5, v. 2, p. 321. [Unless otherwise stated, 'Stalin' henceforth refers to this edition.]
13. Ibid., v. 5, p. 270.
14. Lenin, v. 35, p. 251.
15. Ibid., v. 24, p. 143; v. 48, p. 329.
16. *V.I. Lenin pro Ukrainu*, Kiev, 1969, v. 2, p. 77.
17. *Peremoha Velykoy Zhovtenevoy Sotsialistychnoy Revolyutsii na Ukraini*, Kiev, 1967, v. 1, pp. 359–60.
18. See James Mace, *Communism and the Dilemmas of National Liberation. National Communism in Soviet Ukraine, 1918–1933*, Cambridge, Mass., 1983, p. 24.
19. V. Zatonsky, *Natsionalna problema na Ukraini*, Kharkov, 1926, pp. 33–40.
20. Kommunisticheskaya Partiya (bolshevikov) Ukrainy, *II syezd*, Kharkov, 1927, pp. 174–5.
21. KP(b)U, *II syezd*, pp. 123–4.
22. KPSS, *VIII syezd*, p. 91.
23. Lenin, v. 45, p. 105–106.
24. Ibid., v. 37, pp. 111, 120–21.
25. *Izvestiya*, 3 January 1919.
26. J. Borys, *The Sovietization of the Ukraine*, Edmonton, 1980, pp. 215, 418.
27. Lenin, v. 38, p. 69.
28. P. Fedenko in *Captive Nations in the USSR*, Munich, 1963, p. 107.
29. Kh. Rakovsky, *Borba za osvobozhdenie derevni*, Kharkov, 1920, p. 37.
30. KPSS, *X syezd*, Moscow, 1963, pp. 202–203.
31. KPSS, *XII syezd*, Moscow, 1968, p. 504.
32. *Litopys revolyutsii* no. 6, 1926.

33. M. Ravich-Cherkassky, *Istoriya Kommunisticheskoy partii* (*bolshevikov*) *Ukrainy*, Kharkov 1923 p. 241.
34. *Ukrainskyy istorychnyy zhurnal* no. 4, 1968, pp. 117–19.
35. J. Borys, *The Russian Communist Party and the Sovietization of Ukraine*, Ph.D. diss., University of Stockholm, 1960, p. 275.
36. KPSS, *XII syezd*, p. 504.
37. Ibid., pp. 529–30.
38. N.N. Popov, *Ocherki istorii Kommunisticheskoy Partii bolshevikov Ukrainy*, Kharkov, 1929, pp. 277–80.
39. KPSS, *X syezd*, p. 205.
40. See O.O. Kucher, 'Proty Bolshovystsko povstanniya na Ukraini v 1921,' *Litopys chervonoy kalyni* nos. 6 and 9, 1932.

Chapter 3. *Revolution, Peasant War and Famine 1917–21*

1. Jasny, pp. 144–5.
2. Mitrany, p. 59.
3. John Maynard, *The Russian Peasant and Other Studies*, London, 1943, p. 120.
4. Atkinson, pp. 182–3.
5. Lenin, v. 37, pp. 179–81.
6. Maynard, *The Russian Peasant*, p. 66.
7. Atkinson, p. 176.
8. See speeches by V.V. Ossinsky and others at the Eighth, Ninth and Tenth Party Congresses, etc.
9. Lenin, v. 36, pp. 255, 265.
10. Sergey Trapeznikov, *Leninizm i agrarno-krestyanskiy vopros*, Moscow, 1976, v. 2, p. 188.
11. Yu.A. Polyakov in *Istoriya Sovetskogo krestyanstva i kolkhoznogo stroitelstva v SSSR*, Moscow, 1963, quoted by Willets in Schapiro and Reddaway, p. 224.
12. Davies, p. 51.
13. *Znamya truda*, 16 May, 1918.
14. Lenin, v. 36, pp. 408, 428, 488.
15. Lenin, v. 43, pp. 219–20.
16. V.M. Andreev, *Pod znamenem proletariata*, Moscow, 1981, p. 36.
17. *Komitety bednoty. Sbornik materialov*, Moscow-Leningrad, 1933, pp. 46–7; Lenin, v. 37, pp. 175–82.
18. *Na agrarnom fronte* no. 3, 1930, p. 60.
19. Atkinson, p. 195.
20. Yu. Semenko, ed., *Holod 1933 roku v Ukraini*, Munich, 1963, p. 44.
21. Andreev, *Pod znamenem proletariata*, p. 37.

22. Ibid., p. 40.
23. Ibid., p. 88.
24. Lenin, v. 36, p. 430.
25. Ibid., v. 44, p. 157.
26. Ibid., v. 44, p. 156.
27. Ibid., v. 44, p. 157.
28. L. Kritsman, *Geroicheskiy period russkoy revolyutsii*, Moscow, 1926, pp. 114–22.
29. Quoted in E.H. Carr, *The Bolshevik Revolution*, v. 2, p. 169.
30. Lewin, *Political Undercurrents in Soviet Economic Debates*, p. 79; Lenin, v. 39, pp. 167, 274.
31. Report to the Eighth Party Congress, KPSS, *VIII syezd*, Moscow, 1959, p. 354.
32. N.I. Podvoyskiy, *Kontrrevolyutsiya za 4 goda*, Moscow, 1922, p. 4.
33. M. Heller and A. Nekrich, *L'Utopie au Pouvoir*, Paris, 1982, p. 85.*
34. P.G. Sofinov, *Ocherki istorii VChK*, Moscow, 1960, p. 82; George Leggett, *The Cheka*, Oxford, 1981, p. 103.
35. Leggett, *The Cheka*, p. 329.
36. F. Pigido-Pravoberezhny, *The Stalin Famine*, London, 1953, p. 20.
37. *The Trotsky Papers 1917–1922*, The Hague, 1964, v. 2, pp. 278–9.
38. Heller and Nekrich, *L'Utopie au Pouvoir*, p. 80.
39. N.Ya. Gushchin, *Klassovaya borba i likvidatsiya kulachestva kak klassa v Sibirskoy derevne 1926–1933*, Novosibirsk, 1972, p. 89.
40. Heller and Nekrich, p. 87.
41. For this and other details see Oliver Radkey, *The Unknown Civil War in Soviet Russia*, Stanford, Calif., 1976, passim.
42. Heller and Nekrich, p. 87.
43. *Grazhdanskaya voyna i voennaya interventsiya v SSSR. Entsykolopediya*, Moscow, 1983, p. 158.
44. Quoted in Heller and Nekrich, p. 89.
45. Boris Pasternak, *Doctor Zhivago*, London, 1958, p. 202.
46. Leggett, p. 329.
47. Leonard D. Gerson, *The Secret Police in Lenin's Russia*, Philadelphia, 1976, p. 303.
48. M. Verbytsky, *Naybilshyy zlochyn Kremlya*, London, 1952, p. 71.
49. Ibid., pp. 27–30.
50. Quoted by Heller and Nekrich, p. 87.
51. *Kommunisty Urala v gody grazhdanskoy voyny*, Sverdlovsk, 1959, p. 172.
52. L.I. Shkaratan, *Problemy sotsialnoy struktury rabochego klassa SSSR*, Moscow, 1970, pp. 351–4.
53. Andreev, pp. 173–4.

54. I.Ya. Trifonov, *Klassovaya borba v nachale NEPa*, Leningrad, 1964, p. 90.
55. G. Lelevich, *Strekopytovshchina*, Moscow, 1923, p. 36.
56. *Izvestiya VRK*, Kronstadt, 16 March, 1921.
57. Lenin, v. 43, p. 82.
58. Frank Lorimer, *The Population of the Soviet Union*, Geneva, 1946, p. 40.
59. E.Z. Volkov, *Dinamika naseleniya SSSR*, Moscow, 1930, p. 190.
60. B.Ts. Urlanis, *Voyny i Narodonaselenie Evropy*, Moscow, 1960, p. 188.
61. *Vsesoyuznaya perepis naseleniya 1926 g.*, Moscow, 1929, v. 17, p. 2.
62. M.Ya. Latsis, *Dva goda borby na vnutrennem fronte*, Moscow, 1920, p. 75.
63. As Michael Confino puts it.
64. As computed by Jasny from various Soviet sources, p. 200.
65. Mitrany, p. 277; League of Nations, *Report on Economic Conditions in Russia*, Geneva, 1922, pp. 1–3.
66. *The Russian Famines*, New York, 1923, p. 14.
67. League of Nations, *Report on Economic Conditions*, p. 55.
68. *The Russian Famines*, p. 32.
69. H.H. Fisher, *Famine in Soviet Russia 1919–1922*, New York, 1927, p. 252.
70. *Itogi borby s golodom v 1921–1922*, Moscow, 1922, pp. 4, 335.
71. Fisher, *Famine in Soviet Russia*, pp. 262–3.
72. League of Nations, *Report*, p. 57.

* *Utopia in Power*, English edition, published by Century Hutchinson Ltd, London, 1986.

Chapter 4. *Stalemate, 1921–7*

1. Lewin, *Political Undercurrents*, p. 85.
2. Lenin, v. 44, pp. 208, 487.
3. Ibid., v. 41, pp. 175–6.
4. Ibid., v. 45, pp. 369–77.
5. Lewin, *Political Undercurrents in Soviet Economic Debates*, Princeton, 1974, p. 94.
6. Schapiro and Reddaway, p. 209; and see Lenin, v. 45, pp. 8, 86–7.
7. Lenin, v. 44, p. 161.
8. Lewin, *Political Undercurrents*, p. 89.
9. Lenin, v. 43, p. 206; v. 44, p. 108.
10. Ibid., v. 43, p. 383.

11. Quoted in *Kommunist* no. 6, 1963, p. 26.
12. Lenin, v. 44, p. 9.
13. Ibid., v. 44, p. 428.
14. Adam Ulam, *Lenin and the Bolsheviks*, London, 1966, p. 477.
15. Hryhory Kostiuk, *Stalinist Rule in the Ukraine. A Study of the Decade of Mass Terror 1929–1939*, London, 1960, p. 80.
16. Grigorenko, p. 14.
17. Lewin, p. 95.
18. *Pravda*, 24 April 1925.
19. Stephen F. Cohen, *Bukharin and the Bolshevik Revolution*, Oxford, 1980, p. 176.
20. Lewin, pp. 141, 154.
21. L. Trotsky, *The Third International after Lenin*, New York, 1936, p. 270.
22. E.H. Carr, *The Bolshevik Revolution*, New York, 1950, v. 1, p. 355.
23. Lewin, p. 148.
24. *Byulleten oppozitsii* no. 9, 1930, p. 6.
25. Stalin, v. 8, p. 60.
26. Jerzy Karcz, *The Economics of Communist Agriculture*, Bloomington, Ind., 1979, p. 465. Unless otherwise stated, 'Karcz' henceforth refers to this work.
27. Quoted in Naum Jasny, *Soviet Economists of the Twenties*, Cambridge, 1972, p. 17.
28. Jasny, p. 202.
29. *Postroenie fundamenta sotsialisticheskoy ekonomiki v SSSR 1926–1932*, Moscow, 1960, pp. 258–9.
30. Grigorenko, p. 22.
31. *Ukrainian Review* no. 6, 1958, pp. 145–6.
32. *Sotsialistichesky vestnik*, April 1961.
33. *Na agrarnom fronte* no. 2, 1925, p. 110.
34. Lewin, p. 32.
35. Gushchin, *Klassovaya borba i likvidatsiya kulachestva*, p. 170.
36. *Izvestiya*, 17 December 1922.
37. *Ukrainian Review* no. 6, 1958, p. 156.
38. Ibid., pp. 149–50.
39. *The RSFSR Supreme Court in 1923*, Moscow, 1924, p. 25, report by P. Stuchka.
40. Lewin, p. 81.
41. See especially *Ukrainian Review* no. 6, 1958, pp. 126–69.
42. See Atkinson, p. 300.
43. Lewin, p. 88.
44. Ibid., p. 87.

45. N.I. Bukharin, *Put k sotsializmu i raboche-krestyanskiy blok*, Moscow-Leningrad, 1926, p. 13.
46. Lewin, p. 74.
47. KPSS, *XV syezd* (Moscow, 1962), p. 1334.
48. See Lewin, p. 73.
49. See E.H. Carr, *Socialism in One Country*, v. 1, pp. 306, 324–5.
50. A.I. Khryashcheva, *Gruppy i klassy v krestyanstve*, Moscow, 1924, p. 6.
51. KPSS, *XV syezed*, p. 1183.
52. Yu.V. Arutyunyan, *Sotsialnaya struktura selskogo naseleniya SSSR*, Moscow, 1971, p. 26.
53. Jasny, pp. 176–9.
54. Lewin, p. 176.
55. *KPSS v rezolyutsiyakh i resheniyakh syezdov, konferentsiy i plenumov TsK*, 7th edition, Moscow, 1954, v. 2, pp. 258–67, 414–30.
56. Quoted in Roy Medvedev, *Let History Judge*, New York, 1971, p. 99.
57. Lewin, pp. 72–73.
58. Ibid..
59. Ibid., p. 73.
60. Quoted ibid., p. 47.
61. P.I. Lyashchenko, *Istoriya narodnogo khozyaystva SSSR*, Moscow, 1956, v. 3, p. 240.
62. Lewin, p. 48.
63. Ibid., p. 52.
64. Molotov at the Fifteenth Party Congress, KPSS, *XV syezd*, pp. 1182, 1126.
65. *Bolshevik* no. 2, 1929, p. 90.
66. *Na agrarnom fronte* no. 1, 1928, p. 93.
67. Lewin, p. 57.
68. Fifth Congress of Soviets, *Bulleten* no. 16, p. 4.
69. Lewin, p. 71.
70. Ibid., p. 54.
71. Ibid., pp. 163–4.
72. Stalin, v. 8, p. 99.
73. *Pravda*, 14 December, 24 December 1927, 6 January 1928.
74. *Pravda*, 30 September 1928.
75. See H.J. Ellison in *Slavic Review* 1961, pp. 189–202.
76. Kostiuk, *Stalinist Rule in the Ukraine*, p. 31.
77. Stalin, v. 8, p. 160.
78. KPSS, *XII syezd*, p. 573.
79. *Visti Vseukrainskogo Tsentralnogo Komitetu Robitnichikh, Selyanskikh ta Chervonoarmeyskikh deputativ* (henceforth, *Visti*) no. 3, 1926, pp.

1–8.
80. M. Ravich-Cherkassky, p. 5–6.
81. In his conversation with Kamenev in July 1928.
82. Stalin, v. 8, p. 158.
83. Zatonsky, *Natsionalna problema na Ukraini*, p. 21.
84. *Visti*, 9 May 1930.

Part II: To Crush the Peasantry

Chapter 5. *Collision Course, 1928–9*

1. Lewin, pp. 36–7.
2. Ibid., p. 176.
3. KPSS, *XV syezd*, p. 1134.
4. Davies, p. 44.
5. Lewin, p. 183.
6. KPSS, *XV syezd*, p. 1364.
7. Karcz, p. 55.
8. Ibid., p. 463.
9. Ibid., p. 52.
10. Ibid., p. 37.
11. Ibid., p. 38–9.
12. Ibid., p. 41.
13. Quoted ibid., p. 40.
14. A.M. Bolshakov, *Derevnya 1917–1927*, Moscow, 1927, pp. 8–9.
15. Lewin, p. 173.
16. Stalin, v. 11, pp. 90–91.
17. Ibid., pp. 92, 101.
18. D.L. Golinkov, *Krushenie antisovetskogo podpolya v SSSR*, Moscow, 1978, v. 2, p. 306.
19. Trapeznikov, *Leninizm i agrarno-krestyanskiy vopros*, v. 2, pp. 55–6.
20. Golinkov, *Krushenie antisovetskogo podpolya*, v. 2, p. 306.
21. Stalin, v. 11, pp. 3–11.
22. *Selskoe khozyaystvo SSSR: Statisticheskiy sbornik*, Moscow, 1960, p. 79.
23. See Karcz, p. 48.
24. Trapeznikov, v. 2, pp. 32–4.
25. Golinkov, v. 2, pp. 306–307.
26. See Lewin, p. 285.
27. Y. Taniuchi, 'A Note on the Ural-Siberian Method,' *Soviet Studies* v. 33, no. 4, October 1981, p. 535.
28. *Kollektivizatsiya selskogo khozyaystva. Vazhneyshie postanovleniya*

1927–1935, Moscow, 1957, pp. 105–106.
29. Taniuchi, 'A Note on the Ural-Siberian Method,' pp. 529–31.
30. Lewin, p. 218.
31. *Bolshevik* no. 2, 1928, p. 65.
32. Stalin, v. 11, p. 14.
33. Ibid., p. 215.
34. *Pravda*, 15 July 1928.
35. *Pravda*, 2 December 1928.
36. Stalin, v. 11, pp. 167–9.
37. Ibid., p. 179.
38. Medvedev, *Let History Judge*, p. 80.
39. *Planovoe khozyaystvo* no. 3, 1929.
40. Lewin, p. 174.
41. Jasny, pp. 223–7.
42. *Pravda*, 30 September 1928.
43. Stalin, v. 11, pp. 15–16.
44. *Sotsialistichesky vestnik* no. 6, March 1929, p. 11.
45. *Pravda*, 18 September 1928.
46. *Pravda*, 5 December 1928.
47. Stalin, v. 11, p. 288.
48. Taniuchi, p. 525.
49. Ibid., p. 526.
50. Davies, p. 49.
51. *Izvestiya*, 12 and 13 January 1928.
52. *Derevenskiy kommunist* no. 4, 1928, p. 37.
53. *Byulleten oppozitsii* no. 3–4, 1929, pp. 16–26.
54. *Derevenskiy kommunist* no. 11, 1928, p. 26.
55. *Bolshevik* no. 13–14, 1928, p. 74.
56. *Pravda*, 12 February 1929.
57. *Pravda*, 10 January 1929.
58. *Bolshevik Kazakhstana* no. 12, 1928.
59. *Narodnoe prosveshchenie* no. 6, 1928, p. 79.
60. Smolensk archives, quoted in Sheila Fitzpatrick, *Education and Social Mobility in the Soviet Union 1921–34*, Cambridge, 1979, p. 161.
61. *Pravda*, 14 December 1928.
62. *Materialy po istorii SSSR*, Moscow, 1959, v. 7, p. 243.
63. Merle Fainsod, *Smolensk under Soviet Rule*, Cambridge, Mass., 1958, p. 240.
64. See Davies, p. 62.
65. *Bolshevik* no. 13–14, 1928, pp. 46–7.
66. *Bolshevik* no. 19, 1928, p. 20.

67. Stalin, v. 11, p. 45.
68. *KPSS v rezolyutsiyakh*, v. 2, p. 534.
69. Yu. Semenko, ed., *Holod 1933 roku v Ukraini*, Munich, 1963, p. 44.
70. Stalin, v. 11, p. 275.
71. Atkinson, p. 329.
72. *Pravda*, 18 September 1929.
73. Davies, p. 98.
74. Yu.A. Moshkov, *Zernovaya problema v gody sploshnoy kollektivizatsii selskogo khozyaystva SSSR 1929–1932*, Moscow, 1962, pp. 72–3.
75. *Pravda*, 19 July 1929.
76. Lewin, pp. 321–2.
77. Stalin, v. 12, p. 106.
78. *Pravda*, 24 January 1929.
79. Lewin, p. 453.
80. Jasny, p. 305.
81. Stalin, v. 12, p. 92.
82. See Lewin, p. 490.
83. Ibid., p. 475.
84. Verbytsky, p. 28.
85. Davies, p. 58.
86. *Nauchnye zapiski*, Dnepropetrovsk, 1962, v. 76, p. 58.
87. *Planovoe khozyaystvo* no. 8, 1929, p. 57.
88. Kalynyk, p. 77.
89. Atkinson, p. 334.
90. Lewin, quoted in Sheila Fitzpatrick, ed., *Cultural Revolution in Russia*, Bloomington, 1978, p. 59.
91. Ibid..
92. See Davies, pp. 140–42.
93. *Pravda*, 20 August 1929.
94. V.I. Varenov, *Pomoshch Krasnoy Armii v razvitii kolkhoznogo stroitelstva, 1929–1933. Po materialam Sibirskogo voennogo okruga*, Moscow, 1978, passim.
95. Lewin, p. 241.
96. Golinkov, v. 2, p. 308.
97. Atkinson, p. 336.
98. *Vestnik Moskovskogo Universiteta* no. 6, 1967, pp. 19–33.
99. Golinkov, v. 2, p. 307.
100. M. Fainsod, *Smolensk Under Soviet Rule*, pp. 142–3.
101. See e.g. Davies, pp. 82–5, 88–9.
102. Lewin, p. 120.
103. A. Angarov, *Klassovaya borba v sovetskoy derevne*, Moscow, 1929, p. 76.

104. *KPSS v rezolyutsiyakh*, v. 1, p. 546.
105. Ibid..
106. Lewin, p. 120.
107. *Bolshevik* no. 20, 1929, p. 15.
108. *KPSS v rezolyutsiyakh*, v. 2, p. 661.
109. Lewin, p. 84.
110. Fainsod, p. 240.
111. See Davies, p. 91.
112. N.I. Nemakov, *Kommunisticheskaya partiya – organizator massovogo kolkhoznogo dvizheniya 1929–1932*, Moscow, 1966, p. 191.
113. *Pravda*, 23 May 1929.
114. *Derevenskiy kommunist* no. 18, 1929, p. 4.
115. *Pravda*, 9 October 1929.
116. Semenko, *Holod 1933*, p. 46.
117. V. Belov, *Kanuny*, Moscow, 1976, pp. 116, 295.
118. Davies, p. 90.
119. F.M. Vaganov, *Pravyy uklon v VKP(b) i ego razgrom*, Moscow, 1970, pp. 238–41.
120. *Pravda*, 30 July 1929.
121. *Pravda*, August 1929.
122. Davies, p. 75.
123. Ibid., p. 76.
124. Ibid., p. 85.
125. Oleksa Kalynyk, *Communism the Enemy of Mankind*, London, 1955, p. 25.
126. Nemakov, *Kommunisticheskaya partiya – organizator kolkhoznogo dvizheniya*, p. 198.
127. Karcz, p. 57.
128. Lewin, p. 438.
129. *Pravda*, 27 June 1929.
130. Lewin, p. 107.
131. *Kollektivizatsiya selskogo khozyaystva*, pp. 101–102.
132. Ibid., p. 99.
133. Lewin, p. 421.
134. See Jasny, p. 28.
135. Atkinson, p. 371.
136. *Pravda*, 7 November 1929.
137. *Ekonomicheskaya zhizn*, September 1929, p. 29 and January 1930, p. 75.
138. Stalin, v. 12, p. 138.
139. *Pravda*, 19 February 1930.
140. R.W. Davies, *The Soviet Collective Farm, 1929–1930*, Cambridge,

Mass., 1980, p. 45.
141. Jasny, p. 3.
142. *Annals of the Ukrainian Academy of Arts and Sciences in the US* vol. 9, 1961, p. 93; and see Karcz, p. 48.
143. *Voprosy istorii* no. 5, 1963, p. 22.
144. See Lewin, p. 467.
145. Davies, p. 405.
146. Lewin, pp. 431–2, 435.
147. Ibid., pp. 431–2.
148. *Pravda*, 28 September 1929.
149. *Pravda*, 12 October 1929.
150. Stalin, v. 12, p. 160; *Pravda*, 6 January, 1930.
151. Davies, p. 131.
152. Quoted ibid., p. 148.
153. Lewin, p. 453.
154. Ibid. p. 346.
155. *Pravda*, 20 September 1929.
156. Davies, p. 71.
157. Lewin, *Political Undercurrents*, pp. 99–100.
158. *Pravda*, 7 November 1929.
159. *Voprosy istorii KPSS* no. 4, 1962, p. 71.
160. *Kommunist* no. 3, 1966, p. 95.
161. See Davies, pp. 163–5.
162. *Bolshevik* no. 22, 1929, p. 17.
163. *Bolshevik* no. 2, 1930, p. 17.
164. Davies, p. 70.
165. Nemakov, p. 83.
166. *KPSS v rezolyutsiyakh*, v. 2, p. 663.
167. See Davies, pp. 190–91.
168. *Istoriya kollektyvizatsii silskoho hospodarstva Ukrainskoy RSR 1917–1937. Zbirnyk dokumentiv i materialiv u tryokh tomakh*, Kiev, 1962–1971, v. 2, p. 245.
169. *Pravda*, 29 December 1929.
170. *Pravda*, 25 November 1929.
171. *Pravda*, 30 October 1929.
172. Davies, pp. 188–9.
173. *Pravda*, 29 December 1929.

Chapter 6. *The Fate of the 'Kulaks'*

1. *Pravda*, 27 December 1929.
2. N.A. Ivnitsky, *Klassovaya borba i likvidatsiya kulachestva kak klassa*

1929–1932, Moscow, 1972, p. 178.

3. *Pravda*, 17 September 1929.
4. Moshkov, *Zernovaya problema*, p. 72.
5. *Pravda*, 21 January 1930.
6. Quoted by Davies, p. 233.
7. e.g. I.Ya. Trifonov, *Likvidatsiya ekspluatatorskikh klassov v SSSR*, Moscow, 1975, p. 209.
8. Lewin in Fitzpatrick, pp. 58–9.
9. I.I. Slynko, *Sotsialistychna perebudova i teknichna perebudova silskoho hospodarstva Ukrainy 1927–1932*, Kiev, 1961.
10. Viktor Kravchenko, *I Chose Freedom*, New York, 1946, p. 103. [Unless otherwise stated, 'Kravchenko' henceforth refers to *I Chose Freedom*.]
11. Lewin, p. 503.
12. Lewin in Fitzpatrick, p. 49.
13. Nemakov, p. 147.
14. Ivan Stadnyuk in *Neva* no. 12, 1962.
15. V.P. Danilov, ed., *Ocherki istorii kollektivizatsii selskogo khozyaystva v soyuznykh respublikakh*, Moscow, 1963, p. 185.
16. Carr, *Socialism in One Country*, v. 1, p. 99.
17. S.O. Pidhainy, ed., *The Black Deeds of the Kremlin*, Detroit, 1955, v. 1, p. 502.
18. *Na agrarnom fronte* no. 7–8, 1930, p. 94.
19. See Davies, p. 251.
20. N.Ya. Gushchin, *Klassovaya borba i likvidatsiya kulachestva kak klassa v sibirskoy derevne 1926–1933*, Novosibirsk, 1972, p. 236.
21. Ibid..
22. Ibid..
23. *Pravda*, 21 October 1930.
24. See Davies, pp. 247–8.
25. Fainsod, p. 243.
26. Davies, p. 236.
27. Ivnitsky, *Klassovaya borba i likvidatsiya kulachestva*, p. 214.
28. Quoted in Davies, p. 234.
29. Ibid., p. 236.
30. *Voprosy istorii* no. 4, 1962, p. 68.
31. Yu.V. Arutyunyan, *Sostialnaya struktura selskogo naseleniya SSSR*, Moscow, 1971, p. 26.
32. Nemakov, p. 147.
33. *Voprosy agrarnoy istorii*, Vologda, 1968, pp. 49–50.
34. See Trapeznikov, v. 2, p. 243.
35. Pidhainy, ed., *The Black Deeds of the Kremlin*, v. 2, p. 306.

36. Olexa Woropay, *The Ninth Circle*, London, 1954, p. 46.
37. Stadnyuk in *Neva*, p. 200.
38. Sergey Zalygin, 'Na Irtyshe,' in *Izbrannye proizvedeniya*, Moscow, 1973.
39. Viktor Astafiev, 'Posledniy poklon,' *Roman-gazeta* no. 2–3, 1979; idem., *Tsar-ryba*, Moscow, 1980; Boris Mozhaev, 'Iz zhizni Fedora Kuzkina,' *Novy mir* no. 7, 1966; idem., *Lesnaya doroga*, Moscow, 1973; idem., *Starye istorii*, Moscow, 1978; idem., *Muzhiki i baby*, Moscow, 1979.
40. Fainsod, pp. 241–4, 259.
41. Ibid..
42. Vasily Grossman, *Forever Flowing*, New York, 1972, pp. 140–41.
43. Ivnitsky; Danilov, p. 105.
44. Moshkov, pp. 156–7.
45. Verbytsky, pp. 48–50.
46. Pidhainy, v. 1, p. 466.
47. Quoted in Lewin, pp. 512–13.
48. *Voprosy istorii KPSS* no. 5, 1975, p. 130.
49. Fainsod, p. 248.
50. *Pravda*, 25 January 1930.
51. *Pravda*, 2 February 1930; Pidnainy, v. 2, pp. 410–11.
52. Davies, *The Soviet Collective Farm*, p. 80.
53. Kravchenko, p. 104.
54. *Pravda*, 9 October 1929; *Visti*, 8 October, 10 October, 10 November 1929.
55. Gushchin, p. 218.
56. Fainsod, p. 244.
57. *Sobranie zakonov SSSR* 1932, no. 84, article 516.
58. *Pravda*, 11 February 1930.
59. Pidhainy, v. 2, p. 198.
60. Kalynyk, *Communism the Enemy of Mankind*, p. 85.
61. Ibid..
62. Fred Beal, *Word from Nowhere*, London, 1938.
63. Semenko, p. 48.
64. Verbytsky, p. 68.
65. *Istoriya Sovetskogo krestyanstva i kolkhoznogo stroitelstva v SSSR*, Moscow, 1963, p. 277.
66. Varenov, *Pomoshch Krasnoy Armii*, pp. 39, 42, 59.
67. *Pravda*, 26 January 1930.
68. Ivnitsky, p. 245.
69. Danilov, p. 239.
70. Ivnitsky, p. 299.

71. Medvedev, *Let History Judge*, p. 140.
72. Fainsod, p. 263.
73. Stalin, v. 13, p. 253.
74. *Ukraine: A Concise Encyclopedia*, Toronto, 1963, v. 1, p. 617.
75. See Jasny, p. 312.
76. Lewin, p. 507.
77. Ibid., p. 508.
78. S. Swianiewicz, *Forced Labor and Economic Development*, London, 1965, p. 124.
79. *Pravda*, 7 December 1929.
80. *Voprosy istorii KPSS* no. 5, 1975, p. 130.
81. Gushchin, p. 242.
82. Commission International contre les camps de concentration sovietiques, *Livre Blanc sur les Camps de Concentration Sovietiques*, Paris, 1951, p. 32.
83. I. Solonevich, quoted in B. Souvarine, *Stalin*, London, 1939, p. 545.
84. Varlam Shalamov, *Kolymskie rasskazy*, London, 1978.
85. Grossman, *Forever Flowing*, p. 141.
86. *Kollektivizatsiya selskogo khozyaystva v Zapadnom Rayone RSFSR*, Moscow, 1968, pp. 246–50.
87. Verbytsky, p. 33.
88. Fainsod, p. 248.
89. *Radyanska Ukraina* no. 10, 1930.
90. Grossman, pp. 142–3.
91. Ibid., p. 144.
92. Fainsod, p. 248.
93. e.g. Pidhainy, v. 1, p. 468.
94. Adam Tawdul in *New York American*, 22 August 1935.
95. Grossman, p. 144.
96. Zalygin, 'Na Irtyshe', p. 487.
97. *Narodnoe prosveshchenie* no. 6, 1930, p. 17.
98. Ibid., p. 16.
99. Grossman, p. 147.
100. *Pravda*, 1 February 1930.
101. Fainsod, p. 245.
102. Ibid..
103. Harvard University Refugee Interview Project, Work Section 1719.
104. Grossman, p. 141.
105. Danilov, *Ocherki istorii*, p. 185.
106. *Bolshevik* no. 5, 1930, p. 41.
107. Fainsod, p. 245.

108. Ibid., pp. 180–82.
109. Ibid., pp. 185–6.
110. Ibid. p. 185.
111. *Sovetskaya iustitsiya* no. 9, 1932, p. 7.
112. *Pravda*, 15 January 1930.
113. Fainsod, p. 246.
114. G. Tokaev, *Stalin Means War*, London, 1951, p. 6.
115. Astafiev in *Roman-gazeta* no. 2, 1979, p. 29.
116. *Bolshevik* no. 8, 1930, p. 20.
117. *Pravda*, 5 March 1930.
118. See Davies, p. 257.
119. Fainsod, p. 148.
120. Ibid., pp. 54–5.
121. Lewin, pp. 27–8.
122. Maurice Hindus, *The Great Offensive*, New York, 1933, p. 65.
123. Fainsod, p. 250.
124. Woropay, p. 52.
125. Ibid., p. 51.
126. Lev Kopelev, *The Education of a True Believer*, New York, 1978, p. 270.
127. Pidhainy, v. 1, p. 146.
128. Ibid..
129. Semenko, p. 27.
130. Ibid., pp. 23–4.
131. Kravchenko, pp. 88–90.
132. Pidhainy, v. 2, p. 624.
133. Semenko, p. 7.
134. Ibid..
135. Pidhainy, v. 1, p. 198.
136. Ibid., p. 191.
137. Ibid., p. 467.
138. *Experiences in Russia, 1931*, Pittsburgh, 1932, p. 176 (anonymous).
139. Grossman, p. 145.
140. Pidhainy, v. 1, p. 179.
141. Ibid., p. 144.
142. Ibid., p. 166.
143. Ibid., p. 144; Aleksandr Solzhenitsyn, *The Gulag Archipelago*, New York, 1978, v. 3, p. 360.
144. F. Pigido-Pravoberezhny, *The Stalin Famine*, London, 1953, p. 24.
145. Solzhenitsyn, *Gulag*, v. 3, p. 360.
146. Ibid., p. 361.
147. Pidhainy, v. 1, p. 182.

148. V. Tendryakov, 'Death,' *Moskva* no. 3, 1968.
149. Astafiev, *Tsar-Ryba*, p. 266.
150. Grossman, p. 147.
151. Pidhainy, v. 1, p. 174.
152. Semenko, p. 73.
153. Pidhainy, v. 1, p. 166.
154. Wolfgang Leonhard, *Child of the Revolution*, Chicago, 1958, p. 136.
155. *Voprosy istorii* no. 11, 1964, p. 59.
156. Pidhainy, v. 1, p. 145.
157. *Voprosy istorii* no. 11, 1964, p. 61.
158. Trapeznikov, v. 2, p. 455.
159. Leonhard, *Child of the Revolution*, p. 142.
160. Semenko, p. 10.
161. e.g. Solzhenitsyn, in *Gulag*, v. 3, p. 362.
162. Pidhainy, v. 1, p. 172.
163. *Voprosy istorii* no. 11, 1964, p. 58.
164. *Istoriya Sovetskogo krestyanstva i kolkhoznogo stroitelstva v SSSR*, p. 277.
165. Solzhenitsyn, *Gulag*, v. 3, p. 359.
166. Trapeznikov, v. 2, p. 432.
167. Ivnitsky, p. 304.
168. Grossman, p. 148.
169. *Voprosy istorii* no. 11, 1964, p. 61.
170. Ivnitsky, p. 310.
171. Trifonov, *Likvidatsiya*, pp. 369, 381–2.
172. Ivnitsky, p. 311.
173. John Scott, *Behind The Urals*, Bloomington, 1973, p. 85.
174. John Littlepage, *In Search of Soviet Gold*, New York, 1937, p. 80.
175. Pidhainy, v. 1, p. 167.
176. Mozhaev, *Starye istorii*, p. 152.
177. Solzhenitsyn, p. 366.
178. Ibid..
179. Gushchin, p. 222.
180. Pidhainy, v. 1, p. 177.
181. Ibid., p. 173.
182. Ibid., p. 250.
183. Ibid., p. 467.
184. Ibid., p. 166.
185. Ibid., p. 175.
186. Ibid., p. 179.
187. Solzhenitsyn, p. 303.
188. Lenard Hubbard, *The Economics of Soviet Agriculture*, London, 1939,

p. 177; Swianiewicz, *Forced Labor*, p. 123.

189. Pidhainy, v. 1, p. 173.
190. *The Second Day* by Ilya Ehrenburg, quoted in Anatol Goldberg, *Ilya Ehrenburg*, New York, 1984, p. 141.

Chapter 7. *Crash Collectivization and its Defeat, January–March 1930.*

1. *Marksizm i voprosy yazykoznaniya*, Moscow, 1950, p. 29.
2. *Istoriya SSSR* no. 5, 1982.
3. Isaac Deutscher, *The Prophet Outcast*, Oxford, 1963, p. 123.
4. Alexander Barmine, *One Who Survived*, New York, 1945, p. 123.
5. *History of the CPSU*, Moscow, 1960, p. 435.
6. e.g. *Pravda*, 13 and 17 September 1929.
7. *Voprosy istorii* no. 3, 1954, p. 23.
8. V.M. Selunskaya, *Rabochie – dvadtsatipyatitysyachniki*, Moscow, 1964, p. 201.
9. Fainsod, pp. 254–5.
10. *Materially po istorii SSSR* v. 1, pp. 426, 434, 458.
11. Selunskaya, *Rabochie – dvadsatipyatitysyachniki*, Moscow, 1964, p. 201.
12. Nemakov, p. 179.
13. *Voprosy istorii* no. 5, 1947.
14. *Kolkhozy v 1930 g.: itogi raportov kolkhozov XVI syezdu VKP(b)*, Moscow, 1931, p. 224.
15. Selunskaya, pp. 81, 187.
16. Davies, p. 204.
17. Fainsod, p. 284.
18. Kravchenko, pp. 91–2.
19. Grigorenko, p. 36.
20. Grossman, p. 143.
21. *Nash sovremennik* no. 11, 1978, p. 186.
22. Aleksandr Malyshkin, 'Lyudi iz zakholustya' in *Sochineniya*, Moscow, 1956, v. 2, p. 356.
23. Fainsod, p. 289.
24. Ibid., p. 288.
25. Ibid., p. 289.
26. Ibid..
27. Kravchenko, p. 127.
28. *Radyanska Ukraina* no. 10, 1930.
29. *Pravda*, 28 February 1930.
30. Ibid..
31. P.N. Sharova, *Kollektivizatsiya selskogo khozyaystva v Tsentralno-*

Chernozemnoy Oblasti, 1928–1932, Moscow, 1963, p. 148.
32. *Visti*, 2 July 1932.
33. Fainsod, p. 143.
34. Khataevich quoted in Davies, p. 226.
35. Taniuchi, p. 540.
36. Lewin, p. 393.
37. Fainsod, p. 149.
38. Ibid..
39. Taniuchi, p. 540.
40. Ibid., pp. 540–41.
41. *Vlast Sovetov* no. 20, 1930, p. 9, no. 22–3, p. 20.
42. *Planovoe khozyaystvo* no. 2, 1929, p. 111.
43. Lewin, p. 93.
44. Markoosha Fisher, *My Lives in Russia*, New York, 1944, pp. 49–50.
45. Quoted by Taniuchi, p. 542.
46. O. Volkov in *Nash sovremennik* no. 11, 1978, p. 186.
47. Pidhainy, v. 2, pp. 281-6.
48. Verbytsky, p. 47.
49. Trapeznikov, v. 2, p. 241.
50. *Vlast sovetov* no. 8–9, 1930, p. 34, no. 14–15, pp. 44–6, and no. 16, pp. 17–18.
51. Verbytsky, p. 56.
52. Hubbard, pp. 115–16.
53. See Davies, p. 256.
54. *Pravda*, 11 September 1929.
55. Trifonov, *Likvidatsiya*, pp. 297–8.
56. e.g. Pidhainy, v. 1, p. 247.
57. *Ukrainian Review* no. 6, 1958, p. 168.
58. Fainsod, p. 253.
59. Ibid., p. 55.
60. *Istoriya selyanstva Ukrainskoy RSR*, Kiev, 1967, v. 2, p. 151.
61. A. Yakovetsky, *Agrarnye otnosheniya v SSSR v period stroitelstva sotsializma*, Moscow, 1964, p. 326.
62. G.A. Tokaev, *Stalin Means War*, London 1951, p. 7.
63. Kravchenko, p. 106.
64. Kalynyk, pp. 40–42.
65. Ibid., pp. 42–3, plate xxi.
66. Ibid., pp. 47–54.
67. Kopelev, p. 226.
68. Fainsod, p. 241.
69. *Soviet Ukraine*, Kiev, 1969, p. 137.
70. Pidhainy, v. 1, p. 189.

71. Quoted by Davies, p. 259.
72. Sharova, *Kollektivizatsiya selskogo khozyaystva v TsChO*, p. 155.
73. Pidhainy, v. 1, p. 167.
74. Woropay, p. 12.
75. Ibid., p. 11.
76. Pidhainy, v. 1, p. 218.
77. Verbytsky, pp. 22–3.
78. Pidhainy, v. 1, pp. 219–20.
79. See Kostiuk, pp. 10–11, summing up a number of reports.
80. Woropay, p. 12.
81. Depending on the definition of 'rebel', and not necessarily simultaneously.
82. Gushchin, pp. 94–5.
83. Ibid., pp. 186–7.
84. Ibid., pp. 204–205.
85. Ibid., pp. 222–3.
86. Varenov, pp. 45–6, 41.
87. Alexander Orlov, *The Secret History of Stalin's Crimes*, London, 1954, pp. 41–2.
88. *Genocide in the USSR*, p. 22.
89. Ibid., p. 61.
90. *Zarya Vostoka*, 6 June, 1930.
91. Isaac Deutscher, *Stalin*, London, 1949, p. 325.
92. Stadnyuk, p. 159.
93. *Pravda*, 9 January 1930; *Visti*, 20 and 27 February 1930.
94. Kalynyk, pp. 90–95.
95. Ibid..
96. Fainsod, p. 253.
97. Verbytsky, pp. 71–2.
98. Pidhainy, v. 2, pp. 398–9.
99. Ibid., p. 306.
100. Grigorenko, p. 35.
101. *Pravda*, 11 January 1930.
102. Ibid..
103. *Sibir v period stroitelstva sotsializma i perekhoda k kommunizmu*, Novosibirsk, 1965, pp. 5, 82.
104. Tokaev, p. 7.
105. Danilov, p. 181.
106. Alexander Weissberg, *The Accused*, New York, 1951, p. 146; and see *The USSR in Figures*, Moscow, 1935, pp. 110, 180 ff.
107. Alexander Baykov, *The Development of the Soviet Economic System*, Cambridge, 1946, p. 196.

108. In Danilov, p. 45.
109. Ibid.
110. *Voprosy istorii* no. 5, 1963, p. 27.
111. *Pravda*, 19 February 1930.
112. *Pravda*, 2 March 1930.
113. See Cohen, *Bukharin*, p. 342.
114. *KPSS v rezolyutsiyakh*, v. 2, pp. 649–51.
115. Stalin, 'Reply to the collective-farm comrades,' v. 12, pp. 214, 217.
116. Ibid..
117. See Davies, pp. 319–23, 325–6.
118. Danilov, p. 46.
119. *Istoricheskiy arkhiv* no. 2, 1962, p. 197, quoted by Medvedev, *Let History Judge*, p. 88.
120. Davies, p. 312.
121. *Visti*, 30 March 1930; and see Pidhainy, v. 2, pp. 295–304.
122. Trapeznikov, v. 2, p. 251.
123. Nemakov, pp. 4, 191.
124. *Ocherki istorii Kommunisticheskoy Partii Gruzii*, Tbilisi, 1963, v. 2, p. 105.
125. *Stenograficheskiy otchet Vsesoyuznogo soveshchaniya po usovershenstvovaniyu kadrov v istoricheskoy nauke*, Moscow-Leningrad, 1964, pp. 299–300.
126. *Khrushchev Remembers*, p. 72.

Chapter 8. *The End of the Free Peasantry, 1930–32*

1. *Pravda*, 2 March 1930.
2. Jasny, p. 32.
3. *Pravda*, 17 April 1930.
4. Quoted in Davies, p. 290.
5. Ibid., p. 291.
6. Ibid., p. 296.
7. Ibid., p. 297.
8. Ibid., p. 296.
9. Quoted ibid., p. 293.
10. e.g. Pidhainy, v. 1, p. 292.
11. Kopelev, p. 189.
12. e.g. Pidhainy, v. 1, p. 292.
13. *Pravda*, 17 April 1930.
14. *Sotsialistichesky vestnik*, May, 1930.
15. See Davies, p. 330.
16. *Pravda*, 16 October 1930.

17. Semenko, pp. 52–54.
18. Pidhainy, v. 1, p. 177.
19. P.I. Lyashchenko, *Istoriya narodnogo khozyaystva SSSR*, v. 3, p. 280.
20. Beal, *Word From Nowhere*, p. 242.
21. Moshkov, p. 127.
22. Ibid., p. 135.
23. Ibid., pp. 126, 129.
24. Ibid..
25. Ibid., pp. 124–5.
26. Ibid., pp. 196–7; Nemakov, p. 91.
27. Weisberg, *The Accused*, p. 196.
28. Ibid., p. 189.
29. Ibid., p. 192.
30. Swianiewicz, p. 114.
31. Anne D. Rassweiler in *Slavic Review* 42, Summer 1983, p. 234, citing A.M. Panfilova, *Formirovanie rabochego klassa SSSR v gody pervoy pyatiletki 1928–1932*, Moscow, 1964 and M. Romanov, *Organizatsiya otkhodnichestva na novom etape*, Moscow-Leningrad, 1931.
32. Kalynyk, pp. 93–4.
33. *Bolshevik* no. 7, 1930, p. 19.
34. Stalin, v. 13, p. 55.
35. J. Millar in *Slavic Review* 33, 1974, pp. 750–66; A.A. Barsov in *Istoriya SSSR* no. 3, 1968, pp. 64–82; and see Karcz, pp. 457–8.
36. Karcz, p. 457.
37. *Bolshevik* no. 7, 1930, p. 18.
38. British Embassy despatch of 23 January 1933, see *Public Record Office Handbooks* no. 13. *The Records of the Foreign Office, 1782–1939*, London, 1969.
39. Kalynyk, pp. 20, 28.
40. Fainsod, p. 265.
41. Grigorenko, p. 41.
42. Fainsod, pp. 265–6.
43. Ibid., pp. 255–7.
44. Ibid., p. 450.
45. P.P. Postyshev and S.V. Kossior, *Soviet Ukraine Today*, New York, 1934, p. 31.
46. Roy and Zhores Medvedev, *Khrushchev*, New York, 1978, p. 26.
47. Grigorenko, p. 39.
48. Ibid., p. 38.
49. Gushchin, pp. 231–2; Paul B. Anderson, *People, Church and State in Modern Russia*, London, 1944, p. 86.

50. Fainsod, p. 257.
51. Postyshev and Kossior, *Soviet Ukraine Today*, pp. 21–2.
52. Karcz, p. 456.
53. Ibid., p. 467.
54. Jasny, p. 541.
55. *Sovetskaya istoricheskaya entsiklopediya*, v. 7, article 'Collectivization'.
56. Roy and Zhores Medvedev, *Khrushchev*, p. 27.
57. Moshkov, p. 171.
58. Ibid., p. 169.
59. Davies, p. 367.
60. See Vsevolod Holubnychy in *Annals of the Ukrainian Academy of Arts and Sciences in the US* v. 9, 1961, p. 108.
61. *Sovetskaya istoricheskaya entsiklopediya*, v. 7, p. 494.
62. R. and Zh. Medvedev, *Khrushchev*.
63. *Khrushchev Remembers: The Last Testament*, p. 108.
64. Postyshev and Kossior, p. 28.
65. Verbytsky, p. 17.
66. Danilov, p. 202.
67. *Los Angeles Evening Herald and Express*, 1 May 1935.
68. Weissberg, p. 188.
69. Kalynyk, p. 61.
70. Ibid., p. 60.
71. Jasny, p. 251.
72. *Materialy po istorii SSSR*, v. 7, p. 365.
73. Fainsod, pp. 302–303.
74. *Outline History of the USSR*, English edition, Moscow, 1960, p. 297; also see sources quoted by Holubnychy in *Annals of the Ukrainian Academy*, p. 78, ff.
75. Stalin, v. 12, p. 160.
76. *Izvestiya*, 24 January 1930.
77. *Chislennost skota v SSSR*, Moscow, 1957, p. 6.
78. Leonid Plyushch, *History's Carnival*, New York, 1977, p. 41.
79. *Pravda*, 6 January 1930.
80. *Experiences in Russia*, p. 179.
81. Tokaev, p. 7.
82. Ivan Solonevich, *Soviet Paradise Lost*, New York, 1938, p. 137.
83. *Kolkhozy v 1930 godu: statisticheskiy sbornik*, Moscow, 1931, pp. 110–11.
84. Beal, p. 242.
85. *Experiences in Russia*, p. 197.
86. Beal, p. 246.
87. *Zvezda*, 5 November 1929, quoted in *Nauchnye zapiski*, v. 76,

Dnepropetrovsk, 1962, p. 46.
88. Postyshev and Kossior, pp. 23–4.
89. Pidhainy, v. 2, p. 364.
90. Postyshev and Kossior, p. 29.
91. Fainsod, p. 286.
92. Lewin in Fizpatrick, p. 64.
93. Jasny, p. 32.
94. I. Vinnikova in *Volga* no. 12, 1979, p. 179.
95. Grigorenko, p. 39.
96. Stalin, v. 13, p. 402.
97. Ibid., pp. 213–14.
98. Gushchin, p. 242.
99. Danilov, p. 58.
100. *Visti*, 19 March, 1930.
101. *The Menshevik Trial*, Leningrad, n.d., pp. 59, 62; *Itogi vypoleneniya pervogo pyatiletnego plana*, Moscow, 1934, pp. 103–105; Robert Conquest, *The Great Terror*, London, 1973, p. 736.
102. Medvedev, *Let History Judge*.
103. Jasny, pp. 29–30.
104. *Sibir v period stroitelstva sotsializma i perekhoda k kommunizmu*, Novosibirsk, 1965, v. 5, p. 83.
105. A. Shlikhter, *Vybrany tvory*, Kiev, 1959, p. 533.
106. S.V. Sholtz, *Course of Agricultural Statistics*, Moscow, 1945, p. 37, as quoted by Jasny.
107. Jasny, p. 10.

Chapter 9. *Central Asia and the Kazakh Tragedy*

1. Danilov, p. 245.
2. Ibid., p. 252.
3. Ibid., p. 492.
4. B.A. Tulepbaev, *Torzhestvo Leninskikh idey sotsialisticheskogo preobrazovaniya selskogo khozyaystva v Sredney Azii i Kazakhstane*, Moscow, 1971, p. 199.
5. Yu.A. Polyakov and A.I. Chugunov, *Konets basmachestva*, Moscow, 1976, pp. 144–51.
6. Polyakov and Chugunov, p. 156.
7. Ibid.
8. Ibid; Victor Serge, *From Lenin to Stalin*, p. 61.
9. Danilov, p. 408.
10. Martha Olcutt, 'The Collectivization Drive in Kazakhstan,' *The Russian Review* 40, April 1981, p. 136.

11. Olcutt, 'The Collectivization Drive in Kazakhstan,' p. 123.
12. *Kollektivizatsiya selskogo khozyaystva Kazakhstana*, Alma-Ata, 1967, v. 2, p. 222.
13. A. Kuchkin, *Sovetizatsiya Kazakhskogo aula*, Moscow, 1962.
14. *Revolyutsiya i natsionalnosti* no. 5, 1932, p. 59; Olcutt, p. 132.
15. *KPSS v rezolyutsiyakh*, v. 2, pp. 649–51; *Voprosy Istorii*, 1960, no. 2, p. 36.
16. Olcutt, p. 142.
17. Ibid., p. 140.
18. *Bolshevik Kazakhstana* no. 12, 1938; Tulepbaev, *Torzhestvo leninskikh idey*, pp. 136–7.
19. Tulepbaev, p. 202.
20. Olcutt, p. 133.
21. *Kollektivizatsiya selskogo khozyaystva Kazakhstana*, v. 2, p. 287.
22. Olcutt, p. 129.
23. Tulepbaev, p. 206.
24. Ibid., pp. 203, 206; Olcutt, pp. 129–30.
25. A.B. Tursunbaev, *Pobeda kolkhoznogo stroya v Kazakhstane*, Alma-Ata, 1957, p. 149.
26. Olcutt, p. 130.
27. Tursunbaev, *Pobeda kolkhoznogo stroya v Kazakhstane*, pp. 144–8.
28. Olcutt, p. 127.
29. Polyakov and Chugunov, p. 154.
30. *Krasnaya zvezda*, 10 April 1984.
31. See Olcutt, p. 138.
32. Pidhainy, v. 2, p. 243.
33. *Bolshevik Kazakhstana* no. 1, 1939, p. 87.
34. *Kollektivizatsiya selskogo khozyaystva Kazakhstana*, v. 2, p. 306.
35. Olcutt, p. 137.
36. Ibid., p. 131.
37. *Pravda*, 29 November 1931.
38. Olcutt, pp. 133–4.
39. Pidhainy, v. 2, p. 243.
40. *Bolshevik Kazakhstana* no. 12, 1932, p. 13.
41. *Experiences in Russia*, p. 197.
42. Danilov, pp. 293–4.
43. *Bolshevik Kazakhstana* no. 9–10, 1937, p. 47.
44. Olcutt, p. 134.
45. *Kollektivizatsiya selskogo khozyaystva Kazakhstana*, v. 2, p. 142.
46. Olcutt, p. 133.
47. Ibid., p. 135.
48. Danilov, p. 293.

49. Olcutt, p. 128.
50. Ibid., p. 139.
51. Tulepbaev, p. 203.
52. Lovin, Head of the Chelyabinsk Tractor Plant, quoted by A.J. Tawdul, *New York American*, 19 and 20 August 1935.
53. *Khrushchev Remembers*, Boston, 1970, p. 72.
54. Robert Rupen, *How Mongolia is Really Ruled*, Stanford, 1979, p. 55.
55. *Pravda*, 2 November 1935.
56. Pidhainy, v. 1, p. 164.
57. Littlepage, pp. 109–11.
58. Rupen, *How Mongolia is Really Ruled*, p. 55.
59. Grigorenko, p. 48.

Chapter 10. *The Churches and the People*

1. Lewin, p. 23.
2. Atkinson, p. 175.
3. *Pravda*, 18 April 1928.
4. *Pravda*, 20 April 1922.
5. N. Orleansky ed., *Zakon o religioznykh obyedineniyakh RSFSR*, Moscow, 1930.
6. Fainsod, p. 308.
7. Roy Medvedev, *Stalin and Stalinism*, London, 1979, p. 76.
8. Quoted in Davies, p. 229.
9. *Pravda*, 11 January 1929.
10. e.g. Davies, p. 246.
11. Ivnitsky, p. 130.
12. Davies, pp. 96–7.
13. Pidhainy, v. 1, p. 493.
14. Verbytsky, p. 51.
15. Pidhainy, v. 1, p. 271.
16. Pidhainy, v. 1, p. 499.
17. Ibid., p. 260.
18. Ibid., p. 261.
19. Fainsod, p. 254.
20. Medvedev, *On Stalin and Stalinism*, p. 70.
21. *Visti*, 10 October 1929.
22. e.g. Semenko, p. 46.
23. *Antireligioznik* no. 1, 1930, p. 5.
24. Pidhainy, v. 1, p. 459.
25. Ibid., p. 502.
26. Medvedev, *On Stalin and Stalinism*, p. 70.

27. Fainsod, p. 247.
28. *Visti*, 22–6 December 1929.
29. *Visti*, 5 January 1930.
30. Verbytsky, p. 69.
31. Pidhainy, v. 1, p. 501.
32. Kravchenko, p. 127.
33. *Visti*, 1 January 1930.
34. *Pravda*, 22 February 1930.
35. *Visti*, 5 January 1930.
36. *Visti*, 22 December 1929.
37. *Pravda*, 27 November 1929.
38. *Pravda*, 30 November 1929.
39. *Visti*, 1 January 1930.
40. *Pravda*, 12–15 January 1930.
41. *KPSS v rezolyutsiyakh*, v. 2, pp. 670–71.
42. Pidhainy, v. 1, p. 508.
43. Ibid., p. 505.
44. Medvedev, *On Stalin and Stalinism*, p. 71.
45. V. Rasputin, 'Proshchanie s Materoi' in *Povesti*, Moscow, 1976.
46. Weissberg, p. 461.
47. I.A. Lavrov, *V strane eksperimentov*, Harbin, 1934, p. 216.
48. Paul B. Anderson, *People, Church and State in Modern Russia*, New York, 1941, p. 86.
49. *Bolshaya Sovetskaya Entsiklopediya*, 1st edition, v. 23, p. 811.
50. *Ukrainian Review* no. 6, p. 153.
51. *Visti*, 26 and 27 February 1930.
52. *Visti*, 22–6 December 1930.
53. Pidhainy, v. 1, p. 494.
54. Pidhainy, v. 1, p. 497.
55. Gregory Luznycky, *Persecution and Destruction of the Ukrainian Church by the Russian Bolsheviks*, New York, 1960, pp. 43–4.
56. Luznycky, *Persecution and Destruction*, pp. 59–60.
57. *Ogonek* no. 46, 1963, pp. 30–31.

Part III: *The Terror – Famine*

Chapter 11. *Assault on the Ukraine*

1. *Visti*, 14 March 1930.
2. *Chervony shlyakh* no. 4, 1930, pp. 141–2.
3. Pidhainy, v. 1, p. 27.
4. Semenko, p. 11.

5. *Ukrainian Review* no. 6, 1958, p. 156.
6. Stalin, v. 7, p. 71.
7. *Proletarska pravda*, 22 January 1930, quoted in Dmytro Solovey, 'On the Thirtieth Anniversary of the Great Man-made Famine in Ukraine,' *The Ukrainian Quarterly* 19, 1963, p. 7.
8. e.g. Verbytsky, p. 28.
9. Ibid., p. 65.
10. KPSS, *XVII syezd*, Moscow, 1934, p. 199.
11. Woropay, p. 60.
12. e.g. Swianiewicz, p. 120.
13. Grigorenko, pp. 35–6.
14. Harvard University Refugee Interview Project, p. 482.
15. *Pravda*, 17 January, 1933.
16. *Pravda*, 9 October, 1929.
17. *Pravda*, 5 September, 6 October, 6 November 1929.
18. *Khrushchev Remembers: The Last Testament*, p. 120.
19. Grigorenko, p. 36.
20. Ibid., p. 37.
21. Vasyl Hryshko, *Moskva slyozam ne viryt*, New York, 1963; idem., *Ukrainskyy Golokost – 1933*, New York-Toronto, 1978.
22. Pidhainy, v. 1, p. 243.
23. *Zasukhi v SSSR*, ed. A.I. Rudenko, Leningrad, 1958, p. 164.
24. *Pravda*, 9 June, 1932.
25. *Visti*, 11 July, 1932.
26. *Suchasna Ukraina*, 9 August, 1953, p. 6.
27. *Pravda*, 7 July, 1932.
28. *Pravda*, 14, 15 July, 1932.
29. *Visti*, 17 July, 1932.
30. See *Visti* 5 July, 28 July, 1932, as quoted by Kostiuk, p. 17.
31. e.g. Solovey in *The Ukrainian Quarterly* 19, 1963.
32. Pidhainy, v. 2, p. 107.
33. Stadnyuk in *Neva* no. 12, 1962.

Chapter 12. *The Famine Rages*

1. Grossman, p. 148.
2. Stalin, v. 13, pp. 213–14, 402.
3. A.Ya. Vyshinsky, *Revolyutsionnaya zakonnost na sovremennom etape*, Moscow, 1933, pp. 99–103.
4. *Visti*, 11 June 1933.
5. *Journal de Genève*, 26 August 1933.
6. *Visti*, 27 August, 14 September, 30 November, 1932, 2 February

1933.
7. Pidhainy, v. 1, p. 205.
8. *Los Angeles Herald*, 22 February 1935.
9. Woropay, p. 249.
10. Pidhainy, v. 1, p. 219.
11. Nemakov, p. 254.
12. Beal, p. 247.
13. Verbytsky, p. 66.
14. Pidhainy, v. 2, pp. 450–52.
15. Pigido-Pravoberezhny, p. 45.
16. *Ukrainian Review* no. 6, 1958, p. 134.
17. Woropay, p. 54.
18. Ibid., p. 55.
19. Pidhainy, v. 2, pp. 395–9.
20. *Bilshovyk Ukrainy* no. 19–20, 1932.
21. Ibid., no. 21–2, 1932.
22. Moshkov, p. 215.
23. e.g. *Visti*, 1 September 1932.
24. *Visti*, 9 December 1932.
25. *Kommunist*, Kharkov, 24 November 1932.
26. *Visti*, 30 January 1933.
27. *Pravda*, 16 November 1932.
28. *Pravda*, 8 December 1932.
29. *Visti*, 8 December 1932.
30. *Komsomolskaya pravda*, 23 November 1932.
31. *Ukrainskyy zbirnyk*, p. 96.
32. Danilov, p. 200.
33. *Visti*, 30 November, 21 December 1932, 1 January, 4 January, 9 January 1933.
34. *Visti*, 28 January 1933.
35. Pidhainy, v. 1, p. 247.
36. Pidhainy, v. 2, p. 354.
37. Weissberg, p. 122.
38. Kopelev, p. 234.
39. Kravchenko, *I Chose Freedom*, p. 113.
40. Pidhainy, v. 1, p. 280.
41. Danylo Miroshuk, *Who Organized the Famine in the Ukraine*, MS.
42. Kravchenko, p. 128.
43. Kostiuk, p. 44.
44. Pigido-Pravoberezhny, pp. 44–5.
45. Beal, p. 241.
46. *Ukrainskyy zbirnyk*, p. 83.

47. Verbytsky, p. 61.
48. Woropay, p. 49.
49. Pidhainy, v. 2, p. 108.
50. Verbytsky, p. 55–60.
51. Pidhainy, v. 2, pp. 36–7.
52. Woropay, p. 53.
53. Woropay, pp. 39–41.
54. Pidhainy, v. 2, p. 75.
55. *Pravda*, 10 March 1963.
56. Ibid..
57. Kopelev, p. 235.
58. Ibid., pp. 11–12.
59. Kravchenko, p. 105.
60. Ibid., p. 114.
61. Boris Nicolaevsky, *Power and the Soviet Elite*, New York, 1965, pp. 18–19.
62. See P. Scheibert, 'Ueber Lenins Anfaenge,' *Historische Zeitschrift* v. 182, p. 561.
63. *Visti*, 9 December 1932.
64. Pidhainy, v. 2, pp. 483–4.
65. Pidhainy, v. 1, p. 249.
66. *Visti*, 11 January 1933; Pidhainy, v. 2, pp. 484–5.
67. Stadnyuk, p. 125.
68. Astafiev in *Nash sovremennik* no. 1, 1978, p. 17.
69. Tendryakov, 'Death', *Moskva* no. 3, 1968.
70. Kravchenko, p. 119.
71. Grossman, p. 157.
72. Ibid., p. 134.
73. Pidhainy, v. 1, p. 248.
74. Plyushch, p. 40.
75. Grossman, p. 155.
76. Kravchenko, p. 129.
77. Pidhainy, v. 2, p. 558.
78. Kravchenko, p. 121.
79. Pidhainy, v. 2, p. 581.
80. *Sotsialistichesky vestnik* no. 19, 1933, p. 15.
81. Tawdul in *New York American*, 22 August 1935.
82. M. Karavay, *Nachalnik politotdela Ust-Labinskoy MTS*, Moscow, 1934, p. 12.
83. Harvard University Project, Schedule A, case 285.
84. Verbytsky, p. 30.
85. Semenko, p. 48.

86. Lucy Robins Lang, *Tomorrow is Beautiful*, New York, 1948, p. 262.
87. *Ukrainian Review* no. 2, 1956, pp. 86–120.
88. Pidhainy, v. 2, p. 581 ff.
89. e.g. Ivan Chinchenko, *Vinnytska trahediya*, Winnipeg, 1981, MS.
90. Eugene Lyons, *Assignment in Utopia*, New York, 1937, pp. 469–70.
91. Pidhainy, v. 2, pp. 469–70.
92. *Sotsialistichesky vestnik* no. 14, 23 July 1932.
93. Victor Serge, *Memoirs of a Revolutionary*, London, 1963, p. 64.
94. Pidhainy, v. 2, p. 77.
95. Pigido-Pravoberezhny, p. 38.
96. Pidhainy, v. 2, p. 84.
97. Pidhainy, v. 1, p. 209.
98. *Visti*, 8 December 1932; *Proletarska pravda*, 10 December 1932; Woropay, p. 13.
99. William Henry Chamberlin, *Russia's Iron Age*, Boston, 1934, p. 86.
100. Medvedev, *Let History Judge*, p. 93.
101. Kalynyk, pp. 80–85.
102. Pigido-Pravoberezhny, passim and Harvard Project, passim.
103. *Bolshevik* no. 1–2, 1933.
104. *Pravda*, 26 May 1963.
105. *Bolshevik* no. 1–2, 1933.
106. Ibid..
107. *Pravda*, 24 November 1933.
108. Postyshev and Kossior, pp. 9–10.
109. *Pravda*, 6 February 1933.
110. Ibid..
111. *Pravda*, 26 February 1933.
112. *Pravda*, 6 February 1933.
113. *Hospodarstvo Ukrainy* no. 3–4, 1933, p. 32.
114. *Visti*, 13 February 1933.
115. *Pravda*, 24 November 1933.
116. Postyshev and Kossior, p. 18.
117. Ivan Chinchenko, *Vinnytska trahediya*, MS.
118. *Ukrainske khozyaystvo*, no. 3–4, 1978, pp. 28–30.
119. Joseph Berger, *Shipwreck of a Generation*, London, 1971, p. 23.
120. *Visti*, 12 March 1933.
121. *Izvestia*, 12 March 1933.
122. *Pravda*, 24 November 1933.
123. *Istoriya selyanstva Ukrainskoy RSR*, v. 2, p. 188.
124. Pidhainy, v. 2, p. 52.
125. Selunskaya, p. 233.
126. *Pravda*, 19 February 1933.

127. Pidhainy, v. 2, pp. 558–622.
128. Grossman, p. 157.
129. Pidhainy, v. 2, p. 578.
130. Ibid., p. 712.
131. Vyshinsky, *Revolyutsionnaya zakonnost na sovremennom etape*, pp. 102–103.
132. Pidhainy, v. 2, p. 511.
133. Thomas Walker in *New York Evening Journal*, 18 February 1933.
134. Pidhainy, v. 2, pp. 578–9.
135. Woropay, p. 18.
136. Kopelev, pp. 280–381.
137. Alekseev in *Zvezda* no. 1, 1964, p. 37.
138. Stadnyuk in *Neva*, December 1962.
139. Kravchenko, p. 118.
140. Kalynyk, p. 117.
141. *Los Angeles Evening Herald*, 26 February 1935.
142. M. Solovyev, *Zapiski voennogo korrespondenta*, New York, 1954, pp. 57–61.
143. Grossman, p. 155.
144. Chamberlin, *Russia's Iron Age*, p. 368.
145. Pidhainy, v. 2, p. 576.
146. Ibid., pp. 450–51.
147. Grossman, pp. 148, 155.
148. Stepan Dubowyk, MS.
149. Pidhainy, v. 2, pp. 593–4.
150. Verbytsky, p. 32.
151. Pidhainy, v. 2, p. 80.
152. Solovyev, *Zapiski voennogo korrespondenta*, p. 55.
153. Dmytro Soloviy, *The Golgotha of the Ukraine*, New York, 1953, p. 33.
154. Grossman, p. 88.
155. Semenko, p. 14.
156. Woropay, p. 189.
157. Ewald Ammende, *Human Life in Russia*, London, 1936, p. 62.
158. Weissberg, p. 189.
159. Kostiuk, p. 32.
160. Hindus, p. 289.
161. Danylo Miroshuk, *Who Organized the Famine in Ukraine?*, MS.
162. Grossman, p. 161.
163. Semenko, p. 4.
164. Kravchenko, p. 111.
165. Verbytsky, p. 72.
166. Grossman, p. 161–2.

167. Ibid..
168. e.g. Woropay, pp. 31–2.
169. Verbytsky, p. 95.
170. Semenko, p. 15.
171. Woropay, p. 33.
172. Pidhainy, v. 1, p. 245.
173. Grossman, pp. 162–3.
174. Beal, p. 244.
175. Stepan Dubowyk, MS.
176. Kalynyk, pp. 111–16.
177. Pidhainy, v. 2, p. 695.
178. Woropay, p. 46.
179. Pidhainy, v. 1, p. 269.
180. Ibid., pp. 260–61.
181. Ibid., v. 2, p. 122.
182. Pidhainy, v. 1, p. 253.
183. *Los Angeles Evening Herald*, 29 April 1935.
184. Ibid., 1 May 1935.
185. Pidhainy, v. 2, p. 672.
186. Verbytsky, p. 55.
187. Pidhainy, v. 2, p. 672.
188. U.S. House Select Committee on Communist Aggression. *Special Report no. 4, Communist Takeover and Occupation of Ukraine*, Washington, D.C., 1955.
189. Pidhainy, v. 1, p. 283.
190. Kalynyk, p. 116.
191. William Henry Chamberlin, *The Ukraine: a Submerged Nation*, New York, 1944, pp. 60–61.
192. Chamberlin, *Russia's Iron Age*, p. 368.
193. Semenko, pp. 74–5.
194. Lang, *Tomorrow is Beautiful*, pp. 268–9; Fainsod, p. 244.
195. Woropay, p. 47.
196. Personal communication; and see C. Henry Smith, *The Story of the Mennonites*, Berne, Indiana, 1941, chapter 8.
197. Solovey, *The Golgotha*, pp. 42–3.
198. Pidhainy, v. 1, p. 240.
199. Kalynyk, pp. 22–3.
200. Pidhainy, v. 1, pp. 233, 244.
201. Pidhainy, v. 2, p. 676.
202. Pidhainy, v. 2, p. 68.
203. Woropay, p. 18.
204. Beal, p. 243.

205. Ibid., p. 251.
206. Kravchenko, p. 114.
207. Pidhainy, v. 2, pp. 530–31.
208. Pidhainy, v. 2, p. 533.
209. Chamberlin, *The Ukraine*, p. 61.
210. Woropay, p. 43.
211. Pidhainy, v. 1, p. 295.
212. Pidhainy, v. 2, p. 590.
213. *Dilo*, 31 October 1934.
214. Grossman, p. 160.
215. W.I. Reswick, *I Dreamt Revolution*, Chicago, 1952, pp. 308–309.
216. *Christian Science Monitor*, 29 May 1934.
217. Pidhainy, v. 2, p. 85.
218. Grossman, pp. 164–5.
219. e.g. Kopelev, pp. 240–41.
220. Stepan Dubowyk, MS.
221. Grossman, p. 164.
222. Pidhainy, v. 1, p. 230.
223. Ibid., p. 38.
224. Ukrainian National Council in Canada, *Bulletin* no. 1, p. 1.
225. Plyushch, p. 40.
226. *Komitety nezamozhnykh selyan Ukrainy*, Kiev, 1968, pp. 580–82.
227. Pidhainy, v. 2, p. 36.
228. Woropay, p. 56; Harvard Project, Schedule A. Case 1434, p. 13.
229. Semenko, p. 45.
230. Woropay, p. 48.
231. Ibid., pp. 55–6; Pidhainy, v. 2, pp. 125–6.
232. Verbytsky, p. 33.
233. Pidhainy, v. 1, p. 262.
234. Ibid., p. 266.
235. Ibid., p. 280.
236. Pigido-Pravoberezhny, p. 60.
237. Woropay, p. 24.

Chapter 13. *A Land Laid Waste*

1. *Fortnightly Review*, 1 May 1933.
2. *Answers*, 24 February 1934.
3. Beal, p. 249.
4. Quoted in Hindus, p. 154.
5. Kravchenko, p. 130.
6. *Pravda*, 24 June 1933.

7. Trifonov, *Likvidatsiya ekspluatatorskikh klassov*, pp. 352–3, 359.
8. *Pravda*, 16 December 1933.
9. *Pravda*, 8 February 1933.
10. Ammende, p. 62.
11. Woropay, p. 23.
12. Ibid..
13. e.g. Kopelev, p. 284.
14. *Visti*, 17 March 1933.
15. *Visti*, 3 March 1933.
16. Pidhainy, v. 2, p. 89.
17. *Visti*, 23 April 1933.
18. Woropay, p. 57.
19. *Ukrainskyy zbirnyk*, v. 2, p. 97.
20. Woropay, pp. 25–6.
21. e.g. Pidhainy, v. 1, p. 269.
22. Grossman, p. 165.
23. Pidhainy, v. 2, p. 543; Pigido-Pravoberezhny, p. 58.
24. U.S. House Select Committee, *Report on Communist Aggression*, p. 19.
25. Verbytsky, pp. 47, 59.
26. Ibid., p. 74.
27. *Kommunist*, Kharkov, 26 December 1934.
28. Woropay, p. 58.
29. Ibid..
30. Pidhainy, v. 1, pp. 231–2.
31. *Visti*, 11 June 1933.
32. Ibid..
33. Postyshev and Kossior, p. 10.
34. *Kommunisticheskaya partiya Ukrainy v rezolyutsiyakh i resheniyakh 1918–1956*, Kiev, 1958, p. 569.
35. Solovey in *The Ukrainian Quartely* 19, 1963, p. 23.
36. *Izvestiya*, 21 September 1933.
37. Jasny, pp. 86, 544.
38. Pidhainy, v. 1, p. 232.
39. Postyshev and Kossior, p. 5.
40. *Proletarska pravda*, September 1933.
41. *Molodaya gvardiya* no. 19–20, 1933.
42. *Visti*, 30 July 1933.
43. *Kommunist*, 27 June 1934.
44. British Embassy despatch 4 September 1933.
45. Tawdul in *New York American*, 30 August 1935.
46. British Embassy despatch 4 September 1933.

47. Pidhainy, v. 1, p. 232.
48. Dmitriy Shostakovich, *Testimony*, New York, 1979, pp. 214–5.
49. *Pravda*, 12 March 1933.
50. Kostiuk, p. 50.
51. *Pravda*, 2 December 1933.
52. Kostiuk, p. 93.
53. *Visti*, March 1933.
54. Kostiuk, p. 57.
55. Ibid., p. 48.
56. *Pravda*, 22 June 1933.
57. *Pravda*, 8 July 1933.
58. *Pravda*, 2 December 1933.
59. *Chervony shlyakh* no. 1–2, 1932, p. 92.
60. Postyshev and Kossior, p. 109.
61. *Visti*, 22 June 1933.
62. Postyshev and Kossior, p. 109.
63. *Visti*, 5 June 1933.
64. Postyshev and Kossior, p. 63.
65. Ibid., p. 74.
66. Kostiuk, p. 59.
67. Ibid., p. 143.
68. Postyshev and Kossior, p. 82.
69. Ibid..
70. Kostiuk, p. 56.
71. Ibid., p. 58; U.S. House. Select Committee, *Report*, p. 22.
72. Pidhainy, v. 1, p. 403.
73. *Chervony shlyakh* no. 8–9, 1933, p. 246.
74. Pidhainy, v. 2, p. 57.
75. *Visti*, 21 January 1934.
76. *Bilshovyk Ukrainy* no. 3, 1936.
77. *Visti*, 24 January 1934.
78. *Visti*, 5 June 1937.
79. KPSS, *XVII syezd*, pp. 71, 199.
80. *Pravda*, 18 December 1934.
81. *Pravda*, 10 June 1935.
82. Ibid..
83. Kostiuk, pp. 101–102.
84. Ibid., pp. 105–107.
85. See Pidhainy, v. 1, p. 394; U.S. House Select Committee, *Report*, pp. 19–20.
86. *Byulleten oppozitsii* no. 77–8, 1939, p. 5.
87. *New York Times*, 21 September 1953.

Chapter 14. *Kuban, Don and Volga*

1. *Novoe Russkoe Slovo*, 24 December 1982.
2. *Encyclopedia Britannica* XI edition, v. 7, p. 218, article 'Cossacks' by Prince Kropotkin.
3. *Large Soviet Encyclopedia*, III edition, v. 13.
4. *Novoe Russkoe Slovo*, 24 December 1982.
5. A. Osichko, *Pochemu oni nas unichtozhali* quoted in *Novoe Russkoe Slovo*, 26 December 1982; *Genocide in the USSR* p. 247.
6. KPSS, *XVII syezd*, p. 148.
7. *Slomit sabotazh seva i khlebozagotovok, organizavannyy kulachestvom v rayonakh Kubani*, Moscow, 1932.
8. Ibid..
9. Ibid..
10. *Pravda*, 29 April 1933.
11. J. Maynard, *Collective Farms in the USSR* p. 9.
12. *Novoe Russkoe Slovo*, 24 December 1982.
13. Maynard, *Collective Farms*, p. 9.
14. *Russkoe vozrozhdenie* no. 2, 1981.
15. Verbytsky, pp. 77–8.
16. *Molot*, 17 December 1932, quoted in *Novoe Russkoe Slovo*, 26 December 1982.
17. Pidhainy, v. 1, p. 44.
18. *Novoe Russkoe Slovo*, 26 December 1982.
19. Medvedev, *Let History Judge*, p. 93.
20. Pidhainy, v. 1, p. 44.
21. Solovyev, pp. 73–5.
22. Ibid., pp. 76–80.
23. Kostiuk, p. 96.
24. *Molot* 20, 22 December 1932, quoted in *Novoe Russkoe Slovo*, 26 December 1982.
25. *The Ukrainian Herald* no. 7–8, p. 111.
26. *Brueder in Not! Dokumente der Hungersnot*, Berlin, 1933.
27. Ibid., p. 7.
28. Ibid., p. 14.
29. Ibid., p. 7.
30. Ibid., p. 11.
31. Vyshinsky, p. 104.
32. Harvard Project, Schedule A. Case 296.
33. Pidhainy, v. 2, p. 79.
34. *Genocide in the USSR* p. 247.

35. Verbytsky, pp. 78–9.
36. British Embassy despatch, 27 October 1933.
37. Pidhainy, v. 2, p. 121.
38. Ammende, p. 99.
39. Pidhainy, v. 2, p. 71.
40. Chamberlin, *Russia's Iron Age* p. 83.
41. Semenko, p. 3.
42. Tokaev, p. 10.
43. British Embassy despatch 5 March 1933.
44. British Embassy despatch 27 October 1933.
45. *Sovetskaya Rossiya* 26 August 1975.
46. Alekseev, *Nash sovremennik* no. 9, 1972, p. 96.
47. *Brueder in Not* p. 3.
48. *Hunger Predigt*, Berlin, 1933, p. 23.
49. Ibid., p. 25.
50. Ibid., p. 11.
51. Ibid., pp. 134–5.
52. e.g. *Hunger Predigt* p. 127.
53. Ammende, p. 220.
54. *Brueder in Not* p. 15.

Chapter 15. *Children*

1. Beal, p. 259.
2. *Prosveshchenie Sibiri* no. 4, 1929, p. 111.
3. Fainsod, p. 241.
4. Solzhenitsyn, p. 360.
5. *Na putyakh k novoy shkole* no. 4–5, 1930, p. 25.
6. Beal, p. 248.
7. Kravchenko, p. 98.
8. Seminar on Ukrainian Famine, 1933, Toronto, December 1981.
9. Pidhainy, v. 1, p. 300.
10. Pigido-Pravoberezny, p. 24.
11. Ibid..
12. Pidhainy, v. 2, p. 537.
13. *Los Angeles Evening Herald*, 1 May 1935.
14. Woropay, p. 23.
15. Richard Crossman, ed., *The God That Failed*, London, 1950, p. 68.
16. A Koestler, *The Yogi and the Commissar*, New York, 1946, p. 128.
17. Grossman, pp. 156–7.
18. *Los Angeles Evening Herald*, 20 February 1935.
19. Woropay, p. 42.

20. Pidhainy, v. 2, pp. 535–6.
21. Pidhainy, v. 1, p. 303.
22. e.g. Beal, p. 253.
23. *New York Evening Journal*, 16 April 1935; and see Lang, p. 260.
24. Ammende p. 63.
25. Whiting Williams in *Answers*, 24 February 1934.
26. Pidhainy, v. 2, p. 73.
27. A.J. Tawdul, in *New York American*, 29 August 1935.
28. Pidhainy, v. 1, p. 448.
29. *Khuliganstvo i khuligany*, Moscow, 1929, p. 46.
30. *The Russian Famines*, p. 17.
31. *Kommunisticheskoe prosveshchenie* no. 1, 1934, p. 106.
32. Ibid., no. 2, 1935, p. 97.
33. Ibid., no. 4, 1935, p. 16.
34. *Voprosy istorii KPSS* no. 8, 1966, p. 112.
35. *Kommunisticheskoe prosvescenie* no. 4, 1935, pp. 15–17.
36. Ibid., no. 1, 1934, p. 106.
37. *The Challenge* no. 6, October 1951, pp. 9–16.
38. Viktor Popov in V. Avdeev, ed., *Vchera i segodnya*, Moscow, 1970, p. 18.
39. Weissberg, p. 414.
40. Pidhainy, v. 1, p. 298.
41. Kalynyk, p. 116.
42. Chinchenko, MS.
43. Pidhainy, v. 1, p. 551.
44. Ibid, p. 575.
45. Woropay, p. 39.
46. Pidhainy, v. 2, p. 253.
47. *Narodnoe prosveshchenie* no. 2, 1930, p. 11.
48. *Kommunisticheskoe prosveshchenie* no. 13, 1935, pp. 3–6.
49. e.g. Tawdul in *New York American*, 30 August 1935.
50. Beal, p. 256.
51. *Kommunisticheskoe prosveshchenie*, no. 3, 1935, p. 7.
52. Astafiev in *Roman-gazeta* no. 2, 1979, p. 60; and see his 'Posledniy Poklon' in *Nash sovremennik* no. 6, 1978.
53. See Gerson, p. 128.
54. *The Challenge* no. 12, p. 12.
55. Pidhainy, v. 1, p. 444.
56. Beal, p. 258.
57. Quoted in Pidhainy, v. 1, p. 269.
58. Karavay, p. 88.
59. Ibid..

60. *Pravda*, 24 November 1933.
61. Ibid..
62. F. Shevchenko, *History of the Ukraine*, Kiev, n.d., v. 2, p. 336.
63. S. Pavlov, speech to the November 1962 Plenum of the Central Committee of the Komsomol.
64. *Komsomolskaya Pravda*, 2 September 1962.
65. *Reuters*, 21 May 1934.
66. *Molot*, 30 August 1934.
67. *Pravda*, 20 December 1937.
68. Orlov, p. 53.
69. Peter Yakir, *A Childhood in Prison*, London, 1972, p. 44.
70. Orlov, p. 53.
71. Pigido-Pravoberezhny, p. 46.
72. Seminar on Ukrainian famine, Toronto
73. *Cahiers du Monde Russe et Sovietique* no. 18, 1977, p. 7.
74. Kopelev, p. 282.
75. Quoted in John A. Armstrong, *The Politics of Totalitarianism*, New York, 1961, p. 7.
76. Verbytsky, pp. 55–60.
77. *Ukrainskyy zbirnyk*, v. 2, p. 92.
78. Seminar on Ukrainian famine, Toronto.
79. Pidhainy, v. 1, p. 253.

Chapter 16. *The Death Roll*

1. Yu.A. Korchak-Chepurkovsky, *Tablitsy dozhyvannya i spodivanoho zhyttya ludnosty URSR*, Kharkov, 1929, pp. 33, 72–9; idem, *Visnik statystyky Ukrainy* no. 2, 1928, pp. 154–8; idem, *Izbrannye demograficheskie issledovaniya*, Moscow, 1970, pp. 301–302. Also John F. Kattner and Lydia W. Kulchycka, *The USSR Population Census of 1926: A Partial Evaluation*, U.S. Bureau of Census, International Population Report, Series P. 95 no. 50, October 1957, pp. 100–117.
2. S.I. Pirokov, *Zhizn i tvorcheskaya deyatelnost O.A. Kvitkina*, Kiev, 1974.
3. *Bolshevik* no. 23–4, 1938.
4. *Pravda*, 17 January 1939.
5. *Pravda*, 26 January 1935.
6. *Naselenie SSSR. Chislennost, sostav i dvizhenie naseleniya*, Moscow, 1975, p. 7.
7. *Vestnik statistiki* no. 11, 1964, p. 11.
8. See Karcz, p. 479.
9. *Pravda*, 5 December 1935.

10. *The Second Five Year Plan*, English edition, New York, 1937, p. 458.
11. *Vestnik statistiki* no. 11, 1964, p. 11.
12. Anton Antonov-Ovseenko, *The Time of Stalin*, New York, 1981, p. 207.
13. V.I. Kozlov in *Istoriya SSSR* no. 4, 1983, p. 21.
14. Pidhainy, v. 2, p. 594.
15. I. Kraval in *Planovoe khozyaystvo* no. 12, 1936, p. 23.
16. Tawdul in *New York American*, 18 August 1935.
17. Ibid..
18. Orlov, p. 28.
19. Tawdul in *New York American*, 19 August, 1935.
20. Beal, p. 255.
21. *Los Angeles Evening Herald*, 29 April, 1935.
22. Lang, p. 260.
23. John Kolasky, *Two Years in Soviet Ukraine*, Toronto, 1970, p. 111.
24. Tawdul in *New York American*, 19 August, 1935.
25. Plyushch, p. 42.
26. Swianiewicz, p. 123.
27. David Dallin and Boris Nicolaevsky, *Forced Labor in the Soviet Union*, London, 1948, p. 54.
28. Swianiewicz, p. 59; *Livre Blanc sur les Camps de Concentration*, pp. 31–6; etc.
29. *Khrushchev Remembers: The Last Testament*, p. 120.
30. *Le Matin*, 30 August 1933.

Chapter 17. *The Record of the West*

1. *New York Herald Tribune*, 21 August 1933; Chamberlin, *The Ukraine*, p. 60.
2. *Manchester Guardian*, 21 August 1933.
3. *New York Herald Tribune*, 21 August 1933.
4. Hindus, pp. 146–8, 153–5.
5. *Izvestiya*, 26 February 1933.
6. British Embassy despatch 5 March 1933.
7. Koestler, *The Yogi and the Commissar*, pp. 137–8.
8. Chamberlin, *Russia's Iron Age*, pp. 155–6.
9. *Pravda*, 19 December 1933.
10. Letter dated 3 January 1934, quoted in the *Congressional Record*, v. 80, p. 2110.
11. Quoted in *Famine in the Ukraine*, New York, 1934, p. 7.
12. U.S. Embassy despatch no. 902, 26 September 1935.
13. Lyons, pp. 366–7.

14. Ammende, pp. 230–31.
15. Pidhainy, v. 1, p. 270.
16. Lang, p. 263.
17. Verbytsky, p. 97.
18. Ammende, p. 232.
19. *Figaro*, 16 October 1933; Beal, p. 245.
20. Beal, p. 245.
21. Pidhainy, v. 2, pp. 93–4.
22. Grossman, p. 159.
23. Kalynyk, p. 14.
24. Beal, p. 259.
25. Pidhainy, v. 1, p. 281.
26. Statement to London General Press, 1932.
27. *Antireligioznik* no. 5, 1930.
28. Sherwood Eddy, *Russia Today: What We Can Learn From It*, New York, 1934, p. xiv.
29. Maynard, *Collective Farms in the USSR*, p. 6.
30. Maynard, *The Russian Peasant*, p. 296.
31. Sidney and Beatrice Webb, *Soviet Communism: A New Civilization?*, London, 1937 (the question mark was dropped in later editions).
32. S. and B. Webb, *Soviet Communism*, pp. 235, 245.
33. Ibid..
34. Ibid., p. 245.
35. Ibid., p. 267.
36. Ibid., p. 268.
37. Ibid., p. 563.
38. Ibid., p. 259.
39. Ibid., p. 266.
40. Ibid., p. 262.
41. Ibid., p. 282.
42. Ibid., p. 263.
43. Ibid..
44. Ibid., p. 261.
45. Ibid., p. 248.
46. Ibid., p. 276.
47. Ibid., p. 266–7.
48. *New York Times*, 13 September 1933.
49. British Embassy despatch, 16 September 1933.
50. On Duranty see especially Marco Carynnyk in *Commentary* 76, November 1983, and in *The Idler* no. 1, January 1985, and no. 2, February 1985.
51. Weissberg, p. 194.

Chapter 18. *Responsibilities*

1. *Sotsialistichesky vestnik*, 12 April 1930.
2. *Ukrainskyy Prometey*, pp. 19–20.
3. Woropay, p. 57.
4. *Ukrainskyy Zbirnyk*, pp. 85–6.
5. Beal, p. 255.
6. Pidhainy, v. 2, pp. 491–2.
7. Ibid..
8. *Khrushchev Remembers*, pp. 73–4.
9. *Khrushchev Remembers: The Last Testament*, p. 109.
10. *Samizdat I: La voix de l'opposition communiste en U.R.S.S.*, Paris, 1969, pp. 92–100.
11. *Pravda*, 26 May, 1964.
12. *Khrushchev Remembers: The Last Testament*, p. 124.
13. See Plyushch, p. 179.
14. U.S. House Select Committee on Communist Aggression, *Report*, pp. 19–20.
15. e.g. Deutscher, p. 33; Barmine, p. 264.
16. Orlov, p. 318.
17. See Pidhainy, v. 1, p. 467; Woropay, p. 28; Plyushch, pp. 41, 85.
18. Plyushch, p. 41.
19. Pidhainy, v. 1, p. 236.
20. Ibid., p. 467.
21. Woropay, p. 28.
22. *Novoe Russkoe Slovo*, 29 March 1983.
23. *Vpered* no. 7, 1958, p. 1.
24. Pidhainy, v. 1, p. 251.
25. Ibid., p. 273.
26. Woropay, p. 29.
27. Pidhainy, v. 1, p. 281.

Epilogue *The Aftermath*

1. Pasternak, *Doctor Zhivago*, p. 422.
2. Yakir, p. 86.
3. Weissberg, p. 288.
4. Pidhainy, v. 1, pp. 415–16.
5. Ibid., p. 212.
6. Weissberg, pp. 290–91.
7. Medvedev, *Let History Judge*, pp. 236–7.

8. *Ukrainian Review* no. 6, 1958, pp. 136–40.
9. Elinor Lipper, *Eleven Years in Soviet Prison Camps*, London, 1951.
10. *Ukrainian Herald* no. 7–8, p. 63.
11. E.R. Stettinius, *Roosevelt and the Russians: the Yalta Conference*, Garden City, New York, 1949, p. 187.
12. Ivan Dzyuba, *Internationalism or Russification*, London, 1968, p. 108.
13. *Pravda*, 10 December 1963.
14. *Literary Gazette*, Kiev, 20 November 1947.
15. *Istoriya Akademii Nauk Ukrainskoy SSSR*, Kiev, 1975, p. 802.
16. See Vyacheslav Chornovil, *The Chornovil Papers*, New York, 1968.
17. See Medvedev, *Let History Judge*, p. 106.
18. See Swianiewicz, p. 94.
19. Ibid., p. 100.
20. *Pravda*, 23 September 1935.
21. Jasny, p. 37.
22. A. Avtorkhanov, *The Reign of Stalin*, London, 1955, pp. 176–7.
23. Jasny, p. 458.
24. Swianiewicz, pp. 105–106.
25. Jasny, p. 346.
26. *Planovoe khozyaystvo* no. 7, 1939.
27. See Roy and Zhores Medvedev, *Khrushchev*, p. 27.
28. Danilov, pp. 532–3.
29. Grossman, p. 148.
30. *Istoriya Sovetskogo krestyanstva i kolkhoznogo stroitelstva v SSSR*, p. 276.
31. *Pravda*, 19 September 1947.
32. *Narodnoe khozyaystvo SSSR v 1965 godu*, p. 311.
33. *Partiynaya zhizn*, November 1965.
34. Mozhaev, 'Plyushko pole', in *Lesnaya doroga*, p. 400.
35. F. Abramov, *The Dodgers*, English edition, London, 1963, pp. 86–7.
36. Yefim Dorozh in *Novy mir* no. 6, 1965, p. 8.
37. See *Survey* no. 4, 1980, p. 28.
38. *Izvestiya*, 18 July 1982.
39. *Soviet Analyst* v. 11, no. 15, pp. 4–5.
40. *Trud*, 30 July 1982.
41. Victor Popov on Radio Moscow, 8 September 1982.
42. Mozhaev, 'Polyushko-pole,' in *Lesnaya doroga*, p. 513.
43. *Sovetskaya Rossiya*, 12 September 1980.
44. F. Abramov in *Nash sovremennik* no. 9, 1979, p. 25.
45. Astafiev in *Nash sovremennik* no. 1, 1978, p. 25.
46. Nicolaevsky, pp. 18–19.
47. Kravchenko, p. 107.

48. *Pravda*, 8 October 1965.
49. *Selskaya zhizn*, 29 December 1965, 25 February 1966.
50. Quoted in Karcz, p. 57.
51. Trapeznikov, v. 2, pp. 187–9.
52. *Pravda*, 10 March 1963.
53. *Soviet Ukraine*, (in English) Kiev, 1970, p. 293.

Select Bibliography

Of the seventy-odd periodicals and double that number of books referred to in the text, together with a number of manuscript sources, those listed below are some of the most useful; between them they largely cover the main themes, and in many cases provide much additional and confirmatory detail beyond what could be used in the present work. The reader is, of course, also referred to the major official documents and periodicals and to other basic sources given in the Notes.

General

Ammende, Ewald, *Human Life in Russia*. London, 1936.

Barsov, A.A., *Balans stoimostnykh obmenov mezhdu gorodom i derevnei*. Moscow, 1969.

Carynnyk, Marco, *Commentary* 76, November 1983; *The Idler* nos. 1 and 2, 1985.

Chamberlin, William Henry, *Russia's Iron Age*. Boston, 1934.

Cohen, Stephen F., *Bukharin and the Bolshevik Revolution*. New York, 1983.

Conquest, Robert, ed., *Agricultural Workers in the USSR*. London, 1968.

Dalrymple, Dana, 'The Soviet Famine of 1932–34,' *Soviet Studies* vol. 15, no. 3, January 1964.

Danilov, V.P., ed., *Ocherki istorii kollektivizatsii selskogo khozyaystva v soyuznykh respublikakh*. Moscow, 1963.

Davies, R.W., *The Socialist Offensive. The Collectivization of Soviet Agriculture 1929–1930*. Cambridge, Mass, 1980.

Ellison, Herbert, 'The Decision to Collectivize Agriculture,' in *Russian Economic Development from Peter the Great to Stalin*, ed. William Blackwell. New York, 1974.

Fainsod, Merle, *Smolensk under Soviet Rule*. Cambridge, Mass, 1958.

Ivnitsky, N.A., *Klassovaya borba i likvidatsiya kulachestva kak klassa 1929–1932*. Moscow, 1972.

Jasny, Naum, *The Socialized Agriculture of the USSR*. Stanford, 1949.

Karcz, Jerzy, *The Economics of Communist Agriculture*. Bloomington, 1979.

Kostiuk, Hryhory, *Stalinist Rule in the Ukraine*, London, 1960.

Lewin, Moshe, *Russian Peasants and Soviet Power*. London, 1968.

Lewin, Moshe, *Political Undercurrents in Soviet Economic Debates*. Princeton, 1974.

Mace, James, E., *Communism and the Dilemmas of National Liberation*. Cambridge, Mass, 1983.

Mitrany, David, *Marx Against the Peasant*, Chapel Hill, 1951.

Millar, James R., 'Mass Collectivization and the Contribution of Soviet Agriculture to the First Year Plan,' *Slavic Review* 33, December 1974.

Moshkov, Yu. A., *Zernovaya problema v gody sploshnoy kollektivizatsii selskogo khozyaystva SSSR*. Moscow, 1966.

Nemakov, N.I., *Kommunisticheskaya partiya – organizator massovogo kolkhoznogo dvizheniya 1929–1932*. Moscow, 1966.

Olcutt, Martha Brill, 'The Collectivization Drive in Kazakhstan,' *Russian Review* 40, April 1981.

Postyshev, P.P. and Kossior, S.V., *Soviet Ukraine Today*. New York, 1934.

Radkey, Oliver H., *The Unknown Civil War in Soviet Russia*. Stanford, 1976.

Radziejowski, Janusz, 'Collectivization in Ukraine in the Light of Soviet Historiography,' *Journal of Ukrainian Studies* no. 9, Fall 1980.

Robinson, Geroid Tanquary, *Rural Russia under the Old Regime*. New York, 1932.

Selunskaya, V.M., *Rabochie – dvadtsatipyatitysyachniki*. Moscow, 1964.

Slomit sabotazh seva i khlebozagotovok organizovannyy kulachestvom v rayonakh Kubani. Moscow, 1932.

Sullivant, Robetr S., *Soviet Politics and the Ukraine*. New York, 1962.

Swianiewicz, S., *Forced Labour and Economic Development*. London, 1965.

Taniuchi, Y., 'A Note on the Ural-Siberian Method,' *Soviet Studies* vol. 33, no. 4. October 1981.

Trapeznikov, Sergey, *Leninizm i agrarno-krestyansky vopros*. Moscow, 1976.

Ukraine: A Concise Encyclopedia. 2 vols. Toronto, 1963–1965.

Webb, Sidney and Beatrice, *Soviet Communism: A New Civilization*. Second edition. London, 1937.

Collected Individual Testimonies and Documents

Brueder in Not. Berlin, 1933.

Chynchenko, Ivan M., *Trahediya ditey v Ukraini v proklyatykh rokakh*. MS.
Dolot, Myron, *Execution by Hunger*. New York, 1985.
Kalynyk, O., *Communism the Enemy of Mankind*. London, 1955.
Harvard University Refugee Interview Project. Duplicated Typescript.
Pidhainy, S.O., editor in chief. *The Black Deeds of the Kremlin*. 2 vols. Toronto, 1953.
Soloviy, Dmytro, *The Golgotha of the Ukraine*. New York, 1953.
Verbytsky, M., *Naybilshyy zlochyn Kremlya*. London, 1952.

Accounts by Former Party Activists

Grigorenko, Petro, *Memoirs*. London, 1983.
Kopelev, Lev, *The Education of a True Believer*. New York, 1977.
Kravchenko, Victor, *I Chose Freedom*. New York, 1946.

Soviet Fictional Accounts

Astafiev, Viktor, 'Posledniy poklon,' *Roman-gazeta* no. 2–3, 1979.
Belov, Vasily, *Kanuny*. Moscow, 1976.
Grossman, Vasily, *Forever Flowing*. New York, 1972.
Sholokhov, Mikhail, *Podnyataya tselina. (Virgin Soil Upturned)* Moscow, 1947.
Stadnyuk, Ivan F., *People are not Angels*. London, 1963.

396

Index

408

411

Vyshinksky, A. 39, 132, 225

Wages, anomolies in 169
'War Communism' 47–9, 58, 74, 145, 165
Webb, Beatrice and Sidney 56, 316, 317, 318, 321
Weissberg, Alexander 230
West Siberian Territory Committee 119
Western Province 158, 204, 205
White Sea Canal 168, 257
Witte, Serge 18
Women's Revolts 157–8, 166, 207, 236, 263, 277
Wrangel, General 50

Yablonskaya 97
Yahotyn District 254
Yakir, Iona 325
Yakovlev, A. 114, 243
Yakovlev, Kolya 295
Yalovy, Mykhaylo 267
Yantsenovo 137
Yareski 250, 251
Yaroslavl Prison 212
Yavorsky, Matvei 267
Yayva Penal Encampment 208

Yefremov, Serhii 218
Yemetsk 142
Yezhov, Nikolai Ivanovich 231, 300, 324, 344
Yugovsk 52
Yurynets, Professor 269

Zaporizhia Province 137, 173; closure of churches in 204; death toll from famine in 252; requisitioning of grain 220–1; resettlement of depleted villages 263
Zaporozhe 205, 274
Zasulich, Vera 22
Zatonsky, V. 35, 38, 263, 323, 333
Zavitne 280
Zeleny, (Partisan Leader) 52
Zerov, Mikola 271
Zheleznyany 110
Zhitomir Province 251
Zhornoklovy 250
Zhuky 256
Zhytomyr Province 35, 225, 238, 250, 254
Zidky 249
Zinoviev, Grigori 24, 41, 63, 78, 94, 333